The Dragon's Underbelly

Dynamics and Dilemmas in Vietnam's Economy and Politics

Edited by Nhu Truong and Tuong Vu

The Dragon's Underbelly

Dynamics and Dilemmas in Vietnam's Economy and Politics

 YUSOF ISHAK INSTITUTE

First published in Singapore in 2023 by
ISEAS Publishing
30 Heng Mui Keng Terrace
Singapore 119614

Email: publish@iseas.edu.sg
Website: bookshop.iseas.edu.sg

The responsibility for facts and opinions in this publication rests exclusively with the authors and their interpretations do not necessarily reflect the views or the policy of the publisher or its supporters.

ISEAS Library Cataloguing-in-Publication Data

Name(s): Truong, Nhu, editor. | Vu, Tuong, 1965-, editor.
Title: The dragon's underbelly : dynamics and dilemmas in Vietnam's economy and politics / edited by Nhu Truong and Tuong Vu.
Description: Singapore : ISEAS-Yusof Ishak Institute, 2023. | Includes index.
Identifiers: ISBN 9789815011395 (paperback) | ISBN 9789815011401 (PDF) | ISBN 9789815011814 (epub)
Subjects: LCSH: Vietnam—Economic conditions. | Vietnam—Politics and government.
Classification: LCC DS559.912 D75

Cover photograph by Nhu Truong showing pillar detail from the Temple of Literature, Hanoi.
Cover design by Refine Define
Index compiled by DiacriTech Technologies Pte Ltd
Typeset by Stephen Logan
Printed in Singapore by Mainland Press Pte Ltd

Contents

Contributors

Quang Chau is is a faculty member at the Department of Education Management, University of Education, Vietnam National University Hanoi, and a PhD candidate at the Department of Educational Policy and Leadership, State University of New York at Albany, where he also works as a research assistant at the Program for Research on Private Higher Education (PROPHE). His research interests focus on private higher education, and higher education governance and policy. He is an editorial board member of the Routlege book series Global Realities in Private Higher Education, and the lead editor of the series' volume on Asian Private Higher Education. In addition, Quang has participated in policy research and consultation projects, penned education commentaries, and organized and presented at many conferences.

Hoang Cam Thanh is a Lecturer in the Faculty of International Relations of the University of Social Sciences and Humanities, Vietnam National University. In May 2012, she was awarded a Master of Arts in Political Science from the Graduate School of Texas A&M University–Commerce in the United States. She is currently a PhD candidate in International Relations at the University of Social Sciences and Humanities, Hanoi, Vietnam.

Mai Fujita is the Director of Southeast Asian Studies Department II at the Institute of Developing Economies, Japan External Trade Organization. With interests in the nexus of market-oriented transition, globalization and economic development in Vietnam, she has published extensively on Vietnam's participation in global value chains, industrialization and the development of local firms, including the book *Exploiting Linkages for Building Technological Capabilities: Vietnam's Motorcycle Component Suppliers under Japanese and Chinese Influence* (2013). Recently, she has undertaken research on the development of state-owned and private enterprises, entrepreneurs and state-business relationships.

Mai Van Tinh is a retired senior specialist of the Higher Education Department, Vietnam's Ministry of Education and Training, where he started to work in 1972. After retirement, he joined the Association of Vietnam Universities and Colleges as Deputy Head of the Policy Research and Analysis Unit, and then as Director of the Center for Higher Education Technology – Science Transfer and Research (CETSTR). He has held different positions in various higher education projects and associations, including the Vietnam Community College Association as an Advisory Board Member, and the International Open Frontiers Education Institute as a senior strategic advisor. He received his PhD in Applied Linguistics at the State University in St. Peterburg in 1985.

Nguyen Khac Giang is a researcher on Vietnamese affairs. Giang obtained his PhD in Political Science at Victoria University of Wellington, New Zealand, where he compared Vietnamese and Chinese political developments. He was formerly Head of the Political Research Unit of the Hanoi-based Vietnam Institute for Economic and Policy Research (VEPR). His co-authored book, *Civil Society in Vietnam: An Institutional Approach*, was published in 2018 and received the IRED Vietnam's Best Book in Economics Award in 2019. His academic work appears in, among others, the *Asian Journal of Political Science*, *Constitutional Political Economy*, and *Asia & the Pacific Policy Studies*. He also writes extensively for major Vietnamese and English news outlets, including *VnExpress*, *Saigon Times*, Zing News, Vietnamnet, *The Diplomat*, and the East Asia Forum.

Nguyen Thuc Cuong is currently a PhD Candidate in the Department of Political Science at McGill University. He also holds an MA degree in International Relations at the University of Chicago. His research interests include the philosophy and methodology of social sciences, contemporary nationalism, theories of the state, international relations theories, and social movement, with a geographical focus on Vietnam.

Thuy Nguyen is a Data Scientist at Reason Foundation. She holds a PhD in Political Science from the University of Oregon, where she specializes in Data Science and Quantitative Research Methods.

Yoon Ah Oh is Assistant Professor at the Graduate School of International Studies (GSIS) at Seoul National University. Her research focuses on the political dimensions of asymmetric economic interdependence, with a focus on Southeast Asia. For the last few years she has been examining Southeast Asia's external relations, most notably with China. Her recent articles include "The Patterns of State-Firm Coordination in China's Private Sector Internationalization: China's Mergers and Acquisitions in Southeast Asia" with Suyeon No in the *Pacific Review* (2020), "Chinese Development Aid to Asia: Size and Motives" in the *Asian Journal of Comparative Politics* (2020), and "Power Asymmetry and Threat Points: Negotiating China's Infrastructure Development in Southeast Asia" in the *Review of International Political Economy* (2018). Prior to joining GSIS she was a fellow at the Korea Institute for International Economic Policy, where she conducted research on Southeast Asian economies and Korea-ASEAN economic relations. She received her PhD in political science from Ohio State University and her MA and BA degrees in political science from the National University of Singapore and Seoul National University, respectively.

Duy Trinh is a Data and Statistical Specialist at the Niehaus Center for Globalization and Governance at Princeton University. His research focuses on intra-elite conflicts in single-party regimes, particularly of contemporary Vietnam and China. His most recent peer-reviewed article, titled "Explaining Factional Sorting in China and Vietnam", appears in *Problems of Post-Communism*. Trinh is a Southeast Asia Research Group (SEAREG) fellow. He received his PhD in Political Science from the University of California, San Diego.

Trinh Khanh Ly worked for the Vietnam General Confederation of Labour (VGCL) and the ILO Country Office for Vietnam for many years. Her main research fields include trade unions, social dialogue, industrial conflicts, labour reform and migrant workers. Her studies are published in peer-reviewed journals such as the *Asian Journal of Law and Society*, *Southeast Asian Studies*, and *Global Labour Column*. She is a Jurist-Sworn Interpreter and also an entrepreneur in Belgium.

Nhu Truong is Assistant Professor in the Department of Politics and Public Affairs at Denison University , a Mansfield-Luce Asia Scholars Network Fellow, a Rosenberg Institute Scholar, and a Center For Khmer Studies Senior Research Fellow. Her research is concerned with the repressive-responsiveness of autocracies and democracies, social contention, state formation, and political legitimation in Northeast and Southeast Asia, particularly China, Vietnam and Cambodia. Her work has appeared in the *Journal of East Asian Studies*, *Problems of Post-Communism*, edited books, and policy studies. Previously, she was a Postdoctoral Associate with the Council on Southeast Asian Studies at Yale University, a Shorenstein Postdoctoral Fellow on Contemporary Asia at Stanford University, a Young Southeast Asia Fellow selected by the Southeast Asia Research Group, and a New Faces in China Studies Conference Fellow held at Duke University. She holds a PhD in Political Science from McGill University, an MPA in International Policy and Development from New York University, and an MA in Asian Studies from the University of Texas in Austin.

Truong Quang Hoan is a Research Fellow at the Institute for Southeast Asian Studies (ISEAS), a unit under the Vietnam Academy of Social Sciences (VASS). He also teaches subjects such as Political Economy and the Political Economy of Japan's Economic and Social Development at Vietnam National University, Hanoi. His main research fields include Southeast Asian economies and ASEAN's relations with external partners, particularly the economic aspect. His studies are published in peer-reviewed journals such as *Rian Thai: International Journal of Thai Studies*, *China Report*, *East Asian Economic Review*, *ISEAS Perspectives*, *Journal of Cultural Economics*, and *Sage Open*. He was formerly the Asian Graduate Fellow in Singapore in 2015 and the Taiwan Fellow in Taiwan in 2017. He received his PhD in International Economics from the Graduate Academy of Social Sciences, VASS.

Upalat Korwatanasakul, Associate Professor at the School of Social Sciences, Waseda University, is an international development economist with interest in a wide range of economic and social development topics in East and Southeast Asia; namely, the digital economy, global value chains, the informal economy, labour markets, small and medium-sized enterprises, and trade policy. He has worked with and had research collaborations with major international organizations and research institutes such as the Asian Development

Bank Institute (ADBI), the Economic Research Institute for ASEAN and East Asia (ERIA), the International Labour Organization (ILO), the Japan International Cooperation Agency Research Institute (JICA-RI), and the United Nations Economic and Social Commission for Asia and the Pacific (UNESCAP), among others. He holds a PhD in International Studies, majoring in Development Economic Analysis, from the Graduate School of Asia-Pacific Studies, Waseda University (Tokyo, Japan).

Vu Quang Viet received his PhD in Economics from New York University (1980). He is an expert on national accounts, input-output, and supply and use tables. While he was Chief of National Accounts of the United Nations Statistics Division, he contributed to international efforts to establish standards for economic statistics and national accounts embodied in the 2008 and 1993 System of National Accounts. He is the author of a number of books on GDP compilation, studies on national accounts, input-output, and the financial social accounting matrix. He has also authored numerous articles in Vietnamese and some in English on the economy of Vietnam. After retiring from the UN, he has served as consultant to the African Development Bank, Statistical Center of the Gulf Cooperation Council (GCC), USAID, Rand Corporation, Asian Development Bank, UNSD, UNDP and a number of countries in Asia, the Middle East and Africa.

Thinh-Van Vu is a lecturer at the Department of Human Resource Management, Thuongmai University, Hanoi, Vietnam. He received his PhD in Management Science at the Department of Business Administration, Nanhua University, Taiwan (2022). His research interests include labour relations and trade unions, sustainable human resource management, workplace bullying, employee voice, and CSR. He received the second prize in the "Labor Research Contest" organized by ILO and the Ministry of Labor, Invalids and Social Affairs in 2019. His recent research has appeared in *Human Resource Management*, *Safety Science*, *International Journal of Hospitality Management*, *Journal of Sustainable Tourism*, and *Data in Brief.*

Tuong Vu is Professor and Head of the Political Science Department at the University of Oregon. He has held visiting appointments at Princeton University and the National University of Singapore. A former editor of the *Journal of Vietnamese Studies*, he is the author or editor of seven books, including, most recently, *Building a Republican*

Nation in Vietnam, 1920–1963 (2022), *Toward a Framework for Vietnamese American Studies: History, Community, and Memory* (2023), *The Republic of Vietnam, 1955–1975: Vietnamese Perspectives on Nation Building* (2020), and *Vietnam's Communist Revolution: The Power and Limits of Ideology* (2017) as well as thirty other peer-reviewed publications on the politics of nationalism, revolution and state-building in East and Southeast Asia. Vu is the founding director of the US-Vietnam Research Center at the University of Oregon, and he is consulted frequently on Vietnamese politics by international media, including *The Economist*, the Associated Press, Nikkei Asia and Bloomberg News Service.

Introduction

The Peg of Vietnam's Economic and Political Development

Nhu Truong and Tuong Vu

During an eight-day spectacle of its 13th National Congress in 2021, the Vietnamese Communist Party opened the curtain on a political theatre that reaffirmed the party's ruling leadership. This 13th National Congress also marked thirty-five years since the Vietnamese Communist Party (VCP) ushered in Renovation in order to divert the economy towards a path of market reforms. Having survived the collapse of the Soviet Bloc, today, the high economic growth generated under these reforms has provided the party with a claim to performance-based legitimacy. Between 2016 and 2020, Vietnam continued to attract significant foreign investments that sustained an annual growth rate of 6 per cent. During the global coronavirus pandemic, the country's GDP growth dropped to 2.91 per cent, its lowest growth rate in decades. Yet Vietnam was still recognized as one of the three Asian economies, along with China and Taiwan, to have maintained a positive growth rate despite the severe impact of the pandemic (Lee 2021). This gave the newly elected leadership at the 13th National Congress the confidence to exude continued optimism in the nation's future (Duc Binh et al. 2021).

Now, at this important juncture, it is a timely opportunity to take stock of Vietnam's economic and political developments, and to closely dissect the contradictions behind the VCP's success story. As this volume shows, the previous five years from 2016 to 2020 offered causes for both hopes and concerns. Despite the resilience of the Vietnamese economy, many problems persist, some of which are structural, including the low productivity of the labour force, an inefficient state-owned sector, rising national debt, and the country's low position on the global value chain of production (P.V. 2020).[1] Back in 2010, VCP leaders formally declared 2020 to be the year when Vietnam was to become a modern, industrialized economy (Ng Tong 2010). Ten years later, the goalposts for the party's performance have been expediently shifted. The party now aspires to transform the economy and to achieve national industrialization by 2035 (Song An 2021), but that goal remains elusive to date.

In politics, the VCP has tightened its grip over political elites during the previous five years. Calls for political reforms garnered wide public attention and permeated spheres of political debates during the 2013 constitutional revision, including calls for a multi-party system and a constitutional court. But the VCP has unequivocally rejected demands for deeper political reforms and has moved to centralize party leadership and control. At the 13th National Congress, General Secretary Nguyen Phu Trong broke institutional norms to hold the reins for a third consecutive term, while the majority of membership in the new Politburo are career officials in the party bureaucracies and state security (Le 2021). Under Trong, the party has also launched a vigorous anti-graft campaign that netted more than a hundred officials, including a Politburo member and numerous other top officials in the military, the police, national and provincial governments, and state-owned enterprises. While the VCP propagated this unprecedented campaign as a "deep clean" of the political machinery to safeguard public goods from the maw of corruption and to maintain the people's faith in the party (Phuong Linh 2018), the campaign has principally been motivated by political wrangling and factional infighting.[2]

In this economic and political climate, hundreds of activists and advocates for democracy, land rights, religious freedom and other civil liberties have been arrested and given lengthy sentences in prison (Human Rights Watch 2021). Political openings that facilitated the emergence of the so-called "self-nomination movement" in the 2016 legislative election have also been tightened (Truong 2020). Massive protests against two government draft laws erupted nationwide in 2017, exposing the latent power of anti-government undercurrents in society (Human Rights Watch 2018).[3] Tensions with China in the East Sea/South China Sea remain high despite the VCP's efforts to appease China, making Vietnam's engagement with China a dangerous issue that arouses both strong nationalist sentiments and widespread social discontent (Grossman 2021, pp. 19–23). While Vietnam has revised the Labour Code in 2019 to allow workers to form independent trade unions (Hutt 2019; Chan 2020), how this change will be implemented in practice still remains in question.[4] The government's recent failure to cope with the resurgence of Covid-19 in the summer and autumn of 2021 further exposed deep problems in its economic model as well as in its social and political management styles (Flower 2021; Tatarski 2021).

This edited volume examines these developments and trends in Vietnam's economy and politics over the last five years, while noting that many trends discussed in the volume have occurred since Nguyen Phu Trong's first term, if not earlier. The volume addresses two crucial sets of questions. First, what is the nature of Vietnam's economic growth since market reforms? More specifically, what role has the state played in Vietnam's developmental trajectory? What then are the coming opportunities and challenges for Vietnam's economy? Second, how has economic growth affected Vietnamese politics? To what extent has rapid economic transformation strengthened or weakened the communist party's grip on the political system?

In this introductory chapter, we will first attempt to answer these two sets of questions with economic theories of development. Through this lens, our analysis stresses the resource-based nature of Vietnam's economic growth and the problematics of the current trajectory.[5] It is underpinned by a sharper differentiation of the more limited role of the state in Vietnam's development compared to the region's "East Asian tigers". Systemic vulnerabilities in the current economy now place Vietnam at a particular crossroads in which the regime is confronted not with the mere task of propelling GDP growth but with the greater challenge of generating sustainable growth over the long term. Ironically, while economic growth has emboldened the party's claim to performance-based legitimacy, it has also heightened tensions in contemporary state-society relations that directly challenge and erode the power of the party over society.

In the second part of this chapter, we will introduce the contributing essays in this book, which focus on different aspects of the above sets of questions. Through the latest research represented by a collection of perspectives from Asia, including Vietnam, Japan and South Korea, as well as scholars working within and outside of North America across fields and practices, this volume will provide readers with a better understanding of salient issues facing contemporary Vietnam after more than three decades of market reforms.

Nature of Economic Growth

At the risk of oversimplification, neoclassical economic theory views the development of a national economy as contingent on the efficient use and allocation of scarce resources—namely, labour and capital—throughout the economy.[6] Other things being equal, more workers, more machines and more efficient employment of both are bound to raise national income. Besides the amounts of productive resources employed, the quality of workers and the level of technology also determine productivity and expand growth possibilities. Institutional economics adds to neoclassical economics by stressing market and governmental institutions that reduce transaction costs, ultimately raising efficiency. Development economists further emphasize the importance of trade gains for developing economies because of the limited size of the domestic market and the enormous needs for imported technologies.

The above elementary insights from economic theories are particularly useful, given Vietnam's peculiar conditions when the government embraced market reforms in the late 1980s. At the time, Vietnam was among the poorest countries in the world; in 1988 three million of its population were near starvation and another five million were malnourished (Heng 1993). This dire economic crisis could not be attributed to the country's lack of labour and capital, but rather to the communist government's inept policy that effectively repressed the capacity of the Vietnamese economy. The VCP's initial push for a centrally planned and primarily collective economy severely restricted market activities, leading to a situation in which both physical and human resources were deeply undervalued and underemployed.

According to standard economic theories, the engine of Vietnam's economic growth, at least for the first two decades of reform, came from the unleashing of this "repressed capacity" under the command economy, aided by gains from trade, external aid, investment and remittance (Riedel and Turley 1999; Hill 2010). The willingness of the VCP to retract previous dogmatic policies in favor of alternative pathways to economic growth was instrumental. As government restrictions were lifted, increasing amounts of domestic resources were brought into productive activities for market circulation rather than for meeting government quotas. With private enterprises legalized, individuals seeking better lives for themselves and their families contributed to rising productivity. As the economy opened up to foreign investment and trade, foreign aid and capital expanded the available stock of resources and technologies. Billions of annual remittances from the diaspora, especially in the early years, played a profound role in stimulating domestic consumption, providing hard currencies for the import of machinery, and balancing the current account and the government budget (Dang 2016, pp. 356–57; Vu 2015).

From this analytical viewpoint, the secrets of economic growth in Vietnam appear to be no secrets at all. The often touted "miracle" of Vietnam transitioning from being a starving nation to one of the world's top rice exporters in only a few years speaks not to any miraculous developmental government policy but simply to the government's liberalization of the country's repressed capacity.[7] As Hal Hill (2000, p. 284) argues about Vietnam's unexpected success in export, "the most suitable analytical tool for understanding the success of the reforms is the concept of 'unshackling' exporters, and business in general".

Today, the limits of Vietnam's current growth model are supported by three observations. First, Vietnam's economy has not risen above its expected rank in the region. Assuming Vietnam had not experienced three devastating wars and the failed socialist experiment, one would expect its economy to be at a comparable level of GDP per capita as those of the Philippines, Indonesia and Thailand—neighbouring countries with more or less similar endowments. In fact, between 1990 and 2019, Vietnam's national per capita income remained much lower than that of Thailand as well as those of Indonesia and the Philippines.[8] Second, if we compare Vietnam's national income per capita in the 1980s and today with those of its neighbours, it can be seen that there has been no change in the ranking over those four decades. In the 1980s, Vietnam was the fourth-poorest country in Southeast Asia, ranked above only Burma, Laos and Cambodia and below the rest, including the Philippines. As of 2019, Vietnam's economy maintained the same low ranking, even though its gaps with the Philippines have been sharply reduced.[9] Third, national incomes per capita of Cambodia and Laos, countries that had shared a history of war and socialism with Vietnam before opening up in the 1990s, have also tracked closely that of Vietnam in the last four decades.

The regional comparison above suggests, on the one hand, that Vietnam still has some repressed capacity. Both neoclassical and institutional economics would suggest that the Vietnamese government should further liberalize the economy and craft more effective market institutions to realize the full potentials of the country's resources. On the other hand, the comparison also suggests that sheer reliance on Vietnam's resources or repressed capacity might not be sufficient.

Continuing rapid growth to help Vietnam keep up with its neighbours must count on other development strategies and institutional factors, such as higher productivity and technological upgrading, and deeper rationalization of existing financial institutions.

The Role of the State

Although standard economic theories assign only a limited role to the state in economic development, they are suspect in the context of East Asia, where scholars have pointed out the decisive role of the state in the rapid industrialization of Japan, South Korea, Taiwan and Singapore (Johnson 1982; Amsden 1989; Haggard 1990; Kohli 2004; Suehiro 2008). Industrialization in these nations was achieved less by following neoclassical economic prescriptions and more by direct state interventions through effective industrial policies that successfully promoted strategic sectors and through social policies such as land reform and state investment in education and healthcare that enhanced growth-inducing equality.

On the surface, the experiences of the "East Asian tigers" seem relevant for Vietnam (Turner et al. 2019; Beeson and Pham 2012). After all, Vietnam does have a powerful state that already directly controls major economic sectors. A closer look reveals, however, that the Vietnamese state has much less capacity than the East Asian tigers (Pincus 2015), and much less autonomy or cohesion to pursue the same strategy (Gainsborough 2017; Fforde and Homutova 2017). Furthermore, the state is hamstrung by the party's tenacious clinging to its socialist ideology, which still gives priority to state-owned enterprises (SOEs), regardless of their efficiency, at the expense of private capital (Vu-Thanh 2017). The large state-owned sector, whose interests are intertwined with those of the ruling elites, is quite powerful and has resisted reform (Ishizuka 2020).[10]

If Vietnam were to pursue state-led industrialization, the political system dictates that it would rely on SOEs, which is exactly what has happened. The Vietnamese state under prime ministers Vo Van Kiet and Nguyen Tan Dung championed the consolidation of SOEs to create conglomerates—dubbed "steely fists"—that could lead Vietnam's industrialization (Vu 2009). Yet none turned into a Korean chaebol, and quite a few went bankrupt, losing billions of dollars. The state-owned sector in fact has been "a net drag on the Vietnamese economy" (Malesky and London 2014, pp. 412–13). Periods that have witnessed the most rapid growth and poverty reduction have been when the state sector was weakest.

With such a dismal performance of its industrial strategy, the contributions of the Vietnamese state to the country's economic transformation have been limited to lifting the market restrictions of the socialist era, providing political stability and special treatment for foreign investors (even while domestic private firms are discriminated against), negotiating trade agreements to widen access for Vietnamese exports, and other similar policies. In land management, for instance, between 1986 and 1993, the Vietnamese government had granted individuals a bundle of land-use rights to facilitate land-market transactions. Effective as of the 1993 Land Law, these included the rights to transfer, exchange, inherit, lease and mortgage land-use rights. Subsequent legislative amendments and revisions further broadened and extended these rights to both domestic and foreign investors, enterprises and businesses, including the rights to sublease, donate, provide guarantees and contribute land use as capital.[11] Most notably, the 2003 Land Law swung open the gate for indiscriminate government land seizures, often occurring in collusion with investors, without commensurate compensation for dispossessed villagers for "economic development purposes". Unlike Vietnam, the Chinese Communist Party has more proactively and intently maintained control of the land supply, particularly through government control of rural-to-urban land conversion, as a "tool of macroeconomic management" for boosting and contracting the national economy (Rithmire 2017).[12] Whereas China might be described as a case of "land-centered development" (Lin 2009) or "state-led development" (Ong 2014; Chan 1994), this is less the case for Vietnam. So the role of the state in Vietnam's industrialization is to promote growth within the gradually loosening parameters of ideological and political constraints, rather than to take the bull by the horns in leading the country's economic development.

On social policies to support growth-inducing equality, the role of the state in Vietnam has been similarly passive despite rhetoric to the contrary. While social inequality in Vietnam has been less severe than for many of its neighbours—such as China and the Philippines (Kuhonta and Truong 2020; Kuhonta 2011; Malesky, Abrami and Zheng 2011)—the number of "the super-rich" in Vietnam has increased rapidly in the last decade at a rate estimated to be the world's third-highest during 2019–24 (Wells-Dang and Vu 2019; McCarthy 2020). If arbitrary land seizures have helped political elites amass wealth, state investment in education and healthcare, especially for workers and the urban poor, has been meagre.[13] Moreover, although Vietnam is less corrupt than Cambodia and the Philippines, its public service is still mired in corruption that further limits access for ordinary citizens and labour productivity (Transparency International 2021; Benedickter and Nguyen 2018, p. 29). In catching up with neighbouring countries then, it will be important for the Vietnamese state to invest more in social services while reducing corruption.

Economic Growth and Political Change

How then has economic growth affected Vietnamese politics? To what extent has growth weakened or strengthened the VCP's power? There is a rich body of scholarship in political science about the relationship between economic growth and political change.[14] Although they do not fully apply to Vietnam, some evidence of each theory can be found, and all point to the weakening grip of the ruling communist party on the political system.

Based on the historical experience of European development, modernization theorists focus on the emergence of the bourgeoisie and other urban middle classes as interconnected modernizing processes, such as urbanization, industrialization, secularization and social differentiation, that spread throughout society. It is expected that the rise of new urban classes will lead to increasing demands for political participation (Lipset 1959). As Huntington (1968) argues, the crises observed in many newly independent countries in Asia and Africa in the 1960s came from the failure of their political systems to develop effective political institutions that incorporate or channel those demands.

Without assuming the inevitability of authoritarian collapse or political democratization that modernization theory largely takes for granted,[15] the potential of the middle class as agents of opposition and democratic pushbacks has borne out in part among Vietnam's neighbouring countries. Throughout the post-war history of these countries, while the business elites often cooperated with governments, urban groups from students to teachers to professionals were engaged in numerous protest movements, even though not always for democracy.[16] In South Korea, they toppled the Rhee Syngman regime in 1960 and battled military rule in Kwangju in 1980, eventually contributing to the democratization of the country in 1988 (Lee 2007). In the Philippines, "people power" brought down the Marcos dictatorship in 1986 (Thompson 1995). In Thailand and Indonesia, the Thai government of Kittikachorn and the Indonesian government of

Suharto, respectively, fell in the face of massive urban protests in 1973 and 1998 (Bertrand 2013, chs. 2 and 5).

On the other side of the ideological spectrum are Karl Marx and scholars in his school who draw different lessons from European experiences. The central figures in these accounts are not the bourgeoisie but subordinate classes such as farmers, workers and the urban poor (Marx and Engels 1848; Thompson 1971; Scott 1976). Greater exploitation under capitalism coupled with the destruction of traditional mechanisms for welfare provision by market forces are predicted to lead to riots, protests and revolts by those classes that can pose challenges to the ruling elites. Workers' strikes were indeed a major cause of unrest in South Korea under military rule (Koo 2001). Rural armed struggles led by communist parties threatened government in the Philippines (1950s and 1980s) and Thailand (1960s–70s).

Displaying vestiges of similar dynamics, large public protests have been on the rise in Vietnam during the last decade. Workers' strikes have been common, as have been farmers' protests, some of which involved violence (Kerkvliet 2019). Representing this bleak trend was the recent case of Dong Tam village, where villagers armed themselves and openly challenged the authority for over a year, ultimately resulting in the death of their leader in a night-time raid by security forces (Kerkvliet 2020). While these protests have often been invoked by specific grievances, protests concerned with environmental causes or otherwise fuelled by anti-China sentiments have seen more cross-linkages across societal cleavages. Urban intellectuals, veterans and students led small but persistent demonstrations in 2007, 2011 and 2014 to demand the Vietnamese government take action against China for its perceived violations of Vietnamese sovereign rights in the South China Sea (Vu 2014). Massive protests involving thousands from wider social sectors and classes simultaneously took place in many large cities against the Special Zone and Cybersecurity laws in 2017 (Human Rights Watch 2018). Likewise, the Tree Movement in 2015 rallied public outcry against the Hanoi government's decision to cut down 6,708 trees lining the city streets (Vu 2017). Large demonstrations by farmers and fishermen with wider public support later took place in the aftermath of an environmental disaster caused by a Taiwanese steel complex in Ha Tinh in 2016, demanding accountability and compensation.

Deep and widespread resentment has also been fuelled by restricted outlets for "managed participation" and a constricting space for political dissent. There is little redress in the system against wrongdoers who are powerful officials. Many established intellectuals and young bloggers have risked long prison sentences to write critically about the communist party and the government in their online posts. Several have sought to found autonomous professional associations, such as the Free Journalists' Club (*Cau lac bo Nha bao Tu do*), Independent Writers' League (*Van doan Doc lap Viet nam*), and Independent Journalists' Association (*Hoi Nha bao Doc lap*). Others have formed (illegal) political parties and democracy advocacy groups, such as the Democratic Party (*Dang Dan chu*), Bloc 8406 (*Khoi 8406*) and Brotherhood for Democracy (*Hoi Anh em Dan chu*).

Society-centred accounts, however, do not capture the decisive impacts of economic growth on post-communist Vietnam's political elites and the regime. First, the ability of the market economy to improve living standards has over time deepened the gap between the regime's socialist ideology and the reality of life. With few exceptions, the ruling elites today no longer believe in that ideology even though they still publicly pledge their allegiance to it (Saxonberg 2012). Second, under the market economy, money has increasingly penetrated the communist party and government bureaucracies. Corruption has reached an alarmingly high level; it involves large sums of money that feed insatiable greed and has become endemic in public service.[17] The government monopoly of resources and abuses of power have continually generated widespread grievances that run deep. This also attests to the problem of a development strategy that relies heavily on foreign investment and which subjects the lower classes to exploitation and dispossession. Third, the communist party can no longer retain much of its secrets as rival elite factions resort to the internet to air the dirty laundry of their enemies in public (Bui 2016). This exposure has further diminished the legitimacy of the VCP.

Another source of threats for the regime comes from its relations with the outside world. As Vietnam's economy becomes more integrated into the global economy, it is now vulnerable to external economic shifts over which it has no control. One of the recent shifts involves the trade war and security tensions between the United States and China, the two largest trade partners of Vietnam. Regardless of what will transpire, Vietnam is in a precarious position and is likely to be negatively affected.

In response to dangers from eroding legitimacy and weakened cohesion as a result of corruption and rising popular nationalism, VCP leaders have sought to retool the system in minor ways in order to stem political decay and increase its resilience. Ideologically, they have continued to downplay socialism and relied more on economic performance as a discourse of legitimation (Le 2012). They have loosened control over domestic criticisms of China to reduce pressure and appease popular nationalist sentiments. Institutionally, since 2016 the party has launched a more aggressive anti-corruption campaign than in the past. Other means to increase vertical and horizontal accountability have been instituted (Abrami et al. 2013; Schuler 2021).

The VCP has sought to tighten its control over the military while expanding police power to monitor the internet, crack down on dissent and suppress opposition. Epitomizing the trend in changing state-society relations is the increasing use of violence by protesters and by the government, such as in the case of Dong Tam village above. This trend testifies powerfully to the effects of economic transformation on politics in Vietnam.

Furthermore, it speaks to the need for the party to take greater steps to address societal grievances and demands, as well as to develop political institutions that better respond to and incorporate public interests. As Huntington forewarned, "the primary problem of politics is the lag in the development of political institutions behind social and economic change" (Huntington 1968, p. 5).

Officials of international agencies in Hanoi who were frustrated when their advice for further reform was ignored by the government reportedly joked that Vietnam was neither a developed nor developing country; it belonged to a unique category of "countries that don't want to develop".[18] While the Vietnamese government appears irrational in the joke, it is not. Rather, the regime is walking a tightrope and must navigate a delicate balance between imperatives for rapid development and increased existential threats, particularly in scenarios where the party has failed to be responsive to societal needs and unrest.

Structure of the Book

The chapters in this edited volume are organized thematically in three parts. Part I underscores how the Vietnamese economy is vulnerable across many dimensions despite its impressive growth rates. The first chapter by Tuong Vu and Thuy Nguyen places Vietnam's market reform in a historical perspective by reviewing developments since the 1980s as the country evolved from its socialist system of the war and revolutionary period. Their chapter frames the market reforms of the late 1980s against the backdrop of the Vietnamese communist revolution and the draconian march to socialism in the first post-war decade, which led to a profound social, political and economic crisis.

The authors recount how Vietnamese reformers have embarked on market reform but refused political reform. This principle has fundamentally shaped the reform process and its outcome, including the integration of the economy into the global economy, the rise of "red crony capitalism", the decay of the political system, and the ongoing legitimacy crisis.

In Chapter 2, Vu Quang Viet offers an overview of Vietnam's developmental path since 1985 with a historical discussion about the country's transition from a planned economy to market-oriented economic reforms.[19] Making use of statistical data, the chapter outlines how Vietnam's economy has fallen short of reaching the VCP's alleged goal of achieving industrialization. In doing so, the author calls for a re-evaluation of Vietnam's development strategy and advocates for deeper reforms.

Although Vietnam's rapid economic development has been largely explained by its participation in the global value chain (GVC) and a focus on low-value-added activities and foreign direct investments, Upalat Korwatanasakul argues in Chapter 3 that industries such as food products, textiles and clothing, and electrical and electronic equipment have also contributed significantly to the rapid development of Vietnam's economy. Yet, by depending on foreign inputs and technologies in order to increase the country's total production outputs and exports without further upgrades, Vietnam faces risks of structural stagnation, erosion of national competitiveness, and economic slowdown. Therefore, to steer the economy from falling into a middle-income trap, the VCP should consider integrating a GVC-upgrading development model into its new policy agenda. Policies that facilitate strong institutional reforms, promote strategic GVC engagement and strengthen domestic capabilities, especially of small and medium-sized enterprises, should be the priority.

The next two chapters, Chapter 4 by Truong Quang Hoan and Chapter 5 by Yoon Ah Oh, similarly highlight the negative trends in Vietnam's economy. Specifically, Truong alerts Vietnam to the danger of falling into a middle-income trap as a result of the country's declining labour productivity. Employing data from the Trade-in-Value-Added database, this chapter explores the dynamic pattern of Vietnam's position in the global value chain, focusing on the electronics industry and the textile and apparel industry as well as the extent to which different groups in this industry actually benefit from the global value chain. Analysis in Chapter 5 focuses instead on Vietnam's economic dependence on trade relations with China. In particular, Oh employs a typology of trade shocks based on the intentionality of events that trigger the shocks, and the transmission channels of bilateral trade between Vietnam and China. This typology provides a framework to identify and better understand the nature of Vietnam's vulnerability, as well as the distinctive risks associated with each particular type of trade shock.

Next, Part II focuses on important political developments and changes in state-society relations under the effects of economic growth in contemporary Vietnam, particularly evolving state-business relationships in Vietnam's state-owned enterprises, the mechanisms of VCP leadership in public universities, the role of media in popular protests, and the freedom of workers to organize in Vietnam. In the chapters by Mai Fujita and by Quang Chau and Mai Van Tinh, they suggest that although the VCP maintains certain strongholds of state-owned enterprises and public universities, party control has also eroded. Concerning regime responses to social unrest, the analysis by Nguyen Thuc Cuong and Hoang Cam Thanh suggests that citizen protests channelled through media-infratized politics led the government to respond with policy change in 2018. At the same time, as Thinh Van Vu's chapter points out, whether policy change results in meaningful outcomes is another question.

Focusing on the equitization and divestment of state capital from large state-owned enterprises and the rise of large private family-owned enterprises building close relationships with the party-state, Chapter 6 by Mai Fujita asks who are the individuals leading large state and private enterprises and from where have they emerged? And how have state-business relationships changed? In order to address these questions, her chapter examines the structure of the enterprise sector, features of Vietnam's largest enterprises, and profiles and origins of the top management of the largest state-owned and private enterprises, which draws on an original database of the top managers of listed enterprises. Based on in-depth case studies of the career histories of the managers of selected large private and state-owned enterprises, Fujita concludes that the state-business relationship remains close despite the recent emergence of several large private enterprises.

Using archive documents and extensive interviews, Chapter 7 by Quang Chau and Mai Van Tinh sheds light on a subject insufficiently covered in Vietnam studies—that is, how the VCP controls higher education. Through the analytical framework of elite dualism, the authors argue that party control of public universities is relatively tight at the top level but rather loose at the grass-roots level. First, university presidents, who are de facto the party secretary, normally have both good academic credentials and solid political capital. Second, at the sub-institutional levels, political capital is often outweighed by academic credentials in appointment decisions. Third, the Communist Youth Union appears to be losing ground to international NGOs that provide students with English skills and opportunities to volunteer abroad. Furthermore, the recent enforcement of the US-style governing board structure as part of the public administration system's restructuring, whilst not likely to threaten the party leadership, has the potential to create opportunities for universities to thrive. In contrast to calls for power convergence (*nhat the hoa*) throughout the political system, the party tends to tolerate some power divergence in the realm of higher education. In conclusion, the authors suggest that universities can potentially hold leverage for democratization.

To what extent does space actually exist for citizen participation, societal resistance and the development of civil society in contemporary Vietnam? In addressing this crucial question, Nguyen Thuc Cuong and Hoang Cam Thanh in Chapter 8 capture an increasingly salient dimension of contemporary Vietnamese civil society called mediatized infrapolitics—an unobtrusive realm of everyday state-society struggle on mass media platforms. These two authors conducted a discourse analysis of local newspapers and foreign media outlets on the controversial proposal for land leases of ninety-nine-years' duration for foreign investors in Special Economic Zones (SEZs) and the resultant policy change in 2018. Taking the results, the authors argue that mediatized infrapolitics has increasingly influenced the accountability of the VCP via a three-stage communicative process. In short, unlike noisy, headline-grabbing protests and demonstrations, mediatized infrapolitics, albeit seemingly innocuous, quietly and effectively sets the scene for the former to spread in moments of external crisis.

While the previous chapter suggests that the Vietnamese communist regime could be responsive to social demands, Chapter 9 by Thinh Van Vu highlights some of the inherent limitations in these responses. In December 2019, the National Assembly of Vietnam passed a new labour code, which came into effect in January 2021. It allows workers to form independent unions at the workplace. Examining factors that hinder the freedom of trade unions in Vietnam and workers' participation in such unions, the chapter finds that provisions in the law remain vague and do not specify how to set up and manage new workers representative organizations at the workplace. Moreover, union subservience to the VCP and managerially dependent unions still hinder trade union reform. In effect, many workers do not trust a union's protection or its role of representation.

Chapter 10 by Trinh Khanh Ly discusses another dark side of Vietnam's development—namely, rising inequality in society and the low wages for workers that has resulted in large numbers of them seeking employment opportunities abroad, whether legally or illegally. Rather than providing vocational training or finding other means to raise workers' incomes, the Vietnamese government has aggressively promoted the export of labour. While this policy has brought higher incomes for workers and large amounts of annual remittances to the Vietnamese economy, there have been problems, including steep fees collected by state-designated labour-export agencies and the prevalence of workers overstaying their visas. Despite such labour export programmes, low wages for domestic workers and limited employment opportunities continue to send thousands of young Vietnamese to Europe every year to work illegally. Trinh shows how these workers encounter great risks in their journeys and are exploited in their host countries.

Finally, Part III places Vietnam in comparative perspective, specifically with China, by focusing on political accountability, political factions and government responses to protests. Challenging the assumption that Vietnam and China are identical regimes, Nguyen Khac Giang in Chapter 11 argues that Vietnam exhibits relatively higher accountability than China. Employing nested game analysis, the chapter shows how the two regimes have been involved in different games during certain historical periods, consisting of the game between the ruler and the selectorate (internal accountability game), the regime and the population (external accountability game), and the regime and foreign powers (foreign pressure game). Different payoff expectations in each game affect the characteristics of accountability within the respective regimes. In the long run, regimes with low accountability like China face a higher risk of internal factionalization, whereas regimes with higher accountability like Vietnam are exposed to a higher risk of elite-mass tensions.

Chapter 12 further contributes to a comparative study of Vietnam and China by drawing attention to how factional politics animates the anti-corruption campaigns led by the communist party in each country. Using a new dataset of disciplinary investigations in the Chinese and Vietnamese communist parties, Duy Trinh argues that regimes can resolve this dilemma by selectively protecting officials who are perceived as allied with the dictator. Factional clarity, the extent to which perceived and actual factional affiliation overlap, determines how selective protection manifests. In China, where factional clarity is strong, the regime engages in ex post protection by delaying sanctions and meting out lenient punishments to investigated officials in provinces whose leaders share ties with the incumbent general secretary. In contrast, under Vietnam's weak factional clarity, such officials are protected ex ante by being excluded from investigations. Altogether, these findings shed light on how authoritarian regimes with similar formal institutions produce divergent corruption and anti-corruption outcomes.

Where Vietnam will be headed in the next five years remains to be seen. As a case of a rapidly growing post-communist country, Vietnam has attracted great attention from outside observers. Regardless of how readers view the Vietnamese model of development, we hope they will find this volume useful for understanding its particular strengths and weaknesses, and its accomplishments and failures.

Notes

1. See also the chapters by Vu Quang Viet, Upalat Korwatanasakul and Truong Quang Hoan in this volume.
2. See Chapter 12 by Duy Trinh in this volume.
3. See also Chapter 8 by Nguyen Thuc Cuong and Hoang Cam Thanh in this volume.
4. See also Chapter 9 by Thinh Van Vu in this volume.
5. By "growth", we refer to the increase in gross domestic product (GDP) or GDP per capita, while recognizing that this is an imperfect measure of a country's overall development.
6. For an advanced discussion of the neoclassical and other theories of economic growth, see Acemoglu (2009).
7. A similar conclusion is reached by many studies on China and Vietnam reviewed by Malesky and London (2014, p. 401). The discussion here does not deal with the politics of reform per se. See Chapter 1 by Tuong Vu and Thuy Nguyen in this volume for an overview of political issues related to reform. For studies on the drawn-out policy debates and changes at the central level in accepting local policies that accommodated private incentives, see Fforde and de Vylder (1996) and Dang (2016); on agriculture specifically, see Kerkvliet (2005). For a more positive assessment of Vietnam's transformation than is provided here, see Fforde (2009, pp. 486–87).
8. Data from the World Bank based on constant 2017 international dollar. Available at https://data.worldbank.org/indicator/NY.GDP.PCAP.PP.KD?locations=VN-PH-ID-TH.
9. The Vietnamese government changed its method of GDP calculation in late 2019 resulting in its GDP increasing by 25 per cent and overtaking that of

the Philippines in 2020. See Lien Hiep Quoc Viet Nam (2019). This artificial increase has not been accepted by many economists (email communication with Vu Quang Viet).

10. See also Chapter 6 by Mai Fujita in this volume. Among the East Asian tigers, only Taiwan has had a relatively large state-owned sector, but Taiwanese political elites have been more forthrightly pro-capitalism and pro–United States than Vietnamese communist leaders.

11. See the 1998 and 2001 amendments and the 2003 Land Law.

12. This is not to suggest that Vietnam should follow the so-called "China model", given the many repercussions that resulted from China's path to economic growth. See, for example, Sargeson (2013).

13. The latest available data shows that government spending on healthcare and education as a percentage of GDP in Vietnam is lower than the world average, while spending for defence is higher. See https://www.theglobaleconomy.com/Vietnam/Health_spending_as_percent_of_GDP/; https://www.theglobaleconomy.com/Vietnam/Education_spending_percent_of_government_spending/; and https://www.theglobaleconomy.com/Vietnam/mil_spend_gdp/. Another source confirms that the Vietnamese state is far more concerned about security than development. In 2014, Vietnam's domestic security forces (including the military) consumed 21 per cent of the annual national budget (compared to 11 per cent in the United States), while its spending on education accounted for 16 per cent. Vu Quang Viet, "Tai sao boi chi ngan sach qua lon va keo dai trong nhieu nam o Viet Nam", *Thoi Dai Moi* no. 16 (September 2017): pp. 219, 232, 242. http://www.tapchithoidai.org/ThoiDai36/201736_VuQuangViet.pdf.

14. See Bertrand (2013) for a broad review of the literature as applied to Southeast Asia.

15. Not long ago, some individuals claimed that "China is moving closer to vindicating classical modernization theory", and even predicted that "China will embark on democratization around 2020" (Liu and Chen 2012). Yet, that neither China's nor Vietnam's communist regimes have democratized—and indeed have become more deeply entrenched—has turned the modernization thesis on its head. Both countries are exemplary cases of *growth without democratization*, at least to date.

16. For a discussion of recent anti-democratic protests in Thailand involving "illiberal democrats" against "undemocratic liberals", see Norton (2012). Others—including Berman (1997), Bellin (2000), Wright (2010), and Sinpeng and Arugay (2014)—have also called into question the notion that the middle class is an inherent liberal or progressive force that always provides a bulwark for democracy.

17. According to surveys conducted in 2019 by the United Nations Development Programme, between 20 and 45 per cent of respondents perceived corruption as prevalent in the public sector (UNDP 2020). For corruption involving high-ranking officials and state-owned enterprises, see Vuving (2019, pp. 375–86).

18. Hai Chau (2015) quotes Pham Chi Lan, the former head of the Vietnam Chamber of Commerce and an advisor to former Vietnamese prime ministers.

19. In this volume, the order of Vietnamese names is left to the author's preference.

References

Abrami, Regina, Edmund Malesky, and Yu Zheng. 2013. "Vietnam through Chinese Eyes: Divergent Accountability in Single-Party Regimes". In *Why Communism Did Not Collapse: Understanding Authoritarian Regime Resilience in Asia and Europe*, edited by Martin Dimitrov, pp. 237–75. New York: Cambridge University Press.

Acemoglu, Daron. 2009. *Introduction to Modern Economic Growth*. Princeton, NJ: Princeton University Press.

Amsden, Alice. 1989. *Asia's Next Giant: South Korea and Late Industrialization*. New York: Oxford University Press.

Beeson, Mark, and Hung Pham. 2012. "Developmentalism with Vietnamese Characteristics: The Persistence of State-Led Development in East Asia". *Journal of Contemporary Asia* 42, no. 4: 539–59.

Bellin, Eva. 2000. "Contingent Democrats: Industrialists, Labor, and Democratization in Late-Developing Countries". *World Politics* 52: 175–205.

Benedickter, Simon, and Loan Nguyen. 2018. "Obsessive Planning in Transitional Vietnam: Understanding Rampant State Planning and Prospects for Reform". *Journal of Vietnamese Studies* 13, no. 4: 1–47.

Berman, Sheri. 1997. "Civil Society and the Collapse of the Weimar Republic". *World Politics* 49: 401–29.

Bertrand, Jacques. 2013. *Political Change in Southeast Asia*. New York: Cambridge University Press.

Bui, Thiem Hai. 2016. "The Influence of Social Media in Vietnam's Elite Politics". *Journal of Current Southeast Asian Affairs* 35: 89–111.

Chan, Anita. 2020. "Vietnam's and China's Diverging Industrial Relations Systems: Cases of Path Dependency". *Journal of Contemporary Asia* 50: 321–40.

Chan, Kam Wing. 1994. *Cities with Invisible Walls: Reinterpreting Urbanization in Post-1949 China*. Hong Kong: Oxford University Press.

Dang, Phong. 2016. *Tu duy Kinh te Viet nam, 1975–1989*. Hanoi: Tri Thuc.

Duc Binh, Tien Long, and Vien Su. 2021. "Van kien Dai hoi XIII ket tinh tri tue toan Dang, toan dan". *Tuoi Tre*, 26 January 2021. https://tuoitre.vn/van-kien-dai-hoi-xiii-ket-tinh-tri-tue-toan-dang-toan-dan-20210125164308874.htm.

Fforde, Adam. 2009. "Economics, History, and the Origins of Vietnam's Post-war Economic Success". *Asian Survey* 49, no. 3, 484–504.

Fforde, Adam, and Lada Homutova. 2017. "Political Authority in Vietnam: Is the Vietnamese Communist Party a Paper Leviathan?" *Journal of Current Southeast Asian Affairs* 36, no. 3: 91–118.

Fforde, Adam, and Stefan de Vylder. 1996. *From Plan to Market: The Economic Transition in Vietnam*. Boulder, CO: Westview.

Flower, Barnaby. 2021. "Delta Variant Sets Off Alarm Bells in Vietnam". *East Asia Forum*, 1 August. https://www.eastasiaforum.org/2021/08/01/delta-variant-sets-off-alarm-bells-in-vietnam/.

Global Witness. 2016. "Hostile Takeover: The Corporate Empire of Cambodia's Ruling Family". https://www.globalwitness.org/en/reports/hostile-takeover/.

Grossman, Derek. 2021. *Regional Responses to US-China Competition in the Indo-Pacific: Vietnam*. Santa Monica: RAND Corporation.

Haggard, Stephan. 1990. *Pathways from the Periphery: The Politics of Growth in Newly Industrializing Countries*. Ithaca: Cornell University Press.

Hai Chau. 2015. "Viet nam la mo hinh ky la nhat the gioi: Nuoc ... khong chiu phat trien". *Infonet*, 10 August 2015. https://infonet.vietnamnet.vn/thoi-su/viet-nam-la-mo-hinh-ky-la-nhat-the-gioi-nuoc-khong-chiu-phat-trien-71097.html.

Heng, Russell. 1993. "Leadership in Vietnam: Pressures for Reform and Their Limits". *Contemporary Southeast Asia* 15, no. 1 (June): 98–110.

Hill, Hal. 2000. "Export Success against the Odds: A Vietnamese Case Study". *World Development* 28, no. 2 (February): 283–300.

Human Rights Watch. 2018. "Vietnam: Investigate Police Response to Mass Protests". 15 June 2018. https://www.hrw.org/news/2018/06/15/vietnam-investigate-police-response-mass-protests.

———. *World Report 2021*. https://www.hrw.org/world-report/2021/country-chapters/vietnam#.

Huntington, Samuel. 1968. *Political Order in Changing Societies*. New Haven: Yale University Press.

Hutt, David. 2019. "Vietnam's Workers Finally Lose Their Chains". *Asia Times*, 19 December 2019. https://asiatimes.com/2019/12/vietnams-workers-finally-lose-their-chains/.

———. 2021. Vietnam's Labor Rights Make Two Steps Forward, One Step Back". Deutsche Welle, 22 February 2021. https://www.dw.com/en/vietnams-labor-rights-make-two-steps-forward-one-step-back/a-56653076.

Ishizuka, Futaba. 2020. "Political Elite in Contemporary Vietnam: The Origin and Evolution of the Dominant Stratum". *Developing Economies* 58, no. 4, 276–300.

Johnson, Chalmers. 1982. *MITI and the Japanese Miracle: The Growth of Industrial Policy, 1925–1975*. Stanford: Stanford University Press.

Kerkvliet, Benedict J. 2005. *The Power of Everyday Politics: How Vietnamese Peasants Transformed National Policy*. Ithaca: Cornell University Press.

———. 2019. *Speaking Out in Vietnam: Public Political Criticism in a Communist Party-Ruled Nation*. Ithaca: Cornell University Press.

———. 2020. "January 9, Violent Conflict near Hanoi". *US-Vietnam Review*, 3 February 2020. https://usvietnam.uoregon.edu/en/january-9-violent-conflict-near-ha-no%cc%a3i/.

Kohli, Atul. 2004. *State-Led Development: Political Power and Industrialization in the Global Periphery*. New York: Cambridge University Press.

Koo, Hagen. 2001. *Korean Workers: The Culture and Politics of Class Formation*. Ithaca: Cornell University Press.

Kuhonta, Erik Martinez. 2011. *The Institutional Imperative: The Politics of Equitable Development in Southeast Asia*. Stanford: Stanford University Press.

Kuhonta, Erik Martinez, and Nhu Truong. 2020. "The Institutional Roots of Defective Democracy in the Philippines". In *Stateness and Democracy in East Asia*, edited by Aurel Croissant and Olli Hellmann, pp. 153–78. Cambridge: Cambridge University Press.

Le, Hong Hiep. 2012. "Performance-Based Legitimacy: The Case of the Communist Party of Vietnam and Doi Moi". *Contemporary Southeast Asia* 34, no. 2, 145–72.

Le, Thu Huong. 2021. "Vietnam Picks Control over Reform at 13th National Party Congress". *Foreign Policy*, 10 February 2021. https://foreignpolicy.com/2021/02/10/vietnam-communist-party-congress-reform-coronavirus-economy/.

Lee, Namhee. 2007. *The Making of Minjung: Democracy and the Politics of Representation in South Korea*. Ithaca: Cornell University Press.

Lee, Yen Nee. 2021. "This is Asia's Top-Performing Economy in the Covid Pandemic—It's Not China". CNBC, 27 January 2021. https://www.cnbc.com/2021/01/28/vietnam-is-asias-top-performing-economy-in-2020-amid-covid-pandemic.html.

Lien Hiep Quoc Viet nam. 2019. "Viet nam cong bo GDP sua doi". 13 December 2019. https://vietnam.un.org/vi/28249-viet-nam-cong-bo-gdp-sua-doi.

Lin, Chusheng. 2009. *Developing China: Land, Politics and Social Conditions*. London: Routledge.

Lipset, Seymour Martin. 1959. "Some Social Requisites of Democracy: Economic Development and Political Legitimacy". *American Political Science Review* 53, no. 1, 69–105.

Malesky, Edmund, Regina Abrami, and Yu Zheng. 2011. "Institutions and Inequality in Single-Party Regimes: A Comparative Analysis of Vietnam and China". *Comparative Politics* 43, no. 4: 401–19.

Malesky, Edmund, and Jonathan London. 2014. "The Political Economy of Development in China and Vietnam". *Annual Review of Political Science* 17: 395–419.

McCarthy, Niall. 2020. "The Countries Set for a Super-Rich Population Boom". 6 March 2020. https://www.forbes.com/sites/niallmccarthy/2020/03/06/the-countries-set-for-a-super-rich-population-boom-infographic/?sh=657d4fa36988.

Ng Tong. 2010. "Nam 2020 VN tro thanh nuoc cong nghiep hien dai". *Nguoi Lao Dong*, 29 March 2010. https://nld.com.vn/thoi-su-trong-nuoc/nam-2020--vn-tro-thanh-nuoc-cong-nghiep--hien-dai-2010032810400848.htm.

Norton, Elliot. 2012. "Illiberal Democrats vs. Undemocratic Liberals: The Struggle over the Future of Thailand's Fragile Democracy". *Asian Journal of Political Science* 20, no. 1: 46–69.

Ong, Lynette H. 2014. "State-Led Urbanization in China: Skyscrapers, Land Revenue and 'Concentrated Villages'". *China Quarterly*, no. 217: 162–79.

P.V. 2020. "Khong thanh nuoc cong nghiep, Viet nam con tut hau 20 nam so voi Trung Quoc". *Dan Viet*, 1 January 2020. https://danviet.vn/khong-thanh-nuoc-cong-nghiep-viet-nam-con-tut-hau-20-nam-so-voi-trung-quoc-77771046149.htm.

Phuong Linh. 2018. "Cuoc chien chong tham nhung o Viet Nam: Diem nhan trong xu the chung cua the gioi". *Trang thong tin dien tu Uy ban Kiem tra Trung uong*. https://ubkttw.vn/nghien-cuu-trao-doi/-/asset_publisher/bHGXXiPdpxRC/content/cuoc-chien-chong-tham-nhung-o-viet-nam-iem-nhan-trong-xu-the-chung-cua-the-gioi (accessed 1 November 2021).

Riedel, James, and William Turley. 1999. "The Politics of Economics of Transition to an Open Market Economy in Vietnam". Working Paper no. 152. Paris: OECD Development Centre.

Rithmire, Meg. 2017. "Land Institutions and Chinese Political Economy". *Politics & Society* 45, no. 1: 123–53.

Saxonberg, Steven. 2012. *Transitions and Non-transitions from Communism: Regime Survival in China, Cuba, North Korea and Vietnam*. New York: Cambridge University Press.

Schuler, Paul. 2021. *United Front: Projecting Solidarity through Deliberation in Vietnam's Single-Party Legislature*. Stanford: Stanford University Press.

Scott, James. 1976. *The Moral Economy of the Peasant: Rebellion and Subsistence in Southeast Asia*. New Haven: Yale University Press.

Sinpeng, Aim, and Aries A. Arugay. 2014. "The Middle Class and Democracy in Southeast Asia". In *Routledge Handbook of Southeast Asian Democratization*, edited by William Case. London: Routledge.

Song An. 2021. "Dai hoi Dai bieu toan quoc lan thu XIII cua Dang: Khoi day khat vong phat trien". *Dau Tu*, 27 January 2021. https://baodautu.vn/dai-hoi-dai-bieu-toan-quoc-lan-thu-xiii-cua-dang-khoi-day-khat-vong-phat-trien-d137120.html.

Suehiro, Akira. 2008. *Catch-Up Industrialization: The Trajectory and Prospects of East Asian Economies*, translated by Tom Gill. Hawaii: University of Hawai'i Press.

Tatarski, Michael. 2021. "Vietnam's Workers Struggle Just to Get by under Hard Lockdowns". *China Labor Bulletin*, 13 September 2021. https://clb.org.hk/content/vietnam%E2%80%99s-factory-workers-struggle-just-get-under-hard-lockdown.

Thompson, E.P. 1971. "The Moral Economy of the English Crowd in the Eighteenth Century". *Past and Present* 50, no. 1: 76–136.

Thompson, Mark. 1995. *The Anti-Marcos Struggle: Personalistic Rule and Democratic Transition in the Philippines*. New Haven: Yale University Press.

Transparency International. 2021. "Corruptions Perception Index 2020". https://www.transparency.org/en/cpi/2020/index/nga (accessed 1 November 2021).

Truong, Nhu. 2020. "Opposition Repertoires under Authoritarian Rule: Vietnam's 2016 Self-Nomination Movement". *Journal of East Asian Studies* 21, no. 1: 117–39.

Turner, Mark, Hae-Young Jang, Seung-Ho Kwon, and Michael O'Donnell. 2019. "Does History Repeat Itself? Economic Development and Policy Convergence in Vietnam and South Korea". *Asian-Pacific Economic Literature* 33, no. 2: 27–43.

United Nations Development Programme. 2020. "Press Release on Provincial Governance and Public Administration Performance Index—PAPI 2019". 28 April 2020. http://papi.org.vn/wp-content/uploads/2020/04/PAPI-2019-launch.-Press-Release.ENG_.pdf.

Vu, Ngoc Anh. 2017. "Grassroots Environmental Activism in an Authoritarian Context: The Trees Movement in Vietnam". *VOLUNTAS: International Journal of Voluntary and Nonprofit Organizations* 28: 1180–208.

Vu, Quang Viet. 2009. "Vietnam's Economic Crisis: Policy Follies and the Role of State-Owned Conglomerates". In *Southeast Asian Affairs 2009*, edited by Daljit Singh, pp. 389–417. Singapore: Institute of Southeast Asian Studies.

Vu, Tuong. 2014. "The Party v. The People: Anti-China Nationalism in Contemporary Vietnam". *Journal of Vietnamese Studies* 9, no. 4: 33–66.

Vuving, Alexander. 2019. "Vietnam in 2018: A Rent-Seeking State on Correction Course". In *Southeast Asian Affairs* 2019, edited by Daljit Singh and Malcolm Cook, pp. 375–93. Singapore: ISEAS – Yusof Ishak Institute.

Wells-Dang, Andrew, and Vu Thi Quynh Hoa. 2019. "Shrinking Opportunities: Social Mobility and Inequality Widening in Vietnam". 20 May 2019. https://www.unrisd.org/80256B3C005BE6B5/search/C0838EC429923F AAC125840000323191.

Wright, Teresa. 2010. *Accepting Authoritarianism: State-Society Relations in China's Reform Era*. Stanford: Stanford University Press.

Yu, Liu, and Dingding Chen. 2012. "Why China Will Democratize". *Washington Quarterly* 35, no. 1: 41–63.

Part I

Part I

Chapter 1

"Doi Moi" but Not "Doi Mau": Vietnam's Red Crony Capitalism in Historical Perspective

Tuong Vu and Thuy Nguyen

How has Vietnam transformed from a country undergoing a socialist revolution in the 1970s to having what we call a "red crony capitalist system" today? What is the main dynamic that has shaped this transformation? In answering these questions, this chapter builds on the rich scholarship of the history, politics and political economy of Vietnam's market reform. By reviewing developments in Vietnam as the country slowly evolved from its socialist system of the war and revolutionary period, we locate the cause of the reform in the comprehensive crisis facing socialist Vietnam in the late 1970s and early 1980s when the revolutionary regime sought earnestly to realize its utopian dreams. Originally a temporary solution to a crisis, market liberalization came to acquire a dynamic of its own, releasing vast social and economic potential. Yet, as we argue, the determination of the ruling Vietnamese Communist Party (VCP) to protect its power and privileges has restrained those potentials considerably while being itself corrupted by emerging socio-economic forces, leading to the rise of red crony capitalism and a looming legitimacy crisis confronting the party today. By "red crony capitalism", we mean the prevalence of close family and other forms of political connections between Communist Party members and business owners.[1]

The chapter is arranged in five sections. The first two address the ideological, political and economic context of the reform, beginning with a brief review of the careers of the first generation of communist leaders from the late 1920s who were still at the helm of the Vietnamese state in the late 1980s. Their socio-economic vision was profoundly shaped during the protracted revolution they had led, and that vision played a decisive role in guiding the developmental course of the first post-war decade in Vietnam. During that decade, the VCP sought to establish the socialist system in the South in the same way it had done in the North since 1954. This forced march to socialism led to a profound political, social and economic crisis. Even with generous help from the Soviet bloc, Vietnam was in a dire situation in the early 1980s as already poor economic production and living standards continued to worsen.

The third section recounts how Vietnamese leaders since the mid-1980s have embarked on market reform but refused political reform. As asserted in the *People's Army Newspaper* (*Quan doi Nhan dan*), "renovation but not changing [political] colour is the first principle [of reforms]" (Ha Dang 2017).[2] In Vietnamese: "doi moi", yes, but "doi mau", no! This formula of limited reform has allowed the regime to survive the collapse of the Soviet bloc. For more than three decades, the VCP has overseen rapid economic growth that lifted millions out of poverty and that raised national income many times. By the 2000s, Vietnam's advantages—including its strategic location in a dynamic region, its tropical climate and natural resources such as oil and forests, its relatively large and young population, and its large diaspora—helped it attract billions in foreign investment, aid, and remittance every year, fuelling economic growth and wealth accumulation.

The final two sections are focused on the rise of red crony capitalism and the crisis of legitimacy in contemporary Vietnam. Despite impressive economic achievements, Vietnam's political system has undergone significant decay. The VCP continues to hold on to an outdated ideology that has no resonance with reality. Behind the facade of a market economy, state-owned enterprises still occupy the strategic sectors, while private enterprises have been looked on with deep suspicion. State managers have formed a critical power bloc and successfully resisted structural reform that would take away their privileges. The state bureaucracy is thoroughly penetrated by corrupt patronage networks that peddle offices and influences to serve officials and their cronies. As officials have accumulated wealth, both legally and illegally, social inequality and political unrest have been rising rapidly. Recent years have witnessed the rise of a civil society and an urban middle class that are increasingly vocal in demanding greater political representation and government accountability. Thus, the future of communist rule has come to depend increasingly on whether rapid economic growth can continue and whether force can always keep a restless population in check.

Revolutionaries and Their Vision

To understand the timing, goals and processes of Vietnam's market reform it is essential to understand its top leaders' backgrounds and experiences, which were uniformly narrow to begin with and further ossified over decades of war. Most of the top VCP leaders of the 1970s began their careers as activists within the network of the Third Communist International established in 1919 and directed from Moscow (Vu 2017, chs. 1 and 2). By the late 1920s and early 1930s, when the communist movement began in Vietnam, that network had spread over the entire Eurasian continent from Western Europe to Southeast Asia. The first Vietnamese communists—such as Ho Chi Minh, Le Duan, Truong Chinh, Hoang Quoc Viet and Pham Van Dong—were young when they joined the movement, whether in Paris or in French Indochina. Nguyen Van Linh, who was on the younger side of the first generation and who would become a central figure in economic reform in post-war Vietnam, was only fifteen when he joined the movement.

These men and (a few) women typically came from modest family backgrounds, possessing at most an elementary school education in the modern school system created by the French. Exceptions were Pham Van Dong, Vo Nguyen Giap and Truong Chinh, who received formal education at the secondary or tertiary level.[3] Some received training in Moscow, such as Ho Chi Minh, who was assigned to work in East Asia as a Comintern agent. Others, like Le Duan, joined when they came into contact with those who had been trained abroad. Significantly— besides Ho and a few others who had lived in France, China and the Soviet Union and had travelled to other Western countries—the rest never had any experience outside of Vietnam.

By the 1970s, the dozen or so members of the VCP's Politburo, the top executive body, were all those revolutionaries of the first generation. They had spent decades, if not languishing in colonial prisons, primarily waging war and making revolution. The lower level of leaders was better, but only a few of those Central Committee members of the VCP in post-war Vietnam had had any significant experience outside Vietnam. Several younger members of this group possessed training and worked in technical fields and had accumulated significant experience during 1954–75 in running the economy of

North Vietnam based on the Stalinist-Maoist model.[4] But the vast majority built their careers in war, diplomacy, mass organizing or propaganda.

Vietnam's communist leaders viewed the wars with the French, and later the Republic of Vietnam and the United States, as part of their socialist revolution. Since the 1930s these leaders had dreamed of taking power and building a communist society in their country while contributing to world revolution. Few Vietnamese communists read Karl Marx and other socialist thinkers directly. Most learned the basics of socialism from introductory-level books such as Evgeni Preobrazhensky and Nikolai Bukharin's *The ABC of Communism* (Dang 2005, p. 153). Their model of an ideal society was the Soviet Union under Stalin that they read about or (for a few) observed first-hand (Vu 2017, chs. 1–2). In this model, social classes deemed "exploitative" would be ultimately eliminated even though their support might have been courted in certain phases of the revolution. The state would necessarily own all productive assets, control trade and redistribute wealth across society to ensure development with social equality. The entire economy would operate under central planning, whose goal was to mobilize all resources for industrialization. In the countryside, all agricultural production would be collectivized to achieve large-scale socialist production.

In general, Ho Chi Minh and his comrades believed that the effective mobilization of all resources together with workers' and farmers' enthusiasm about socialism under the power of a strong state and the wise and caring leadership of the vanguard party would inevitably produce the miracle of a socialist paradise in a reasonable time, regardless of the level of development where a country began.[5] Vietnamese leaders, like their dedicated communist comrades elsewhere at the time, passionately believed that the success of the Russian Revolution and the rapid industrialization of the Soviet Union under Stalin were evidence of "the Age of Revolution" that would bring about the ultimate triumph of communism on a global scale.

After having taken control of North Vietnam in 1954, the communist leaders remained deeply committed to that worldview (Dang 2005, pp. 74–83). They embarked on realizing their dream: collectivization of agriculture and the nationalization of trade and industry were mostly completed by 1960, paving the way for the First Five-Year Plan during 1961–65 (Nguyen T. 1999; Dang 2005, pp. 179–210, 250–311; Kerkvliet 2005). Even in the first year of the plan, however, agricultural production fell. With a rising population and stagnant production in subsequent years, living standards continued to deteriorate even before the war in the South began in earnest and also before the United States started bombing North Vietnam in 1964 (Vo 1990, p. 19). Throughout the war, it was not the collective farms but the five per cent of farm land reserved for private cultivation, along with food aid from the Soviet bloc, that helped keep Northerners from starving. War contributed to the economic hardships the North Vietnamese experienced. Near the end of the war, the government sought to enlarge collective farms in the hope of making them more productive despite evidence to the contrary (Dang 2005, p. 303).

The March to Sorghum Socialism, 1975–86

After the war, North Vietnam took over a largely intact Southern market economy that was much more developed and productive than the Northern economy.[6] While heavily dependent on foreign aid and trade, the Southern economy was dynamic. It possessed fully commercialized agriculture and burgeoning industries oriented towards producing for consumption and connected to other vibrant economies in the region (Dang 2009, pp. 21–22). A predominantly commercial culture and a significant entrepreneurial class dominated by ethnic Chinese made the Southern economy similar to those of other Southeast Asian countries such as Thailand, Malaysia and Indonesia but distinguished it sharply from the Northern economy, which was Stalinist-Maoist by design.

Touring the South after the war, top North Vietnamese leaders grudgingly admired the Southern capitalist economy for its productive capacity and its dynamic agriculture and modern industries (Dang 2016, pp. 90–99). There was some discussion in the leadership about whether Hanoi should leave the Southern economy as it was for some time to exploit the existing advantages or to immediately transform it into a socialist economy (Huy Duc, vol. 1, pp. 251–67, 279–83). The VCP eventually opted for the latter at the twenty-fourth plenum of the Central Committee in August 1975, likely expecting that the Southern economy would perform even better under the Stalinist model (Vo 1990, p. 59). A number of factors explained this decision: the hope that the complementary resource bases of the two economies would mean they would both benefit from immediate unification; the fear of losing political control over the South again if its economy was not immediately subject to Hanoi's control; overall disdain for the Southern enemy and the capitalist system in general; the belief in socialism and an ambition to realize the socialist dream as quickly as possible; and the idea that victory against the Americans in war meant any future challenge would be surmountable.[7]

The socialist transformation of the Southern economy was draconian. Thousands of residents in Southern cities were resettled in former war zones, dubbed "new economic zones", with little government support, ostensibly to start a new life as farmers. Between 1975 and 1976, in an operation codenamed "X1", the government confiscated thousands of enterprises, private houses and other valuable personal property owned by 670 families of "comprador capitalists" in nineteen Southern cities (Vo 1990, pp. 66, 77–80, 88–90). Many of these families were ethnic Chinese. A large number were sent to the above new economic zones, while many joined hundreds of thousands of members of the former regime in "re-education camps". In the second campaign, codenamed "X2", during 1977–1978, the targets were small and medium-sized industrial and trading enterprises that belonged to about 40,000 families of private owners.

These campaigns to nationalize industry and trade were accompanied by the introduction of new currencies in 1975 in the South and in 1978 in the whole country (Vo 1990, pp. 71, 90). In each case, households were tightly restricted in the amount of the old currency they could exchange, so to all practical purposes they were robbed of most of their savings on the day the old currency went out of circulation. From mid-1977, the government began to pressure farmers to give up their land, draught animals and tools to join cooperatives. The goal was to organize all farmers in low-level cooperatives by the end of 1979. The campaigns for socialist transformation and the retribution taken on former supporters and officials of the Republic of Vietnam were the primary causes of a massive exodus of Southerners and ethnic Chinese from Vietnam in the late 1970s—the largest wave of refugees in modern history up to that point. "Boat people"—the term coined to refer to those refugees who risked their lives on rickety boats in the journey to escape from Vietnam—was an original contribution of Vietnamese socialism to the English lexicon.

The imposition of the socialist economic system on the South was carried out in conjunction with the Second Five-Year Plan (1976–80), unveiled at the 4th Party Congress in December 1976. The congress set the goal of achieving large-scale socialist industrial production within about twenty years. Towards that goal, ambitious targets were set, such as food production to reach 21 million tons by 1980 and industrial output to increase by 16–18 per cent per year (Vo 1990, pp. 74–76). Yet this plan ignored the war-ravaged conditions of the country, its dependency on foreign aid (both North and South), and the already apparent failure of the socialist model in North Vietnam. Without any knowledge of economics, party leaders thought commercialized Southern farmers could be coerced into cooperatives, be paid little for their work, and yet agricultural production would increase.

Post-war Vietnam's forced march to socialism failed completely and resulted in extreme misery for its people.[8] Agricultural and industrial outputs increased only marginally—by 2 and 0.6 per cent per year, respectively—despite more than $4 billion in foreign aid and loans during this period, mostly from the Soviet bloc (Vo 1990, pp. 79, 83, 93–94, 100–102). About 10,000 out of more than 13,000 collective farms set up in 1979 collapsed in 1980 because of resistance from farmers. Stagnant production and a rising population led per capita national income to fall by about 10 per cent during the Second Five-Year Plan. The whole country was on the verge of famine by 1979, and the already tightly rationed food supply for urban residents was drastically reduced. The main staple of rice was substituted by emergency food aid in the form of Soviet wheat and sorghum grains, which were used in some countries as animal feed. The Vietnamese who survived this period coined the term "sorghum socialism" (*chủ nghĩa xã hội ăn bo bo*) to mock their government for its radicalism that ended in disastrous failure (personal observation, Ho Chi Minh City).

Even before Vietnam went to war with Cambodia and China, the situation was already dire. In 1979, the party decided to relent, allowing local governments more autonomy, authorizing the use of material incentives to stimulate production, and tolerating small private businesses (Fforde and de Vylder 1996, pp. 130–43; Dang 2016, ch. 2). In 1981, the government allowed collective farms to enter into contracts with individuals and groups of farmers that set production quotas for fulfilment—the farmers were free to sell on the market anything they produced above the quota. At the 5th Party Congress in 1982, the leaders approved those 1979 and 1981 decisions and the Third Five-Year Plan for 1981–85. In the new plan, the party pledged to improve living standards by adjusting the balance between agriculture and light industry on the one hand and heavy industry on the other, while still aiming to complete collectivization of the Mekong delta by 1985.

The new policies stimulated production for the first two years, but farmers quickly found out that the quotas imposed by cooperatives were too high for them to make a surplus. It was estimated that farmers got only 16–17 per cent of the contract output after fulfilling all their obligations to the government (for comparison, they had the right to at least 20 per cent of the crop while working as tenants in the colonial period) (Vo 1990, pp. 132–33, 163). The Second Five-Year Plan did witness industrial growth thanks to Soviet aid and loans of nearly $5 billion in the form of 150 infrastructural and industrial projects. Soviet influence in Vietnam reached a peak during this period; Russian was taught throughout Vietnam, thousands of Vietnamese students and officials studied in the Soviet Union, and hundreds of Soviet experts lived in Vietnam (Dang 2016, pp. 174–80).

The Second Five-Year Plan helped Vietnam to recover from the crisis caused by the First Five-Year Plan, and the country's national income per capita in 1985 returned to the level of 1976. Yet food production was still insufficient to feed a growing population. The already extremely low living standards were deteriorating rapidly in 1985 because of hyperinflation as the government had been printing money to sustain its rising budget deficit (Vo 1990, pp. 144, 160, 167). At the same time, the thriving black market was threatening government control over the economy, and its corrupt cadres were causing mounting popular resentment. To solve the problem, the party decided to liberalize some prices and issue a new currency, but these clumsy attempts pushed inflation to about 600 per cent, threatening an imminent economic collapse (Dang 2016, pp. 275–88). Fortunately for the party, Le Duan died in office in July 1986, opening the way for reformist leaders who had been inspired by Gorbachev's *perestroika* (economic restructuring) in the Soviet Union. It was very unlikely that the reformist leaders in the VCP would have been able to push through their agenda without Gorbachev's protection (Vu 2017, pp. 249–50).

Market Reform without Political Reform, 1986–97

That was the context of the market reform that the 6th Congress of the VCP embraced in late 1986. At the congress, three other top leaders (Truong Chinh, Pham Van Dong and Le Duc Tho) who were in their mid-seventies retired, and Nguyen Van Linh became the new party chief. The congress sharply criticized policy since 1975 as having been driven by wild dreams rather than reality (Dang 2016, pp. 296–320). It called for the whole party to face the truth and speak the truth (*nói thẳng nói thật*). The resolution issued by the congress supported a general toleration of the private sector and accepted the legitimate role of market factors in the operation of the economy. Economic reform was to be accompanied by foreign policy changes:

Vietnam was to withdraw its troops from Cambodia and to seek peace and normal relations with China, the United States and the Association of Southeast Asian Nations (ASEAN).

In the next three years, the VCP authorized limited measures to liberalize the economy, including raising real interest rates, dismantling controls over domestic trade, increasing prices paid to farmers, cutting subsidies, giving greater autonomy to state-owned enterprises (SOEs), and removing many restrictions on foreign trade (Dang 2016, pp. 320–85). A new Land Law enacted in late 1987 is an example of the tentative character of these initial reform measures. The law allowed collective farms to distribute their land to farming households for long-term use but also imposed a ceiling on what each household could receive. The state retained ownership of all land, and no land sales or transfers would be permitted. The distribution of land to households marked the end of collective agriculture while guarding against the potential rise of new landlords. A foreign investment law enacted in late 1987 followed a similar pattern: foreign investors were welcomed but were required to team up with a local state-owned enterprise. The party wanted to attract foreign funds to develop Vietnam's economy, but it would not permit the re-emergence of a domestic capitalist class that could challenge its power.

Despite being limited in their extent, early market reform policies offered immediate relief to the economy, especially with respect to hyperinflation, which was brought down to about 100 per cent in 1989 (Dang 2016, p. 378). The overall situation remained dire, however, as the Soviet Union was reducing its aid and famine was reported in some provinces in the central region. At the same time, the new policies also generated many new problems. Thousands of incidents of disputes over land erupted in many parts of the country, some involving violence (Kerkvliet 1995, pp. 72–80). Inspired by Gorbachev's *glasnost* (openness and political democratization) and similar democratizing trends in Eastern European communist countries at the time, a movement emerged among many Vietnamese intellectuals, writers and retired officials demanding democratization (Abuza 1999). As the movement was gaining momentum, a sympathetic Nguyen Van Linh responded by calling on writers "to save [themselves] before Heaven can save [them]", signalling strong institutional resistance to political liberalization within the leadership (Nguyen 1987; Abuza 1999, pp. 132–37).

Here it is important to bear in mind the various views about market reform among the top party leaders. Three main groups within the leadership held different views about reform. The numbers of moderates and conservatives represented a delicate balance, whilst liberals formed a small third faction. The conservatives, who were still numerous, opposed market reform and wanted the party to continue the march to socialism. In contrast, moderates under Truong Chinh and Nguyen Van Linh supported reform in certain areas but viewed it as a tactical step back to raise production and improve living conditions before proceeding with socialism. They did not view reform as representing a rejection of socialism. Like Gorbachev who inspired them, reform was to entail more, not less, socialism. Finally, there were the liberals, who were inspired not only by Gorbachev's *perestroika* but also by his *glasnost*. They called for political reform and democratization. The liberals were composed mostly of intellectuals, writers, technocrats, Southern veterans and some retired leaders. They received support from Tran Xuan Bach, the only incumbent Politburo member who advocated political as well as economic reform (Abuza 1999; Stern 1993, ch. 4).

In early 1989, the Polish Roundtable Agreement between the communist government and the Solidarity movement was concluded that allowed free legislative elections. This event raised alarms among Vietnamese leaders about the dangers of political reform. In a Central Committee Plenum, VCP chief Nguyen Van Linh rejected calls from liberals for democratization as misguided and dangerous (Vu 2017, pp. 258–61). He declared that the nature of imperialism had not changed and the party needed to maintain vigilance against the plot of imperialist powers seeking to subvert socialist countries. Subsequent events further hardened the VCP's stand towards political reform. That summer, Tiananmen protests nearly brought down the Chinese government, and tanks had to be brought in to crush them. By the end of the year, nearly all communist regimes in Eastern Europe had fallen like dominoes.

At this critical juncture, moderates and conservatives in Vietnam closed ranks and cracked down on supporters of political reform (Abuza 2001, ch. 3). The latter lost their official positions and some were placed under house arrest. Market reform that had brought some early results was allowed to continue. To the outside the party still talked about renovation ("doi moi"), but internally the full motto was renovation without changing political colours ("doi moi nhung khong doi mau") (Ha Dang 2017). Gorbachev was considered a traitor, and the VCP was quick to voice public support for the coup against him that eventually failed. Vietnam rushed to normalize relations with

China in 1990 even though Beijing refused to form an alliance with Hanoi to save world socialism as the Vietnamese proposed (Tran 2003). Despite the loss of Soviet patronage, Vietnamese leaders could now feel more secure as they had the giant socialist China by their side.

The years from 1990 to 1996 were the best years of the reform period in terms of growth rate—about 8 per cent per annum on average (the rates since have been lower). As one of the poorest countries in the world in 1990, Vietnam benefited from a very low starting point. Human and material resources were extremely undervalued and underemployed under the socialist system, which had mostly abolished real prices and economic incentives. Now that market mechanisms had returned, the values of resources soared and efficiency gains were large (Riedel and Turley 1999). Vietnam also benefited from a dynamic region. South Korea, Taiwan, Thailand, Malaysia, Singapore and Indonesia were at the time seeing the highest growth rates in the world, and they were all eager to explore new opportunities in Vietnam. As a result, registered foreign investment accumulated from a few hundred million dollars to $5.5 billion between 1990 and 1995 (Vu 2015, p. 13). The value of Vietnam's exports, which were mostly crude oil and other commodities, doubled in the same period (Beresford and Dang 2000, pp. 60–61). As relations with the United States improved and eventually normalized, by 1995 Vietnam had received pledges of official aid from international institutions of close to a billion dollars (Vu 2015, p. 31). Annual remittances from abroad by diasporic Vietnamese, estimated to be about $100–200 million in the 1980s, continued to rise to about $660 million by the mid-1990s (Nguyen 2017, p. 82). Given the country's nominal GDP of about $20 billion in 1995, the amounts of aid and remittance were substantial, giving a boom to economic activities in urban areas.

As the economic situation improved, the government "equitized" (privatized) about six thousand small enterprises but retained an equal number, all of which were large enterprises in strategic sectors (Painter 2003). A new land law was promulgated in 1993 that permitted the sale, lease and transfer of land-use rights (not land itself) and that raised the time limit of those rights up to fifty years (Nguyen 2007). The law also empowered local governments with the authority to repossess land to be used for "public purposes" with compensation. This clause would turn out to be a big loophole for local officials to grab land, pay farmers as little as possible, lease them to private developers at high prices, and pocket the profits.

With the dissolution of collective farms, Vietnamese farmers produced enough not only for domestic needs but also for export (Chirot 2016, ch. 5). Rice exports made up about 11 per cent of total exports throughout the 1990s, and Vietnam became the world's second-largest rice exporter in 1996—a miracle given the country had suffered from famine throughout the 1980s (Yoon and Nguyen 2009, pp. 945–46). With more employment opportunities and new freedom to employ personal and family resources to gain the highest returns in the marketplace, the national poverty rate fell sharply from nearly 60 per cent to less than 40 per cent between 1992 and 1998.

The economy remained fragile. Although increased tax revenues and foreign aid helped reduce the budget deficit significantly, trade deficit increased sharply and amounted to nearly half the value of exports. Vietnam's 1990s boom was driven primarily by one-time boosts in productivity and by remittances and foreign investments largely from neighbouring Asian countries. The boom ended in 1997 when the Asian financial crisis led to the collapse of the South Korean, Malaysian, Indonesian and Thai economies. The Vietnamese economy was yet to be integrated into the global economy and the impact of the regional crisis on Vietnam was mild, seeing only weakened demand for its exports and the suspension of many foreign investment projects (Dinh 2000, pp. 368–72).

In politics, the 1990s witnessed a continuing transition after the VCP had recovered from the shock of the Soviet bloc's collapse in 1991. Changes were implemented to "regularize politics", which saw a retirement age, term limits, qualifications and regional representation formally or informally established for the Politburo and Central Committee (Thayer 1992, pp. 1–4). This process allowed leadership changes to occur at the top. Nevertheless, the party found it difficult to catch up with the times. Its leaders were in their seventies, and more than a quarter of its membership was in retirement (Vasavakul 1997). Its membership of three million was composed mostly of males from the North, and veterans were a significant component. The party still operated with much secrecy, like a revolutionary clique, and policymaking remained a top-down process that permitted little dissent or criticism from outsiders.

In a mid-term Party Congress in 1994, the leaders began to promote the formula of "market economy with socialist orientations", which appeared to duplicate China's "socialism with Chinese characteristics". This formula basically meant that the leadership remained loyal to its revolutionary past and committed to the protection of communist rule, but was open to experimenting with market mechanisms to facilitate economic growth. The congress also defined the threats to Vietnam as being fourfold, including economic backwardness, corruption, deviation from socialism, and subversive "hostile forces" (i.e., the United States) (Vu 2017, pp. 268–69). Economic reform was acceptable but only to the extent it would not threaten communist rule.

As Vietnam opened up to the outside world, its society was changing in ways beyond the party's ability to control (Thayer 1995, 2009). Towards the end of the 1990s, intellectuals and students with access to contacts in the outside world—whether through travel, study or work—began to question one-party rule and the relevance of Marxism-Leninism. At foreign-invested enterprises, workers frequently participated in wildcat strikes to demand higher wages and better working conditions (Tran 2013, p. 202). Disputes over land between farmers and local governments ballooned, leading to many violent protests. As religious establishments gained more freedom to operate, resentment that had long accumulated towards the government began to surface among the groups that had been most suppressed: Northern Catholics, Southern Buddhist Hoa Hao and Cao Dai, and Protestant ethnic minorities in the Central Highlands (Abuza 1999, ch. 6).

By the late 1990s the situation in the countryside had become tense. Despite being "the world's second-largest rice exporter", Vietnamese farmers did not get rich because government rice export monopolies allowed them only low profit margins in good years when there was high demand from the world market, while refusing to buy their rice in bad years when world demand was low (Chirot 2016, ch. 5). Government investment into agriculture had been consistently low, and village governments imposed numerous levies on farmers to pay for local budgets and to line their pockets. Farmers' anger eventually exploded in Thai Binh province in 1997 when villagers in several districts revolted en masse, seized local governments and held officials captive until the military descended to suppress them (Abuza 2001, pp. 83–88). Following this incident, the government issued a decree ordering local governments to publicize their budgets and involve farmers in making important decisions concerning duties and land development. According to a survey in 2012, this so-called "grassroots democracy" decree was reportedly implemented only in a limited manner (Vasavakul 2019, pp. 47–49).

Global Integration and the Rise of Red Crony Capitalism, 1998–2011

Vietnam was not severely affected by the Asian financial crisis of the late 1990s because its economy was still largely insulated. Still, the regional crisis might have given Marxist-Leninist loyalists the ammunition to slow down market reforms. Since the mid-1990s, following the successful normalization of Vietnam's relations with the United States and with ASEAN, reformers in the party such as Vo Van Kiet, Phan Van Khai and Vu Khoan had aimed for more substantial reforms in the development of private enterprises and the full integration of Vietnam into the global and regional economy. Their most significant achievements were a 1997 Central Committee resolution to allow the development of agricultural estates for cash crops and the 1999 Company Law in support of private sector development. The estates policy was to circumvent the limits on landholding imposed by the land law, and was followed by amendments in 1998 and 2001 to the Land Law to further stipulate land-use transfer rights and the procedures of land acquisition, including compensation and addressing complaints. The Company Law was to provide legal protection for private entrepreneurs and investors' property and to limit the arbitrary powers of state regulators.

The reformers' efforts in international integration met greater resistance. In 1999 they secured the party's approval for a bilateral trade agreement (BTA) with the United States that would greatly expand Vietnam's exports to America. In response to a provocative question about the future of socialism by Secretary of State Madeleine Albright during her visit to Hanoi, and in light of China's disapproval of the deal, hardcore loyal Marxist-Leninists—such as Do Muoi, Le Kha Phieu, Nguyen Duc Binh and Nguyen Phu Trong, who were suspicious of Washington's subversive motives—at the last minute ordered the planned signing ceremony to be cancelled (Huy Duc 2012). After China acceded to the World Trade Organization (WTO) in 2000, loyalist opposition to integration within the VCP leadership relented. Vietnam concluded the BTA in 2001 and became a member of the WTO in 2007.

Despite such resistance, a more liberal environment allowed Vietnam to overcome the economic slump caused by the Asian financial crisis and achieved growth throughout the next decade. Annual growth rates were lower, however, than those in the mid-1990s. Growth was still driven primarily by foreign investment, aid and the billions of dollars of annual remittance by overseas Vietnamese. Registered foreign direct investment (FDI) rose sevenfold from less than $3 billion in 2000 to about $22 billion in 2014. The total value of exports increased tenfold from about $15 billion in 2000 to $150 billion in 2014 (Vu-Thanh et al. n.d., p. 8; Nguyen and Nguyen 2015, p. 342). Not only did the value of exports increase but the exported commodities also shifted to more labour-intensive manufactured goods. In the early 2000s, the four largest categories of Vietnam's exported goods were crude oil, textiles and garments, shoes, and seafood, in that order. A decade later the value of exports in textiles and garments became three times larger than that of crude oil, and the four top exports were textiles and garments, shoes, electronics, and seafood. Despite rapid growth, labour productivity across the economy did not increase and remained low compared to that in Vietnam's Southeast Asian neighbours (Nguyen 2005, pp. 23–25).

Under the Company Law, Vietnam's private sector grew rapidly from about 15,000 registered companies in 2000 to about 75,000 by the mid-2010s (Cheshier 2009, p. 137). In terms of total national industrial output, the share for private enterprises increased from less than 24 per cent in the late 1990s to about 36 per cent a decade later (compared with 47 per cent for foreign-invested enterprises and 17 per cent for state-owned enterprises). The private sector continues to face many constraints; the VCP has always proclaimed its intention to preserve the leading position in the economy for the state-owned sector, and this policy was manifest in preferences given to state-owned enterprises in access to land, credit and state contracts (Vu-Thanh 2014). Private entrepreneurs also face higher hurdles in opening businesses, greater scrutiny of their operations, and arbitrary treatment and even extortion by local officials—all resulting in higher costs and a volatile business environment.[9]

While the government discriminates against Vietnam's private businesses for fear of a domestic capitalist class that may one day challenge its power, foreign investors to Vietnam have frequently been given red-carpet treatment (Vasavakul 2019, pp. 40–41). Provincial governments usually relax regulations to compete for FDI since the rate of economic growth in their province is key if officials are to be promoted to higher offices. FDI also brings local governments lucrative construction contracts, of which it is estimated up to a billion dollars lined the pockets of officials in 2019.[10] Given such conditions, it is unsurprising that foreign-invested enterprises formed the largest sector in Vietnam's economy by the early 2000s, and which accounted for 43 per cent of total national industrial output (compared with 17 per cent a decade earlier) (Vu-Thanh et al. n.d., p. 34).

As private and foreign-owned sectors expanded, the state-owned sector's share of total national industrial output fell from 29 per cent in the early 2000s to 17 per cent by the early 2010s. State-owned enterprises still controlled all strategic sectors from energy to steel, and from textiles to foodstuff. Despite being assigned the leading role in the economy and being granted many privileges, the state-owned sector continues to underperform (Vasavakul 2019, pp. 42–43). The government's policy of "equitization"—which has the dual purpose of improving efficiency and complying with WTO terms for a "market economy"—made little headway as managers, executives and supervising ministry officials dragged their feet (Guild 2021).

After Nguyen Tan Dung replaced Phan Van Khai as prime minister in 2006, he moved quickly to take personal control of major state conglomerates and use them as venues for his patronage network. In public, Dung promoted those conglomerates as "steely fists" in the mould of Korean chaebols to spearhead Vietnam's economic development. His government even underwrote bonds in the international market to raise funds for these conglomerates. Whether because of collusion or lax oversight (perhaps both), these conglomerates expanded into banking and real estate rather than focusing on production. By the first years of Dung's second term in office, some of these conglomerates had become bankrupt, losing billions of dollars in state investment as a result of corruption at the highest level. For example, Vinashin, the state-owned ship-building conglomerate, went bankrupt in 2010 after having lost $4.5 billion (equivalent to about 4.5 per cent of Vietnam's GDP at the time) (Vu 2009).

Corruption was also rampant in connection with foreign aid, and one of the largest cases involved a project management unit (PMU) of the Ministry of Transportation, which managed infrastructure projects worth $2 billion financed by official development aid.[11] In this case officials were found to have embezzled millions of dollars for gambling and lavish spending on personal items. The scandal led to the resignation of the minister of transportation, the arrest of his deputy, and the convictions of several executives. Ironically, two reporters who revealed the case were also convicted of "abusing democratic freedoms" and spreading "false information". The government apparently did not want to encourage anyone to expose more corruption.

As Vietnam became more open, clear signs of a civil society appeared (Thayer 2009). On the eve of Vietnam's accession to the

WTO, dozens of political dissidents who lived in different parts of Vietnam, including several Catholic priests and Buddhist monks, set up the group named "8406" (the date of their founding, 8 April 2006) to demand democratization. The government tolerated this group until the formalities for accession were concluded, then police were sent to arrest them. In 2007, a group of public intellectuals, including many who had advised the former prime minister, founded an independent think tank, the Institute of Development Studies. This group, which organized public events to critically discuss government policies, was forced to disband after the government issued a decree banning research institutes from publicizing their reports.

Following pressure from party members who wanted to open their own companies, and following China's policy of admitting business executives into the Communist Party, the VCP began to permit party members to run private businesses in 2006. As the ruling elite, party members were now free to leverage political connections and privileges to enrich themselves. Despite the sharp increase in corruption and graft reaching to the top, the party took one further step in 2011 to admit entrepreneurs (Son Tra 2012). These moves heralded the rise of red crony capitalism—a capitalist system dominated by people with political and often family connections to the ruling Communist Party.[12] As two researchers and long-time policy consultants to the government recently observed about the "informally commercialized administrative culture", which is "highly institutionalized" and which undergirds Vietnam's red crony capitalism,

> At present, off-budget operations and illicit activities are commonplace in all state organizations at all levels.... Informal practices go far beyond ordinary modes of bureaucratic corruption. They are much more strategic, systemic, and highly institutionalized in an *informally commercialized administrative culture*. Examples include *running private firms under the names of relatives and straw men* to feed them with public contracts, trading state positions for cash and favors, auctioning off licenses, informally renting out public property, grabbing land in the context of fuzzy property regimes, collecting informal levies, capitalizing on insider information on land speculations, bid-rigging in public procurement, *nurturing private firms in the shadow of state enterprises*, and siphoning off large profits in state monopolies.... Whether bureaucrats are individually or collectively organized, the ingenuity by which they capitalize on their public offices and privileged access to state resources knows little limit. (Benedickter and Nguyen 2018, p. 29; italics added)

Institutional Decay and the Crisis of Legitimacy

After three decades of economic liberalization, Vietnam has escaped extreme poverty. Despite some media hype about Vietnam soon becoming the next "Asian tiger", that moment has not arrived. Growth since 2007 has been slower than in the previous period. While the gap between Vietnam and its neighbours has shrunk considerably, Vietnam's national income per capita in 2019 ranked fourth from the bottom in Southeast Asia, exactly where it had been in 1986 when market reform began.[13]

With five million members, the VCP accounts for six per cent of the population. Party membership is a key requirement for promotion to leadership positions in all government bureaucracies, including universities, public schools and hospitals, publishing companies, and media organizations (no private media are allowed).[14] The party has invested massive resources into controlling public opinion and culture. Two key bodies in charge of strengthening and disseminating the party's ideology and political messages are the Central Theoretical Council and Central Propaganda and Training Commission (CPTC). The Central Theoretical Council is tasked with advising the party's leadership on ideological issues. The Propaganda Department oversees the content of newspapers, radio and television, education, cultural and scientific publications, and information regarding external matters and international cooperation. This department has branches down to provincial and district levels to make sure party propaganda reaches Vietnamese wherever they live and work. The party has recently created a new cyberforce code-named "AK47", which consists of tens of thousands of online undercover agents and hackers to monitor social media, spread misinformation, hack into private accounts of dissidents and inundate Facebook with requests for closing down certain pages for "violation of community norms" (which Facebook now routinely complies with) (Mai Hoa 2017).

Despite the regime not tolerating an independent civil society, Vietnamese continue to form a variety of clubs, groups and associations out of shared interests (Wischermann 2010). A few of these have been involved in political activism, but most such have shut down after the police arrested their leaders.[15] Confronting nearly a thousand state-owned newspapers that serve as the mouthpieces of various government and party organs, a few independent online newspapers have emerged since the early 2000s to offer alternative channels of information.[16] Joined by social media a few years later, independent media have strived to serve as a counterbalance to the state-controlled media. Although these media are forced to operate behind a firewall, they have had a significant impact by fact-checking official media, publishing historical documents revealing long-held secrets of the VCP and presenting alternative perspectives on numerous social and political topics. Together with political groups, these media face constant harassment by the police, but they help nurture a growing civil society in Vietnam.

It is not a coincidence that the emergence of an incipient civil society in Vietnam is taking place amidst rising unrest. Whereas the regime blames external "hostile forces" for unrest, its own socialist system—namely, public ownership of land, one-party dictatorship, and repression of civil rights—is the true cause. Since the state is the sole authority to manage land, officials have grabbed land ostensibly for "public needs" but in reality to rent it to developers at high prices. The farmers whose lands are taken rarely have any voice in land deals and are often forced to accept any price offered by the government. The 2013 Land Law has sought to curb such predatory behaviour of local officials, resulting in a decline in the percentage of nationwide land-related petitions to the National Assembly from 71 per cent of total petitions to 60 per cent by 2017 (Truong 2020, p. 225).

While the number of disputes and protests involving land has decreased, it remains substantial. The law might have reduced the excesses but it does not appear to have prevented land grabbing, especially when it involves a powerful central SOE, such as in the recent case of Dong Tam village where the government sided with the developer (Kerkvliet 2020; Nguyen 2020). The law also cannot undo past injustices. Over the past decades people whose lands and homes were seized throughout the country have formed a new class of "victims of injustice" (*dan oan*) comprising hundreds of thousands. The visibility of this *dan oan* class has raised collective awareness among many Vietnamese about the injustice of the system and has fuelled other collective actions such as anti-China demonstrations, environmental protests and workers' strikes. Unrest has spread across the country and become increasingly common. Some recent protests have involved thousands of people.

To protect the regime from collapsing in the face of such unrest, the enormous public security forces have frequently relied on brute force. It is estimated that the Public Security Organization now employs nearly twelve per cent of the Vietnamese workforce (Thayer 2017). Uniformed and undercover police, the armed forces, Communist Youth members and local officials have been mobilized to prevent activists and other citizens from participating in protests. When they have taken place, peaceful protests have frequently been met with violent crackdowns involving beatings, mass arrests and long prison sentences for activists.

The other key socialist institutions—namely, one-party dictatorship and repression of civil rights—have allowed officials to pursue misguided policies and engage in corruption that has devastating effects on the environment and the livelihoods of millions. The most serious environmental disaster thus far occurred in 2016 when the Taiwanese-invested Formosa Ha Tinh Steel Company illegally discharged toxic industrial waste into the ocean and caused massive fish deaths along the four coastal provinces of Central Vietnam. It was later discovered that the provincial government in collusion with some central officials had rushed to approve the investment with only a perfunctory assessment of its environmental impact. Nor did they care whether the company later complied with environmental regulations. In response to a sustained public outcry and massive protests by people in the affected provinces, the government negotiated with Formosa to offer compensation to fishing households who lost their sources of livelihood, but it has refused to prosecute the company executives and officials responsible (Cam 2016).

As an attempt to stem the rapid decay of the regime, VCP general secretary Nguyen Phu Trong has since 2013 waged a campaign against corruption. In his campaign, Trong appears to have learned from the earlier campaign to "catch both tigers and flies" implemented by Xi Jinping in China to consolidate his power. While Trong has so far been unable to prosecute former prime minister Nguyen Tan Dung and his family for corruption, he has succeeded in sending Dung's associates to prison, including a Politburo member, several deputy ministers of defence and public security, and many executives of state-owned banks and conglomerates. At least a hundred officials have been arrested and convicted since 2013 (Huong Giang 2020). Although the campaign targets corruption at all levels in many sectors, those known to be close associates of Trong who appear to have been extremely corrupt have avoided persecution. The campaign is therefore as much about factional struggle as about fighting corruption. The strategy is strictly top-down with little reliance on public inputs in any form. As Trong once stated, he wanted to "catch mice without breaking the vase" (Xuan Linh 2014). The seemingly tough campaign has not translated into regulations or new institutions since the VCP does not want its power restricted.

Conclusion

Vietnam has witnessed enormous changes in politics, the economy and society since the implementation of market reform. Overall, general living standards have improved greatly and the country has become more open and dynamic. The economy has generated a greater amount of materials and services. But the distribution of wealth and well-being have been heavily skewed to the ruling class comprising officials and their families and cronies. In the name of economic development, the regime has neglected environmental protection while tolerating unbridled corruption. There has been little improvement in political freedom and human rights. The policy of opening the economy without reforming the political system now entrenches a red crony capitalism that impairs the Vietnamese economy from taking full advantage of its favourable conditions. The totalitarian power of the old communist state is now being converted into money in a market economy, generating institutional decay at every level of government.

Thanks to reform, Vietnam avoided the fate of fellow communist regimes in Eastern Europe and has made impressive achievements since then. Yet Vietnam's transformation over the last three decades does not signal the triumph of capitalism as some Western journalists have naively remarked (Kirk 2019). In fact, Vietnam remains a frontier where imported capitalist institutions continue to be tested against the harsh local realities of a renegade communist state bent on preserving its power and privileges at any costs.

Notes

1. Our definition borrows in part from Christine Ngo and Vlad Tarko (2017, pp. 484–85).

2. In Vietnamese, *"doi moi* nhung khong *doi mau* la nguyen tac dau tien" (emphasis added). "Doi moi" means renovation, whereas "doi mau" literally means changing colour and metaphorically refers to the abandonment of socialism and Communist Party rule.

3. For their official biographies, see the book series available at https:// tulieuvankien.dangcongsan.vn/van-kien-tu-lieu-ve-dang/book/sach-chinh-tri.

4. The general organization of the North Vietnamese economy followed the Soviet model. Major aspects, however, such as the land reform (1953–56) and the massive mobilization of labour for public projects in the late 1950s were strongly influenced by Maoist thinking as displayed in similar campaigns in China at the time. See Nguyen (1977) and Holcombe (2020).

5. Dang (2005, pp. 108–50) offers an overview of the economic thinking of Ho Chi Minh and Le Duan, as well as the direction of economic policy they implemented in North Vietnam during 1955–75.

6. On different aspects of the Southern economy compared with the North, see Dang (2005, chs. 17–22) and Beresford (1988, pp. 95–108). Sansom (1970) offers a cogent analysis of the dynamic Southern agriculture despite the ongoing war.

7. In early 1976, Le Duan actually promised each Vietnamese family a radio set, refrigerator and TV set within ten years. *Nhan Dan*, 2 February 1976, cited in Vo (1990, p. 167).

8. On socialism as the cause for the underdevelopment in Southeast Asia, including Vietnam, see Vu (2013).

9. Surveys of Vietnamese businesses about their opinions on government regulations show significant improvements over time but the level of red tape and official graft remains substantial. For example, see the 2019 report by the Vietnam Chamber of Commerce and Industry (2020, pp. 49–59).

10. Thanks to the anti-corruption campaign by the VCP in recent years, the so-called "bribe tax", or the average cost of bribe payments for foreign-invested enterprises, was 1.1 per cent of sales in 2019 (equivalent to $1.1 billion). This was a significant decline from the ratio of 1.6 per cent in 2016. Vietnam Chamber of Commerce and Industry (2020, p. 75).

11. For a detailed summary of this case in the aftermath of the arrests of reporters, see H.L. (2008).

12. See Mai Fujita's chapter in this volume on the latest patterns of state-business collusion.

13. See Nhu Truong and Tuong Vu's introduction to this volume.

14. See Quang Chau and Mai Van Tinh's chapter in this volume on the weakening grip of the VCP on universities.

15. Examples include Hoi Bau bi Tuong than (see http://baubituongthan.blogspot.com/2013/12/ieu-le-hoi-bau-bi-tuong-than.html); Dang Dan chu and Hoi Nha bao Viet nam Doc lap. Three leaders of the latter—namely, Pham Chi Dung, Nguyen Tuong Thuy and Le Huu Minh Tuan—were arrested recently and sentenced to 15, 11 and 11 years, respectively. See the announcement by remaining members at https://baotiengdan.com/2021/01/06/tuyen-bo-cua-hoi-nha-bao-doc-lap-viet-nam/.

16. Examples include boxitvn.blogspot.com, vandoanviet.blogspot.com, luatkhoa.org, thevietnamese.org and https://www.facebook.com/nhatkyyeunuoc1/.

References

Abuza, Zachary. 2001. *Renovating Politics in Contemporary Vietnam*. Boulder, CO: Lynne Rienner.

Benedikter, Simon, and Loan Nguyen. 2018. "Obsessive Planning in Transitional Vietnam: Understanding Rampant State Planning and Prospects for Reform". *Journal of Vietnamese Studies* 13, no. 4: 1–47.

Beresford, Melanie. 1988. "Issues in Economic Unification: Overcoming the Legacy of Separation". In *Postwar Vietnam: Dilemmas in Socialist Development*, edited by David Marr and Christine White, pp. 95–110. Ithaca: Cornell SE Asia Program, Cornell University.

Beresford, Melanie, and Dang Phong. 2000. *Economic Transition in Vietnam: Trade and Aid in the Demise of a Centrally Planned Economy*. Cheltenham: Elgar.

Cam, Van Kinh. 2016. "Formosa boi thuong 500 trieu USD". *Tuoi Tre*, 1 July 2016. https://tuoitre.vn/formosa-boi-thuong-500-trieu-usd-van-con-qua-it-1128220.htm.

Cheshier, Scott. 2009. "The New Class in Vietnam". PhD dissertation, University of London.

Chirot, Laura. 2016. "The Politics of New Industrial Policy: Sectoral Governance Reform in Vietnam's Agro-Export Industries". PhD dissertation, Massachusetts Institute of Technology.

Dang Phong. 2005. *Lich su Kinh te Viet nam 1945–2000*, vol. 2 (1955–1975). Hanoi: Khoa hoc Xa hoi.

———. 2009. *"Pha rao" trong kinh te vao dem truoc doi moi*. Hanoi: Tri Thuc.

———. 2016. *Tu duy Kinh te Viet nam, 1975–1989*. Hanoi: Tri Thuc.

Dinh, Xuan Quan. 2000. "The Political Economy of Vietnam's Transformation Process". *Contemporary Southeast Asia* 22, no. 2 (August): 360–88.

Fforde, Adam, and Stefan de Vylder. 1996. *From Plan to Market: The Economic Transition in Vietnam*. Boulder, CO: Westview.

Gainsborough, Martin. 2010. *Vietnam: Rethinking the State*. London: Zed Books.

Guild, James. 2021. "A Dream Deferred? The 'Equitization' of Vietnam's State-Owned Enterprises". *The Diplomat*, 11 February 2021. https://thediplomat.com/2021/02/a-dream-deferred-the-equitization-of-viet-nams-state-owned-enterprises/.

H.L. 2008. "2 nha bao Thanh nien va Tuoi tre bi bat vi dua tin vu PMU 18". *Thanh Nien*, 13 May 2008. https://thanhnien.vn/thoi-su/2-nha-bao-thanh-nien-va-tuoi-tre-bi-bat-vi-dua-tin-vu-pmu-18-209439.html.

Ha Dang. 2017. "Doi tu bo chu nghia xa hoi la mot sai lam lon". *Quan doi Nhan dan*, 16 January 2017. https://www.qdnd.vn/chong-dien-bien-hoa-binh/doi-tu-bo-chu-nghia-xa-hoi-la-mot-sai-lam-lon-497501.

Holcombe, Alec. 2020. *Mass Mobilization in the Democratic Republic of Vietnam, 1945–1960*. Honolulu: University of Hawai'i Press.

Hugo, Graeme. 2005. "Asian Experiences with Remittances". In *Beyond Small Change: Making Migrant Remittances Count*, edited by Donald Terry and Steven Wilson, pp. 341–72. Washington, DC: Inter-American Bank.

Huong Giang. 2020. "8 nam phong chong tham nhung". *Thanh Tra*, 20 December 2020. https://thanhtra.com.vn/chinh-tri/doi-noi/8-nam-phong-chong-tham-nhung-18-can-bo-dien-trung-uong-quan-ly-bi-xu-hinh-su-175520.html.

Huy Duc. 2012. *Ben Thang Cuoc* [The winning side], 2 vols. Los Angeles: Osinbook.

Kerkvliet, Benedict. 1995. "Rural Society and State Relations". In *Vietnam's Rural Transformation*, edited by Benedict Kerkvliet and Doug Porter, pp. 65–98. Boulder, CO: Westview Press.

————. 2005. *The Power of Everyday Politics: How Vietnamese Peasants Transformed National Policy*. Ithaca: Cornell University Press.

————. 2020. "January 9, Violent Conflict near Hanoi". *US-Vietnam Review*, 3 February 2020. https://usvietnam.uoregon.edu/en/january-9-violent-conflict-near-ha-no%cc%a3i/.

Kirk, Donald. 2019. "Vietnam is Unique Ally for US in Decades Ahead". *Waco Tribune-Herald*, 28 February 2019.

Mai Hoa. 2017. "Hon 10.000 nguoi trong 'Luc luong 47' dau tranh tren mang". *Tuoi Tre*, 25 December 2017. https://tuoitre.vn/hon-10-000-nguoi-trong-luc-luong-47-dau-tranh-tren-mang-20171225150602912.htm.

Ngo, Christine, and Vlad Tarko. 2018. "Economic Development in a Rent-Seeking Society: Socialism, State Capitalism and Crony Capitalism in Vietnam". *Revue Canadienne D'études Du Développement* 39, no. 4: 481–99.

Nguyen, Duc Thanh, and Nguyen Thi Thu Hang, eds. 2015. *Bao cao thuong nien kinh te Viet nam 2015*. Hanoi: Vietnam National University Publishing House.

Nguyen, Gregory Tien Hung. 1977. *Economic Development of Socialist Vietnam, 1955–80*. New York: Praeger.

Nguyen, Phuc Hien. 2017. "Remittances and Competitiveness: A Case Study of Vietnam". *Journal of Economics, Business, and Management* 2, no. 5 (February): 79–83.

Nguyen, Thi Ngoc Thanh. 1999. "The Reform of Capitalists and Capitalism in North Vietnam, 1958–1960". MA thesis, Vietnam Institute of Economics.

Nguyen, Tien Trung. 2020. "The Dong Tam Trial: Violations of the Criminal Procedure Law at the Court of First Instance". *US-Vietnam Review*, 2 October 2020. https://usvietnam.uoregon.edu/en/the-dong-tam-trial-violations-of-the-criminal-procedure-law-at-the-court-of-first-instance/.

Nguyen Van Linh. 1987. "Dong chi Nguyen Van Linh noi chuyen voi van nghe si". *Van Nghe*, 17 October 1987. http://www.viet-studies.net/NhaVanDoiMoi/NguyenVanLing_NoiChuyenVanNgheSi.htm.

Nguyen, Van Suu. 2007. "Contending Views and Conflicts over Land in Vietnam's Red River Delta". *Journal of Southeast Asian Studies* 38, no. 2 (June): 309–34.

Nguyen, Van Thuong, ed. 2005. *Tang truong kinh te Viet nam: Nhung rao can can phai vuot qua*. Hanoi: Ly Luan Chinh Tri.

Painter, Martin. 2003. "The Politics of Economic Restructuring in Vietnam: The Case of State-Owned Enterprises 'Reform'". *Contemporary Southeast Asia* 25, no. 1 (April).

Pham Huyen. 2014. "Bauxite lo dai, Viancomin vat nai xin uu dai". *Bao Dau Tu*, 4 January 2014. https://baodautu.vn/bauxite-lo-dai-vinacomin-vat-nai-xin-uu-dai-d4534.html.

Sansom, Robert. 1970. *The Economics of Insurgency in the Mekong Delta of Vietnam*. Cambridge, MA: MIT Press.

Sidel, Mark. 2007. "Vietnamese Diaspora Philanthropy to Vietnam". Report prepared for the Philanthropic Initiative, Inc., and the Global Equity Initiative, Harvard University. https://www.tpi.org/sites/default/files/pdf/vietnam_diaspora_philanthropy_final.pdf (accessed 31 March 2021).

Son Tra. 2012. "De ket nap nhung nguoi la chu doanh nghiep tu nhan vao Dang". *Xay Dung Dang*, 12 November 2012. http://xaydungdang.org.vn/Home/

Dang-vien/2012/5720/De-ket-nap-nhung-nguoi-la-chu-doanh-nghiep-tu-nhan-vao.aspx.

Stern, Lewis. 1993. *Renovating the Vietnamese Communist Party: Nguyen Van Linh and the Programme for Organizational Reform, 1987–91*. Singapore: Institute of Southeast Asian Studies.

Thayer, Carlyle. 1992. *Political Developments in Vietnam: From the Sixth to Seventh National Party Congress*. Discussion Paper Series No. 5. Canberra: Research School of Pacific Studies, Australian National University.

————. 1995. "Mono-Organizational Socialism and the State". In *Vietnam's Rural Transformation*, edited by Benedict Kerkvliet and Doug Porter, pp. 39–64. Boulder, CO: Westview Press.

————. 2009. "Vietnam and the Challenge of Political Civil Society". *Contemporary Southeast Asia* 31, no. 1: 1–27.

————. 2017. "Vietnam: How Large Is the Security Establishment?" *Thayer Consultancy Background Brief*, 12 April 2017.

Tran, Ngoc Angie. 2013. *Ties That Bind: Cultural Identity, Class, and Law in Vietnam's Labor Resistance*. Ithaca: Cornell Southeast Asia Publications, Cornell University.

Tran, Quang Co. 2003. "Hoi uc va Suy nghi". https://anhbasam.files.wordpress.com/2015/06/hoi-ky-tran-quang-co.pdf (accessed 31 March 2021).

Truong, Nhu. 2020. "In the Shadow of Authoritarian Expropriation: From Reactive to Institutionalized Responsiveness in Vietnam and China". PhD dissertation, McGill University.

Vasavakul, Thaveeporn. 1997. "Sectoral Politics and Strategies for State and Party Building from the VII to the VIII Congress of the Vietnamese Communist Party (1991–1996)". In *Doi Moi: Ten Years after the 1986 Party Congress*, edited by Adam Fforde. Canberra: Research School of Pacific Studies, Australian National University.

————. 2019. *Vietnam: A Pathway from State Socialism*. New York: Cambridge University Press.

Vietnam Chamber of Commerce and Industry. 2020. Provincial Competitiveness Index 2019 (May). https://pcivietnam.vn/en (accessed 31 March 2021).

Vo, Nhan Tri. 1990. *Vietnam's Economic Policy since 1975*. Singapore: Institute of Southeast Asian Studies.

Vu-Thanh, Tu-Anh. 2017. "The Political Economy of Industrial Development in Vietnam, 1986–2013". In *The Practice of Industrial Policy: Government-business Coordination in Africa and East Asia*, edited by John Page and Finn Tarp, pp. 167–87. New York: Oxford University Press.

Vu-Thanh, Tu-Anh, et al., n.d. "A Retrospective on Past 30 Years of Development in Vietnam". Unpublished paper.

Vu, Quang Viet. 2009. "Vietnam's Economic Crisis: Policy Follies and the Role of State-Owned Conglomerates". *Southeast Asian Affairs 2009*, edited by Daljit Singh, pp. 389–417. Singapore: Institute of Southeast Asian Studies.

Vu, Tuong. 2013. "Socialism and Underdevelopment in Southeast Asia". In *Handbook of Southeast Asian History*, edited by Norman Owen, pp. 188–98. New York: Routledge.

————. 2017. *Vietnam's Communist Revolution: The Power and Limits of Ideology*. New York: Cambridge University Press.

Vu, Van Chung. 2015. "Foreign Capital Inflows and Economic Growth: Does Foreign Capital Inflows Promote the Host Country's Economic Growth? An Empirical Case Study of Vietnam and the Intuitive Roles of Japan's Capital Inflows on Vietnam's Economic Growth". Tokyo: Policy Research Institute, Ministry of Finance. https://www.mof.go.jp/pri/international_exchange/visiting_scholar_program/ws2015_vu2.pdf.

Vuving, Alexander. 2010. "Vietnam: A Tale of Four Players". In *Southeast Asian Affairs 2010*, edited by Daljit Singh. Singapore: Institute of Southeast Asian Studies.

Wischermann, Joerg. 2010. "Civil Society Action and Governance in Vietnam: Selected Findings from an Empirical Survey". *Journal of Current Southeast Asian Affairs* 2: 3–40.

Xuan Linh. 2014. "Tong Bi thu: Diet chuot dung de vo binh". *Vietnamnet*, 6 October 2014. https://vietnamnet.vn/vn/thoi-su/tong-bi-thu-diet-chuot-dung-de-vo-binh-200746.html.

Yoon, Heo, and Nguyen Khanh Doanh. 2009. "Trade Liberalization and Poverty Reduction in Vietnam". *World Economy* 32, no. 6 (June): 934–64.

Chapter 2

A Comparative Statistical View
of the Vietnamese Economy
under Reform since 1985

Vu Quang Viet

As of 2020, Vietnam's per capita income was estimated to be
US$2,400, which is at the middle position of countries in the category
of "lower middle income" set by the World Bank (between US$1,036
and US$4,045). While Vietnam's economy has been widely viewed
as a success story, comparatively it is not so successful, and many
key features of the country's economic expansion may not be fully
understood. As Table 2.1 indicates, Vietnam achieved much lower
growth rates (4.3, 7.4 and 6.6 per cent, respectively) for the three
decades between 1980 and 2000 when compared with the growth rates
over the three decades of 1960–80 for South Korea (9.5, 10.5 and 8.8
per cent) and 1980–2000 for China (9.7, 10 and 10.4 per cent).[1]

As I will argue in this chapter, there are two main reasons for
Vietnam's lower performance even after its economic reforms. First
is the strategy of industrialization that assigns too powerful a "leading
role" to the state-owned enterprises (SOEs) at the expense of the private
sector. The SOEs have generated corruption and driven up public debt
(both for the government and the SOEs) to an extremely high level
that almost bankrupted the economy in the early 2000s. Second is the
strategy of growth that courts foreign direct investment (FDI) simply
for the employment of low-skilled labour instead of focusing on FDI
projects that stimulate the development of human capital resources
and the transfers and exchanges of knowledge, technologies and
skills. As shown in Table 2.12, the foreign invested sector made up a

significant share of GDP (22.5 per cent) in 2018, clearly at the expense of the private domestic corporations (10.1 per cent of GDP), although its productivity was even lower than that of the state-owned sector.

This chapter develops a statistical analysis that attends to the following four tasks: (1) to comparatively assess Vietnam's development through a closer look at Vietnam's GDP; (2) to examine the views of the ruling Vietnamese Communist Party (VCP) about industrialization; (3) to explore the role of FDI in Vietnam's economy and the country's development strategy for it; and (4) to provide a cross-country comparison of Vietnam's labour productivity in industry.

Assessing Vietnam's Development Comparatively: A Closer Look at GDP

In light of Vietnam's rapid growth since the early 1990s, one may conclude that Vietnam's economic policies have been quite successful. But they do not appear nearly as successful as those of South Korea or China. This, it will be argued later, is mostly owing to the leadership of Vietnam, which has lacked a clear vision for the country. While GDP as a measure of economic performance has many known limitations, an analysis of Vietnam's economy in terms of GDP is also quite revealing, both for the purposes of understanding structural features of Vietnam's economy and for viewing Vietnam from a comparative international perspective.

As can be seen in Figure 2.2, Vietnam's GDP growth rates were brought from a low 4 per cent in the 1980s to an annual percentage of 6.8 per cent for the three decades between 1990 and 2018. This compares with rates of 9.3 per cent in China and 6.3 per cent in India. In terms of per capita GDP, which is more important, the average annual growth rate of Vietnam was 5.5 per cent, whilst for China it was 8.6 per cent and for India 4.7 per cent.

In 2018, Vietnam's per capita GDP reached US$1,964 at current market prices and it joined the club of lower-middle-income countries (see Figure 2.3 and Table 2.1). This figure, however, is still 54 per cent lower than that of the Philippines and less than a quarter of China's, a third of Thailand's and one sixth of Malaysia's (see last column, Table 2.3). In contrast, South Korea, which in the 1960s had per capita GDP lower than Malaysia and more or less the same as the Philippines, has joined the OECD community of wealthy countries. Its per capita GDP in 2018 was 13.6 times that of Vietnam's (see Table 2.2).

In terms of per capita GDP, the performance of Vietnam has been good, but not as good as China's or South Korea's. In its periods

FIGURE 2.1
Vietnam's GDP Growth Rates and Annual CPI Changes, 1985–2018

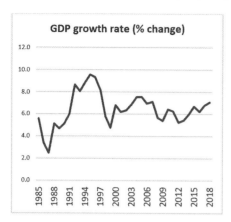
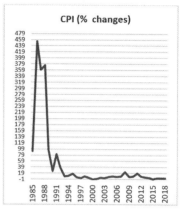

Sources: World Bank data, although 1985–90 data for Vietnam are from United Nations Statistics Division.

FIGURE 2.2
Average Annual Growth Rates per Capita GDP, 1990–2018

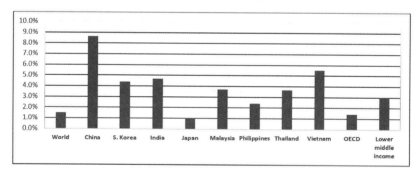

of rapid growth, China achieved four decades of annual growth in per capita GDP of almost 7–9 per cent, while South Korea achieved three decades of growth at 7–8 per cent. In contrast, over the last three decades Vietnam achieved only one decade of high growth of only almost 6 per cent (see Table 2.3). Nor does Vietnam's performance compare favourably with countries in Southeast Asia. At the present growth rates, Vietnam would take twenty-four years to catch up with Thailand if Thailand stood still, and sixty-four years if Thailand grew at the same rate as now (see last column of Table 2.3 and the accompanying note for a more realistic evaluation).

In many respects, the pattern of GDP growth in Vietnam is closely linked with its poorly conceived and executed industrial policies, which is the topic of the next section.

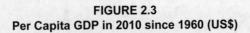

FIGURE 2.3
Per Capita GDP in 2010 since 1960 (US$)

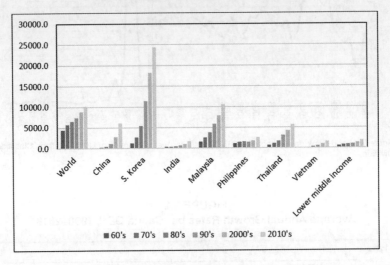

TABLE 2.1
GDP Average Annual Growth Rates

	1960s	1970s	1980s	1990s	2000s	2010s
World	5.6	4.0	3.0	2.7	2.9	3.0
China	3.4	7.4	9.7	10.0	10.4	7.8
South Korea	9.5	10.5	8.8	7.1	4.7	3.4
Japan	10.4	4.3	4.3	1.5	0.5	1.4
India	3.9	2.9	5.7	5.8	6.3	7.0
Malaysia	6.5	8.2	5.9	7.2	4.8	5.4
Philippines	5.1	5.8	2.0	2.8	4.5	6.3
Thailand	7.8	7.5	7.3	5.2	4.3	3.8
Vietnam		4.3	7.4	6.6	6.2	
OECD	5.7	3.6	3.0	2.6	1.8	2.0
Lower-middle-income	3.9	4.8	4.0	3.2	5.7	5.6

Notes: GDP growth rates and per capita GDP of countries other than Vietnam are based on the World Bank's database on per capita GDP and the ADB's Key Indicators (2019). Data on Vietnam are from the United Nations database on national accounts, which draws on data produced by the General Statistics Office of Vietnam. Data on GDP growth rates of Vietnam from the World Bank seem to be in error as they differ significantly from other sources for the years 1985–89 and 1997–2001. Thus, they have not been used. Instead, data for Vietnam for these years have been taken from the ADB and UN and converted to 2010 US dollars by the author.

TABLE 2.2
Per Capita GDP in 2010 (US$)

	1960s	1970s	1980s	1990s	2000s	2010s	2018	2018
World	4,466	5,749	6,544	7,424	8,816	10,185	10,894	5.55
China	170	267	515	1,170	2,766	6,119	7,753	3.95
S. Korea	1,238	2,698	5,459	11,385	18,258	24,366	26,777	13.63
India	357	402	483	668	1,023	1,682	2,101	1.07
Japan	13,332	21,931	30,378	40,157	43,598	46,551	48,920	24.90
Malaysia	1,624	2,532	3,758	5,887	7,835	10,527	12,120	6.17
Philippines	1,163	1,446	1,551	1,518	1,801	2,522	3,022	1.54
Thailand	713	1,103	1,716	3,180	4,205	5,656	6,362	3.24
Vietnam	–	–	395	561	993	1,608	1,964	1.00
OECD	14,158	19,190	23,596	29,039	34,814	37,750	39,990	20.36
Lower-middle-income	610	760	882	1,008	1,324	1,941	2,262	1.15

Note: VN = 1.0.

TABLE 2.3
Average Growth Rate in Per Capita GDP in 2010 (US$)

	1970s	1980s	1990s	2000s	2010s	Annual average 1990–2018	Years for VN to catch up*
World	2.6	1.3	1.3	1.7	1.5	1.5	36
China	4.6	6.8	8.5	9.0	8.3	8.6	29
S. Korea	8.1	7.3	7.6	4.8	2.9	4.4	54
India	1.2	1.9	3.3	4.3	5.1	4.7	1
Japan	5.1	3.3	2.8	0.8	0.7	1.1	67
Malaysia	4.5	4.0	4.6	2.9	3.0	3.7	38
Philippines	2.2	0.7	-0.2	1.7	3.4	2.5	9
Thailand	4.5	4.5	6.4	2.8	3.0	3.7	24
Vietnam	—	—	3.6	5.9	4.9	5.5	0
OECD	3.1	2.1	2.1	1.8	0.8	1.4	63
Lower-middle-income	2.2	1.5	1.4	2.8	3.9	3.1	3

Note: *The years required for Vietnam to catch up in terms of per capita GDP with the country in the row, for instance Thailand, would be 24 years, assuming that Vietnam would continue to grow annually at 4.9 per cent (the average rate of the 2010s) while Thailand would not grow. Let V stand for Vietnam's per capita income and T for Thailand's. Then, at present, T = 3.24V. In N years, assuming that T does not grow, then V x (1.049)N = T = 3.24 x V. Thus N=Log (3.24)/Log (1.049) = 24. Of course, Thailand does not stand idly by. Should Thailand grow at 3 per cent, for example, N = Log (3.24)/[log 1.049/Log (1.03)] = 64. The calculation presented is mainly for fun because, more importantly, the number of years required to catch up may be much less because as an economy becomes richer the value of its currency will appreciate more quickly, which would close the income gap more quickly. As one can see from the past, 1 dollar used to be worth 10 Chinese yuan; now it is only worth 7. Or, in 1960–70, 1 dollar was 360 yen but is now worth 107. In other words, the increase in GDP in terms of the US dollar is simply closing the gap in the cost of living.

The Communist Party's View of Industrialization

In 2000, the VCP set the goal to achieve industrialization by 2020 (Dang Cong San Viet Nam 1996). The resolution was repeated at the 11th Party Congress in 2011 (Dang Cong San Viet Nam 2010, 2016). Both congresses emphasized the leading role of the state sector, and the government took concrete action under the 2011 plan to promote shipbuilding, bauxite mining and aluminium production as leading industries. These were all poor choices. By 2000 the world market in ships was already saturated by South Korea, China and Japan—countries with superior shipbuilding capabilities across virtually all dimensions. And the focus on bauxite and aluminium was doomed to achieve little more than providing raw materials for China using obsolete Chinese technologies. As I have shown earlier (Vu 2009), the plan drove Vietnam's economy to the brink of bankruptcy. By 2020, Vietnam had failed to reach the goal of per capita GDP of US$3,200–3,500 that had been set out at the 12th Party Congress in 2016. In fact, per capita GDP of Vietnam was at only US$2,600 measured at current prices by the end of 2019, and per capita income was even lower because of the net payment of property income abroad for foreign investors and lenders.

From 2018, the VCP's Politburo seemed to adopt a different approach to achieving the same goal, but set it back ten years to 2030. In preparation for the 13th Party Congress in 2021, the Politburo issued an important directive on industrial development in 2018 that laid out some reasonable ideas, including an emphasis on the role of private enterprises; the prioritization of the information technology and electronics industry and the green economy; and the selection of science, technology, education and training as keys to create a breakthrough in national industrial policy (Dang Cong San Viet Nam 2018a). The directive then specified that by 2030 manufacturing should make up 30 per cent of GDP, out of which 20 per cent should be in high-tech industries. Party leaders seemed to be oblivious, however, to the fact that manufacturing in 2019 made up only 16.8 per cent of GDP and employed only 20.7 per cent of the workforce (Asian Development Bank Key Indicators 2019).

Even so, the directive seemed to lack unified political support because, in the same year, the Politburo took an opposite approach by issuing a directive for the government to enact the proposed law for free economic zones (FEZ) at three sites with ninety-nine-year land leases for foreign investors and visa waivers for foreigners: at Van Don, a town in the north bordering China; Bac Van Phong in Central

Vietnam; and Phu Quoc, an island located in the Gulf of Thailand (Dang Cong San Viet Nam 2018b). These tourist destinations are not close to any university or research centre that could provide technical support or high-skilled workers to the FEZ. After furious public opposition, the National Assembly decided to postpone the decision.[2] But the impulse behind this misbegotten initiative was revealing. In particular, it reflected a strikingly unsophisticated approach to utilizing foreign direct investment.

Overall, modernization from the point of view of the Vietnamese policymakers appears to centre principally on FDI and exports, but its undiscriminating approach to FDI has generated its own costs. At first glance, Vietnam appears to be an FDI and export success story, and in certain respects it is. By 2018 Vietnam was second in the world only to Singapore in obtaining the highest ratio of external merchandise trade over GDP and the highest ratio of FDI over total investment on fixed assets in Asia (see Table 2.4).

Upon closer scrutiny, however, Vietnam can be seen to be, at least for now, hardly utilizing FDI in ways observed in China or Korea. On the contrary, it is serving mainly as an export platform for China and Korea; a place where FDI from China and Korea are exported to exploit low-skilled and low-paid labour in order to process goods imported from their own countries for export to other advanced countries. There are few backward linkages in Vietnam's industrial sector. This is reflected in the fact that Vietnam has a huge surplus in balance of trade with the United States and the European Union (around US$30 billion with each), while having a correspondingly huge deficit with China and Korea (US$20–30 billion with each). This, in turn, has brought

TABLE 2.4
External Trade and Foreign Direct
Investment over GDP (%), 2018

	External trade/ GDP (%)	FDI/GDP (%)
Vietnam	196	6.3
China	34	1.7
South Korea	74	0.8
Japan	66	0.5
Malaysia	130	2.4
Thailand	99	2.6
Philippines	57	3.0
Singapore	215	25.0
World	46	1.6

Vietnam into a serious dispute with the United States and in violation of a requirement under the free trade agreement with the European Union (EVFTA), which requires Vietnam to raise domestic content to 45 per cent for garments and shoe products and at least 30 per cent for other products in order to benefit from low tariffs on its exports to the European Union (Vu 2020). Further, Vietnam's failure to cultivate backward linkages reflects a failure to deepen industrialization and expand manufacturing, in contrast to South Korea and China.

It is quite clear that Vietnam is still substantially agricultural—in the same league as India. Vietnam's agriculture still accounts for 17.4 per cent of GDP, in comparison with 9.9 per cent for Thailand (see Table 2.5) and much lower shares in high-income countries. The drastic reduction in agriculture as a percentage of GDP in all countries in the world reflects contributions from scientific knowledge to productivity. The share of agriculture in GDP of the world economy is currently at 4 per cent, and less than 2 per cent in advanced countries. In the United States it accounts for only 0.9 per cent of GDP but the country can produce more than it needs and US farmers even need to be paid by the government to keep their land idle.[3] In contrast, agriculture in Vietnam reflects very slow improvements in productivity and a lack of sophisticated private or state corporations. It is interesting to analyse the backward and forward linkages between agriculture and specific manufacturing industries such as food production, but unfortunately

FIGURE 2.4
Trade Balance of Vietnam to the EU, US and Japan, 2014–18 (billion US$)

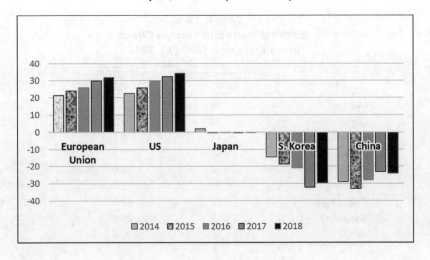

the data published by Vietnam's General Statistical Office is only at the aggregate manufacturing level, which does not allow such analysis.

Vietnam's ruling party aspires to raise industry to account for 30 per cent of GDP by 2030. In Asia, only in China and Malaysia

TABLE 2.5
Share of Agriculture, Forestry and Fishing in GDP (%)

	1960s	1970s	1980s	1990s	2020s	2010s
World				6.3	4.2	3.6
China	37.0	31.9	28.9	20.1	12.0	8.5
South Korea				1.7	3.0	2.1
Japan				1.7	1.2	1.1
India	40.5	36.4	29.5	25.6	18.5	16.4
Malaysia	35.9	29.0	20.5	13.1	9.0	9.1
Philippines	27.5	29.5	23.9	19.9	13.0	10.9
Thailand			17.9	10.0	9.2	9.9
Vietnam			41.4	30.2	21.1	17.4
OECD				2.1	1.6	1.5
Lower-middle-income	37.0	34.3	26.1	22.9	18.0	15.9

TABLE 2.6
Share of Industry (Manufacturing, Mining and Construction) in GDP (%)

	1960s	1970s	1980s	1990s	1920s	2010s
World				30.2	28.2	26.3
China	34.9	44.2	44.1	45.0	46.1	43.1
South Korea				34.1	33.3	35.0
Japan				34.1	30.2	28.0
India	21.2	23.4	26.5	27.3	29.2	28.2
Malaysia	28.5	35.0	39.5	42.5	45.8	39.2
Philippines	31.1	34.9	36.8	33.0	33.7	31.2
Thailand			32.0	37.3	38.2	36.8
Vietnam			26.3	28.9	38.3	33.1
OECD				26.1	24.5	22.6
Lower-middle-income	21.7	23.6	28.9	30.5	31.8	30.0

TABLE 2.7
Share of 2018 GDP of Industry and Manufacturing (%)

	Industry	Manufacturing
OECD	22.3	14
United States	18.2	11
Japan	29.1	10
Korea	35.1	27
China	40.7	29
Malaysia	38.3	22
Thailand	35.0	27
Philippines	30.7	19
India	26.7	15
Vietnam	34.2	16
Lower-middle-income	28.8	15

has industry ever exceeded 40 per cent of GDP (see Table 2.6). This might be a desirable goal for Vietnam if industrialization would aim at backward linkages to the national economy, and if a long-term view on technological change is considered.

Vietnamese leaders must note that the decline in the role of industry is in line with the general trend in advanced economies, and even in lower-middle-income countries, to move away from manufacturing and into information and other services. This trend, again similar to that for agriculture, is because of the increase in technology and labour productivity in industry. The decline in the share of manufacturing in GDP is particularly significant when the economy reaches high stages of modernization. The share of manufacturing used to be 30 per cent in the United States but it is now 11 per cent (see Table 2.7).

The Role of FDI in Vietnam

FDI has played an important role in the Vietnamese economy, at least in providing jobs and in raising the level of per capita GDP. Whether it has helped modernize the economy though is a different issue. No country in Asia has relied on FDI inflows as much as Vietnam; with respect to industrial deepening, it is likely that few countries have benefited less from high levels of FDI.

It is important to observe differences in policies and practices regarding FDI and its contributions to national industrialization. At various times, Japan and South Korea relied on their own investment and loan capital for economic development. In South Korea, FDI played a relatively more important role but at a very low level; on average, less than 1.5 per cent (see Table 2.11 and Figure 2.4), except for one year (1972) when it reached 4.6 per cent of GDP (World Bank Database on Foreign Direct Investment n.d.). In both countries, states and firms crafted strategies to learn from more advanced countries and develop their own technical capabilities over time. China benefited from massive FDI flows in numerous ways, but FDI was always a part of a broader strategy. Beyond and perhaps ultimately more importantly than employment creation, FDI has been used as a means of gaining access to foreign technology, both through pervasive and massive technology theft and through leveraging access to its huge domestic market by making investment conditional upon technology transfer. Vietnam, by comparison, has done little to none of the above.

The point is not to understate the contributions of FDI to Vietnam's growth, but rather to recognize the VCP's failure to harness FDI to the process of industrial transformation. While it is certainly true that FDI in Vietnam has contributed to employment, construction and revenues, it is equally the case that, thus far, the state has not managed FDI strategically. The danger (and in some respects reality) is that Vietnam has relatively little to show for FDI beyond significant though possibly temporary gains in low-wage employment and damaging levels of economic dependence on foreign capital and investment.

The following sections will review the increasing role of FDI in the Vietnamese economy since 2010 as compared with Korea and China. It grew at the expense of the state sectors but provided no benefit to the private sector. Statistics show that FDI doubled its share of fixed investment in Vietnam, to 24 per cent of total fixed investment during the 2015–18 period (see Table 2.10). This ratio reflects the extremely high reliance on FDI, unlike the cases of South Korea and China either in the past or at the present time.

As a result, the FDI corporate enterprises sector increased its share of gross value added (GVA)—i.e., GDP less taxes on products—from 13.3 per cent to 22.5 per cent (see Table 2.12), while GDP from the state-owned sector declined from 38.5 per cent in 2000 to 30.7 per cent in 2018. GDP share of the private domestic sector remained the same at around 10 per cent of GDP. Clearly, the FDI sector grew at the expense of the state sectors (which includes state-owned enterprises and the state bureaucracy) and has had little effect in the development of private domestic enterprises.

More importantly, foreign investment in Vietnam, instead of helping to improve the overall labour productivity of the nation

TABLE 2.8
Some Basic Indicators on Incorporated Enterprises in Vietnam, 2017

	Labour/capital (capital valued in 10 billion VN dong)	Profit before taxes/equity capital (%)	Debt/equity capital (%)
Total incorporated enterprises	5.0	8.4	231.2
State-owned	1.6	10.7	331.6
Private domestic	5.7	4.1	225.4
FDI	8.2	16.2	152.3

Source: Tong dieu tra doanh nghiep 2017 (2017 Census of enterprises).

TABLE 2.9
Percentage Share of Investment in Fixed Assets (GFCF) over GDP and FDI/GFCF of Vietnam, China and South Korea

	2000–2004	2005–9	2010–14	2015–18
Vietnam				
GFCF/GDP (%)	29.2	32.7	26.2	24.0
FDI/GFCF (%)	12.6	19.1	18.2	24.3
China				
GFCF/GDP (%)	36.7	40.8	45.3	42.9
FDI/GFCF (%)	8.3	7.8	5.2	0.7
South Korea				
GFCF/GDP (%)	31.0	30.6	29.6	30.2
FDI/GFCF (%)	−2.1	1.7	4.9	4.1

TABLE 2.10
FDI Investment/GDP

	1970s	1980s	1990s	2000s	2010s
China	0.0	0.5	3.9	3.7	2.6
South Korea	0.7	0.4	0.7	1.3	0.8
Japan	0.0	0.0	0.1	0.2	0.3
India	0.0	0.0	0.4	1.5	1.7
Malaysia	3.1	3.2	5.8	3.1	3.5
Philippines	0.5	0.6	1.8	1.5	1.9
Thailand	0.6	1.0	2.5	3.4	2.3
Vietnam	0.0	0.0	6.8	5.1	5.2
Lower-middle-income	0.6	0.4	1.2	1.9	2.0

Sources: Asia Development Bank Key Indicators (2020) and World Bank database on foreign direct investment (n.d.).

FIGURE 2.5
FDI as a Percentage of GDP

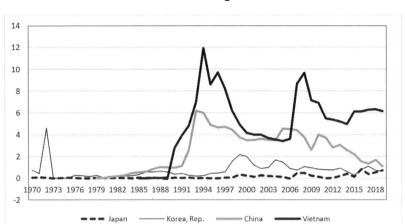

TABLE 2.11
Shares of Gross Value Added (GVA) by Institutional Sectors in Vietnam

	State sectors	Collective sector	Household sector	Private domestic corporate sector	FDI corporate sector
2000	38.5	8.5	32.3	9.7	13.3
2005	37.6	6.7	32.1	8.5	15.2
2006	36.7	6.4	31.9	9.0	16.1
2007	35.4	6.1	31.9	9.7	17.0
2008	35.1	5.9	31.4	10.2	17.4
2009	34.7	5.8	31.7	10.5	17.3
2010	33.6	4.6	36.7	7.9	17.3
2011	32.8	4.5	36.8	8.3	17.7
2012	32.6	4.4	36.3	8.9	17.8
2013	32.3	4.5	35.3	8.7	19.3
2014	31.9	4.5	35.0	8.7	19.9
2015	31.9	4.5	34.8	8.8	20.1
2016	32.0	4.4	33.8	9.1	20.7
2017	31.8	4.2	32.6	9.6	21.8
2018	30.7	4.2	32.5	10.1	22.5

Notes: Data is from the General Statistics Office of Vietnam (GSO). Data from the GSO do not separate SOEs from other state activities and therefore labour productivity cannot be calculated separately for SOEs for comparison purposes. But this does not affect the overall conclusions on differences in labour productivity. Because of the low level of productivity of public services, the labour productivity of SOEs may be biased downward. Also, the data was more accurate from the year 2010 onwards as GSO has separated taxes on products from gross value added of sectors and thus shares are not affected by tax policy.

FIGURE 2.6
Shares of Gross Value Added (GVA) by Institutional Sectors in Vietnam

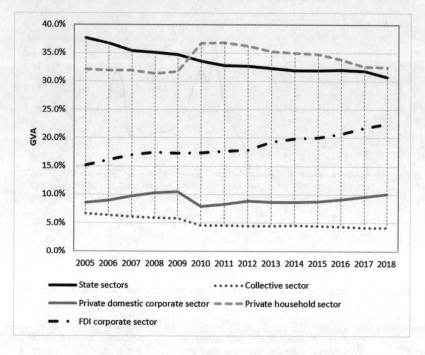

TABLE 2.12
Labour Productivity Measured by Value Added
per Worker in Vietnam (million 2010 VND)

	State sector	Non-state domestic sector	FDI sector	FDI/State sector
2005	114	21	217	1.9
2006	122	22	209	1.7
2007	127	23	200	1.6
2008	131	23	199	1.5
2009	137	24	232	1.7
2010	126	22	189	1.5
2011	133	23	168	1.3
2012	141	24	169	1.2
2013	148	25	163	1.1
2014	157	26	155	1.0
2015	168	28	155	0.9
2016	181	29	150	0.8
2017	192	31	144	0.7
2018	202	33	149	0.7

Figure 2.7
Industry Labour Productivity – GVA per Worker
(million 2010 VND) in Vietnam

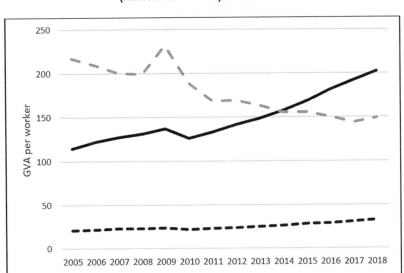

and the development of its economy through backward linkages to domestic suppliers, has been simply aimed at exploiting low paid, unskilled Vietnamese labour. We observe that labour productivity in the FDI sector measured as gross value added per worker has actually been declining relative to the state-owned sector. Specifically, in 2005 labour productivity of the FDI sector (measured by gross value added per employee at constant prices) was almost twice that of the state sector. But by 2018 it had declined drastically to only 70 per cent of the state sector (see the last row, Table 2.13). There are two reasons for this. First, the share of FDI in the mining and extraction sector, which is always more capital-intensive, has declined. This has been particularly so for petroleum and gas.[4] Another reason, and one that is more worrying, is that the FDI Vietnam has attracted has remained overwhelmingly concentrated in industries with low technology and that entails unskilled labour such as the garment and electronic assembly industries.[5] These industries, which are characterized by a very high ratio of labour over capital, are highly profitable for foreign investors, while contributing little to Vietnam's industrialization or the skilling of its workforce (see Table 2.9). In the meantime, Vietnam has made very little progress in attracting FDI into higher value sectors.

FIGURE 2.8
Vietnam: Annual FDI Inflow and Investment
Income Outflows, 2000–2018

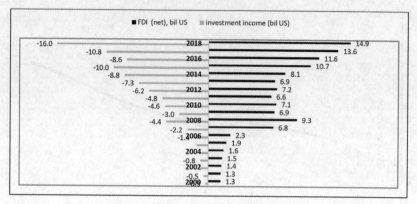

Note: See World Bank database on foreign direct investment for foreign direct investment, net inflows (% of GDP) from the World Bank data, and Asian Development Bank Key Indicators (2019) for net investment primary income for Vietnam.

The final point to be made about foreign direct investment is that the FDI investors have clearly benefited from their investments in Vietnam, seeing a rate of profit before taxes at 18 per cent. The repatriation of investment incomes abroad has also become quite significant: in 2018, investment income outflows totalling US$16 billion surpassed FDI inflows (US$14.9 billion) for the first time (see Figure 2.7). The rate of return before taxes was reported by Vietnam's Ministry of Planning and Investment at 17 per cent in 2017, which is high compared to the global rate of return of 8 per cent in 2010 and 6.8 per cent in 2019 (Qiang and Kusek 2010).

Cross-Country Comparison of Labour Productivity in Industry

FDI in Vietnam has been shown to not be contributing to any increase in labour productivity for the Vietnamese economy and has in fact been pulling it down. Labour productivity as measured by gross value added per worker in Vietnam increased from an annual value of US$2,000 (in 2010 US dollars) in 1991 to US$5,000 in 1999 and has been hovering around US$5,000 a year since then (for a period of twenty years).

China, by contrast, starting at a low base compared with Vietnam in 1991, has seen a tenfold increase in labour productivity, reaching US$22,000 in 2018 measured in the same 2010 constant prices.

FIGURE 2.9
Labour Productivity of Industry of China, Vietnam and South Korea

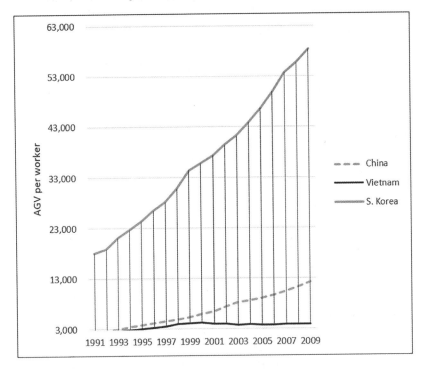

TABLE 2.13
Gross Value Added per Worker in Industry in 2010 (US$)

	1990s	2000s	2010s
World	19,699	26,266	28,075
China	3,790	8,971	18,611
South Korea	24,973	46,206	67,165
India	3,489	4,424	5,994
Japan	74,018	88,270	104,731
Malaysia	24,099	30,545	32,304
Philippines	9,250	10,003	12,683
Thailand	12,552	13,694	16,958
Vietnam	3,133	3,897	4,104
OECD	61,038	72,535	82,227
Lower-middle-income	5,925	6,595	7,695

Source: World Bank DataBase on value added per workers (n.d.).

Having said that, China's labour productivity is still only a third of South Korea's, which was US$71,000 as of 2018 (see Figure 2.9). Vietnam is at the same rank as India and is far below the average of lower-middle-income countries.

Re-examination of Vietnam's Development Strategy

This chapter has been written with a critical view of Vietnam's development strategy. It has focused on FDI as this represents a potentially vital but so far disappointing contributor to national development. I have examined how and why this is the case and explained that, while FDI has contributed to employment generation and other development goals, its contributions to Vietnam's long-term development are in doubt owing to the lower labour productivity of the new FDI projects, which have lowered overall productivity of the FDI sector and have had a negligible effect on the private domestic sector (see Table 2.12 and Table 2.13).

That Vietnam's industrial strategy is faltering owes not only to the management of FDI but also to problems in the broader economy and to its political maladministration. With respect to FDI, Vietnam needs to adopt and implement policies that can make foreign investment contribute to gains in labour productivity and industrial deepening through an expansion of links to the domestic economy. This requires real political commitments to improving hitherto underdeveloped capacities and infrastructures. Beyond this, two issues of special concern include the continued outsized role and poor performance of the state sector and problems in human capital formation that will not develop without management autonomy and freedom of thinking in higher education.[6]

Technically, it is easy for Vietnam to change the system in such a way that foreign direct investment choices can be made that would improve labour productivity in the long run and would improve the capability to build the necessary infrastructure for development—the physical assets that any modern economy needs, such as a clean water supply, electricity and natural gas, road and rail connections, ports and telecommunications.

To be successful in modernization, it is urgent for Vietnam to invest successfully in the human capital of its society, which would allow it to build its own intellectual infrastructure for the future. Overall, it can be said that Vietnam was successful in increasing per capita GDP, but it has failed to modernize the country in terms of building human capital. Efforts to develop human capital, although promoted in official rhetoric, have been dismally implemented because of the VCP's need to have full management and political control over higher education, whether private or public. This topic deserves a serious analysis. Only a few points, however, are related here.

The first example is about the failure of the plan formed in 2010 to produce twenty thousand PhDs by 2020, half of them within the country and half abroad (TTXVN/Vietnam+ 2010). This declaration was made in the official mid-term review of the State Auditing Commission. According to the commission, by 2016 the target of 12,800 PhDs should be met. In reality, only 23 per cent of the domestic PhDs had been met. For the target of earning PhDs overseas, only 34 per cent received approval to go abroad, and of these many have not completed their studies and some did not return after completing them (Yen Anh 2018). It is unclear why the overseas programme failed to make sufficient selections or whether the PhDs that have been completed are meaningful. As it stands, among all state sectors, the public security sector has the highest number of PhDs.

The second example concerns brain drain. By 2017, 130,000 students from Vietnam were abroad on their own volition to study and had spent in the region of US$3–4 billion a year doing so. The ratio of students returning home after completing their degrees is unknown, though it is probably small. The press in Vietnam cited an example of well-trained people not willing to return: out of thirteen students who received top prizes in student competitions, only one came home after completing their study abroad—a figure of less than 8 per cent (Le Kien 2015). In China, in 2016 the number of students going abroad was 544,000, and the number coming home was 432,000 (MBA Crystal Ball 2018). The reason for Vietnamese graduates not coming home is simple: they cannot get a decent-paying job in Vietnam. In contrast, China ran two hundred talent recruitment programmes within the Thousand Talents Plan to attract to China not only Chinese scientists but also foreign scientists, offering better salaries than those offered at top posts in the United States and Europe. In 2017 alone, according to a report to the US Senate, China was able to recruit seven thousand "high-end professionals", including several Nobel Prize winners.[7]

No university from Vietnam has been rated among the top one hundred universities in Asia by the London-based Times Higher Education ranking. In 2020 there was one each from the Philippines and Malaysia, 42 from China, 14 from Japan, 11 from South Korea and 8 from India in the list (Times Higher Education 2020). R&D expenditure is too low to attract any talent. Data on R&D is rare, but

TABLE 2.14
R&D over GDP (%), 2015

China	2.1
South Korea	4.2
Japan	3.2
Malaysia	1.3
Philippines	0.1
Thailand	0.6
Vietnam	0.4

Source: Asia Development Bank Key Indicators (2020).

according to the Asian Development Bank, R&D was very low in 2015, accounting for only 0.4 per cent of GDP (see Table 2.14). There is in fact a long way for Vietnam to go, but the first thing to do is to set the right vision for modernization.

Acknowledgement

I am extremely thankful to Professor Jonathan London at Leiden University and Professor Tuong Vu at the University of Oregon for their valuable comments on a draft of this chapter.

Notes

1. These periods reflected the effects of reforms in the three countries. The 1990–2000 period in Vietnam used for comparison should be viewed as appropriate as it was fifteen years after the war, which ended in 1975, and two years after the elimination of price controls by the state.
2. On public protests against the law, see Nguyen Thuc Cuong and Hoang Cam Thanh's chapter in this volume.
3. In 2017 the United States produced US$447 billion of gross output from agriculture, forestry and fisheries and exported US$140 billion (31 per cent). It also imported, however, a value of US$120 billion.
4. Between 2010 and 2019, the share of value added of the mining sector declined from 11 per cent to 7.5 per cent.
5. For an analysis of Vietnam's position in the global value chain in these industries, see Chapter 3 by Upalat Korwatanasakul and Chapter 4 by Truong Quang Hoan in this volume.
6. On how the party controls Vietnamese universities, see Chapter 7 by Quang Chau and Mai Van Tinh in this volume.
7. US Senate (2019), Federal Bureau of Investigation (2015), Barry and Kolata (2020).

References

Asian Development Bank. 2019. https://www.adb.org/publications/key-indicators-asia-and-pacific-2019 (accessed 15 December 2020).

———. 2020. "17 Sustainable Development Goals". https://kidb.adb.org/kidb/sdg#9 (accessed 15 December 2020).

Barry, Ellen, and Gina Kolata. 2020 "China's Lavish Funds Lured U.S. Scientists. What Did It Get in Return?" *New York Times*, 7 February 2020. https://www.nytimes.com/2020/02/06/us/chinas-lavish-funds-lured-us-scientists-what-did-it-get-in-return.html.

Dang Cong San Viet Nam. 1996. "Nghi quyet ve dinh huong chien luoc phat trien khoa hoc va cong nghe trong thoi ky cong nghiep hoa, hien dai hoa van hiem vu den nam 2000". 24 December 1996. https://thuvienphapluat.vn/van-ban/Linh-vuc-khac/Nghi-quyet-02-NQ-HNTW-dinh-huong-chien-luoc-phat-trien-khoa-hoc-va-cong-nghe-127646.aspx.

———. 2010. "Báo cáo chính trị của Ban Chấp hành Trung ương Đảng khoá X tại Đại hội đại biểu toàn quốc lần thứ XI của Đảng". December 2010. http://chinhphu.vn/portal/page/portal/chinhphu/NuocCHXHCNVietNam/ThongTinTongHop/noidungvankiendaihoidang?categoryId=10000716&articleId=10038382.

———. 2016. "Nghi quyet dai hoi dai bieu toan quoc lan thu 12 cua dang". 28 January 2016. https://dangcongsan.vn/xay-dung-dang/nghi-quyet-dai-hoi-dai-bieu-toan-quoc-lan-thu-xii-cua-dang-368870.html.

———. 2018a. "Nghi quyet so 23-NQ/TW ngay 22/3/2018 cua Bo Chinh tri ve dinh huong xay dung chinh sach phat trien cong nghiep quoc gia den nam 2030, tam nhin den nam 2045". 22 March 2018. https://tulieuvankien.dangcongsan.vn/he-thong-van-ban/van-ban-cua-dang/nghi-quyet-so-23-nqtw-ngay-2232018-cua-bo-chinh-tri-ve-dinh-huong-xay-dung-chinh-sach-phat-trien-cong-nghiep-quoc-gia-den-nam-4125.

———. 2018b. "Du thao luat don vi hanh chinh -kinh te dac biet Van Don, Bac Van Phong, Phu Quoc". 12 June 2018. https://thuvienphapluat.vn/tintuc/vn/thoi-su-phap-luat/thoi-su/20379/toan-van-du-thao-luat-dac-khu.

Federal Bureau of Investigation. 2015. "Chinese Talent Program". September 2015. https://info.publicintelligence.net/FBI-ChineseTalentPrograms.pdf.

Le Kien. 2015. "Vi sao 13 chau di du hoc, 12 chau khong ve?" *Tuoi tre News*, 2 November 2015. https://tuoitre.vn/vi-sao-13-chau-di-du-hoc-12-chau-khong-ve-995404.htm.

MBA Crystal Ball. 2018. "More International Students Returning Home to China, India after Graduation than Before". 19 February 2018. https://www.mbacrystalball.com/blog/2018/02/19/international-students-returning-home-after-graduation/.

Ministry of Planning and Investment. 2020. *Sach Trang Doanh Nghiep Viet Nam 2020*. Hanoi: General Statistics Office Publishing House. https://www.gso.gov.vn/wp-content/uploads/2020/04/Ruot-sach-trang-2020.pdf (accessed 15 December 2020).

Qiang, Christine Zhenwei, and Peter Kusek. 2020. "Overview". In *Global Investment Competitiveness Report 2019/2020: Rebuilding Investor Confidence in Times of Uncertainty*. Washington, DC: The World Bank.

Time Higher Education. 2020. "Asia University Rankings 2020". https://www.timeshighereducation.com/world-university-rankings/2020/

regional-ranking#!/page/0/length/25/sort_by/rank/sort_order/asc/cols/ stats (accessed 6 April 2021).

TTXVN/Vietnam+. 2010. "Dao tao it nhat 20.000 tien si trong vong 10 nam toi." 26 June 2010. https://dantri.com.vn/xa-hoi/dao-tao-it-nhat-20000-tien-si-trong-vong-10-nam-toi-1277773376.htm.

United Nations. n.d. United Nations Data Base on National Accounts. https:// unstats.un.org/unsd/snaama/Basic (accessed 15 December 2020).

US Senate Staff Report. 2019. *Threats to the U.S. Research Enterprise: China's Talent Recruitment Plans.* 18 November 2019. https://www.hsgac.senate. gov/imo/media/doc/2019-11-18%20PSI%20Staff%20Report%20-%20 China%27s%20Talent%20Recruitment%20Plans.pdf.

Vu, Quang Viet. 2009. "Vietnam's Economic Crisis: Policy Follies and the Role of State-Owned Conglomerates". In *Southeast Asian Affair 2009*, edited by Daljit Singh, pp. 389–417. Singapore: Institute of Southeast Asian Studies.

Vu, Quang Viet. 2020. "Vietnam: de dat loi ich cao nhat ve thuong mai va dau tu nuoc ngoai". *US-Vietnam Review*, 17 April 2020. https://usvietnam. uoregon.edu/viet-nam-de-dat-loi-ich-cao-nhat-ve-thuong-mai-va-dau-tu-voi-nuoc-ngoai-ky-1-nhan-xet-tong-quat/; and https://usvietnam. uoregon.edu/viet-nam-de-dat-loi-ich-cao-nhat-ve-thuong-mai-va-dau-tu-voi-nuoc-ngoai-ky-2-chinh-sach-cua-my-va-phan-ung-cua-viet-nam/.

World Bank. n.d. World Bank database on per capita GDP (constant 2010 US dollars). https://data.worldbank.org/indicator/NY.GDP.PCAP.KD/ (accessed 15 December 2020).

———. n.d. World Bank database on foreign direct investment (net inflows as % of GDP). https://data.worldbank.org/indicator/BX.KLT.DINV.CD.WD.

———. n.d. World Bank database on value added per workers (constant 2010 US dollars). https://data.worldbank.org/indicator/NV.IND.EMPL.KD (accessed 15 December 2020).

Yen Anh. 2018. "Tieu tung de an dao tao 23.000 tien si". *Nguoi Lao Dong News*, 9 January. https://nld.com.vn/thoi-su/tieu-tung-de-an-dao-tao-23000-tien-si-20180108224405108.htm (accessed 15 December 2020).

Chapter 3

Global Value Chains and Vietnam's Economic Development: A Path to Perils or Prosperity?

Upalat Korwatanasakul

The Sixth National Congress of the Vietnamese Communist Party (VCP) was an important milestone in Vietnam's development path as it marked the significant transformation of the Vietnamese economy. With the economic reform of Doi Moi (Renovation) in 1986, Vietnam transitioned to a socialist-oriented market-based economy. This structural transformation, particularly in trade liberalization and the promotion of foreign direct investment (FDI), facilitated Vietnam's participation in regional and global production networks or value chains. Participation in the global value chain (GVC) benefited the country in various ways, including enhancing its capabilities and competitiveness, improving its product quality, bringing financial stability, and expanding its markets (Korwatanasakul and Warunsiri 2020, p. 1). As a result of participating in the GVC, Vietnam—once one of the world's poorest countries—reached an average growth rate of nearly 7 per cent in the period from 1990 to 2019, which is one of the highest growth rates in the world, and it became a lower-middle-income country in 2010 (World Bank 2020). Moreover, GDP per capita increased almost thirteenfold from US$210 in 1989 to US$2,700 in 2019 (World Bank 2020). The reform also attracted a large amount of FDI into the country: Vietnam's FDI net inflows rose sharply from US$0.18 billion in 1990 to US$15.5 billion in 2018 (World Bank 2020).

In 2021, the 13th National Congress may mark another turning point in Vietnamese history. Despite the past economic success, the slowdown of growth has signalled to the VCP the need for another major structural transformation after thirty-five years of Doi Moi reform. In a fast-changing world, the economic policies implemented in the past (e.g., the focus on labour-intensive activities) are unlikely to apply to the current market environment and conditions. While enjoying the benefits of the GVC, Vietnam is continuing over time to lose competitiveness in its strategic industries. Without a well-planned economic strategy, the benefits from GVC participation may be illusory and leave the country with structural stagnation, particularly in terms of innovation and technological development.

This study provides a novel analysis through the lens of the GVC framework and empirical data of trade in value-added to examine issues related to the dilemma of development and global integration in Vietnam. To date, this has been little explored in the political economy literature. The results of the study suggest that Vietnam's successful participation in the GVC explains its rapid economic and social development. Vietnam raised the volume of its total output and exports by using foreign inputs and technologies. At the same time, the study data also indicates that heavy reliance on foreign inputs and technologies that resemble intensive backward GVC participation without further upgrading will result in structural stagnation, erosion of national competitiveness, a slowdown of growth, and ultimately a failure to escape from the middle-income trap. Therefore, to steer the economy towards prosperity and sustainability, the VCP may consider integrating a GVC-upgrading development model into its new policy agenda. Policies that facilitate substantial institutional reforms, promote strategic GVC engagement, and strengthen domestic capabilities, especially of small and medium-sized enterprises (SMEs), should be the priority for Vietnam.

The study is structured as follows. The second section provides a brief overview of Vietnam's economic development. The third section discusses the mechanisms and benefits of GVC participation for Vietnam. The fourth section presents the dilemma confronted by Vietnam regarding its GVC participation and the possibility of it falling into a middle-income trap. The fifth section lays out the challenges for Vietnam to maintain competitiveness in its strategic value chains, particularly in textiles and clothing, electrical and electronic equipment, and the automotive industry. The last section discusses policy implications and proposes several policy recommendations, which is followed by the conclusion.

Global Value Chain Participation and Vietnam's Economic Miracle

Vietnam was one of the fastest-growing economies in the world. From 1985 to 2019, the average annual growth rate of real GDP was 6.5 per cent, while GDP per capita has also grown substantially (Figure 3.1). Vietnam went through a structural transformation from a primitive agriculture-based economy to a newly industrialized one. In 1994, the net output share of the manufacturing sector outweighed that of agriculture for the first time, and it became more critical in the 2000s and afterwards (Figure 3.2). The economy reached its peak in 1995, manifesting the benefits of the Doi Moi reforms and witnessing real GDP growth of 9.5 per cent. Its worst performance was in 1999, when its growth rate dropped to 4.8 per cent because of the 1997 Asian financial crisis (Figure 3.1). The Vietnamese economy was quite resilient though as the growth was still optimistic and bounced back to 7 per cent within two years after the crisis. According to Anh, Duc and Chieu (2014, p. 5), Vietnam's high GDP growth was the result of the socialist market mechanism and a series of economic reforms such as the withdrawal of price controls in the consumer market, liberalization of trade and investment, equitization of state-owned enterprises (SOEs), and enforcement of private property rights. In 2010, Vietnam became a lower-middle-income country; it aims to reach the status of an upper-middle-income country by 2035.

FIGURE 3.1
Real GDP Growth and Per Capita GDP in Vietnam, 1985–2019

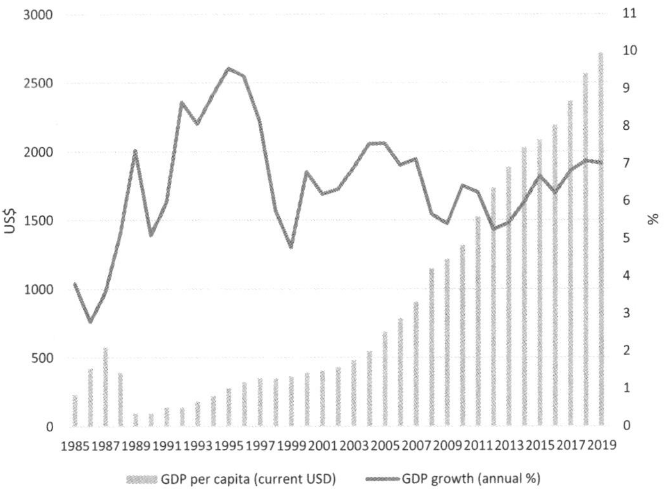

Source: Author, based on the World Bank.

The country's success in GVC participation largely explains its rapid economic development.[1] The share of domestic value added (DVA)[2] in gross exports fell from 77 per cent in 1990 to 68 per cent in 2018 (see Figure 3.3). Vietnam has been expanding the share of foreign value added (FVA)[3] in gross exports during the same period.

FIGURE 3.2
Structural Transformation of the Vietnamese Economy, 1985–2019 (Net output as % of GDP)

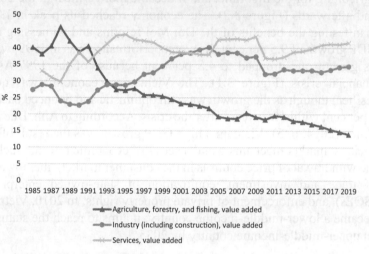

Source: Author, based on the World Bank.

FIGURE 3.3
Vietnam's Value-Added Content of Exports in 1990 and 2018

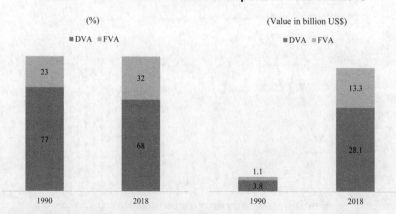

Note: DVA = domestic value added, FVA = foreign value added.
Source: Author, based on ASEAN-Japan Centre (n.d.).

The decrease in the DVA share (or the increase in the FVA share) was accompanied by a sharp rise in DVA volume in exports from US$3.8 billion to US$28.1 billion and a hike in gross exports from US$4.9 billion to US$41.4 billion. The DVA volume, FVA volume and gross exports grew significantly at between 11 and 13 per cent from 1990 to 2018. Depending more on foreign input such as intermediate goods and technologies has allowed the country to achieve higher productivity and gain access to a larger market. As shown in Figure 3.4, Vietnam has relied heavily on foreign intermediate goods, particularly in the

FIGURE 3.4
Share of Foreign Value Added in Vietnamese Exports, by Sector, Industrial Group and Selected Industries, 2015

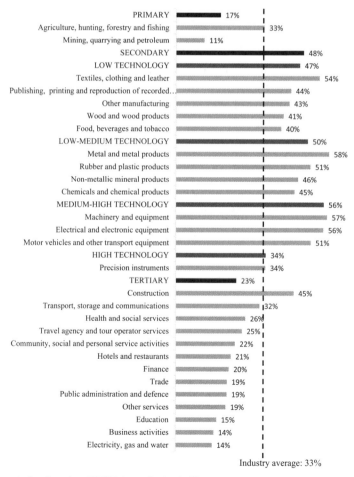

Source: Author, based on ASEAN-Japan Centre (n.d.).

manufacturing sector. FVA share accounted for almost half of gross exports (48 per cent) and was significantly above the industry average (33 per cent). The most considerable portion of foreign inputs is found in the medium- to high-tech industrial group (56 per cent), covering industries such as electrical and electronic equipment (56 per cent), machinery and equipment (57 per cent), and motor vehicles and other transport equipment (51 per cent). Moreover, the low- to medium-tech industrial and low-tech industrial groups also manifest remarkable high FVA shares: 50 per cent and 47 per cent, respectively. The textiles and clothing industry, one of Vietnam's strategic industries, shows the highest FVA share (54 per cent) within the low-tech industrial group.

The higher FVA share, volume and higher gross exports reveal the significance and success of the Doi Moi economic reforms that promoted trade liberalization and attracted FDI, particularly in the manufacturing sector. In 2018, Vietnam attracted a total of US$30.8 billion worth of registered FDI, while FDI in the manufacturing sector amounted to US$14.2 billion (Figure 3.5). Through foreign investment, technologies, innovation and technical know-how (e.g., management) are transferred to local firms located along value chains. Local firms also have an incentive to catch up with the new technologies and know-how since they must meet international production standards. Therefore, local firms in Vietnam have for

FIGURE 3.5
Foreign Direct Investment Inflow into Vietnam, 2018 (billion US$)

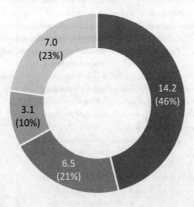

▪ Processing & manufacturing ▪ Property business ▪ Wholesale & retail sale ▪ Others

Note: The number in brackets indicates a percentage in total foreign direct investment.
Source: Author, based on the Ministry of Planning and Investment (Vietnam).

TABLE 3.1
Vietnam's GVC and RVC Participation, 1990–2018 (%)

Year	FVA Share			DVX Share			GVC Participation	RVC Participation
	non-ASEAN countries	ASEAN countries	Total	non-ASEAN countries	ASEAN countries	Total		
1990	20.1	2.6	22.7	16.7	1.5	18.2	40.8	4.1
1995	23.4	4.2	27.6	14.2	3.3	17.4	45.0	7.5
2000	19.7	4.1	23.8	17.6	4.3	21.9	45.7	8.4
2005	24.3	5.4	29.7	18.9	4.4	23.4	53.1	9.9
2010	34.1	7.9	42.1	16.1	3.6	19.6	61.7	11.5
2015	26.7	6.7	33.3	16.7	3.5	20.2	53.5	10.1
2018	25.6	6.5	32.1	14.3	2.9	17.3	49.4	9.4

Note: GVC participation = Total FVA share + Total DVX share, RVC participation = FVA share by ASEAN countries + DVX share in ASEAN countries, DVX share = share of Vietnam's domestic value added incorporated in other countries' exports, FVA share = share of foreign value added in Vietnam's exports, GVC = global value chain, RVC = regional value chain.

Source: Author, based on ASEAN-Japan Centre (n.d.).

the past decades benefited considerably from imported technology or backward GVC participation. Trade liberalization attracts foreign investment and facilitates Vietnam's smooth participation in regional and global value chains. There has been a positive trend of Vietnam's regional value chain (RVC) and GVC participation from 1990 to 2018, in which the level of RVC and GVC participation increased substantially (Table 3.1). In addition, Vietnam deepened the degree of intra-industry trade in various industries with its regional trading partners, including food, beverages and tobacco; electronics and motor vehicles; wood and wood products; chemicals and chemical products; and other manufacturers (Figure 3.6). As a result of its

FIGURE 3.6
Vietnam's Regional Value Chain Participation by Industry, 2015 (%)

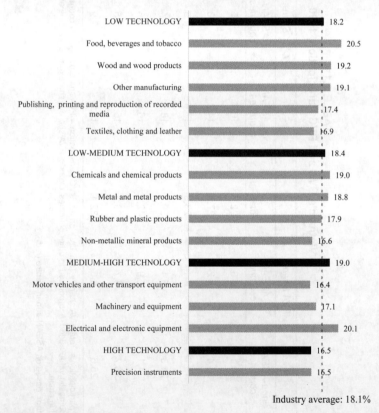

Industry average: 18.1%

Note: Regional value chain participation is the sum of the share of foreign value added created by other ASEAN countries in Vietnamese exports and the share of Vietnam's domestic value added incorporated in other ASEAN countries' exports.

Source: Author, based on ASEAN-Japan Centre (n.d.).

GVC participation, Vietnam has become a new production hub for some industries, including electrical and electronic equipment (e.g., smartphones, integrated circuits, micro assemblies and TVs), textiles and clothing, and food processing.

The Double Edges of a GVC-Oriented Development Strategy

Before the Doi Moi reform, Vietnam was in *stage zero* of catch-up industrialization,[4] in which the country was characterized by monoculture, subsistence agriculture and dependency. Without the help of foreign input and technology, Vietnam would not have achieved its current level of social and economic development. Thus, dependence on FVA was unavoidable and necessary for the initial industrialization and further economic development. The degree of reliance on foreign input depends on several factors; for example, the condition of supporting industries, advancement of domestic technology and innovation, and size of the domestic and foreign markets. An industry inevitably relies on foreign investment because of insufficient local supporting industries, limited domestic capabilities and technology, and low domestic demand. Such investments potentially benefit local firms in the form of imported resources such as raw materials, intermediate products, technology, business know-how, and access to the international market. Like other developing countries, Vietnam has abundant labour and therefore its competitiveness lies mainly in cheap labour. Vietnam entered the GVC predominantly by specializing in low-value-added activities of industries such as food products, textiles and clothing, and electrical and electronic equipment. Even though these industries—except for the food industry—show a relatively smaller share of DVA in their exports, their DVA volume has increased remarkably. Vietnam could benefit significantly from the high *volume of production* as a result of trade and investment liberalization.

But Vietnam is unlikely to further boost or even maintain its current growth level if the country continues its dependence on the large share of FVA in gross exports, particularly in its strategic industries—namely, the automotive industry, electrical and electronics, and textiles and clothing (Korwatanasakul and Intarakumnerd 2020, pp. 36–38; 2021, p. 21). These industries are not listed among the top industries in terms of being able to generate multiplier effects in the Vietnamese economy (see Figure 3.7). In other words, an increase in the production volume in these industries translates to a limited level of production in other domestic industries and therefore only slightly raises the overall output of the economy. The multiplier effects of the electrical, electronics, and textiles and clothing industries (1.63, 1.38 and 1.60, respectively) are even less than the industry average (1.77). The electronics industry is ranked second-worst in terms of its multiplier effect. On the other hand, industries such as wood, coke and refined petroleum products and food products, beverages and tobacco show higher multiplier effects as they are highly integrated with other domestic industries and mainly utilize input produced locally.

Furthermore, it is often the case that the importance of the manufacturing sector is overestimated in traditional trade statistics (Korwatanasakul 2019, p. 13). In the case of Vietnam, the manufacturing

FIGURE 3.7
Multiplier Effects by Industry, Vietnam, 2015

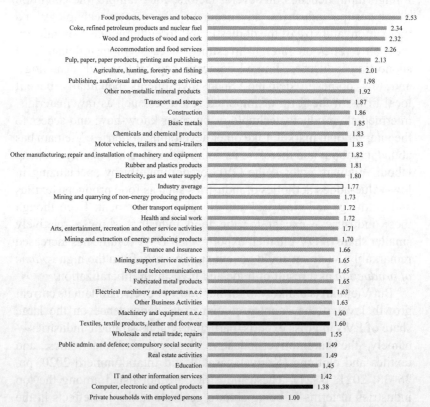

Food products, beverages and tobacco — 2.53
Coke, refined petroleum products and nuclear fuel — 2.34
Wood and products of wood and cork — 2.32
Accommodation and food services — 2.26
Pulp, paper, paper products, printing and publishing — 2.13
Agriculture, hunting, forestry and fishing — 2.01
Publishing, audiovisual and broadcasting activities — 1.98
Other non-metallic mineral products — 1.92
Transport and storage — 1.87
Construction — 1.86
Basic metals — 1.85
Chemicals and chemical products — 1.83
Motor vehicles, trailers and semi-trailers — 1.83
Other manufacturing; repair and installation of machinery and equipment — 1.82
Rubber and plastics products — 1.81
Electricity, gas and water supply — 1.80
Industry average — 1.77
Mining and quarrying of non-energy producing products — 1.73
Other transport equipment — 1.72
Health and social work — 1.72
Arts, entertainment, recreation and other service activities — 1.71
Mining and extraction of energy producing products — 1.70
Finance and insurance — 1.66
Mining support service activities — 1.65
Post and telecommunications — 1.65
Fabricated metal products — 1.65
Electrical machinery and apparatus n.e.c — 1.63
Other Business Activities — 1.63
Machinery and equipment n.e.c — 1.60
Textiles, textile products, leather and footwear — 1.60
Wholesale and retail trade; repairs — 1.55
Public admin. and defence; compulsory social security — 1.49
Real estate activities — 1.49
Education — 1.45
IT and other information services — 1.42
Computer, electronic and optical products — 1.38
Private households with employed persons — 1.00

Note: (a) The total domestic backward linkage effects are calculated from the Leontief inverse matrix of the input-output table. For the full description of each sector, refer to the OECD Input-Output table; (b) Industries indicated by a black bar are Vietnam's strategic industries.

Source: Author, based on the Organisation for Economic Co-operation and Development (OECD).

TABLE 3.2
Contribution of Vietnam's Strategic Industries to Gross Exports
and Total Domestic Value Added, 2015 (million US$ and %)

Industry	Gross exports	Domestic value-added (DVA)	% of gross exports	% of total DVA
Total	30,331	20,224	100.0	100.0
Total of strategic industries	8,129	3,871	26.8	18.9
Electrical and electronic equipment	1,007	444	3.3	2.2
Motor vehicles and other transport equipment	194	95	0.6	0.5
Other manufacturing	1,497	854	4.9	4.2
Textiles, clothing and leather	5,431	2,478	18.0	12.0

Source: Author, based on ASEAN-Japan Centre (n.d.).

sector accounted for 48 per cent of gross exports versus 37 per cent of the total DVA (Table 3.2). In contrast, the agricultural and services sectors accounted for 38 per cent and 24 per cent, respectively, of total DVA. The share of the agricultural sector is even higher than that of the manufacturing sector. Considering the export value of value-added creation that manifests in this sector, the agricultural sector contributes the most to the Vietnamese economy. Thus, policies to improve productivity and innovation in the agricultural sector should also be incorporated in the national economic development plan in order to ease labour transition from the agricultural sector to the manufacturing sector. Such policies are considered prerequisites to achieving higher economic development.

Vietnam's economic growth is based mainly on low-value-added and resource-related industries that entail limited technological transfer from foreign to domestic enterprises. Indigenous suppliers find it difficult to catch up with headquarter economies such as Japan and South Korea, especially in terms of technology and innovation, and therefore cannot move up the value chains. In 2015, Samsung began constructing a new electronics factory in Ho Chi Minh City and requested Vietnam to provide 170 supporting products and services. Only twelve out of a thousand Vietnamese enterprises (1.2 per cent) met Samsung's requirements and standards. Nevertheless, these enterprises have faced high production and investment costs because of their manual processes and obsolete technology (Le 2015, p. 7). Apart from the readiness of indigenous enterprises, a more fundamental concern is the lack of foreign and domestic supporting industries, which prevents Vietnam from economic agglomeration and industrial clustering (Truong 2008, pp. 157–58). Only 40 per cent of materials are locally produced for the textiles and clothing industries, while the electrical and electronic equipment producers import almost 60 per cent of their inputs. Compared with Thailand, where 2,390 foreign and local suppliers coexist, less than 250 supporting suppliers exist in Vietnam's automotive industry (Korwatanasakul and Intarakumnerd 2020, pp. 32–37).

Moreover, the chance of technological absorption is slim in the case of Vietnam because of the paucity of foreign suppliers in the upper production tiers. The technological transfer process often begins with interaction between foreign and domestic enterprises, yet only a handful of foreign suppliers have invested in Vietnam. Furthermore, unlike the case with other developing economies, Vietnam's export-oriented firms have mainly been state-owned enterprises (SOEs) and not FDI firms (Goto 2020, p. 27).

In addition, Vietnam has started losing its competitiveness because of the recent rise of wages and is benefiting less from the slower growth of the strategic industries and global market. The concentration in low-value-added activities and industries means the country is unable to maintain its current economic growth level. As multinational enterprises (MNEs) are sensitive to wage costs and are constantly seeking new locations with lower wage levels, new emerging economies (e.g., Cambodia, Laos and Myanmar) may steal the production share of labour-intensive and low-value-added activities from Vietnam. Vietnam would enjoy less production volume than before. On the positive side, this allows Vietnam to reallocate the resources previously used in low-value-added production to more sophisticated ones. To this end, the country must upgrade its operations and technology to move higher in the value chains. Nevertheless, it is difficult for Vietnam to seize this opportunity. As previously discussed, indigenous suppliers are unprepared in terms of technology and financial resources and have experienced only limited technology absorption.[5]

In summary, the Vietnamese economy will soon reach a crossroads where the economy can either advance to a higher economic level or fall into a middle-income trap. Heavy reliance on foreign inputs and technologies (intensive backward GVC participation) without further upgrading will lead Vietnam to structural stagnation, a slowdown in growth, and failure to transition appropriately to an innovation-driven economy. Vietnam is most likely to end up being

FIGURE 3.8
Stages of Catch-Up Industrialization

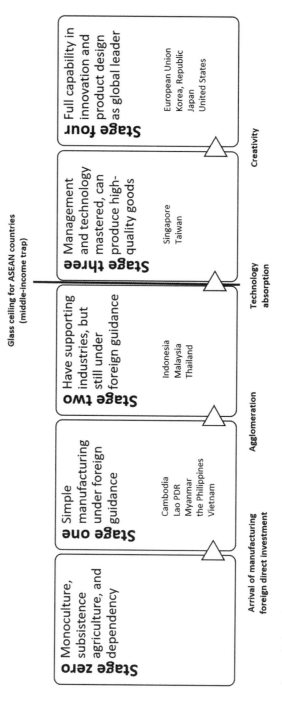

Source: Author, adapted from Ohno (2009, pp. 7–9).

confined in the (lower) middle-income trap because of a lack of basic and sophisticated supporting industries and technological absorption (Tran 2013, p. 126; Hue 2019, p. 248). The country is still located in *stage one* of catch-up industrialization; that is, it is considered a country with simple manufacturing under foreign guidance (Figure 3.8). Cambodia, Laos and Myanmar have recently received attention from MNEs and are categorized under the same stage. Although their industries are substantially less developed than those of Vietnam, they are catching up with the help of FDI. In contrast, upper-middle-income economies such as Indonesia, Malaysia and Thailand are classified under *stage two*, in which the countries play a supportive role in GVCs.

Vietnam's Competitiveness in its Strategic Value Chains

Overall, Vietnam ranks 67th out of 141 countries in the Global Competitiveness Index 4.0 (GCI 4.0) (Schwab 2019, p. 594)—up ten places from 2018.[6] Its score increased by 3.5 points driven by a significant boost in the adoption of information and communications technology (ICT). Despite its improvement, Vietnam's competitiveness is still below the average competitiveness of the ASEAN-6,[7] and it ranks seventh within the Association of Southeast Asian Nations (ASEAN), behind Singapore (1st), Malaysia (27th), Thailand (40th), Indonesia (50th), Brunei Darussalam (56th) and the Philippines (64th). Vietnam's main strengths lie in its health, macroeconomic stability, market size and ICT adoption as these pillars are closer to the optimal situation (100 points) than other pillars (Figure 3.9). Vietnam's performance in these is even better than ASEAN-6 standards (Figure 3.10). With respect to Vietnam's performance for the other pillars, however, there is considerable room for improvement—the distance to the frontier ranges from 30 to 60 points. The pillars achieving only a low performance (low score) and less competitiveness (low rank) are of great concern. These pillars include capacity for innovation, product markets, institutions, business dynamics, skills, and the labour market. On the other hand, pillars such as the financial system and infrastructure are a lower priority. Their performance is already high and close to the frontier (high score) even though they are less competitive than other economies (low rank).

A limited capability for innovation and low human capital development are among the factors preventing Vietnam from moving up the value chains and achieving *stage two* of catch-up industrialization. Scores in innovation capability, skills and the labour market pillars

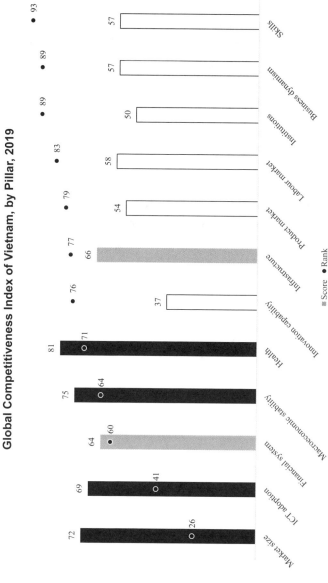

FIGURE 3.9
Global Competitiveness Index of Vietnam, by Pillar, 2019

■ Score   ● Rank

Note: Ranking is calculated from 141 countries, whereas scores are on a 0 to 100 scale, where 100 represents the optimal situation or 'frontier' (Schwab 2019).
Source: Author, based on Schwab (2019).

of 37, 57 and 58, respectively, indicate that Vietnam is far from the frontier (100 points). Furthermore, out of 141 economies, the three pillars rank 76th, 93rd and 83rd, respectively, which manifests low competitiveness compared to other economies. In 2019 there were just 0.21 patent applications per million population, and 0.12 international co-inventions per million population. The degree of multi-stakeholder collaboration is also considerably low. Without a high-quality workforce and adequate support from the government, local innovation and the development of technology are nearly impossible. Vietnam's investment in research and development (R&D) accounts for only 0.4 per cent of GDP, while the average number of years of schooling for its current workforce is 7.6. Insufficient education and training have resulted in an unskilled labour force that lacks the necessary vocational,

FIGURE 3.10
Global Competitiveness Index of ASEAN-6,
Cambodia and Vietnam, 2019

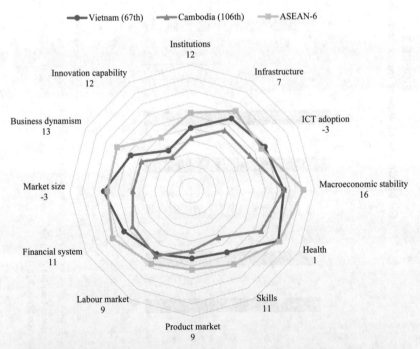

Note: The ASEAN-6 includes Brunei Darussalam, Indonesia, Malaysia, the Philippines, Singapore and Thailand. The number in brackets indicates a rank in the Global Competitiveness Index 2019. The number below each pillar indicates the difference between the performance scores of ASEAN-6 and Vietnam.
Source: Author, based on Schwab (2019).

business-related and digital skills. Consequently, it is possible that the inadequate supply of skilled labour discourages FDI and cross-border innovation.

The quality of institutions, particularly government institutions, is also an important determinant of national competitiveness. Through the Doi Moi reform, the VCP made impressive progress in terms of economic and social development. Vietnam has remained a one-party communist state under the VCP's rule since 1975. SOEs have been playing a significant role in the economy despite it being a market-oriented one. But according to the GCI 4.0, in terms of institutions Vietnam ranks 89th with a score of 50. The country faces challenges such as a lack of state transparency, a limited mechanism for checks and balances, weak corporate governance (because of the presence of SOEs), underdeveloped and poorly implemented legislation for property rights, and other issues to do with state regulations. In addition, underachieving pillars such as product markets (e.g., domestic competition and trade openness) and business dynamism (e.g., administrative requirements) negatively reflect the VCP's vision, transparency and working efficiency. After three decades of reform, the role of the VCP in the market, especially in the form of SOEs, has gradually declined. As a result of equitization, the number of SOEs dropped from twelve thousand in 1990 to three thousand in 2014 (Fujita 2017, p. 7). Nevertheless, SOEs dominate strategic sectors as equitization is limited to small or underperforming enterprises (Painter 2003, p. 1), while the state occupies a large share of equitized enterprises (Fujita 2017, p. 7).

Moreover, state influence over large firms persists through either the appointment of a top political leader as one of the firm's owners or in a less transparent manner (e.g., through family members of a political leader; see Mai Fujita, Chapter 6 in this volume). Therefore, SOEs maintain their strategic economic role, representing a third of GDP, a half of exports and contributing to a quarter of government revenue (West 2018, p. 50). Through government support such as policies and regulations in favour of SOEs and easy access to cheap capital, the existence of SOEs effectively distorts market competition and creates market inefficiency. The high involvement of the state in the private sector may also adversely affect Vietnam's competitiveness in terms of technological innovation, productivity and corruption.

The following sections will focus on Vietnam's competitiveness in its strategic industries: the textiles and clothing industry, the electrical and electronics sector, and the automotive industry.

Textiles and Clothing

Because of its relatively less-capital-intensive nature in comparison with other industries, Vietnam has been able to participate from an early stage in GVCs of the textiles and clothing industry and to realize its current level of industrialization. It is therefore considered one of Vietnam's strategic industries. The nature of the textiles and clothing industry is rather different from other industries, especially in terms of technology requirements and capital intensity. On the one hand, the clothing industry is highly labour-intensive, where its main activities involve cut, make and trim (CMT) operations. On the other hand, it is more capital and technology oriented and covers a wide range of operations; for example, spinning, yarn producing, weaving, knitting, dyeing and finishing. Vietnamese enterprises were initially concentrated in labour-intensive and low-value-added activities—that, is CMT operations—in which they have a comparative advantage.

For the past decade, Vietnam has manifested strong competitiveness in the textiles and clothing industry at regional and global levels. Within ASEAN, Vietnam is the largest export country in this sector, accounting in 2018 for almost half of the combined export value of ASEAN's textiles and clothing (48 per cent, or US$33.7 billion) (Table 3.3). Except for man-made staple fibres (HS55), Vietnam is the leading exporter in all product categories—namely, cotton (HS52),

TABLE 3.3
Global Exports of Textiles and Clothing in ASEAN, 2018 (million US$)

Country	HS52	HS54	HS55	HS60	Textiles	HS61	HS62	Clothing	Total
Brunei	0	0	0	0	0	4	5	9	9
Cambodia	1	3	7	26	38	6,586	1,241	7,827	7,865
Indonesia	811	872	2,177	104	3,964	4,074	4,495	8,569	12,533
Laos	0	0	5	0	5	61	129	190	195
Malaysia	360	459	325	209	1,352	967	343	1,310	2,662
Myanmar	13	3	11	31	57	854	3,263	4,116	4,173
Philippines	2	12	19	4	37	562	321	883	920
Singapore	37	236	122	72	466	728	708	1,436	1,902
Thailand	495	854	1,400	380	3,128	1,679	827	2,506	5,634
Vietnam	2,843	1,144	605	983	5,574	13,850	14,301	28,152	33,726
ASEAN total	**4,561**	**3,581**	**4,671**	**1,809**	**14,623**	**29,365**	**25,633**	**54,998**	**69,621**

Note: HS52: Cotton; HS54: Man-made filaments, strips and the like of man-made textile materials; HS55: Man-made staple fibres; HS60: Fabrics, knitted or crocheted; HS61: Apparel and clothing accessories, knitted or crocheted; HS62: Apparel and clothing accessories, not knitted or crocheted. Clothing = HS61 + HS62; Textiles = HS52 + HS54 + HS55 + HS60; Total = Textiles + Clothing.
Source: Author, based on the United Nations Statistics Division.

man-made filaments (HS54), fabrics (HS60), and apparel and clothing accessories (HS61 and HS62). Vietnam ranks third for man-made staple fibres (HS55)—only behind Indonesia and Thailand. Vietnam is among the world's top ten exporters of textiles and clothing in all product categories apart from man-made staple fibres (HS55) (Table 3.4).

The fundamental issue for the textile and clothing industry—and the same applies in other industries—is its heavy reliance on foreign inputs (e.g., imported fabrics), or the high FVA share (Figure 3.11). This is typical for a country specializing in low-value-added activities (e.g., CMT operations), and it is unable to realize functional upgrading or move up value chains. In contrast with Vietnam, most of the world's top exporters in the textiles and clothing industry are from developed economies that focus on high-value-added activities (e.g., designing, marketing and product branding, and they utilize their advanced technologies in production; see Table 3.4). Since Doi Moi, Vietnam's competitiveness has lain mainly in apparel and clothing accessories (HS61 and HS62) or the clothing industry (Figure 3.12), where it has achieved economic agglomeration in the labour-intensive and low-value-added activities (Goto 2020, p. v). Moreover, the export volume of cotton (HS52) has been rising gradually for the past ten years. Even though cotton is part of the textile industry, its production requires less investment and technological capacity than other products in the same

TABLE 3.4
World's Top Exporters of Textiles and Clothing, 2018

Rank	HS52	HS54	HS55	HS60	HS61	HS62
1	China	China	China	China	China	China
2	USA	Taiwan	USA	S. Korea	Vietnam	Vietnam
3	India	S. Korea	Indonesia	Taiwan	Germany	Italy
4	Pakistan	India	S. Korea	Hong Kong	Italy	Germany
5	Vietnam	Japan	India	Turkey	Turkey	Spain
6	Turkey	Italy	Turkey	Italy	India	India
7	Brazil	USA	Thailand	Vietnam	Hong Kong	France
8	Hong Kong	Germany	Austria	Germany	Cambodia	Turkey
9	Italy	Turkey	Japan	USA	Belgium	Hong Kong
10	Uzbekistan	Vietnam	Germany	Japan	Spain	Netherlands
15			Vietnam			

Note: HS52: Cotton; HS54: Man-made filaments, strips and the like of man-made textile materials; HS55: Man-made staple fibres; HS60: Fabrics, knitted or crocheted; HS61: Apparel and clothing accessories, knitted or crocheted; HS62: Apparel and clothing accessories, not knitted or crocheted.
Source: Author, based on the United Nations Statistics Division.

FIGURE 3.11
Value Added Exports from Textiles, Clothing and
Leather in ASEAN Countries, 2017 (%)

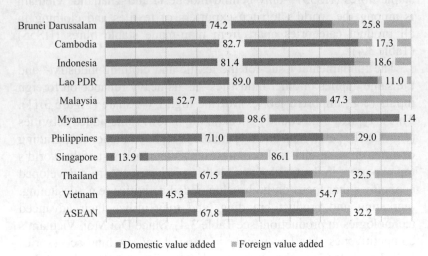

Source: Author, based on ASEAN-Japan Centre (n.d.).

industry. Hence, Vietnam's competitiveness is still and will continue to be concentrated in low-value-added production. There will be no reversal of this trend any time soon as exports of textile products—except for cotton—have remained relatively constant for the past two decades.

In focusing on labour-intensive activities, Vietnam has enjoyed high economic growth by expanding the textiles and clothing industry. And the wages in the industry have inevitably kept pace with the higher living standards. But these higher wages coupled with the recent labour shortage poses new challenges for Vietnam and its competitiveness. In addition, the rise of neighbouring countries such as Cambodia, Laos and Myanmar is likely to complicate the situation as they offer more competitive wages. Despite its limited participation in the value chain, Laos can attract FDI and could join the value chain in the future. And Cambodia and Myanmar have already been active players in the clothing industry. In 2018, among ASEAN countries, Cambodia and Myanmar ranked third and fourth with export values of 7,827 and 4,116, respectively (Table 3.3). In contrast with the situation in Vietnam, FDI firms are relatively more welcome in these two countries (Natsuda, Goto and Thoburn 2010, p. 474). Therefore, the process of technology transfer can happen quicker and more

FIGURE 3.12
Trends of Vietnam's Textiles and Clothing Exports
in ASEAN Countries, 2000–2019 (billions of US$)

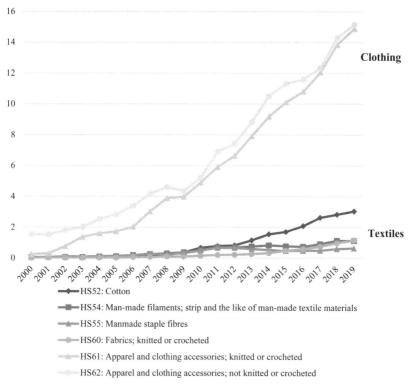

HS52: Cotton
HS54: Man-made filaments; strip and the like of man-made textile materials
HS55: Manmade staple fibres
HS60: Fabrics; knitted or crocheted
HS61: Apparel and clothing accessories; knitted or crocheted
HS62: Apparel and clothing accessories; not knitted or crocheted

Notes: Clothing = HS61 + HS62; Textiles = HS52 + HS54 + HS55 + HS60.
Source: Author, based on the United Nations Statistics Division.

efficiently.[8] Regardless of their high dependence on imported inputs, the FVA shares for Cambodia and Myanmar are significantly lower than that of Vietnam (Figure 3.11). This partly indicates a more well-established network among indigenous firms in the chain (Goto 2020, p. 10).

Electrical and Electronic Equipment[9]

In the 2000s, the assembly activities of MNEs in the electrical and electronics (E&E) industry were relocated from more advanced ASEAN economies to Vietnam because of the relatively lower wages and lower land prices. After Vietnam joined the World Trade Organization in 2007, its E&E industry grew even more rapidly to become one of the country's most crucial strategic industries. Vietnam managed to firmly establish its competitiveness in this industry, which now accounts for approximately 4 per cent of the country's GDP. Initial dependence on foreign inputs brought high growth and development to the industry. In terms of E&E exports—in 2018 totalling US$86.6 billion (Table 3.5)—Vietnam ranked second in ASEAN, after only Singapore, and twelfth in the world. In 2018 the E&E export volume constituted 36 per cent of total exports; it has grown over the last two decades by a factor of 151. In contrast with other industries, the E&E industry is primarily dominated by MNEs, which are mainly from Japan (e.g., Canon, Nintendo and Panasonic), South Korea (e.g., LG and Samsung) and the United States (e.g., Apple and Intel). These companies account for 80 per cent of the domestic market and 90 per cent of total exports (Bich Ngoc and Binh 2019, p. 4).

Nevertheless, depending solely on foreign input and technology, Vietnam's E&E industry is finding it difficult to sustain its competitiveness and move up the value chain. Vietnam participates in the middle of the E&E value chain as its specialization is in labour-intensive activities. The production activities are mainly in low value-added activities, including assembly and testing (Table 3.6). In general, electronic manufacturing service providers and global subsidiaries are concentrated in tiers 3 and 4 of the value chain,[10] which indicates their limited capital and technological capabilities. They rely

TABLE 3.5
Electrical and Electronics Industry Exports in
ASEAN, 1990–2018 (million US$)

Country	1990	1995	2000	2005	2010	2015	2016	2017	2018
Brunei	—	—	—	—	54	30	63	36	37
Cambodia	—	—	1	2	6	321	434	444	511
Indonesia	236	2,545	6,464	7,328	10,373	8,562	8,148	8,467	8,854
Laos	—	—	—	—	18	315	342	419	493
Malaysia	8,521	29,375	37,648	48,195	55,775	59,643	58,279	68,756	83,027
Myanmar	—	—	—	—	2	15	214	74	151
Philippines	—	—	20,532	20,169	14,198	25,974	25,225	32,534	32,874
Singapore	12,881	40,349	54,738	86,560	118,655	118,213	114,794	124,133	128,784
Thailand	2,681	9,693	15,509	20,673	28,945	29,788	29,902	34,090	35,309
Vietnam	—	—	572	1,543	7,081	47,400	57,193	75,323	86,600
ASEAN total	**24,320**	**81,961**	**135,464**	**184,471**	**235,105**	**290,261**	**294,594**	**344,276**	**376,639**

Note: Header 85 is used to approximately represent the electrical and electronics industry. It includes electrical machinery and equipment and parts thereof; sound recorders and reproducers; television image and sound recorders and reproducers, and parts and accessories of such articles.
Source: Author, based on the United Nations Statistics Division.

TABLE 3.6
Structure of Electrical and Electronics Global Value Chain

Players/Tiers	Lead firms/OBMs	Electronic manufacturing service (EMS) providers & global subsidiaries					Lead firms/OBMs
		Original design manufacturers	Component & subsystem suppliers	Tiers 3 & 4	Tier 2	Tier 1	
Functions	R&D, design	R&D, design, assembly and testing	Component design and/ or R&D, wafer fabrication / Component design and/ or R&D wafer fabrication	Assembly and testing			Branding, marketing, manufacturing (for some), sales and distribution
Products	Product concepts, overall design, specifications of product	Product concepts, overall design, specifications of product, and finished products	Electronics: 1. Semiconductors & wafers (IC & active discrete) 2. Passive IC components 3. Bare circuit boards. Electrical: 1. Wires & cables 2. Switchgear/panel boards 3. Transformers	Consumer and industrial E&E products (Indonesia), mobile phones (**Vietnam**), office equipment (Philippines), personal computers (**Vietnam**), storage (Philippines)	Computers (Malaysia and Thailand), Consumer E&E products (Malaysia and Thailand), Storage (Thailand)	Computers, consumer electronics, and communications and networking	Aerospace and defence (USA), automotive (Germany, Japan), communications (all), computers/ office equipment (Japan, Taiwan, USA), consumer electronics (China, Japan, South Korea) industrial E&E products (EU, USA), medical (UK)
Producer countries	China, EU, Japan, South Korea, Taiwan, USA	China, Taiwan, USA	China, Hong Kong, South Korea, Malaysia, Singapore, USA / Cambodia, Indonesia, Laos, Malaysia, Myanmar, Philippines, Thailand, **Vietnam**	Cambodia, Indonesia, Laos, Myanmar, Philippines, **Vietnam**	Malaysia, Thailand	China	China, EU, Japan, South Korea, Taiwan , USA
Value added	High	High	High	Low-Medium	Low-Medium	Low-Medium	High

Note: The electronics manufacturing service industry is divided into the following tiers based on revenues: Tier 1: > US$5 billion; Tier 2: US$500 million to US$5 billion; Tier 3: US$100 million but less than US$500 million, Tier 4: less than US$100 million. E&E = electrical and electronics; IC = integrated circuit; OBM = original brand manufacturer.

Source: Author, based on Frederick and Gereffi (2016, p. vi).

FIGURE 3.13
Value Added Exports from Electrical and
Electronics in ASEAN Countries, 2017 (%)

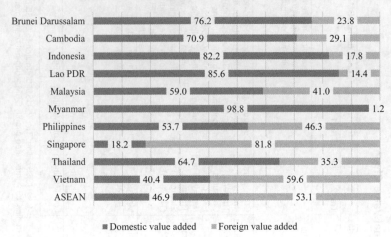

■ Domestic value added   ■ Foreign value added

Source: Author, based on ASEAN-Japan Centre (n.d.).

on imported components and subsystems, foreign technology, and the product design, branding and marketing of leading firms. Vietnam's E&E industry is exposed to a considerably high FVA share, while its upstream and downstream activities are still underdeveloped. Despite its growing exports, Vietnam's competitiveness in the E&E industry has begun to erode because of higher production costs from imported input coupled with the recent increase in wages.

The lack of supporting industries and low domestic technological capabilities are two entangled challenges for Vietnam's E&E industry. Apart from Vietnam, most of the other ASEAN countries—such as Cambodia, Malaysia, the Philippines and Thailand—participate in the E&E value chain in final product assembly and the production of components and subsystems (Table 3.6). Even though more enterprises have recently taken part in the E&E supporting industry in Vietnam, they are not indigenous firms. Vietnam's heavy dependence on foreign inputs jeopardizes the future of the E&E industry as indigenous enterprises have been facing high costs of production. Other than Singapore, which has already been at the higher level of the E&E value chain, Vietnam manifests the highest FVA share among ASEAN countries, emphasizing its vulnerability[11] (Figure 3.13). As local firms focus on labour-intensive activities, they have limited technological and functional upgrading and little international exposure or marketing capabilities. Only a few MNEs offer some limited R&D activities (e.g., the Samsung R&D centre).

And similar to the situation with the textiles and clothing industry, the recent rise in wages complicates the situation for the E&E industry. The industry is being pushed to upgrade its processes, products and functions before it loses its comparative advantage in cheap labour. But it is not well prepared for the upgrading because of its low rate of technological transfer and absorption and on account of insufficient technology and capital among local firms.

Automotive Industry

The automotive industry is relatively new and is still at an early stage of development in comparison with other strategic industries such as E&E, food processing, and textiles and clothing. Since its inception, the industry has not been performing well and has demonstrated only low competitiveness. The export volume has been rather trivial and has only increased very slightly over the past decades (Table 3.7). Despite the country's large population, Vietnam's automotive industry is still relatively small, accounting for only 7.5 per cent of automobile sales in ASEAN.[12] While ranking fourth within the region, the industry produced 200,000 and sold 289,000 passenger cars and trucks in 2018 (Figure 3.14). The larger figure of sales compared with that of production indicates that the automotive industry mainly serves the domestic market. The industry enjoyed higher exports of auto parts through participation in the automotive value chain, in which it relied more on foreign raw materials and inputs (higher FVA share). The

TABLE 3.7
Automotive Industry Exports in ASEAN, 1990–2018 (million US$)

Country	1990	1995	2000	2005	2010	2015	2016	2017	2018
Brunei	—	—	—	—	6	7	7	4	3
Cambodia	—	—	5	5	104	281	354	380	405
Indonesia	39	324	492	1,298	2,900	5,419	5,868	6,835	7,552
Laos	—	—	—	—	3	20	29	28	20
Malaysia	128	409	436	830	1,508	1,784	1,698	1,718	1,979
Myanmar	—	—	—	—	0.003	2	5	10	15
Philippines	—	—	642	1,611	1,861	1,429	1,418	1,183	1,116
Singapore	556	1,219	947	2,734	4,161	3,793	3,538	3,423	3,724
Thailand	136	658	2,519	8,152	18,583	26,556	27,206	28,618	30,763
Vietnam	—	—	74	365	709	1,910	2,068	2,330	2,646
ASEAN total	**858**	**2,610**	**5,116**	**14,996**	**29,836**	**41,201**	**42,189**	**44,528**	**48,224**

Note: Under the Harmonized Commodity Description and Coding Systems, or Harmonized System, the automotive industry's imports and exports are classified mainly under "Header 87 Vehicles; other than railway or tramway rolling stock, and parts and accessories thereof".
Source: Author, based on the United Nations Statistics Division.

FIGURE 3.14
Motor Vehicles Sales and Production, 2017 (thousands of units)

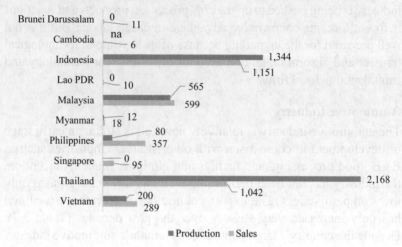

Note: na = not available.
Source: Author, based on Korwatanasakul and Intarakumnerd (2020, p. 1).

large drop in the DVA share (from 69 per cent in 2000 to 50 per cent in 2010) was accompanied by the expansion of production after 2000 (Figure 3.15), while the DVA volume grew by a factor of about nineteen during the period 1990–2015. The sharp increase in DVA volume came mainly from the labour cost advantage rather than domestic technology and innovation because the supporting industries still largely depend on foreign basic materials and inputs. Without sufficient domestic and foreign demand—as well as limitations in technological capability— Vietnam is struggling to move up the automotive value chain and is falling into a vicious cycle of underperforming automobile and supporting industries.

Vietnam's automotive industry has fallen into the same vicious cycle that affected the Philippines, where the small domestic automobile market has led to underdeveloped automobile and supporting industries. Production by Vietnamese automotive assemblers has been inefficient and has not achieved economies of scale because the industry is oriented towards the domestic market, which has only limited demand. In Vietnam the passenger vehicle density is 16 per 1,000 people, whereas the density is as high as 55 for Indonesia, 341 for Malaysia, and 196 for Thailand. Accordingly, local supporting industries such as auto parts and components have remained immature and cannot achieve economies of scale, leaving the costs of parts and

FIGURE 3.15
Structure of Vietnam's Value Added Exports in
the Automobile Industry, 1990–2015

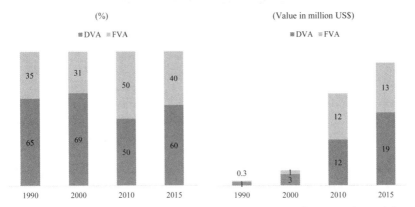

Note: DVA = domestic value added; FVA = foreign value added; US$ = United States dollar.
Source: Author, based on ASEAN-Japan Centre (n.d.).

components high. The localization rate of the supporting industries is meagre and accounts for only ten per cent of total auto parts and components. Most raw materials and intermediate goods are therefore imported. In addition, the nature of the industry, in which production is highly fragmented, also prevents auto suppliers from reaching economies of scale. Inadequate basic industries such as modern machinery and the absence of more advanced industries that produce high-value-added parts and components are the significant challenges faced by Vietnam. The ratio of automakers to auto parts suppliers in Vietnam is 1:11, whereas for Thailand it is 1:170. In 2018 there were twenty automobile assemblers and more than two hundred auto part suppliers (Figure 3.16). Even though several domestic assemblers, including both SOEs and private enterprises such as Truong Hai and Xuan Kien, are active in the industry, most of the market share is dominated by MNEs—for example, Daewoo, Honda, Suzuki and Toyota. But all the production tiers are largely controlled by local SMEs that have low production capacities. Because of the high costs of domestic and imported inputs, locally produced automobiles are expensive and cost even more than imported ones. That is, imported automobiles cost less for consumers in Vietnam and they are usually of higher quality. Consequently, the demand for imported automobiles increases. This again leads to small-scale production by domestic assemblers and creates a vicious cycle whereby insufficient demand is fed to the supporting industries.

FIGURE 3.16
Structure of Vietnam's Automotive Industry, 2018

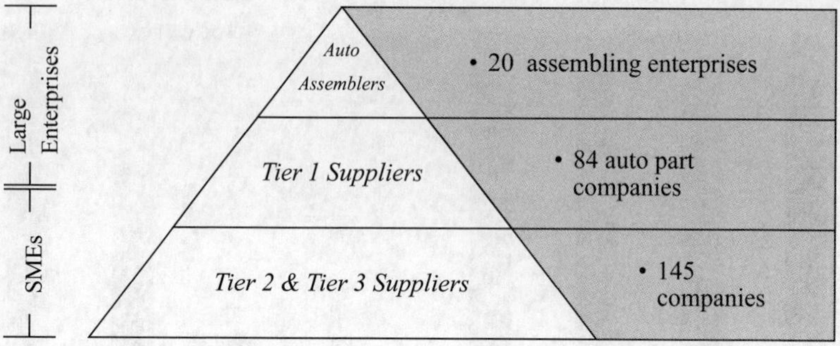

Source: Author, based on Ministry of Industry and Trade (Vietnam)

GVC-Led Development Policies

A *proper* GVC-led development model halts economic stagnation and helps a country graduate to high-income status, while an *unbalanced* one leads the economy in the opposite direction. Successfully participating in GVCs requires sophisticated and complex industrial, institutional, macroeconomic and trade structures that encourage economic and social development. A series of structural reforms under Doi Moi brought Vietnam impressive economic growth and social development. Nevertheless, the slowing increase in recent years raises questions about its sustainability and the quality of the development strategy. Possible GVC-led development policies involve three main areas: leveraging the existing strategic industries that have high competitiveness, facilitating labour movements across sectors, and undergoing structural and institutional reforms.

Leveraging Existing Strategic Industries with High Competitiveness

Leveraging the existing strategic industries that have high competitiveness is one of the policy options that Vietnam may consider. Since 1986, Vietnam has been developing its strategic industries through different channels, including enhancing R&D, formalizing government-business relationships and participating in GVCs. Vietnam was prosperous in process upgrading (improving production efficiency) and well established its strategic industries, including food processing, E&E, and textiles and clothing. Further upgrading of these industries would be more efficient than developing new strategic industries, particularly in terms of expertise, technology, and investment costs. But there is still room for improvement as these industries are still deficient in terms of product and functional upgrading, which requires large-scale capital endowment and high technology and innovation.

SMEs represent the majority of domestic private enterprises. They are usually concentrated in the lower tiers of production (low-value-added activities) and have limited capital. Thus, developing a more efficient financial system is necessary to allow the private sector, especially SMEs, easier access to capital. Secondly, domestic private enterprises face a problem of limited capability in terms of innovation and technology. Adequate government support is vital, including more government spending on R&D, the development of legislation on intellectual property rights, and the enforcement of research collaboration among foreign and domestic multi-stakeholders that guarantees technological transfer.

The role of the services sector has been growing in terms of GVC participation and economic development. While value added in exports of the services sector is approximately two-thirds of that of the manufacturing sector, large FDI inflows account for over half of total inward FDI (53.8 per cent in 2018; Figure 3.5). Thus, preparations to ease towards a services economy are also essential. To this end, the VCP needs to identify the key trends of the future economy and offer support to nurture a competitive domestic services sector. As part of functional upgrading programmes, a potential policy area could be the development of service industries that have high connectivity with existing strategic manufacturing industries. Services such as branding, product design, marketing, and sales and distribution are high-value-added activities.

Facilitating Labour Movements across Sectors

Despite significant labour absorption in the manufacturing sector, most labour (37.4 per cent in 2019) still engages in agricultural activities. Facilitating labour movements by developing the set of modern skills required by the labour market, particularly for high-skilled labour, and simultaneously improving productivity in the agricultural sector may help alleviate the current labour shortage problem in the manufacturing sector. Human capital development is another key policy area that is heavily interrelated with the capacity of the domestic private sector since a high-quality labour force is an essential ingredient for successful upgrading in GVCs, especially in terms of technology and innovation. The VCP may provide more training courses and programmes that promote necessary skills such as vocational skills, business-related skills and digital skills to respond to the business sector's needs. For the long-run development, more practical and relevant knowledge can be integrated into the school curriculum in which creativity, analytical skills and soft skills are emphasized.

Undergoing Structural and Institutional Reforms

Vietnam's economic and social development is a complex issue as it involves a political ideology that many believe is not compatible. Vietnam was able to achieve its current economic and social development under the visionary leadership of the VCP. Nevertheless, Thang (2000, pp. 24–25) has pointed out that the present structural and institutional factors hinder the development of the private sector and, in turn, slow down economic growth. The quality of institutions, particularly that of the VCP, along with its legacies such as the dominance of SOEs and incomplete market institutions, raises concerns about the future of the Vietnamese economy. The VCP's vision and issues of working efficiency such as the lack of transparency, weak governance and poor rules of law have been identified as acting as drags on national competitiveness and potential growth. The dominance of SOEs in the economy and the heavy intervention of the government in the market has caused market distortions that adversely affect innovation, technological development and productivity. It has also limited the effectiveness and efficiency of other reforms (Thanh and Ha 2004, p. 63) and could be a source of corruption.

Despite its struggles to boost the economy and the criticism it has received for its political ideology, the VCP has maintained its socialist convictions and has often reiterated its commitment to socialism in the National Congress. The VCP has been facing a dilemma over political stability and economic growth as radical changes to economic and social structures could lead to changes in the superstructure (Thayer 2008, p. 17). Socialist ideology and a market-oriented economy both have their pros and cons, but the issue for the VCP is how to balance the two. Problems of transparency, governance, legal enforcement and systematic corruption are prevalent in any political ideology—they are not specific to a socialist system—and they should therefore be identified contextually and systematically. In contrast, the issue of market freedom may be more challenging for the VCP as the key is to minimize its intervention in the market. Singapore's "guided or managed democracy" may be an excellent example from which the VCP could learn. The Singapore government can maintain political power and stability while keeping its involvement in the market at a minimum. As long as there is a way to root out systematic corruption and allow more market freedom, maintaining a socialist ideology should not prevent Vietnam from advancing to a higher economic level.

Concluding Remarks

Vietnam is still in the process of transitioning from a centrally planned to a market-based economy. Liberalization of trade and investment under the Doi Moi reforms allowed Vietnam to benefit from GVC participation. An increase in productivity largely explains Vietnam's rapid growth through the utilization of foreign inputs and technology. Nevertheless, heavy reliance on foreign inputs and technologies (intensive backward GVC participation) without further upgrading can be a path to perils. The growth has remained constant for the past two decades, seeing an average growth rate of 6.5 per cent.

The factors that enabled Vietnam's past growth appear weaker, while the recent wage increases, aging population, declining effects of factor accumulation, and underdeveloped structural factors may cause future economic slowdowns. In addition, political obstacles such as the VCP's vision (i.e., the dilemma of political stability and economic development), low institutional quality and issues of transparency, and weak governance and rules of law have the potential to hinder national competitiveness and future growth. The Vietnamese economy could eventually fall into a middle-income trap as the competitiveness of its strategic industries has been eroding over time.

Failing to escape from the trap would exacerbate poverty and economic inequality, cause social instability and segregation, and, in turn, jeopardize the existence of the VCP. Thus, another round of structural transformation and policy reforms in all relevant sectors may be crucial in order to facilitate Vietnam advancing to a higher economic level. Accordingly, the VCP may adopt a more balanced GVC-led development model focusing on functional upgrading to steer its economy towards prosperity. The priority is for policies that strengthen domestic capabilities, especially SMEs, promote strategic GVC engagement, and facilitate strong institutional reforms.

Notes

1. According to Korwatanasakul, Baek and Majoe (2020, p. 20), individual economies can participate in global value chains (GVCs) through either backward or forward participation, which reflect the upstream and downstream links in the chain. Typical GVC participation refers to backward GVC participation (backward linkage), where an individual economy imports foreign inputs to produce its intermediate or final goods and services to be exported. The backward linkage is measured by the share of foreign value added in gross exports. On the other hand, forward GVC participation (forward linkage) occurs when exporting domestically produced intermediate goods or services to another economy that then re-exports them through the value chain to third economies as embodied in other goods or services for further processing. The forward linkage is captured by the share of domestic value added incorporated in the third countries' exports (indirect value-added exports) in gross exports.

2. Domestic value added is the part of a country's exports created within the country; i.e., the part of exports that contributes to GDP (Korwatanasakul and Intarakumnerd 2020, p. 11).

3. Foreign value added indicates the part of a country's gross exports that consists of inputs that have been produced in other countries. The foreign value-added share is the share of the country's exports that do not add to its GDP (Korwatanasakul and Intarakumnerd 2020, p. 11). The sum of foreign and domestic value added equates to gross exports.

4. Ohno (2009, pp. 7–9) categorized catch-up industrialization into five stages from stage zero to stage four. For more details, refer to Figure 3.8.

5. According to the Global Competitiveness Index (GCI) 2019, Vietnam's innovation capacity manifests poor performance and limited competitiveness. The next section, "Vietnam's Competitiveness in its Strategic Value Chains", provides more detailed discussion on the GCI of Vietnam.

6. Based on growth accounting theory, the Global Competitiveness Index 4.0 (GCI 4.0) assesses a country's competitiveness in terms of efficient use of factors of production by examining twelve pillars of the factors that determine productivity. The pillars include institutions, infrastructure, ICT adoption, macroeconomic stability, health, skills, the product market, the labour market, the financial system, market size, business dynamism, and innovation (Schwab 2019, p. 2).

7. The ASEAN-6 includes Brunei Darussalam, Indonesia, Malaysia, the Philippines, Singapore and Thailand.

8. For instance, in Cambodia, as a result of the 100 per cent foreign ownership law since 1994, FDI firms account for over 90 per cent of garment factories, while local ownership is much more significant in Vietnam in the textiles and clothing industry (Natsuda, Goto and Thoburn 2010, p. 474).

9. For complementary analysis, see Chapter 4 by Truong Quang Hoan in this volume.

10. The electronic manufacturing service industry is divided into tiers based on revenues. Tier 1: greater than US$5 billion; Tier 2: US$500 million to US$5

billion; Tier 3: US$100 million to US$500 million; Tier 4: less than US$100 million.

11. Yoon Ah Oh, in Chapter 5 of this volume, discusses Vietnam's vulnerability as being due to its heavy reliance on foreign inputs and provides the case study of Vietnam-China trade relations.

12. The automobile industry is broadly defined as an industry of motorized vehicles consisting of four wheels and powered by internal engines, while narrowly defined as the car industry. The automobile industry is considered part of the automotive industry covering a wide range of motor vehicles, including automobiles (cars), buses, motorcycles, off-road vehicles, light trucks and regular trucks.

References

Anh, Nguyen Thi Tue, Luu Minh Duc, and Trinh Duc Chieu. 2014. "The Evolution of Vietnamese Industry". WIDER Working Paper 2014/076. United Nations University World Institute for Development Economics Research (UNU-WIDER), Helsinki.

ASEAN-Japan Centre. n.d. "AJC-UNCTAD-Eora Database on ASEAN GVCs". https://www.asean.or.jp/en/centre-wide/centrewide_en/ (accessed 31 July 2020).

Bich Ngoc, Tran Thi, and Dao Thanh Binh. 2019. "Vietnam's Electronics Industry: The Rise and Problems of Further Development". *Humanities & Social Sciences Reviews* 7, no. 4: 1–12.

Frederick, Stacey, and Gary Gereffi. 2016. *The Philippines in the Electronics & Electrical Global Value Chain*. North Carolina: Duke University Center on Globalization, Governance and Competitiveness. https://hdl.handle.net/10161/12485.

Fujita, Mai. 2017. "Vietnamese State-Owned Enterprises under International Economic Integration". RIETI Discussion Paper Series 17-E-121. Research Institute of Economy, Trade and Industry, Tokyo. https://www.rieti.go.jp/jp/publications/dp/17e121.pdf.

Goto, Kenta. 2020. "Global Value Chains in ASEAN: Textiles and Clothing". Global Value Chains in ASEAN, paper 14, March 2020. https://www.asean.or.jp/ja/wp-content/uploads/sites/2/GVC_Textiles-and-clothing_Paper-14_full_web.pdf.

Hue, Tran thi. 2019. "The Determinants of Innovation in Vietnamese Manufacturing Firms: An Empirical Analysis Using a Technology-Organization-Environment Framework". *Eurasian Business Review* 9, no. 3: 247–67.

Korwatanasakul, Upalat. 2019. "Global Value Chains in ASEAN: Thailand". Global Value Chains in ASEAN, paper 10, March 2919. https://www.asean.or.jp/ja/wp-content/uploads/sites/2/GVC-in-ASEAN-paper-10_Thailand.pdf.

Korwatanasakul, Upalat, Youngmin Baek, and Adam Majoe. 2020. "Analysis of Global Value Chain Participation and the Labour Market in Thailand: A Micro-level Analysis". ERIA Discussion Paper Series 311. Economic Research Institute for ASEAN and East Asia, Jakarta. https://www.eria.

org/uploads/media/discussion-papers/Analysis-Of-Global-Value-Chain-Participation-And-The-Labour-Market-In-Thailand.pdf.

Korwatanasakul, Upalat, and Patarapong Intarakumnerd. 2020. "Global Value Chains in ASEAN: Automobiles". Global Value Chains in ASEAN, paper 12, January 2020. https://www.asean.or.jp/ja/wp-content/uploads/sites/2/GVC_Automobiles_Paper-12_January-24-2020-web-_edited.pdf.

————. 2021. "Global Value Chains in ASEAN: Electronics". Global Value Chains in ASEAN, paper 13, March 2021. https://www.asean.or.jp/ja/wp-content/uploads/sites/2/GVCs_Electronics_Paper-13_full_web.pdf.

Korwatanasakul, Upalat, and Sasiwimon Warunsiri. 2020. "Trade, Global Value Chains, and Small and Medium-Sized Enterprises in Thailand: A Firm-Level Panel Analysis". ADBI Working Paper 1130. Asian Development Bank Institute, Tokyo. https://www.adb.org/sites/default/files/publication/604661/adbi-wp1130.pdf.

Le, Dang Doanh,. 2015. "The Past and the Hopeful Future of Vietnam's Economy". *Asian Management Insights* 2, no. 1: 28–35.

Ministry of Industry and Trade (Vietnam). n.d. "Viet Nam Industries Development: Investment Opportunities". https://www.asean.or.jp/ja/wp-content/uploads/sites/2/3_MOIT_English.pdf (accessed 31 July 2020).

Ministry of Planning and Investment (Vietnam). n.d. "FDI Inflow into Vietnam Reaches 30.8 Billion USD". https://infographics.vn/ (accessed 31 July 2020).

Natsuda, Kaoru, Kenta Goto, and John Thoburn. 2010. "Challenges to the Cambodian Garment Industry in the Global Garment Value Chain". *European Journal of Development Research* 22, no. 4: 469–93.

Ohno, Kenichi. 2009. "Overcoming the Middle Income Trap: The Challenge for East Asian High Performers". In *The Middle Income Trap: Implications for Industrialization Strategies in East Asia and Africa*, pp. 1–20. Tokyo: GRIPS Development Forum.

Organization for Economic Co-operation and Development. n.d. "Input-Output Tables 2018 Edition". https://stats.oecd.org/Index.aspx?DataSetCode=IOTSI4_2018 (accessed 31 July 2020).

Painter, Martin. 2003. "The Politics of Economic Restructuring in Vietnam: The Case of State-Owned Enterprise 'Reform'". *Contemporary Southeast Asia* 25, no. 1: 20–43.

Schwab, Klaus. 2019. *The Global Competitiveness Report 2019*. Geneva: World Economic Forum. http://www3.weforum.org/docs/WEF_TheGlobalCompetitivenessReport2019.pdf.

Thang, Bui Tat. 2000. "After the War: 25 Years of Economic Development in Vietnam". *NIRA Review* 7, no. 2: 21–25.

Thanh, Vo Tri, and Pham Hoang Ha. 2004. "Vietnam's Recent Economic Reforms and Developments: Achievements, Paradoxes, and Challenges". In *Social Inequality in Vietnam and the Challenges to Reform*, edited by Philip Taylor, pp. 63–89. Singapore: ISEAS – Yusof Ishak Institute.

Thayer, Carlyle A. 2008. "Upholding State Sovereignty through Global Integration: The Remaking of Vietnamese National Security". Paper presented to Workshop on "Viet Nam, East Asia & Beyond", Southeast Asia Research Centre, City University of Hong Kong. http://citeseerx.ist.psu.

edu/viewdoc/download;jsessionid=4D356C7E7613639CA5DFE68DF-B0EEF31?doi=10.1.1.698.2037&rep=rep1&type=pdf.

Tran, Van Tho. 2013. "Vietnamese Economy at the Crossroads". *Asian Economic Policy Review* 8: 122–43. https://doi-org.ez.wul.waseda.ac.jp/10.1111/aepr.12012.

Truong, Chi Binh. 2008. "Factors of Agglomeration in Vietnam and Recommendations". In *Analyses of Industrial Agglomeration, Production Networks and FDI Promotion*, edited by Mohamed Ariff, pp. 155–89. Jakarta: Economic Research Institute for ASEAN and East Asia.

United Nations Statistics Division. n.d. "UN Comtrade Database". https://comtrade.un.org/data/ (accessed 31 July 2020).

West, John. 2018. "Asia's Stunted Economic Development". In *Asian Century ... on a Knife-Edge*, pp. 19–55. Singapore: Palgrave Macmillan.

World Bank. n.d. "World Bank Open Data". https://data.worldbank.org/ (accessed 31 July 2020).

World Trade Organization. 2018. "Trade in Value-added and Global Value Chains Profiles: Explanatory Notes". https://www.wto.org/english/res_e/statis_e/miwi_e/Explanatory_Notes_e.pdf.

Chapter 4

Vietnam's Participation in Global Value Chains: Achievements, Challenges and Policy Implications

Truong Quang Hoan

A study of UNCTAD (2013a) indicates that about eighty per cent of global trade (in terms of gross exports) is associated with the international production networks of multinational enterprises (MNEs). It means that a large number of products are produced from different locations across borders around the globe.

It is believed that developing economies embedded in low-value-added chains can improve their position in GVCs. One of the most useful ways to do this, and one which is widely applied, is by further attracting and improving the quality of inward FDI flows. FDI may create both direct and indirect effects on a country's participation in GVCs. The direct effect is that foreign and domestic enterprises in a joint venture are likely to produce sophisticated products and deepen their participation in GVCs, while the indirect effect is that FDI can create spillover impacts (including horizontal and vertical spillovers) on the level of innovation of local firms (Javorcik 2004, 2008). After having accumulated sufficient capabilities, many of these local firms undertake outward international expansion and become MNEs. Alternatively, to enhance their position within GVCs, firms from developing economies that started off at the lowest position can use international expansion as a way to move up to a higher value-added position. The primary direction of their move depends on the governance structure of the value chain.

FIGURE 4.1
Vietnam's International Trade with the Rest of the World, 1995–2019

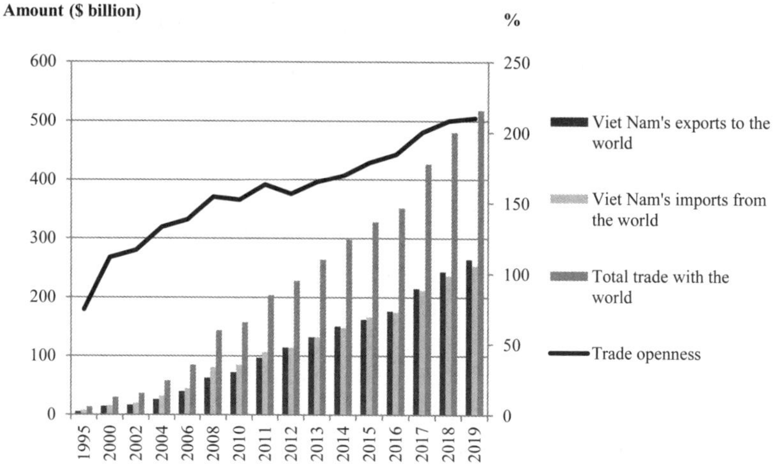

Source: Author's compilation from United Nations Comtrade Database, and World Development Indicators of the World Bank.

Thanks to the growing importance of global FDI and trade, particularly of the manufacturing sector, a large body of research on the nexus between GVCs, FDI and economic growth has concentrated on China (Yao 2009; Fu 2011; Zhu and Fu 2013; Swenson and Chen 2014; Wang and Chen 2020). Meanwhile, little attention has been paid to the GVC participation of smaller developing countries such as Vietnam. A large number of studies on Vietnam have focused on the country's conventional trade (Tran and Heo 2009; McCaig 2011; Truong et al. 2019; Nguyen et al. 2016; Nguyen 2015; Ha and Tran 2017).

Along with the implementation of economic renovation, total commodity trade exchange between Vietnam and the rest of the world grew rapidly from only $13.6 billion in 1995 to $157 billion in 2010 and $518 billion in 2019. Vietnam's exports to the world market expanded to $265.6 billion in 2019 compared with $72.2 billion in 2010 and $5.4 billion in 1995. By contrast, the amount of imports increased to $253.4 billion in 2019 from only $8.1 billion in 1995 and $84.8 billion in 2010. This resulted in a huge extension of the ratio of trade to GDP (trade openness) of Vietnam, climbing from 74.7 per cent in 1995 to 152.2 per cent in 2010 and 210.4 per cent in 2019 (see Figure 4.1). Vietnam has also made significant headway in improving its export basket by increasing the share of sophisticated manufactured products (Tran et al. 2020). For example, data processing from the

World Integrated Trade Solution (WITS) of the World Bank shows that the contribution of machinery and electronic products in Vietnam's total export value to the global market reached 40.2 per cent in 2017, up from 7.9 per cent in 2000 and 14.1 per cent in 2010. In contrast, the export share of less-sophisticated products such as fuels dropped to 2.2 per cent in 2017 from 26.4 per cent in 2000.

Similarly, data processing from the United Nations Conference on Trade and Development (UNCTAD) demonstrate an impressive extension of realized inward FDI flows into Vietnam's economy, increasing from $1.7 billion in 1995 to $8 billion in 2010. Despite the slowdown of the global economy in recent years, FDI flows into Vietnam were on the rise, reaching $11.8 billion in 2015 and $15.5 billion in 2018. In terms of sectoral distribution, data from the General Statistics Office (GSO) of Vietnam demonstrate that the manufacturing and processing sector garnered the highest interest from foreign investors in 2018, accounting for 47 per cent of the registered capital.

Trade and FDI are considered to be among the main driving factors for the impressive economic growth in Vietnam, which reached 6.1 per cent on average between 2008 and 2018. The country now ranks among the fastest growing economies in the world. This has led to a considerable improvement in Vietnam's income per capita, reaching nearly $2,600 in 2018—about nine times higher than in 1995 (World Development Indicators of the World Bank). But Vietnam's growth rates were substantially lower in the first decade of the twenty-first century and lower still after 2008, and this puts the country in danger of falling into a middle-income trap (Herr et al. 2016). In order to overcome this huge challenge, Vietnam needs to achieve greater GVC participation, and in particular it needs to increase the involvement of its domestic enterprises in this.

Against this backdrop, this chapter is a study of the current dynamic pattern of Vietnam's GVC participation. I have selected two export sectors as case studies in order to explore the achievements and limitations of Vietnam's GVC participation—the computers, electronics and electrics industry and the textile and apparel industry. I also delve into the extent to which different groups (both foreign and domestic companies) participate in and gain benefit from GVCs in these export sectors. Specifically, I examine the role of MNEs, particularly Samsung Electronics of South Korea, in Vietnam's GVC participation in the electronics industry. I then present policy recommendations for Vietnam to enhance and deepen its GVC participation, thereby contributing to accelerating the country's economic growth in the future. There are several reasons for selecting these two sectors for the case studies. First, the two represent major export product groups from Vietnam to the world market. Second, there are differences in terms of firm characteristics and the patterns of GVC participation between these two sectors. For instance, the contribution of domestic value added in Vietnam's exports of textiles and apparel was found to be significantly higher than in Vietnam's exports of computers, electronics and electrics. This may indicate a larger role of local production in the textile and apparel industry. Third, I aim to investigate the GVC participation between a labour-intensive sector (the textile and apparel industry) and a technology-intensive sector (the computers, electronics and electrics industry). The chapter principally employs data from the OECD-WTO TIVA database and other sources to analyse Vietnam's GVC participation.

While there are certain common points, my chapter differs from the previous chapter by Upalat Korwatanasakul in at least the following. First, I employ the OECD-TIVA database, while Korwatanasakul's work uses the statistics from the AJC-UNCTAD-Eora database. Second, his chapter compares Vietnam's GVC participation with its ASEAN peers, while my work includes both ASEAN countries and China. Third, Korwatanasakul's work mainly provides overall assessments about Vietnam's GVC participation. My chapter moves beyond macro-trend data to examine sectoral dimensions via case studies. In particular, I focus on examining the role of Samsung in Vietnam's exports and GVC participation in the electronics industry. Similarly, I also deeply analyse the situation and the challenges that Vietnam's textile and apparel industry faces in seeking to improve the country's GVC participation. Finally, Korwatanasakul's chapter provides policy implications for Vietnam's GVC participation at the aggregate level; my work discusses policy implications for deepening Vietnam's GVC participation in the computers, electronics and electrics industry and the textile and apparel industry.

The chapter is structured as follows. After the introduction there is an overview of Vietnam's industrial development policy. The next section explores Vietnam's GVC participation. After that the case studies are presented, followed by a discussion. And the last section discusses the policy implications.

Vietnam's Industrial Development Policy

In 1991, Vietnam introduced the concept of "industrialization-modernization", which aimed to promote economic diversification, reduce the overdependence on heavy industries, and combine the industrialization of traditional industries with the development of advanced and modern industries in order to meet the requirements of globalization and the knowledge economy (Do 2016). After 1996, Vietnam had set a target of turning the country into a modern and industrial economy by 2020. In 2001, the "Strategy for Acceleration of Socialist-oriented Industrialization" to modernize the country by 2020 was launched. Its aim was to develop important heavy industries using high technology. The following lead industries were earmarked for this: electronics, steel, leather and footwear, construction materials, mineral processing, beverages, dairy, and pulp and paper.

In 2007 the Vietnamese government approved a list of priority industries for the period 2007–10 and introduced a number of incentive policies for these industries by Decision No. 55/2007/QD-TTg of 23 April 2007. In 2014 the government established a series of measures to support the development of these industries, including the ratification of "Vietnam's Industrial Development Strategy to 2025 with a vision by 2035", in which the electronics industry and telecommunications were emphasized as key industries (Government Port of Vietnam 2014).

The government applied various privileges and incentives to the FDI sector, including improving the attractiveness of the investment environment. According to Law No. 32/2013/QH13 of 19 June 2013, on amending and supplementing some articles of the Law on Enterprise Income Tax and other acts, any enterprise is entitled to certain privileges and support from the state, including exemptions from payments for leasing of land or water surfaces, and tax exemptions for new high-technology projects (National Assembly of Vietnam 2013). The government also implements exemptions from import duties on goods imported to create fixed assets and on materials, supplies and components to implement investment in Vietnam (Tran and Dao 2019). These exemptions are considered to be more attractive than those of Vietnam's peers. For example, in Thailand, state benefits include an exemption from corporate income tax for eight years and a fifty per cent reduction for the next five years. In the region, the corporate income tax rate in Thailand is 20 per cent, for Singapore it is 17 per cent, and for Malaysia and Indonesia it is 25 per cent (Hirunya 2013).

In early 2017 the Vietnamese government issued Decision 68/2017/QĐ-TTg on a development plan for the supporting industries over the 2016–25 period. The aim is to promote, support and attract domestic and foreign investments into the supporting industries—namely, the electronics and mechanical engineering industries, the garment and textile industry, the leather and footwear industry, the hi-tech industries, and the automotive industry—to create outputs that meet the needs of domestic production and exports and create a gateway for Vietnamese enterprises to enter the GVCs. Under the programme, the output should satisfy 45 per cent of the input demand of domestic manufacturing by 2020 and 65 per cent by 2025 (The Prime Minister of Vietnam 2017).

Other government's efforts include land rental fee incentives. Accordingly, investment projects involved in the supporting industries, also known as secondary projects, shall be exempted from land rent for seven years. Investment projects in craft villages and projects on technical infrastructure located in the supporting industry zone will receive an exemption for eleven years. The government also provides tax incentives. Pursuant to Decree 111/2015/NĐ-CP issued by the government, tax incentives are available for organizations and individuals manufacturing products from the list of prioritized supporting industrial products. Other incentives include exemption of corporate income tax (CIT), import duties, and value added tax (VAT) (Government of Vietnam 2015).

Additional financial incentives are also provided, including research and development (R&D) incentives, investment credit, and an environment protection scheme. In addition, projects carried out by small and medium enterprises (SMEs) shall receive additional incentives related to investment credit and water surface/land prices, subject to some conditions (Dezan Shira and Associates 2018).

Vietnam's Participation in Global Value Chains

A number of recent studies have employed trade in value added as a proxy to examine GVC participation between economies, focusing on East Asia (Ando 2006; OECD and WTO 2013; Kowalski et al. 2015; Kwon and Ryou 2015). According to a study of UNCTAD (2013b), nearly a third of the global export value in 2010 was the result of so-called "double counting". More crucially, trade in value added is found to be closely related to a country's role in regional and global production networks; those economies dominating the upstream of a supply chain are likely to gain the highest value added in their export activities (Ando 2006; World Bank 2017). In this study, I utilize the OECD-WTO TIVA database—a joint effort between the OECD and the WTO—to examine Vietnam's GVC participation. The database is based on OECD input-output tables and provides estimations of value-added trade flows for many economies, including for Vietnam during the period 2005–16.

First, we will consider domestic value added (DVA) content embodied in total commodity exports between Vietnam and the rest of the world, along with a comparison to China and other Southeast Asian economies. The DVA content of exports represents the exported value added that has been generated anywhere in the domestic economy. Statistics from the OECD-WTO TIVA database show that Vietnam's DVA exports to the world market had expanded dramatically, from $23 billion in 2005 to $46 billion in 2010 and $92.9 billion in 2016. Meanwhile, between 2005 and 2016, DVA in exports of Thailand had increased from $75.3 billion to $177.1 billion, while those for Singapore had gone from $81.3 billion to $180.6 billion. This means that Vietnam's DVA exports had increased much faster than those of Thailand and Singapore.

When considering the DVA as share of gross exports, however, there was a different trend between Vietnam and its peers. Table 4.1 shows that Vietnam's DVA share of gross exports was the lowest, and that it had a decreasing trend over time. This trend contrasts with those of other East Asian economies, particularly China and Malaysia, highlighting Vietnam's weak domestic industries.

A closer look at sectoral heterogeneity from Figure 4.2 reveals the remarkable performance of the electricity, gas and water supply

TABLE 4.1
DVA Share of Gross Exports of Vietnam and
Other East Asian Countries (%)

	China	Indonesia	Malaysia	Philippines	Singapore	Thailand	Vietnam
2005	73.73	81.64	55.01	73.70	57.2	61.57	63.92
2006	74.10	85.1	56.57	68.28	55.42	62.89	61.93
2007	75.23	85.67	55.94	75.78	58.56	63.90	59.17
2008	77.05	85.04	59.73	75.20	54.8	60.97	58.49
2009	80.51	87.88	60.23	78.10	57.95	65.60	62.8
2010	78.92	87.55	59.43	76.14	58.73	63.98	59.49
2011	78.26	87.19	60.56	76.48	56.48	61.18	58.20
2012	79.16	86.67	61.94	76.14	56.24	61.58	59.15
2013	79.65	86.11	62.81	79.00	57.17	62.54	58.31
2014	80.47	85.93	63.44	79.64	56.97	63.28	57.58
2015	82.68	87.07	63.09	77.96	59.07	66.44	55.48
2016	83.35	88.68	63.92	76.61	60.55	67.49	56.40

Source: Author's combination from OECD-WTO TIVA database.

FIGURE 4.2
DVA Share of Vietnam's Gross Exports by Sector (%)

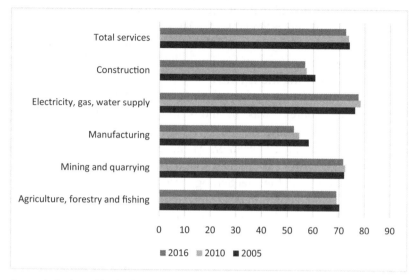

Source: Author's combination from OECD-WTO TIVA database.

FIGURE 4.3
DVA Share of Vietnam's Gross Exports by
Sub-sector of Manufacturing (%)

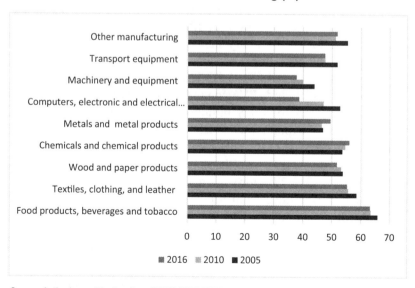

Source: Author's combination from OECD-WTO TIVA database.

sector and the services sector; the average DVA share of gross exports of these industries reached over 70 per cent. In contrast, the lowest performance was found in the manufacturing and construction sectors. These results are understandable as a large proportion of intermediate goods for the electricity, gas and water supply industry are produced domestically, whilst Vietnam has imported a significant share of input for the manufacturing industries.

For the manufacturing sector, Figure 4.3 demonstrates that the highest DVA content was in industries that are low-technology intensive such as food products, beverages and tobacco; chemicals; and textiles, clothing and leather. At the other end of the scale, the DVA content of gross exports was found to be very low for industries that are medium- and high-technology intensive—namely, machinery and equipment, and computers, electronics and electrics. Similar to the argument made in Upalat's chapter in this volume, this trend indicates that because of its limited production capacity Vietnam's domestic enterprises were limited to only being able to produce a large share of intermediate goods in industries that are low-technology intensive, and far fewer for those industries that are medium- and high-technology intensive.

Another crucial aspect in considering the GVC participation of a country is the amount of foreign value added (FVA) content of gross exports. Another useful measure is FVA share of gross exports. This is an "FVA intensity measure". It is often referred to as the "import content of exports", and is considered a measure of "backward linkages" in analyses of GVCs. In other words, it reveals how much the export sector of a country depends on imports of intermediate products from other countries.

Statistics from the OECD-WTO TIVA database show that between 2005 and 2016 Vietnam's FVA content of gross exports had increased from $13.0 billion to $71.8 billion. In 2016 the FVA content of Vietnam's gross exports was much lower than for China ($325.6 billion), Singapore ($117.7 billion) and Thailand ($85.3 billion) but was significantly higher than those of Indonesia ($19.8 billion) and the Philippines ($18.7 billion). Compared with China, Singapore and Thailand, however, the growth rate in FVA content of gross exports in Vietnam was much higher. This indicates a rapidly expanding role of FVA in Vietnam's exports.

We will turn now to the importance of the foreign factor in Vietnam's exports. Table 4.2 reveals a rising FVA share of gross exports from Vietnam—from 36 per cent in 2005 to 43.6 per cent in

TABLE 4.2
FVA Share of Gross Exports of Vietnam and East Asian Countries (%)

	China	Indonesia	Malaysia	Philippines	Singapore	Thailand	Vietnam
2005	26.27	18.36	44.99	26.30	42.8	38.43	36.08
2006	25.90	14.9	43.43	31.72	44.58	37.11	38.07
2007	24.77	14.33	44.06	24.22	41.44	36.10	40.83
2008	22.95	14.96	40.27	24.80	45.2	39.03	41.51
2009	19.49	12.12	39.77	21.90	42.05	34.40	37.2
2010	21.08	12.45	40.57	23.86	41.27	36.02	40.51
2011	21.74	12.81	39.44	23.52	43.52	38.82	41.80
2012	20.84	13.33	38.06	23.86	43.76	38.42	40.85
2013	20.35	13.89	37.19	21.00	42.83	37.46	41.69
2014	19.53	14.07	36.56	20.36	43.03	36.72	42.42
2015	17.32	12.93	36.91	22.04	40.93	33.56	44.52
2016	16.65	11.32	36.08	23.39	39.45	32.51	43.60

Source: Author's combination from OECD-WTO TIVA database.

2016. Interestingly, while Vietnam witnessed an increasing FVA share of gross exports, other East Asian countries showed the reverse trend; the highest declines took place in China, Malaysia and Indonesia. This implies that those East Asian economies had remarkably reduced their dependence on imports of intermediate goods from other countries. In contrast, Vietnam over time had come to rely more on foreign inputs for its production and export activities.

Looking at this in greater detail, Figures 4.4 and 4.5 illustrate the FVA share of Vietnam's gross exports by manufacturing sectors and sub-sectors. Figure 4.4 shows that the FVA share was growing in almost all export sectors—except, that is, for the electricity, gas and water supply sector. The largest FVA share of gross exports was found in the manufacturing sector, followed by the construction sector. The electricity, gas and water supply sector contained the lowest FVA share. This is understandable as this sector is largely monopolized by domestic state-owned enterprises (SOEs), and a large part of intermediate goods can be produced domestically. Figure 4.5, focusing on the manufacturing sector, indicates that the machinery and equipment industry along with the computers, electronics and electrics industry had the highest FVA share in Vietnam's gross exports. It is worth noting that the latter showed the largest expansion. In contrast, there was a declining trend in the FVA share of gross exports in the chemicals industry and the metals industry. This pattern is likely due to the large inward FDI flows into Vietnam's manufacturing sector.

FIGURE 4.4
FVA Share of Vietnam's Gross Exports by Sector (%)

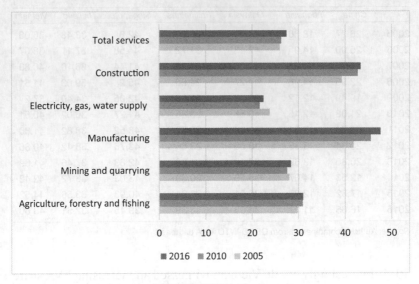

Source: Author's combination from OECD-WTO TIVA database.

FIGURE 4.5
FVA Share of Vietnam's Gross Exports
by Sub-sector of Manufacturing (%)

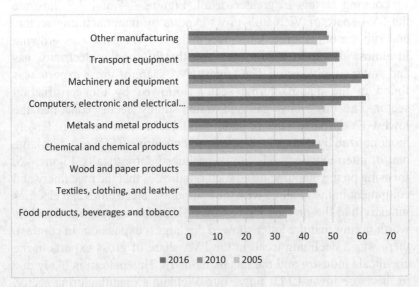

Source: Author's combination from OECD-WTO TIVA database.

This FDI increases the imports of parts and components from other countries. As of 20 December 2019, the total amount of newly registered, adjusted and contributed capital from foreign investors into Vietnam was nearly $38.02 billion. Of this amount, investment focused on the processing and manufacturing industries—totalling capital of $24.56 billion—accounted for 64.6 per cent of total inward FDI (Foreign Investment Agency 2019).

To gain insight into Vietnam's GVC participation at the sectoral level, the next section will analyse the two case studies—namely, the computers, electronics and electrics industry, and the textile and apparel industry.

Case Studies

Computers, Electronics and Electrics Industry

In the early 1990s, most of the electronics manufacturers in Vietnam were state-owned small-sized enterprises focused on assembling televisions, radio cassette recorders, and VCD and DVD players from imported components. From 100 companies in the 1990s, growing to 256 companies in 2005, the big boom happened after Vietnam joined the WTO in 2007 (Tractus Asia Vietnam 2019). In 2016 there were nearly 1,400 enterprises employing 612,000 workers in the country, having increased from 613 enterprises and nearly 168,000 workers in 2010 (see Table 4.3). The electronics industry alone accounted for 28.9 per cent of total exports from Vietnam in 2017—up from 5 per cent in 2010. The industry contributed 14 per cent of Vietnam's GDP in 2017, having grown from a figure of 5.2 per cent in 2010 (Tractus Asia Vietnam 2019). Vietnam saw the most rapid expansion in exports

TABLE 4.3
Number of Enterprises and Labour Force
in Vietnam's Electronics Industry (2010–16)

Year	Number of enterprises	Number of employees
2010	613	167.562
2011	629	238.661
2012	739	289.757
2013	839	327.659
2014	1,021	410.994
2015	1,145	497.037
2016	1,399	612.306

Source: GSO Statistical Year Book 2018.

of computers, electronics and electric products among East Asian economies (see Table 4.4).

Figure 4.6 shows that Vietnam significantly increased exports of intermediate inputs for computers, electronics and electric products to the world—from $918 million in 2005 to $10.2 billion in 2015, and the industry's share of total exports reached 52.8 per cent and 57.6 per cent, respectively. This implies that Vietnam's computers, electronics and electrics industry has increasingly engaged with regional and global production networks.

Despite such an expansion, Table 4.5 reveals a remarkable decrease in the DVA share of gross exports of computers, electronics and electric equipment from Vietnam to the global market—dropping from 52.8 per cent to 38.6 per cent over the period 2005–15. In contrast, there was a rising trend in DVA share of gross exports of computers, electronics and electric equipment in almost all the East Asia economies—except Singapore. For example, the DVA share of gross exports from China increased from 60 per cent in 2005 to 75 per cent by 2015, while those for Indonesia grew from 65 per cent in 2005 to 73 per cent in 2015. The decreasing trend for Vietnam indicates a declining role in this industry of domestic producers in creating value added for total exports. We have seen this trend for all of Vietnam's exports in the previous section, so the trend of the computers, electronics and electrics industry is the same as that broad trend.

TABLE 4.4
Export Value of Computers, Electronic and Electric Products from Vietnam and East Asian Countries ($ million)

Year	China	Indonesia	Malaysia	Philippines	Singapore	Thailand	Vietnam
2005	238,089.3	8,734.6	64,928.6	8,879.9	37,061.3	28,775.3	1,738.4
2006	301,560.3	7,152.2	63,548.1	16,803.4	45,840.4	26,000.6	2,324.5
2007	376,773.1	7,207.7	73,836.1	12,877.3	38,677.8	31,115.9	3,863.3
2008	433,058.7	7,802.5	60,611.6	15,277.9	45,703.6	34,507.8	4,360.8
2009	379,100.0	7,756.1	60,196.8	14,494.8	37,822.1	32,106.9	4,427.8
2010	488,309.9	9,267.4	71,522.7	17,527.9	52,642.0	45,315.4	7,064.5
2011	573,293.6	9,785.7	72,893.1	16,885.4	58,217.7	42,279.3	10,033.9
2012	626,634.9	9,928.1	69,984.6	21,753.4	54,999.0	43,595.8	11,927.2
2013	688,632.4	9,032.5	67,036.6	21,096.7	58,069.7	43,352.2	13,335.1
2014	717,826.4	8,628.5	70,157.6	22,749.5	61,273.4	44,896.6	14,972.6
2015	704,116.1	7,381.5	63,010.8	24,433.3	54,732.9	42,847.3	17,757.3

Source: Author's combination from OECD-WTO TIVA database.

FIGURE 4.6
Vietnam's Exports of Computers, Electronic and Electric Products
by Stages of Processing by Value ($ million) and Share

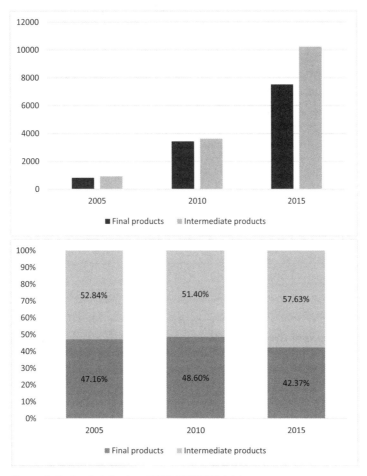

Source: Author's calculation from OECD-WTO TIVA database.

The decline of DVA was accompanied in the parallel rising trend of FVA in Vietnam's exports in this industry. Figure 4.7 shows the significant expansion of FVA share of gross exports of computers, electronics and electric equipment from Vietnam to the world market, reaching 47.1 per cent in 2005 and 61.4 per cent in 2016. Meanwhile, except for Singapore, other East Asian countries experienced a decreasing share of FVA in their gross exports of computers, electronics and electric equipment, particularly China, Malaysia and Indonesia,

TABLE 4.5
**DVA Share of Gross Export of Vietnam and East Asian Countries
in Computers, Electronics and Electrics Industry (%)**

Year	China	Indonesia	Malaysia	Philippines	Singapore	Thailand	Vietnam
2005	59.93	65.34	34.33	57.75	58.52	44.26	52.81
2006	60.31	68.08	36.92	53.28	52.37	43.48	48.91
2007	62.03	67.14	35.73	59.15	61.10	45.53	46.10
2008	65.65	61.10	38.75	60.02	55.14	43.70	45.75
2009	70.20	66.44	38.70	63.59	61.51	47.11	49.65
2010	68.61	65.17	38.38	60.50	59.64	46.10	47.06
2011	68.61	64.54	39.59	64.12	54.10	42.39	45.27
2012	69.24	63.23	41.84	61.83	56.39	46.26	41.94
2013	69.75	65.68	43.05	65.87	56.83	47.06	41.65
2014	71.02	66.03	43.81	66.95	55.17	48.02	41.38
2015	73.02	70.55	44.22	63.35	56.03	50.70	38.75
2016	74.94	73.56	45.37	61.06	56.40	52.10	38.60

Source: Author's combination from OECD-WTO TIVA database.

FIGURE 4.7
**FVA Share of Gross Exports of Vietnam and East Asian Countries
in Computers, Electronics and Electrics Industry (%)**

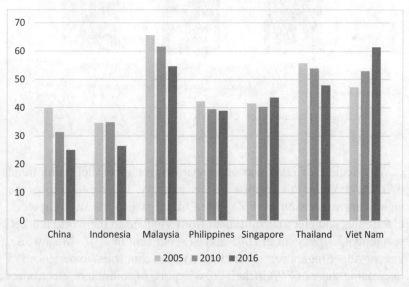

Source: Author's combination from OECD-WTO TIVA database.

which indicates a lower dependence on imports of intermediate inputs in this industry.

While the value added generated in Vietnam's computers, electronics and electrics industry had grown in absolute terms, that a large proportion of this continues to accrue to foreign economies is problematic for the country as it hopes to increase the local content

FIGURE 4.8
Vietnam's Imports of Computers, Electronics and Electric Products by Stages of Processing by Value ($ millions) and Share

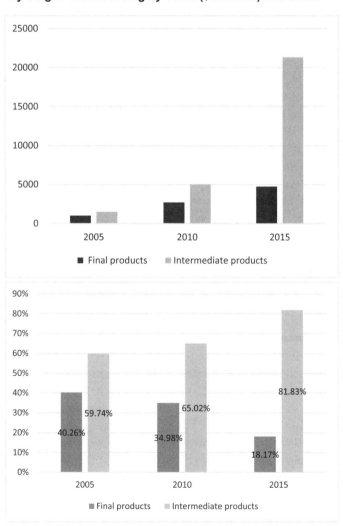

Source: Author's combination from OECD-WTO TIVA database.

of the industry. This can be observed in and explained clearly by reference to Figure 4.8. Between 2005 and 2016, Vietnam had rapidly increased the import value of intermediate computers, electronics and electric products from $1.5 billion to $21.3 billion. This resulted in the large rising share of intermediate inputs to total imports of computers, electronics and electric equipment, from 55.7 per cent in 2005 to 81.8 per cent in 2015. Conversely, the proportion of final import products of this industry declined to 18.1 per cent in 2015 compared with 40.2 per cent in 2005. This trend is also helpful to explain the sharp decline in the DVA share of gross exports of computers, electronics and electric equipment from Vietnam to foreign partners, and even the rapid increase in the absolute export value of these products.

The case of Samsung offers a glimpse into the expansion of Vietnam's participation in the GVC in this industry and the government's efforts to promote local sourcing. Among MNEs operating in Vietnam, the Samsung Group has largely dominated the electronics industry in particular and the whole of exports from the country in general. By the end of 2017, Samsung had committed total investments of $17.3 billion in Vietnam, of which over $14 billion had been disbursed, making it the largest foreign investor in the country. Some $7.5 billion of this was invested in the SEV factory complex in Bac Ninh province and the SEVT factory complex in Thai Nguyen province. About 75 per cent of SEV's products were exported to over fifty countries and territories worldwide, while nearly all of the products by SEVT were destined for export markets. Samsung alone accounted for a staggering 25 per cent of Vietnam's total merchandise exports in 2017, and the group had a significant impact on employment in Vietnam. As of late 2017, Samsung's three factories in Vietnam employed more than a hundred thousand employees, making the group one of the country's largest employers (Nguyen 2018).

Recognizing Samsung's importance, the Vietnamese government has maintained a good relationship with this group at both the national and local level. On several occasions this has gone beyond the government's normal treatment in order to accommodate Samsung's business and production needs. For example, when Samsung's factories were affected by a fire, the provincial government quickly deployed its staff to help with loading so Samsung would not miss its shipment schedule (Tong and Kokko 2019). The same provincial government also timed the planned shutdowns of its electricity supply facilities in a way that would not disrupt Samsung's production schedule. Another example took place in 2016. In order to protect local producers the government had imposed higher tariffs on steel imports from China, which increased the price of specific steel plates that Samsung bought from Korean steelmaker Posco's affiliates in China. Samsung appealed to the central government for a tariff revision, which was subsequently translated into a waiver for steel plates (ibid.).

Government officials felt that regular meetings could be a useful channel to convince Samsung and other MNEs to make changes in important areas such as expectations for increasing local sourcing. Using both closed meetings and open media statements in addition to appeals and persuasion, instead of using outright policy and threats, the Vietnamese government aimed to achieve its policy objectives without affecting subsequent inflows of FDI from incumbent investors. Interestingly, the approach seems to have achieved some results in getting foreign companies to help improve the participation of local firms in their GVCs. For example, shortly after a key meeting with local officials in 2014, Samsung announced it would collaborate with the Vietnamese government in holding an annual workshop—namely, the Samsung Sourcing Fair—and the group would invite Vietnamese firms to present their product offerings. Since 2014, through these events, Samsung has announced its sourcing policy and identified specific parts and components with the potential to be outsourced. It has held meetings with interested local suppliers and provided instructions on the application process and requirements for becoming a Samsung supplier (Tong and Kokko 2019). Accordingly, as of 2016, the number of tier-1 Vietnamese suppliers had increased from 4 to 12, and the number of tier-2 Vietnamese suppliers had reached 178, bringing the total number of Vietnamese enterprises participating in Samsung's supply chain to 190 enterprises. The number of Vietnamese enterprises in the supply chain of two Samsung projects in Bac Ninh and Thai Nguyen (SEV and SEVT) reached 6 tier-1 suppliers and 155 tier-2 suppliers. For the projects of Samsung in Ho Chi Minh City (SEHC), there were 6 tier-1 suppliers and 23 tier-2 suppliers (Logistics4vn 2016).

Textile and Apparel Industry

In addition to the electronics industry, the textile and clothing industry also plays an important role in Vietnam's economy, especially for the export sector.

After the reunification of the country in 1975, Vietnam's textile and apparel industry was very small, and because of the embargo it only operated domestically. A small quantity of textile and clothing products were exported to the socialist countries in Eastern Europe. After the collapse of the Soviet bloc this industry was plunged into crisis (Do 2020). Reforms that began in the late 1980s were the premise for Vietnam's textile and garment industry to participate in GVCs. In particular, since 2000, after the signing of a bilateral trade agreement with the United States, several foreign investors have come to Vietnam to invest in the textile and garment industry thanks to abundant and cheap labour, low electricity prices, and tax incentives. Vietnam's textile and garment industry has seen a remarkable growth in major indicators such as the number of firms, overall scale, total turnover, number of workers, inward FDI value, and export value (Table 4.6).

For example, the number of firms in the textile and clothing industry rapidly expanded after Vietnam's accession to the WTO. Specifically, from 2,994 firms in the textile and clothing industry in 2007, the number of firms in this sector increased to 5,943 in 2011 and to 10,604 in 2017 (General Statistics Office of Vietnam 2018). Inward FDI flows into the textile and clothing industry increased to about $18 billion in 2018. The country's textile and clothing export products to the world had grown rapidly from $1.85 billion in 2000 to $36.5 billion by 2018 (see Table 4.6). Textile and clothing products number among the most important export items for the country, accounting for 14.8 per cent of Vietnam's total exports to the globe in 2018. Vietnam in that year became the third-largest textile and garment exporter in the world (after China and India) (Vietnam Cotton and Spinning Association 2019).

Looking now at the GVC participation of the textile and apparel industry, Figure 4.9 shows that the share of intermediate products in Vietnam's textile and apparel exports to the world has significantly

TABLE 4.6
Major Indicators of Vietnam's Textile and Apparel Industry

Indicator	2000	2018	Growth rate
Scale of the industry ($ billion)	2.00	26.00	13.0
Total turnover ($ billion)	2.00	42.00	21.0
Exports ($ billion)	1.85	36.50	20.0
Size of labour force (million)	0.20	3.60	18.0
Number of spindles (million)	1.00	9.70	9.7
Inward FDI ($ billion)	0.00	18.00	
Share of FDI firms %	0.00	70.00	

Source: Vietnam Cotton and Spinning Association (2019).

expanded, reaching 45 per cent in 2015. On the import side, Vietnam's imports from overseas were heavily concentrated on intermediate products, increasing from 81 per cent to 89 per cent (Figure 4.10). Despite the higher share of intermediate export products, the DVA

FIGURE 4.9
Vietnam's Exports of Textile and Apparel Products
by Stages of Processing (share)

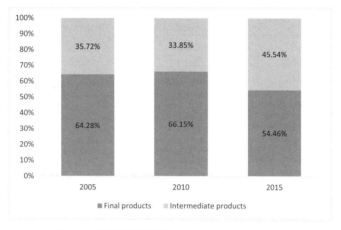

Source: Author's calculation from OECD-WTO TIVA database.

FIGURE 4.10
Vietnam's Imports of Textile and Apparel Products
by Stages of Processing (share)

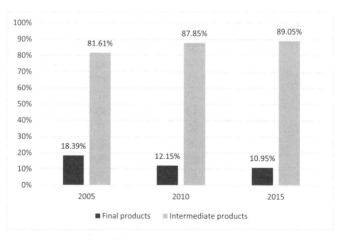

Source: Author's calculation from OECD-WTO TIVA database.

share of the textile and apparel industry in Vietnam's gross exports was much lower compared with other East Asian countries (Table 4.7). Meanwhile, the high rate of intermediate textile and clothing products explains why the FVA share of textile and apparel exports in Vietnam's gross exports of this industry was the largest among other East Asian

TABLE 4.7
DVA Share of Gross Export of Vietnam and East Asian Countries in the Textile and Apparel Industry (%)

Year	China	Indonesia	Malaysia	Philippines	Singapore	Thailand	Vietnam
2005	82.52	77.67	62.33	83.26	52.98	72.38	58.49
2006	83.24	82.92	65.15	76.24	51.05	74.24	57.73
2007	84.70	83.3	64.19	84.43	52.57	76.39	54.76
2008	86.05	79.66	64.83	85.75	50.68	74.02	56.63
2009	88.79	83.51	68.54	87.64	54.89	77.86	59.11
2010	87.93	80.12	63.47	86.60	54.93	73.33	55.65
2011	86.88	77.87	64.94	82.24	62.15	74.14	54.51
2012	87.67	77.44	66.32	83.67	60.81	74.76	54.53
2013	88.15	76.88	66.59	85.67	61.93	75.86	55.56
2014	88.53	76.57	67.22	85.61	63.20	75.8	55.25
2015	89.80	77.76	64.94	84.65	62.55	77.69	53.85
2016	90.63	79.96	64.74	83.81	65.34	79.25	55.25

Source: Author's combination from OECD-WTO TIVA database.

TABLE 4.8
FVA Share of Gross Exports of Vietnam and East Asian Countries in the Textile and Apparel Industry (%)

Year	China	Indonesia	Malaysia	Philippines	Singapore	Thailand	Vietnam
2005	17.48	22.33	37.67	16.74	47.02	27.62	41.51
2006	16.76	17.08	34.85	23.76	48.95	25.76	42.27
2007	15.30	16.70	35.81	15.57	47.43	23.61	45.24
2008	13.95	20.34	35.17	14.25	49.32	25.98	43.37
2009	11.21	16.49	31.46	12.36	45.11	22.14	40.89
2010	12.07	19.88	36.53	13.40	45.07	26.67	44.35
2011	13.12	22.13	35.06	17.76	37.85	25.86	45.49
2012	12.33	22.56	33.68	16.33	39.19	25.24	45.47
2013	11.85	23.12	33.41	14.33	38.07	24.14	44.44
2014	11.47	23.43	32.78	14.39	36.80	24.20	44.75
2015	10.20	22.24	35.06	15.35	37.45	22.31	46.15
2016	9.37	20.04	35.26	16.19	34.66	20.75	44.75

Source: Author's combination from OECD-WTO TIVA database.

countries (see Table 4.8). This demonstrates that Vietnam's textile and apparel industry has a much higher dependence on foreign inputs than the textile industries of other East Asian countries.

Compared with the computers, electronics and electrics industry, however, the DVA share of the textile and apparel industry in Vietnam's gross exports was much higher. Meanwhile, the role of FVA in Vietnam's textile and clothing exports is much less significant than that of the country's exports of the computers, electronics and electrics industry. To some extent this implies the higher degree of localization of the former than that of the latter. But it should be noted that a large part of DVA textile and apparel exports was also created by FDI firms, while the role of Vietnamese firms in this indicator remains modest.

Discussion

Along with the rapid growth in trade and investments, Vietnam has become more integrated in GVCs, allowing the country to expand its own DVA through exports. Vietnam has shown higher integration in GVCs as a buyer and seller since 2000, and the country is considered a typical case of a country that imports goods or services which are then incorporated into exports to another country. Measures of ratios of imports to exports consider that much of the country's exports consist of FVA. Vietnam's export basket has also diversified over time, showing a transition from exporting primary commodities to exporting low- and medium-tech manufactured goods (apparel, furniture and footwear) and subsequently more sophisticated products (machinery and electronics). At the sectoral level, Vietnam's DVA in gross exports expanded in most sectors and exhibited the highest growth rates among its peers (Trinh et al. 2019).

Nevertheless, Vietnam faces numerous constraints to innovating its export basket to allow for the capture of more value addition and to move up the value chain into higher-value-added functions. Most export occupations remain in the unskilled-worker range, and the unskilled component of labour value added is much larger in Vietnam than in its other East Asian peers. This pattern can be observed in most manufacturing industries, including processed foods, machinery and equipment, and textiles and apparel.

Despite the increasing FVA share in gross exports, backward linkages with the domestic economy in Vietnam are weak. The expansion in DVA exported largely came directly from export activities rather than indirectly through domestic inputs. In 2016, data processed from the OECD-WTO TIVA database showed that the contribution of direct DVA from exports was 61.6 per cent of the total, while the value added generated by the domestic pipeline supplying exports was 38.3 per cent. Weak backward linkages are largely the result of weak linkages from FDI firms to a domestic private sector and between local suppliers. It is common for institutions to play a constructive role in integrating FDI with the domestic economy, but in Vietnam it seems that none of the key institutional variables matter (Hollweg et al. 2017).

The lack of backward supply linkages ("local sourcing") in the production of Samsung's mobile phones offers an insightful glimpse at the micro level to help understand the challenges for Vietnam's GVC participation. Attracting MNEs in high-tech industries is not enough to generate the positive spillover effects and demand multipliers necessary to create sustainable industrial development. If supply linkages are weak, then there are few direct contacts between foreign MNEs and local firms, resulting in less learning, fewer spillover benefits, and weaker prospects for the upgrading and development of competitive local firms (Tong and Kokko 2019). A crucial question for the Vietnamese government therefore is how to promote stronger backward supply linkages and ensure the participation of local enterprises in the GVCs.

At the same time, the contribution of Vietnam's services in value added remains low by international standards; its forward linkages to manufacturing export sectors from the backbone services sectors necessary for competitive industry are weak. Because the high-value-added segments of GVCs are often rich in services content, enhancing the competitiveness of the services sector to enable the role of services, both as inputs into the economy and as a means to change the way value is created, should be a priority of the Vietnamese government's upgrading strategy in GVC participation (Hollweg 2017). When the domestic services sector obtains a certain competitive level by international standards, then services exports themselves could foster Vietnam's export diversification.

In terms of the electronics industry, Vietnam only engages in the lowest midstream activities of the electronics value chain, such as sub-assemblies and finished products. Its economy depends heavily on imported components and sub-assemblies. Local production is very limited. As a result, Vietnam has no other option than to rely on component imports to support export activities. Upstream activities in Vietnam's electronics industry are very weak: designing is carried out abroad; the main components (such as electronic chips) are largely imported from foreign countries. Only a few MNEs have R&D activities in the country, and these are limited. One such is the recent R&D centre of Samsung in Hanoi, which has a value of $220 million (Nguyen 2020). At the downstream level these activities are carried out by foreign companies and produced outside Vietnam, while local companies have limited international exposure and marketing capabilities because of a lack of experience and capital (Tractus Asia Vietnam 2019).

This can be seen clearly in Samsung's operations in Vietnam. Samsung's factories in Vietnam rely heavily on Korean suppliers that have co-located in Vietnam to produce intermediate inputs, or they depend on imports from Korea and third countries. As noted, despite the recent expansion, the number of Vietnamese local suppliers— particularly tier-1 suppliers—remains very low. In addition, most of these local suppliers provide only the lowest-value-added inputs to any manufacturing operation, such as packaging. Thus, while 38 per cent of the export value of computers, electronics and electric equipment in 2016 was generated domestically, most of that accrues to global suppliers in Vietnam; Vietnamese suppliers account for only a small proportion of total local content. Efforts to increase local content by local enterprises have obtained only limited results. For example, Samsung held a workshop with the Vietnamese government and two hundred local firms to see which components could be sourced locally; none among the two hundred local firms were able to meet Samsung's requirements.

Vietnam has a weak domestic private sector that is constrained by both an FDI- and SOE-centric business environment and by a lack of skilled labour. Meanwhile, the majority of Vietnam's foreign investors operate in the electronics sector—a high-skilled industry with high barriers to supplier entry. The original equipment manufacturers (OEMs) hold suppliers to some of the highest quality and reliability standards, and they often require the majority of tier-1 suppliers to hold patent protection on supplied parts and components (Grozier and Keene 2020). In the electronics industry, Vietnam's domestic private sector and its labour force have struggled to meet the high requirements from MNEs. This is considered one of the principal reasons that has forced foreign firms operating in Vietnam's electronics industry to import intermediate input and relocate their existing suppliers to the country.

In addition, Vietnam lacks strong electronics clusters. The Vietnamese firms operating in the electronics sector are characterized by their specific products, and they have weak cooperation among themselves as a result of their ownership. In other Southeast Asian countries such as Singapore, Thailand and Malaysia, electronics clusters have been created, while in Vietnam such clusters are only at the initial stages of formation. They are based on groups in the outlying districts of the two largest urban areas—Ho Chi Minh City and Hanoi—and in several provinces such as Bac Ninh, Thai Nguyen and Hai Phong.

Another problem is that currently there is an imbalance between imports for trading and manufacturing in Vietnam's electronic components industry because the import tax imposed for electronic parts and components is lower than that of materials to produce such components. As a result, Vietnamese firms lacking capital and cutting-edge technology tend to import sophisticated electronic parts and components rather than manufacture them, and the participation of local firms in GVCs and the supply chains of FDI firms in this industry remain weak.

Similarly, Vietnam's textile and clothing industry has many shortcomings and faces many challenges in deepening its GVC participation. First, there are weak backward linkages to textiles as textile production and the finishing function have not been proportional to the growth in apparel assembly (Frederick 2017). Second, Vietnam is facing limitations in production capability and the quality of products. For example, in fabric production, existing production is mainly for domestic use, while the processing segment (dyeing and finishing, yarn, fabric and apparel) is the most limited stage of the chain in Vietnam. The country is also facing difficulties in diversifying the types of textile and clothing products with sufficient quality to meet the high requirements of MNEs, thereby expanding the GVC participation of domestic firms in this industry. Third, domestic firms have focused mainly on vertically integrating within Vietnam and in selling their products domestically rather than to international markets through efforts to establish global supply and distribution relationships with MNEs. Local firms lack information about GVCs and ways they could participate in global markets. Fourth, as with the electronics industry, Vietnam's textile and clothing industry lacks a skilled workforce. For apparel, local firms do not have enough workers with soft skills (such as the ability to do business with global buyers), good critical thinking, or marketing and technical skills (such as using automated equipment). For textiles, the shortage of skilled labour is mainly in chemistry-related areas (such as dyeing, finishing, synthetic production, and processing) (Frederick 2017). And finally, the export activities and GVC participation of Vietnam's textile and apparel industry are significantly dependent on FDI firms.

Policy Implications

From a long-term perspective, continued GVC participation in the form of labour-intensive production activities with low productivity and low value added will mean it will be difficult for the Vietnamese economy to sustain its economic growth and overcome the danger of the "middle income trap" (Taguchi et al. 2019). Historically, the growth rates of real GDP per capita in Vietnam during the last decade were not sufficient for a quick catch up, and the level of labour productivity has remained low in recent years. A report of the International Labour Organization in 2014 revealed that the labour productivity of Vietnam is among the lowest in the Asia-Pacific. It is 15 times lower than in Singapore, 11 times lower than in Japan, 10 times lower than in South Korea, 5 times lower than in Malaysia and 2.5 times lower than in Thailand. Worse still, Vietnam has a downward trend for the growth of labour productivity. From 2002 to 2007, labour productivity increased by an average of 5.2 per cent a year, but it reduced to 3.3 per cent between 2008 and 2013 (ILO 2014). To deal with this challenge, the Vietnamese economy needs to transform its structure from one of factor-driven growth to a productivity-driven one through industrial upgrading. In the context of increasing GVC participation, while the Vietnamese economy accepts foreign firms in its production activities, it should also upgrade its domestic productive capacities by obtaining technological transfers from MNEs. The specific recommendations are as follows.

At the aggregate level, the country should facilitate the entry of domestic companies into GVCs by improving the drivers of investment, especially the functioning of market institutions (such as asset protection) and by improving the functioning and quality of the domestic segment of value chains and the quality of service inputs. Strengthening linkages between buyers and sellers in GVCs, along with maximizing the absorption potential of local firms (especially their innovation capacity), would help the domestic sector to benefit from GVC spillovers as well as expand opportunities for upgrading. The country should concentrate on skills development because this could speed up economic upgrading and the densification of the GVC space with more domestic suppliers, while increasing the benefits of GVC participation via promoting social upgrading and cohesion.

Foreign enterprises should not be privileged vis-à-vis domestic companies. In other words, there should be an equal playing field between all companies in Vietnam. For instance, the country should not give too many incentives to MNEs as this could only boost their market (and political) power over Vietnamese policymakers. As a result, there is no motivation for MNEs to increase forward and backward linkages with local suppliers. Additionally, efforts to attract FDI should not be limited to the large MNEs at the core of GVCs but should also aim at large supplier firms in upstream industries across the MNE value chains. By establishing contacts with tier-1 suppliers, local firms would benefit from learning and spillovers as well as having more opportunities to participate in value chains (even as lower-tier suppliers).

For the electronics industry, there are advantageous conditions for the development of this sector over the next few years. Since Vietnam has successfully contained the coronavirus, this Southeast Asian economy is on track for GDP expansion. The electronics industry has retained a positive growth rate in recent months, indicating its great potential for recovery and development. In addition, the trend for many suppliers to move a part of their production from China to other Asian economies, including Vietnam, brings more opportunities for local firms. These factors, along with the initiatives of the Vietnamese government to support the electronic components industry, are expected to enhance the production of local firms and their GVC participation in the future.

The capacity to develop along the electronic GVC, however, will depend heavily on supportive services. Investing, therefore, in a technically skilled workforce with professional qualifications could boost the development of supporting industries for the electronics industry. Improving the managerial skills and the other soft skills of employees will also be necessary to improve the competitiveness of domestic electronic firms. To ensure that supplier development programmes work effectively, foreign firms or industry associations with a high degree of participation from foreign firms should be involved. For instance, MNEs could provide valuable information to help the government determine the required types of local suppliers (tier 1, tier 2 or tier 3) and then direct support and assistance resources to them. As the electronics industry is expected to expand, additional support services (such as an R&D institute and quality control centres) will be needed to create more specialized but high-value-added services jobs. Meanwhile, access to finance (especially tax credits) is important for companies operating in supporting electronics industries so they can develop and move into higher-value-added activities. Vietnam will need to invest more in transport and logistics to boost the competitiveness of its electronics industry as the competitive pressure from its East and Southeast Asian peers will be much higher in the future. This is also necessary because of the greater pressure of moving production activities outside the big cities such as Hanoi and Ho Chi Minh city. Thus, it is necessary to ensure there are no constraints to the availability of third-party transport companies, which can reduce costs for smaller firms. In a similar vein, access to reliable utilities such as the electricity system is vital to improve the competitiveness of domestic electronics firms in the international market.

For Vietnam's textile and apparel industry, the following recommendations should be taken into consideration in order to foster the GVC participation of this sector. First, Vietnam should enhance its participation in high-value-added segments along the GVCs of the textile and apparel industry. This requires improving the skills of the domestic workforce. Training institutions will need to upgrade their curriculum in consultation with firms in the textile and apparel industry. The government should also strengthen collaboration between institutions and enterprises by creating policies that support formal and ongoing training (through grants, subsidies and tax concessions for training expenditure). Second, Vietnam should continue to attract high-quality FDI projects by creating incentives in the textile and apparel industry. There are advantages for Vietnam to do this as the country has a very open economy and has also participated in many free trade agreements (FTA), particularly new-generation FTAs such as the Comprehensive and Progressive Agreement for Trans-Pacific Partnership (CPTPP) and the EU-Vietnam Free Trade Agreement (EVFTA). Third, greater autonomy and more resources should be provided for Vietnamese firms (especially private enterprises) to enhance their innovative capability and develop domestic brands for export, thereby diversifying connections to international markets. Finally, Vietnam's textile and apparel industry needs to find a balance whereby the sector does not depend too much on FDI but is still able to capitalize on the resources provided by MNEs to eventually enhance the GVC participation of domestic firms in higher-value-added activities.

References

Ando, M. 2006. "Fragmentation and Vertical Intra-industry Trade in East Asia". *North American Journal of Economics and Finance* 17, no. 3: 257–81.

Brian, M. 2011. "Exporting out of Poverty: Provincial Poverty in Vietnam and US Market Access". *Journal of International Economics* 85, no. 1: 102–13.

Dezan Shira and Associates. 2018. "Supporting Industries in Vietnam". *Vietnam Briefing.* 30 March 2018. https://www.vietnam-briefing.com/news/supporting-industries-vietnam.html/.

Do, D.D. 2016. "Manufacturing and Industry in Vietnam: Three Decades of Reform". Brenthurst Discussion Paper No. 6. Johannesburg: The Brenthurst Foundation.

Do, Q.C. 2020. "Social and Economic Upgrading in the Garment Supply Chain in Vietnam". IPE Working Papers no. 137. Berlin: Institute for International Political Economy.

Frederick, S. 2017. "Vietnam's Textile and Apparel Industry and Trade Networks". In *Vietnam at a Crossroads: Engaging in the Next Generation of Global Value Chains*, edited by C. Hollweg, T. Smith, and D. Taglioni, pp. 101–9. Washington DC: World Bank.

Foreign Investment Agency. 2019. "Tình hình thu hút đầu tư nước ngoài năm 2019". 7 January 2019. https://dautunuocngoai.gov.vn/tinbai/6318/Tinh-hinh-thu-hut-dau-tu-nuoc-ngoai-nam-2019.

Fu, X. 2011. "Processing Trade, FDI and the Exports of Indigenous Firms: Firm-Level Evidence from Technology-Intensive Industries in China". *Oxford Bulletin of Economics and Statistics* 73, no. 6: 792–817.

Government of Vietnam. 2015. "Decree on Development of Supporting Industry". 3 November 2015. https://vanbanphapluat.co/decree-of-government-no-111-2015-nd-cp-development-of-ancillary-industry.

Government Port of Vietnam. 2014. "Prime Minister Nguyen Tan Dung on June 9, 2014 Signed Decision No. 879/QD-TTg to Approve the Industrial Development Strategy through 2025, Vision toward 2035". 9 June 2014. http://www.chinhphu.vn/portal/page/portal/English/strategies/strategiesdetails?categoryId=30&articleId=10054959.

Grozier, B., and K. Jason. 2020. "Vietnamese Development Policy: Upgrading the Domestic Private Sector through FDI Linkages". MA thesis, John F. Kennedy School of Government, Harvard University.

GSO. 2018. "Statistical Year Book 2018". General Statistics Office of Vietnam.

Ha, V.H., and Q.T. Tran. 2017. "International Trade and Employment: A Quantile Regression Approach". *Journal of Economic Integration* 32, no. 3: 531–57.

Herr, Hansjörg, E. Schweisshelm, and M.H.V. Truong. 2016. "The Integration of Vietnam in the Global Economy and Its Effects for Vietnamese Economic Development". Global Labour University Working Paper No. 44. Geneva: International Labour Organization.

Hirunya, S. 2013. "Thailand Investment Environment and BOI Investment Promotion Policy". Thailand Board of Investment. Changwon, South Korea.

Hollweg, C. 2017. "Servicifying the Vietnamese Economy". *Vietnam at a Crossroads: Engaging in the Next Generation of Global Value Chains,* edited by C. Hollweg, T. Smith, and D. Taglioni, pp. 39–53. Washington DC: World Bank.

Hollweg, C., T. Sturgeon, and D. Taglioni 2017. "Overview". In *Vietnam at a Crossroads: Engaging in the Next Generation of Global Value Chains*, edited by C. Hollweg, T. Smith, and D. Taglioni, pp. 1–26. Washington, DC: World Bank.

ILO. 2014. "Education-Business Mismatch Worsens Already Low Workforce Quality and Productivity". International Labour Organization: ILO Country Office for Vietnam.

Javorcik, S.B. 2004. "Does Foreign Direct Investment Increase the Productivity of Domestic Firms? In Search of Spillovers through Backward Linkages". *American Economic Review* 94, no. 3: 605–27.

———. 2008. "Can Survey Evidence Shed Light on Spillovers from Foreign Direct Investment?" *World Bank Research Observer* 23, no. 2: 139–59.

Kowalski, P., J.L. Gonzalez, A. Ragoussis, and C. Ugarte. 2015. "Participation of Developing Countries in Global Value Chains: Implications for Trade and Trade-Related Policies". OECD Trade Policy Papers No 179. Paris: Organisation for Economic Cooperation and Development.

Kwon, T., and J.W. Ryou. 2015. "Global Value Chains of East Asia: Trade in Value Added and Vertical Specialization". *Asian Economic Journal* 29, no. 2: 121–43.

Logistics4vn. 2016. "Samsung Và "Sự Mở Đường" Cho Công Nghiệp Hỗ Trợ". 30 June 2016. https://logistics4vn.com/samsung-va-su-mo-duong-cho-cong-nghiep-ho-tro.

National Assembly of Vietnam. 2013. "The Law No. 32/2013/QH1". 19 June 2013. https://vanbanphapluat.co/law-no-32-2013-qh13-on-the-amendments-to-the-law-on-enterprise-income-tax.

Nguyen, D. 2018. "Samsung Electronics Việt Nam – 10 năm kiến tâm – tạo tầm – vượt kỳ tích". *Bao dau tu*, 14 May 2018. https://baodautu.vn/samsung-viet-nam-tu-canh-dong-trong-tron-den-chiec-dien-thoai-thu-1-ty-d81544.html.

———. 2020. "Samsung Erects $220 Mln R&D Center in Vietnam". *Vnexpress*, 2 March 2020. https://e.vnexpress.net/news/business/companies/samsung-erects-220-mln-r-amp-d-center-in-vietnam-4062882.html.

Nguyen, D.X. 2016 "Trade Liberalization and Export Sophistication in Vietnam". *Journal of International Trade & Economic Development* 25, no. 8: 1071–89.

Nguyen, P.Q., T.A.T. Le, and Le M.T. 2016. "The Role of Foreign Direct Investment in Improving Value Chains: Evidence from Vietnam and other Developing Countries". The Vietnam Economist Annual Meeting (VEAM), in Da Nang, 11–12 August 2016.

Nguyen, V.C. 2015. "The Impact of Trade Facilitation on Poverty and Inequality: Evidence from Low- and Middle-Income Countries". *Journal of International Trade & Economic Development* 24, no. 3: 315–40.

OECD and WTO. 2013. "Trade in Value-Added: Concepts, Methodologies and Challenges". Joint OECD-WTO Note.

OECD-WTO TIVA database. n.d. https://stats.oecd.org/.

The Prime Minister of Vietnam. 2017. "Quyết Định Về Việc Phê Duyệt Chương Trình Phát Triển Công Nghiệp Hỗ Trợ Từ Năm 2016 Đến Năm 2025".

18 January 2017. https://thukyluat.vn/vb/quyet-dinh-68-qd-ttg-2017-phe-duyet-chuong-trinh-phat-trien-cong-nghiep-ho-tro-tu-2016-den-2025-528f9.html.

Swenson, D.L., and H. Chen. 2014. "Multinational Exposure and the Quality of New Chinese Exports". *Oxford Bulletin of Economics and Statistics* 76, no. 1: 41–66.

Taguchi, H., M.D. Nguyen, and S.D. Pham. 2019. "The Involvement in Global Value Chains and its Policy Implication: Evidence of Vietnam". *Social Science Review* 156: 103–18.

Tong, Y.S., and A. Kokko, A. 2019. "Linking FDI and Local Firms for Global Value Chain Upgrading: Policy Lessons from Samsung Mobile Phone Production in Viet Nam". Inclusive and sustainable industrial Development Working paper series No. 5. Vienna: The United Nations Industrial Development Organization (UNIDO).

Tractus Asia Vietnam. 2019. "Electronics 2019". http://tractus-asia.com/wp-content/uploads/2019/04/Vietnam-electronics-Industry.pdf.

Tran, N.K., and H. Yoon. 2009. "Impacts of Trade Liberalization on Employment in Vietnam: A System Generalized Method of Moments Estimation". *Developing Economies* 47, no. 1: 81–103.

Tran, T.B.N., and T.B. Dao. 2019. "Vietnam's Electronics Industry: The Rise and Problems of Further Development". *Humanities & Social Sciences Reviews* 7, no. 4: 1–12.

Tran, T.H., Q.H. Truong, and C.V. Dong. 2020. "Determinants of Product Sophistication in Viet Nam: Findings from the Firm–Multi-Product Level Microdata Approach". ERIA Discussion Paper Series No. 314. Jakarta: Economic Research Institute for ASEAN and East Asia.

Trinh, Q.L., M. Helble., and T.T. Le. 2019. "Global Value Chains and Formal Employment in Viet Nam". ERIA Discussion Paper Series No. 298. Jakarta: The Economic Research Institute for ASEAN and East Asia.

Truong, Q.H., V.C. Dong, and H.H. Nguyen, 2019. "Taiwan–ASEAN Trade Relations: Trade Structure and Trade in Value Added". *China Report* 55, no. 2: 102–24.

UNCTAD. 2013a. "Global Value Chains and Development: Investment and Value Added Trade in the Global Economy". United Nations Conference on Trade and Development.

———. 2013b. "World Investment Report, Global Value Chains: Investment and Trade for Development". New York: United Nations Conference on Trade and Development.

United Nations. n.d. "United Nations Comtrade Database". https://comtrade.un.org/data/.

Wang, Y., and S. Chen. 2020. "Heterogeneous Spillover Effects of Outward FDI on Global Value Chain Participation". *Panoeconomicus* 67, no. 5: 607–26.

World Bank. 2017. "Global Value Chain Development Reports 2017: Measuring and Analyzing the Impacts of GVCs on Economic Development". Washington, DC: World Bank Group.

Zhu, S., and X. Fu. 2009. "Drivers of Export Upgrading". *World Development* 51: 221–33.

Yao, S. 2009. "Why Are Chinese Exports Not So Special?" *China & World Economy* 17, no. 1: 47–65.

Chapter 5

Vietnam's Economic Dependence on China: Understanding Vulnerability through a Typology of Trade Shocks

Yoon Ah Oh

China's role in Vietnam's rapid economic development is significant but contentious. In the past two decades, Vietnam has significantly benefited from integration into the regional production network anchored in China. Yet there have been mounting concerns in Vietnam that close economic ties between the two countries are asymmetrical, and that the Vietnamese economy is increasingly *dependent* on China. For years, policymakers, experts and observers have expressed worries about the country's high reliance on Chinese inputs in its export industries and the deep penetration by Chinese firms in its domestic consumer and construction markets (Tran 2019; Tuoi Tre News 2013; Ngan 2014). Of particular concern is that, despite the exponential growth in Vietnam's exports and the number of free trade agreements (FTAs) signed by Vietnam to diversify its trade relations, raw materials and equipment used by the country's manufacturing exporters continue to be dominated by Chinese products, and there is no evident sign that the situation is improving (Ngan Anh 2014).

That this is taking place amid increasingly complex geopolitical competition between the United States and China adds another layer of complexity (Vu 2015; Vu 2017, pp. 297–8). China has increasingly leveraged its economic might to achieve foreign policy goals by employing various inducements and sanctions (Chheang 2018; Reilly 2013). Inducements, such as infrastructure projects under the Belt and Road Initiative, may be attractive to many, although simultaneously

China is increasingly using economic sanctions to change the behaviour of other states (Hufbauer and Jung 2020). It is unsurprising that economic dependence is considered to pose a much greater political risk in Vietnam because of its territorial dispute and historical tensions with China (Tuoi Tre News 2013).

Concerns over Vietnam's economic dependence largely arise from the fact that China is its largest trading partner. Moreover, Vietnam continues to record a large trade deficit with China. The asymmetric nature of bilateral trade between Vietnam and China worries many. For Vietnam, China is too big and too important. In contrast, for China, Vietnam is a relatively small trading partner in its global trade. Vietnam may though have particular significance for China's Southeast Asia policy given that it is China's largest trading partner in the region, and a large share of China's overall trade surplus with the region comes from Vietnam. Nonetheless, the asymmetry is unmistakable at the global scale.

The current debate frames this issue as Vietnam's economic "dependence" on China, but one can gain a better understanding by examining the actual source of the concern more closely; that is, the vulnerability in, or asymmetrical control over, the bilateral trade relations. This chapter examines Vietnam's vulnerability to China in its economic ties, focussing on trade. The focus is on trade because trade forms the primary channel of current Vietnam-China economic ties. Foreign direct investment and development cooperation still largely play a limited, secondary role.[1] In taking this approach, I present an analytical framework consisting of two structural dimensions that combine to produce a typology of trade shocks. The typology maps out the range of possible trade shocks and offers the full domain of Vietnam's vulnerability. Distinguishing different types of shocks is useful because different types of shocks require different, although interrelated, responses from Vietnam. Popular accounts tend to conflate them, which results in a lack of rigorous investigation into the issue, and this hinders better policy responses.

The next section briefly discusses the rise of Chinese economic power and growing economic dependence on China across the world. The section after that examines recent trends in and characteristics of Vietnam-China trade relations. Based on a discussion of these recent trade patterns, the fourth section then presents a typology of trade shocks and illustrates the vulnerabilities reflected in each category, which are drawn from the experiences of Vietnam and other countries. This typology exercise suggests that distinctive risks exist for each type of trade shock. I conclude by discussing Vietnam's policy responses.

Economic Dependence on China

The issue of Vietnam's economic dependence on China needs to be examined in the wider context of the contemporary geopolitical landscape. Vu (2015) describes contemporary Vietnam-China relations as "struggling co-evolution", where economic affairs between the two countries entail a constant interplay of actions and reactions that have strong political ramifications. Over the past few decades, the world economy has been reorganized by a shift in production from advanced economies to developing countries. China has been at the centre of this shift because of its role in international production and trade networks created by transnational firms (Gereffi 2014). As China became the top manufacturer for the world, it also became the world's most important export market for raw materials such as iron ore, copper, coal and many other commodities. As a result, China's demand largely determined global commodity prices and the subsequent economic performance of many commodity exporting countries such as Australia and Indonesia (Coxhead 2007). These countries benefited tremendously from close economic ties with China during the commodity boom years in the 2000s, but they soon came to realize the political vulnerabilities of this asymmetric relationship. One of the key examples of this is Australia (Beeson and Wilson 2015).

That China became the industrial power in the age of global product networks led to another important development. Many countries export and import intermediate goods such as parts and components to and from China; some countries export inputs, and others import for final assembly and processing. This creates China's dominance and its disproportionate influence in global supply chains, the extent of which was clearly demonstrated by the severe global supply chain disruptions when China locked down its economy during the early weeks of the Covid-19 pandemic (Gao and Ren 2020).

Finally, China's economic dynamism combined with its massive size gave it powerful leverage in relation to foreign countries and firms that seek access to its market. Ranging from agricultural products and consumer products to tourism, China has emerged as the key market for both advanced and developing economies. These forces converge to make China a major trading partner for a large number of economies. Trade ties with China is one of the key external economic priorities for many, and China's leverage over bilateral relations has increased.

In the wider literature, asymmetric economic interdependence has powerful implications for interstate relations. In his seminal work on the relationship between trade dependence and political power before

World War II, Hirschman (1945) discussed how a dominant state like Germany may create a condition under which it can effectively influence weaker states in Eastern Europe. Subsequently, the modern notion of economic statecraft—the use of economic tools for foreign policy gains—has been developed in a large body of literature in which scholars have expanded the concept of vulnerability, the issue of actors, and the effectiveness of sanctions (Baldwin 1985; Hufbauer, Schott and Elliott 1990; Keohane and Nye 1977). With the rise of China, scholars of economic statecraft have been paying increasing attention to China as an important new actor (Hufbauer and Jung 2020; Norris 2010).

China's revisionist ambitions and increasingly aggressive deployment of economic tools in its diplomacy have made countries particularly concerned about close economic relations with China. What is different about China in economic statecraft from the United States is that, for the most part, it explicitly seeks to deploy its economic power for security purposes (Norris 2010, p. 12). And its unique state capitalist nature gives itself unparallel control over its domestic economic resources (Oh and No 2020). This supports the view that economic dependence on China may create a unique vulnerability that has politico-security implications.

Vietnam-China Trade

Policy discussions of Vietnam's economic dependence on China are largely motivated by chronic trade imbalances between the two countries. China has emerged as Vietnam's largest trading partner and Vietnam continues to record a large trade deficit with China. Large and chronic bilateral trade deficits with China have been the source of much concern in Vietnam. Yet an excessive focus on bilateral trade deficits obscures more important underlying issues. This section examines recent trends in Vietnam's economic relations with China that could have contributed to the dependence debate in question and discusses what other issues need to be brought in to understand the full nature of bilateral relations.

Bilateral trade between Vietnam and China surged in the 2000s after both countries accelerated their integration with the international trade system. The major watershed events were China's accession to the World Trade Organization (WTO) in 2001 and Vietnam's accession in 2006. These were complemented by the China-ASEAN Free Trade Area (CAFTA) that went into effect in 2005. Under CAFTA, ASEAN member states and China agreed to eliminate tariffs for ninety per cent of all traded goods by 2010, while tariff elimination was set for 2015 for Vietnam, along with Cambodia, Laos and Myanmar.[2] As a part of CAFTA, China offered the Early Harvest Program for agricultural products from ASEAN as early as 2003.

The rapid expansion of bilateral trade since the early 2000s made China Vietnam's largest trading partner. Vietnam's merchandise exports to China increased from US$1.5 billion in 2000 to US$41.5 billion in 2019.[3] Its imports from China rose much faster, with an increase from US$1.4 billion to US$75.5 billion in 2019 (Figure 5.1). Since the early 2000s, Vietnam has been running a substantial trade deficit with China. The ratio of imports to exports reached 1.4 as early as 2002 and peaked in 2007 at 3.5. For more than half of the 2010s, Vietnam imported from China more than twice the amount it exported to it. This is reflected in Vietnam's large, chronic trade deficit with its northern neighbour. In 2019, Vietnam's trade deficit with China reached US$35 billion, which accounted for 35 per cent of its total trade deficit. Its second-largest trade deficit was recorded with South Korea (28 per cent), followed by Taiwan (10 per cent).

FIGURE 5.1
Vietnam's Trade with China, 2001–2019 (million US$)

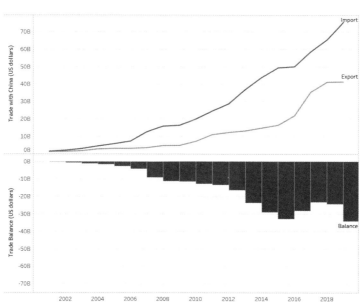

Source: IMF DOTS.

Although China has been one of the largest trading partners of Vietnam, the import side of things has dominated. China's share in Vietnam's total merchandise imports ranged from 24 to 31 per cent during 2001–19 (Figure 5.2). Although its share peaked in 2014 and has been on a downward trend in recent years, this is far higher than experienced by other Southeast Asian countries, excepting Myanmar and Cambodia. On the export side, China's share in Vietnam's exports is large, but still comparable to most of its regional neighbours, seeing figures between 12 and 18 per cent (Figure 5.2). Between 2000 and 2019, China's share in Vietnam's exports rose slightly from 11 to 14 per cent after peaking at 17 per cent in 2018, whilst China's share in imports has been on a stronger upward trend. Although China is Vietnam's largest trade partner, the significance of this requires more nuanced interpretations. China's dominance of Vietnam's exports is at a high level but is not as high as some other Asia-Pacific countries, such as Australia (34 per cent), South Korea (27 per cent) and Japan

FIGURE 5.2
China's Share in Vietnam's Exports and Imports,
Compared with Southeast Asian countries, 2001–19

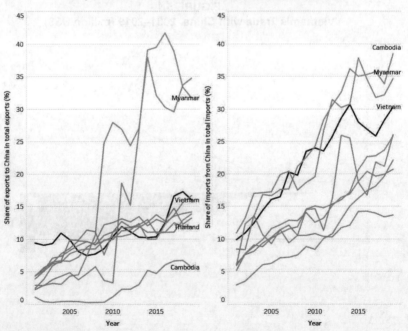

Note: The dark line represents Vietnam.
Source: IMF DOTS.

(20 per cent), as of 2018. Still, combined with a large, chronic trade deficit, this can be a source of serious policy concerns.

Over the past few years, Vietnam has been the country with the largest trade deficit with China in Southeast Asia (Figure 5.3). The deficit reached a record US$33 billion in 2015. In fact, Vietnam's trade deficit accounted for 43 per cent of ASEAN's total trade deficit with China that year.[4] The rapid increase in Vietnam's trade deficit with China started around 2007. Vietnam's accession to the WTO in 2006 may have contributed to an increase in processing and assembly using imported Chinese supplies.

In an economic sense, overall trade balances, not bilateral trade balances with a specific country, should be the focus of policy discussions (IMF 2019). Moreover, in the era of global value chains (GVCs) and global production networks (GPNs), a trade deficit is not a straightforward issue. For many countries participating in GVCs or GPNs, trade deficits are the result of importing intermediate goods for assembly or processing for export to final destinations. In fact, Vietnam itself is the prime example. The rapid expansion of Vietnam-China trade and the surge of Vietnam's trade deficit with China are largely driven by the global production networks established across

FIGURE 5.3
Vietnam's Trade Balance with China, Compared with Southeast Asian Countries, 2000–2019 (million US$)

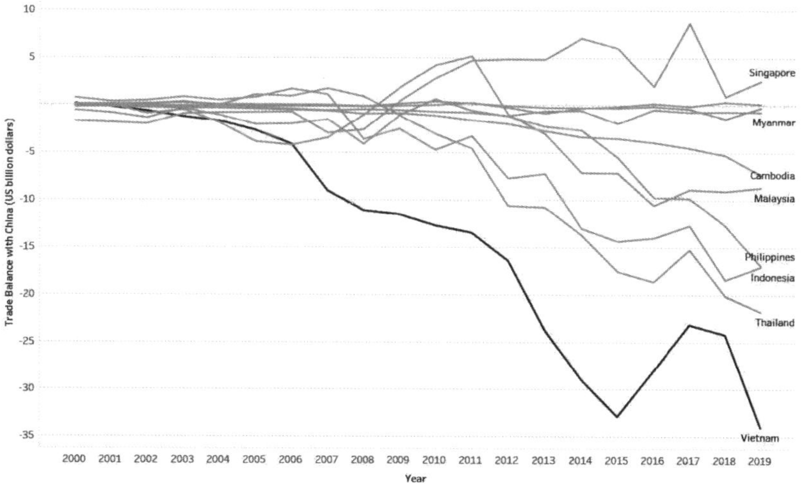

Note: The dark line represents Vietnam.
Source: IMF DOTS.

China, Vietnam and many other Asian countries. Vietnam is the top trading partner for China in Southeast Asia and it has the largest trade deficit with China in the region. But forming a regional production network with China allowed Vietnam to dramatically increase its exports to the United States. As a result, Vietnam has a huge trade surplus with the United States and has a more or less balanced trade account as a whole.

The composition of trade between Vietnam and China reflects the regional production network. Machinery and electrical products accounted for almost half of both Vietnam's exports to and imports from China in 2017 (Table 5.1). The top product groups in both exports and imports are largely the same, except the vegetable group, including fruits, which is the second-largest export product and represents 15 per cent of bilateral exports to China.

The share of intermediate goods in Vietnam's imports from China was 42 per cent in 2000. This increased to about 60 per cent in 2005 and to 72 per cent in 2015, before stagnating in 2019 (Table 5.2). The imports of intermediate goods rose much faster than total imports from China. This accounted for most of the rise in trade deficits. It should be emphasized that the high levels of imports of intermediate products does not necessarily indicate technological dependence, either at the aggregate or bilateral levels. Moreover, advanced economies use imported goods and services extensively to support export competitiveness. As a result, domestic value-added ratios in overall manufacturing exports are often low for these countries (Dollar, Khan and Pei, 2019). Nonetheless, Vietnam's reliance on overseas parts and components is a result of technological underdevelopment and not managerial decisions, and this should be a subject of serious policy discussion.

TABLE 5.1
Top Products in Vietnam's Trade with China, 2017

Product Group	Export Product Share (%)	Product Group	Import Product Share (%)
Machinery and electronics	43.7	Machinery and electronics	47.1
Vegetables	14.6	Textiles and clothing	13.6
Textiles and clothing	9.2	Metals	12.7
Miscellaneous	8.9	Chemicals	6.6
Plastic or rubber	5.3	Plastic or rubber	5.8
Others	18.3	Others	14.1
Total	100.0	Total	100.0

Source: WITS, World Bank.

TABLE 5.2
Share of Intermediate Goods in Vietnam's Imports from China

Year	Intermediates Import (US$ millions)	Total Import (US$ millions)	Share (%)
2000	580	1,401	41.4
2005	3,503	5,900	59.4
2010	12,475	20,204	61.7
2015	35,342	49,441	71.5
2019	54,656	75,586	72.3

Source: Author's calculations using data from UN Comtrade.

Now we turn to recent changes in Vietnam's export competitiveness. A common way to evaluate a country's export competitiveness is by using the revealed comparative advantage (RCA) index (Balassa 1965). The RCA measures the ratio of the share of exports of a product in a country's total exports to the share of exports of that product in total world exports. An RCA value can range from zero to infinity, and it is conventional to interpret a value above one as indicating a comparative advantage in the product and a value below one meaning a comparative disadvantage. RCA measures across countries are also used to compare export competitiveness.

Figure 5.4 shows the trends in RCA measures for China and Vietnam in two manufacturing-related product categories. The first product group is machinery and electrical products categorized by the Harmonized System (HS), 1988/92, while the second is the general manufactures according to the Standard International Trade Classification (SITC), Revision 2. In both product groups, China's export competitiveness is higher than that of Vietnam. Yet the gaps between the countries narrowed in the 2010s, especially in machinery and electronics. This suggests that, although the gap still exists, Vietnam has indeed transformed itself into a formidable exporter of some manufactured goods, especially electronics.[5] Among products whose values are greater than one, Vietnam vastly outperforms China in office machines (SITC 751) and telecommunications equipment and parts (SITC 764). Overall, the data confirm the well-known view that Vietnam has significantly increased its export competitiveness for certain products.

The presence of Vietnam's large and persistent bilateral trade deficit with China is the result of its integration into the East Asian regional production network (Korwatanasakul n.d.; Truong n.d.; Vũ n.d.). This has been the driver of Vietnam's successful transformation

FIGURE 5.4
RCA Trends for China and Vietnam in Manufactures

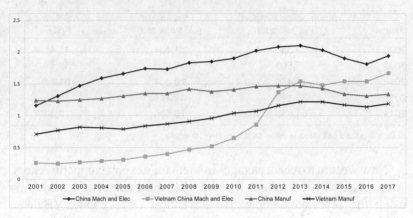

Note: Mach and Elec represents product groups 84–85 in HS 1988/92.
Source: World Bank WITS

into a major global manufacturer of consumer electronics. A case can be made that Vietnam's bilateral trade deficit with China contributes to its overall trade balance. Therefore, reducing its bilateral trade deficit with China may not be a policy priority from a strictly economic point of view.

Nonetheless, bilateral trade balance has important political ramifications. On the other side of the coin, Vietnam's persistent trade surplus with the United States puts increasing pressure on Vietnam-US relations. One of the significant consequences of the recent US-China trade disputes has been the expansion in Vietnam's exports to the US market. This has been facilitated and accelerated, although not exclusively, by the diversification strategies pursued by multinational firms of moving their production bases away from China to Vietnam. The subsequent surge in Vietnam's trade surplus with the United States put Vietnam on the US government currency manipulator watchlist in 2019 (Nakano and Kawanami 2019), and Vietnam was labelled a currency manipulator in 2020 in the last days of the Trump administration (Politi and Szalay 2020). One could argue that the current arrangement may not be sustainable given increasing US pressure on the one hand and Vietnam's dependence on Chinese inputs on the other. Certainly, Vietnam needs to manage bilateral trade surplus with these countries for its immediate and medium-term goals.

From a long-term perspective, a more important point is that policy discussions should be focused on the structure of a country's trade rather than its bilateral trade balance. Close to half of Vietnam's exports to China are of machinery and electrical parts, and a substantial share of exports are accounted for by agricultural products. These factors create different types of vulnerability for Vietnam, and they will be discussed in greater detail in the next section.

Typology of Trade Shocks and Vietnam's Vulnerability

Vietnam's vulnerability in its increasingly close economic ties with China can be systematically analysed by constructing a typology of trade shocks, where shocks are understood as events that exist outside the control of Vietnam. The typology can be constructed by combining two dimensions: the *intentionality* of shocks from China and the type of *transmission channels* for those shocks, particularly in the type of trade between the two countries.

For the intentionality dimension, the distinction between unintentional shocks and intentional shocks is crucial. *Unintentional* shocks are the result of unintended events in China such as natural disasters, outbreaks of infectious disease, or political crises that could suddenly disrupt Vietnam's export linkages, supply chains, tourism networks, and other economic activities tied to China. The suspension of Vietnam's exports to China through border-crossings or production disruptions experienced in Vietnam and many other countries as a result of the lockdowns in China during the Covid-19 pandemic are examples. The risk of disruptions increase as Vietnam's integration with China intensifies.

The other type of shock involves those to Vietnam's economy created by measures *intentionally* imposed by the Chinese government. Such measures include a wide range of decisions by the Chinese government made for economic, administrative and political purposes.

TABLE 5.3
A Typology of Trade Shocks

		Intentionality of the events in China		
		Unintentional	Intentional	
			Economic or administrative	Political
Transmission channels	Vietnam's exports to China	Market access disruptions	Import restrictions	
	Vietnam's imports from China	Supply disruptions	Export controls	

They can be further divided into two groups based on their motives: (1) economic and administrative motives, and (2) political or foreign policy motives. The former can be understood as usual non-trade barriers in the form of health, safety and environmental standards. The latter, politically motivated measures, also known as economic sanctions, have been used increasingly by the Chinese government in recent years. It should also be noted that although the motives may differ between these two subcategories, the tools are often identical. This is because China's coercion is rarely officially announced or codified in the manner that Western nations would, and it often takes the form of implementing safety and labour standards.

China's use of economic punishment to influence the policies of other countries has increased over the past decades as its economic might and political influence have risen. China has previously applied sanctions in relation to territorial disputes, foreign arms sales to Taiwan, meetings of foreign leaders with the Dalai Lama, or international criticism of its human rights record (Zhang 2018). But in recent years the scope of policies that trigger sanctions have expanded to any developments across the globe that in China's view could threaten its security, undermine its global prestige or be interpreted as critical of or offensive to China. China's punitive measures imposed in response to South Korea's deployment of the Terminal High Altitude Area Defense (THAAD) missile system in 2016 is another well-known example. The most formidable weapon China has at its disposal is its large domestic market, which most of the world has been vying to gain and to maintain access to. Any country that relies on China for a substantive part of its exports is vulnerable to these shocks imposed by China.

The *transmission channels* of shocks constitute another dimension of the framework. This channel can be divided into two categories based on the direction and type of trade between Vietnam and China. The first category is Vietnam's exports to China. Here, the likelihood of shocks may differ depending on the sectors. The largest export sector, as discussed in the preceding section, is electronics. This is the key to the global production networks that Vietnam belongs to, along with China. The other important export sectors are agricultural products and tourism. The latter two need serious attention because they are locally controlled export sectors that Vietnam has greater influence over compared with the export-oriented electronics industry, which is largely dominated by multinationals. Both groups are important to Vietnam's export performance, but the likelihood that they will suffer from shocks differs when it comes to intentional shocks. This is because China has chosen non-strategic imports such as agriculture and tourism as a more likely domain for economic sanctions. Economic sanctions impose costs on the sanctioning state, so often the least costly sector will be chosen for such as policy. It is also the case that, unlike the multi-country production of electronics, Vietnam's agricultural exports—largely driven by fresh fruits—and tourism exports are bilateral in nature, thus lowering the risk of the involvement of other countries for China.

The second category is Vietnam's imports from China. For Vietnam, the major part of this flow is captured by its imports of parts and components and of industrial machinery from China for assembly and processing in the country for export. In fact, this second category has driven the sharp rise in Vietnam's trade volume and trade deficits with China. This channel can be most vulnerable to supply chain disruptions. What we have seen most in Vietnam is import disruptions as a result of a pandemic such as Covid-19, but it is possible that Vietnam may experience export controls that China imposes for political reasons in the future.

These two dimensions combine to produce the four categories in Table 5.3. *Market access disruptions* and *Supply disruptions* describe the risks of experiencing unintentional shocks to Vietnam's trade with China. A political crisis, a natural disaster such as an earthquake or flood, or an outbreak of an infectious disease in China could disrupt Vietnam's exports and imports. Exports can be negatively affected by border closures or other logistical challenges, while imports may also be disrupted, which will damage Vietnam's industrial production and its exports to the global market. *Import restrictions* and *Export controls*, on the other hand, represent the risks associated with intentional shocks. Intentional shocks to Vietnam's exports to China are currently the most important category. In addition, although they can be driven by both economic and political motives, the politically motivated shocks require particular attention, and this matter will be discussed in greater detail below. The last category, *Export controls*, represents shocks created by export controls enacted by China on its exports to Vietnam. In the worst-case scenario, this could restrict the supply of crucial parts and components to Vietnam in a strategically important manufacturing sector. Global examples of this type of scenario include US export restrictions aimed at the Chinese telecommunication equipment company Huawei in 2020 and Japan's curbs on exports of materials used for semiconductors in Korea in 2019.

Among the four types of shocks, the category of *Import restrictions*, which includes Chinese economic coercion, warrants further discussion. Beijing's punitive economic measures on other countries have been selective. Such an imposition is often determined by the industry trait of whether the sector to be targeted is "strategic". This is consistent with long-held observations about Chinese state capitalism that the state intervenes in industries that have strategic value to the national economy (Hsueh 2006). This is why China's retaliations against countries normally target consumer products and non-strategic service imports such as media products and tourism. The well-known cases of sanctions by China on Norwegian salmon (Kolstad 2020), bananas from the Philippines (Zhang 2019), and South Korea's cosmetics, entertainment and tourism (Yang 2019) fit such a pattern. Restricting imports of dispensable food products and tourism services is less costly on the Chinese economy than bans on key strategic products such as semiconductors that are hard to substitute. This suggests that technological innovation has important security implications.

Trade Shocks and Vulnerabilities Illustrated

This section discusses examples of each category and it will help to clarify Vietnam's vulnerability. Cases from other countries will also be presented to illustrate some types that are potential risks for Vietnam that have not yet been realized.

Market access disruptions is the first category of trade shocks. These are disruptions that constitute sudden changes in market access for Vietnamese products in the Chinese markets. The level of vulnerability increases as Vietnam's exports to China in both goods and services increase. Such a case could take place when unintentional events in China disrupt the access of Vietnamese exports. A useful example is the sharp decline of Vietnamese fruit exports to China during the Covid-19 pandemic in 2020 because of border closures and other complications (Nitta and Phoonphongphiphat 2020). Vietnam's fruit exports to China declined by 26 per cent during the first eight months of 2020 compared with the same period the previous year (CEIC n.d.). China has emerged as a key market for Vietnam's agricultural exports in recent years. Supported by an expanding middle class, China's demand for imported fruit has been on the rise over the past decade. Vietnam's exports of fruits and vegetables increased from US$302 million to US$2.8 billion in 2018. China accounted for 66 per cent of Vietnam's fruit and vegetable exports in 2019, a figure down from 76 per cent in 2017, as seen in Figure 5.5. The main fruits exported are dragon fruit, watermelons and lychees, along with many other tropical fruits. In addition to market access restrictions, a sudden change in consumer confidence could trigger a demand shock. Chilean cherries were also hit hard by the sharp decline in demand in the Chinese market after the onset of the Covid-19 pandemic. Demand for imported high-end fruit such as cherries and grapes is supported by discretionary spending. The economic downturn could sharply reduce consumer spending in 2020 (Hu 2020). These are examples of demand shocks created by natural disasters or economic slowdowns as unintended events taking place in China.

Supply disruptions is the second category of shock. This is where unexpected events in China disrupt the supply of important industrial inputs to Vietnam. As Vietnam's integration with China-centred supply chains intensifies, this type of vulnerability may become more severe. As the previous section shows, major Chinese imports to Vietnam are intermediate goods. Again, the recent Covid-19

FIGURE 5.5
Vietnam's Exports of Fruits and Vegetables
to China, 2013–19 (million US$)

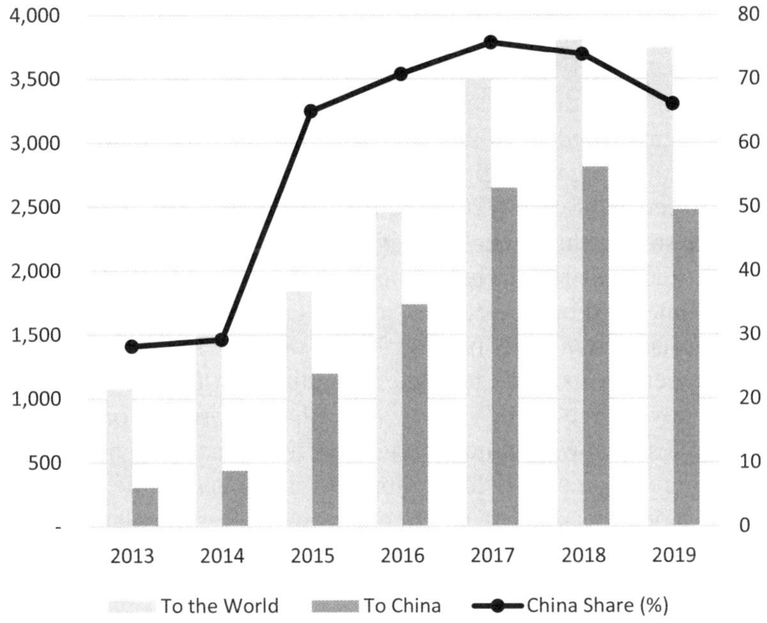

Source: CEIC.

FIGURE 5.6
China's Share in Vietnam's Tourist Arrivals, 2011–18

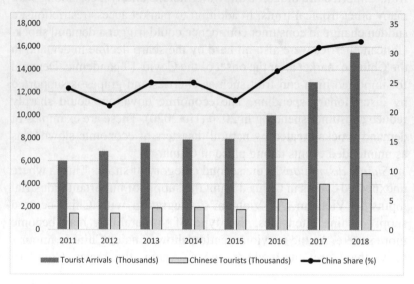

Source: ASEANstats.

pandemic provides an example. Vietnam's export industries rely heavily on China for materials, components and equipment for industrial production. When the coronavirus pandemic forced border closures between China and Vietnam from both sides, manufacturers in Vietnam faced difficulties acquiring parts and other supplies from China (Nguyen and Vu 2020). Samsung, a global smartphone maker and Vietnam's largest single investor, had to fly supplies of parts from China (Reed and Song 2020). South Korean phone manufacturers in Vietnam source thirty per cent of phone components from China, making them particularly vulnerable (Reed and Song 2020). Smartphones and other electronic devices number among Vietnam's top exports, driving the recent rise in Vietnam's exports and the improvement in its trade balance. In addition to travel restrictions, another key source of the shock was the halt of production in China during the shutdown. Although factories in Vietnam did not have to close as a result of supply disruptions during the pandemic, Hyundai, a South Korean carmaker, had to close down all of its plants after it ran out of components—specifically, engine wire-harnesses—from China (White et al. 2020).

Import restrictions is the third category. This category involves shocks to Vietnam's exports that are intentionally created by China.

Vietnam has not seen a clear type of this shock. Thus, the experiences of other countries may be useful. China's punishment of South Korea in 2016–17 for the latter's deployment of the THAAD missile defence system is a recent example. South Korea experienced unprecedented economic retaliation by China as a result of its deployment of the THAAD system in July 2016. The THAAD system was intended as protection against North Korean nuclear ballistic missiles, but China opposed it because it felt the system had the potential to compromise China's deterrent against a nuclear attack by the United States. China strongly protested the deployment of the THAAD and threatened retaliation if South Korea and the United States proceeded with it. After the deployment was under way, a wide range of economic measures were introduced by China. These included the cancelation of media and entertainment events featuring Korean artists in China; the suspension of Chinese group tours, charter flights and cruise ships to South Korea; restrictions on the issuing of business visas to South Koreans; the exclusion of South Korean electronic batteries from Chinese government subsidies; and anti-dumping investigations against South Korean chemical products (YTN 2017). Lotte Mart—a subsidiary of the Korean conglomerate Lotte Group, who provided a golf course as a site for the THAAD system—saw twenty-three of its stores in China forced to shut down on the grounds of "safety violations" (HRI 2017). Lotte Mart eventually backed out of the Chinese market in 2018, while other Lotte businesses faced tax investigations, delays in licensing approval, investigations for fire code violations, and property seizures (Lim 2019). In addition, popular boycotts for South Korean consumer products and a deteriorating environment for South Korean businesses negatively affected overall South Korean goods and services exports to and investment in China during this period. Chinese unofficial sanctions ended only in early 2018 after the new government in South Korea made concessions to Beijing on the THAAD missile shield.[6]

South Korea's tourism industry suffered severely during this period because it relied heavily on the Chinese market. In 2016, forty-seven per cent of all tourists who visited South Korea came from China (UNWTO 2018). It is ironic that one of the reasons for the surge of Chinese tourists in South Korea in the early 2010s was the Chinese government's encouragement of shifting Chinese tourist flows away from Japan in the wake of the maritime disputes over Diaoyudao/ Senkaku island (Paik 2020). Overall, the economic damage was substantial. A research institute under the Export-Import Bank of Korea estimated the damage at between 730 and 1,620 hundred billion

Korean won in lost exports of goods and content, investment earnings, and tourism revenue (2017). China's economic sanctions in the wake of the THAAD deployment brought to prominence in the public mind South Korea's "overdependence" on China for many of its economic sectors (Paik 2020).

Vietnam could face similar economic coercion from China in the future. Vietnam's consumer goods, agricultural products and tourism services to China would be vulnerable to similar sanctions. As discussed above, the Chinese market accounted for 66 per cent of Vietnam's fruit and vegetable exports in 2019 (Figure 5.5). China's importance to Vietnam's tourism industry holds a similar position. Chinese tourists represented 32 per cent of total tourist arrivals in 2018 (Figure 5.6).[7] The level of reliance on Chinese markets shows a strong upward trend. This inevitably increases Vietnam's vulnerability to economic coercion motivated by China's foreign policy interests.

Export controls, the final category, has not been experienced at a noticeable scale by Vietnam, but it could certainly happen in the future. It is another type of economic coercion, which can be defined as targeted supply disruptions imposed for strategic reasons (Seaman 2012). China's unofficial embargo of rare earth shipments to Japan in 2010 in retaliation for a territorial dispute in the East China Sea is a typical example. Japan detained a Chinese fishing boat captain in September after he had his trawler ram Japanese Coast Guard vessels in disputed waters near the Diaoyudao/Senkaku Islands. The captain was later released. His detention led to a diplomatic standoff between the two countries. Soon after this, China was accused of halting shipments of rare earth elements to Japan at its ports in retaliation. Rare earth elements are a group of seventeen metallic elements used in the production of a wide range of high-technology consumer electronics such as batteries for smart phones and electronic vehicles, clean energy products and weapons systems. China controlled ninety-seven per cent of global supply and Japan was the largest market for Chinese rare earth elements (Shen et al. 2020). The Chinese government consistently denied the existence of a ban and attributed the incidents to overzealous local actors such as military and local government officials, customs officers and port workers who held up rare earth shipments to punish Japan in the absence of an official directive from the central government (Seamen 2019). This bears the hallmark of China's economic sanctions, which can be seen in other cases.

The 2010 embargo brought attention to the vulnerability of Japan and other industrialized economies to their dependence on China for the supply of its strategic minerals. China's control over and willingness to use rare earth elements as a diplomatic weapon alarmed many because it could directly affect the global manufacturing of high-tech information and communication technology (ICT), which could have grave security implications. Japan had managed to reduce its dependence on rare earth supplies from China between 2010 and 2012 when there had been another flare up of a territorial dispute with China (Seaman 2012). Nine years later, in 2019, China threatened to cut supplies of rare earth elements to the United States amid escalating trade tensions. This time, China officially announced it would use the supply of rare earth elements as a diplomatic weapon. *The People's Daily*, the official newspaper of the Communist Party of China, literally warned that China would cut off rare earth minerals as a countermeasure in the escalated trade battle after President Xi Jinping visited rare earth mining and processing facilities in Jiangxi a few days earlier (*People's Daily* 2019).

Vietnam's industrialized economy is growingly vulnerable to China's economic coercion since its supply chains are now deeply integrated with China. China has already demonstrated to the world that it is willing to use such interdependence to its strategic advantage. Vietnam's reliance on Chinese inputs for its export-oriented industries thus has additional security implications.

Economic Dependence, Responses and Technological Progress

Vietnam's responses to the risk of economic dependence on China can be divided into two domains. The first response, largely to unintentional trade shocks, comprises market and supply chain diversification and risk management. The first type of response is represented by supply chain risk management and diversification of economic relations. Even before the Covid-19 pandemic in 2020, this was high on the economic policy agenda for the Vietnamese government. It bears emphasis that the choice of markets and supply chains are sticky. Realignment, including diversification and reshoring, has been rare after previous crises (Freund et al. 2020).

The second response, directed at intentional shocks, requires technological superiority in addition to the first type of strategy. What I want to focus on here is the second type of response. China's willingness to take advantage of the vulnerability of its trade partners for foreign policy gains means that Vietnam's trade dependence on China can readily turn into security vulnerability, as evidenced by the recent experiences of its Asian neighbours. While China is more willing to restrict the imports of consumer and agricultural products as well as non-strategic services such as tourism, it is less willing to restrict imports of critical parts and components that are hard to replace in its high-tech industries. This has been confirmed by past cases. During the Chinese sanctions on South Korea over the THAAD deployment, South Korea's ICT exports to China, dominated mainly by semiconductors and display panels, were barely affected (IITP 2017). South Korean semiconductors were critical to China's electronics industries and no alternatives were readily available. China imports the majority of its semiconductors and has long relied on foreign technology despite it being the world's largest market for semiconductors (Ernst 2015). This is another reason why it is important to achieve technological competitiveness by moving up the value chain and through industrial upgrading.

Vietnam faces a daunting task of technological upgrading despite its recent success in transforming itself as a global manufacturer of electronics and other consumer products. Vietnam relies heavily on China for intermediate goods for its export-oriented manufacturing sector, while its technological innovation lags significantly behind China. In fact, this is consistent with the broader patterns in Southeast Asia. Expert observations and academic studies suggest that over the past years Southeast Asia in general has struggled to upgrade or move up the value chain relative to China, particularly in ICT exports (Tham et al. 2016).

It is also the case that this challenge has been well known to Vietnamese policymakers. A policy response has been pursued as part of Vietnam's development strategy to avoid the so-called "middle-income trap" after its initial industrial take-off (Ohno 2009). To escape the trap, transforming Vietnam to be an innovative and technologically advanced economy has been placed high on the country's reform agenda (World Bank and Ministry of Planning and Investment of Vietnam 2016). Despite policy commitment to a bold investment in the country's science and technology system and higher education reform, progress has been limited (Klingler-Vidra and 2020). The challenges on the input side are even reflected in Vietnamese students' overseas education, which constitutes another important source of human capital in science and engineering. Recent data show that business—not science, technology, engineering or mathematics—was the top area of study for Vietnamese students studying at US universities in 2013–14 (Desilver 2015).

One way of assessing the outcome of Vietnam's technological catching up and innovation is to analyse global patent data. The comparative advantage and export competitiveness discussed in the early sections do not necessarily indicate technological advancement or dependence. Table 5.4 shows the trends of Vietnam's patent filing performance in the US market using data from the United States Patent and Trademark Office (USPTO). It also reports the number of patent applications and patents granted in each year from 2006 to 2015. Vietnam's overall performance is disappointing. Before 2011, the filings were in the single digits and accounted for less than 0.2 per cent of all foreign filings with the USPTO. The number of patents actually granted stayed below ten for most years, accounting for about 0.1 per cent of total patents of foreign origin for most of the period. In 2015 Vietnam was in 65th place out of 143 countries, with at least a single filing, and 85th place out of 125 countries, with at least one patent. What should receive particular attention is that Vietnam's relative position among countries has barely improved over ten years. This is in stark contrast to China's performance. In 2015 China filed 21,386 patent applications in the United States and 9,004 patents were granted. China's improvement over time is noteworthy. China's share of foreign applications rose from 1.8 per cent in 2006 to 7.1 per cent in 2015. And its share of total patents of foreign origin rose from 1.0 per cent to 5.3 per cent over the same period.

One can further argue that Vietnam's excessive reliance on Chinese inputs and the country's limited technological progress may not be separate issues. Economic dependence on China may be discussed

TABLE 5.4
Vietnam's Recent Patent Application Filings and
Grants at the US Patent and Trademark Office

Country	2006	2007	2008	2009	2010	2011	2012	2013	2014	2015	Ranking in 2015*
Vietnam's patent applications filed in the US	5	6	10	1	9	13	12	18	32	32	65/143
% foreign origin	0.1	0.2	0.2	0.0	0.1	0.1	0.1	0.1	0.2	0.1	
Vietnam's patents granted by the US	0	1	0	2	2	0	4	10	7	5	85/125
% foreign origin	0.0	0.1	0.0	0.1	0.1	0.0	0.1	0.2	0.1	0.1	

Note: * Rankings in foreign countries with at least one application or grant.
Source: USPTO.

in relation to Vietnam's so-called middle-income challenge. Being able to use Chinse inputs and equipment made it easier for Vietnam and many other developing countries to jump-start manufacturing-led industrialization rather than develop their export industries from scratch. The problem, however, is that a country's economic structure is disincentivized to pursue technological progress, as can seen by Vietnam's limited success in nurturing local supporting industries. The risk of the China boom is that the structure of Vietnam's economy is reshaped as a result of short-term largess at the expense of long-term sustainable development, and that the country loses an opportunity of growing into a high-income economy (Booth 2020; Coxhead 2007).

Conclusion

The first key finding of this chapter is that the concerns over Vietnam's economic dependence on China are legitimate and important, at least in the domain of trade relations, but they require a nuanced understanding. Vietnam is an extreme case in Southeast Asia, although not an outlier, in terms of its trade ties with China. On the import side in particular, Vietnam's dependence on China is unusually high in comparison with Southeast Asia's other industrialized economies, and is closer to the levels of countries that are much less developed (Figure 5.2). Vietnam's trade deficit with China is also outside the normal range of other Southeast Asian countries. This was the result of Vietnam's successful integration with the China-centred "Factory Asia" system by importing critical parts and components from China and turning itself into an efficient processing hub, which enabled its rapid economic growth. In that sense, Vietnam effectively took advantage of its proximity to and supply chain complementarity with China for export-led industrialization.

The more important issue is that Vietnam has asymmetrically limited control over its regional production network with China. The structure of bilateral trade shows that Vietnam continues to rely on imported Chinese materials for its export industries, and there are few signs of it moving up the value chain. The typology exercise clearly shows that Vietnam is exposed to various types of trade shocks arising from China. Diversifying its trade markets and foreign investment profile alone will not make it less vulnerable to more serious types of shocks such as economic coercion by China. Vietnam needs to tackle industrial upgrading more aggressively in order to improve its power in its relations with China. The experiences of other countries show that Chinese economic sanctions are sector-specific, even within a single country. But this may be an even greater challenge for Vietnam than trading partner diversification because it is tied to the more general development challenge of industrial upgrading and achieving technological progress by indigenous firms.

Going forward, Vietnam is in a position to benefit in the short term from the supply chain shift currently under way in Asia. The Covid-19 pandemic accelerated the relocation of manufacturing bases out of China that had already been taking place. This has created opportunities for many countries in Asia, and Vietnam is expected to benefit the most because of its uniquely favourable combination of business environment, infrastructure and labour costs. How such a realignment will affect Vietnam's vulnerability to China depends on the structure of new supply chain arrangements. GVC realignment may reduce Vietnam's imports of intermediate goods from China by producing supplies in Vietnam or by finding alternative trading partners. If realigned GVCs simply result in further shifting the assembly and production hub from China to Vietnam, Vietnam will continue to need large volumes of imported inputs from China. This will put double pressure on Vietnam by exposing it to greater trade tensions with the United States and to intentional and unintentional shocks from China.

Finally, what are the implications of Vietnam's economic dependence for its foreign policy towards China? One of the key mediating factors in this process is how the Vietnamese Communist Party and its government respond to the anti-China nationalism currently so pervasive in Vietnamese society. Domestic policy suggestions could prompt fierce protests if they are perceived to pave the way for China's encroachment on Vietnamese territory and the loss of Vietnam's sovereignty. The politicization of the China threat during the 2018 protests against the Special Economic Zone (SEZ) Law is a good example. From June to September 2018, popular protests took place across Vietnam against the proposed SEZ Law. These protests were driven by the fear that the ninety-nine-year land lease available to foreign investors under the SEZ Law could lead to Chinese control over Vietnamese land in the three strategic locations of Quang Ninh, Khanh Hoa and Kien Giang. Because of the intensity and scale of the protests, the government delayed the passage of the proposed law, and it has been on hold since then. That the Vietnamese government made concessions in response to popular protests was a rare event in the country's political process. It has important foreign policy implications and will be discussed in Chapter 8 of this book.

In domains where China's provocation is direct and palpable, the political task of managing nationalist reactions could be even more challenging for the Vietnamese government. The large-scale anti-China protests that took place during the 2014 Haiyang Shiyou 981 oil rig crisis was one such test. Although the government was able to restrain anti-China sentiments during this particular crisis using an effective propaganda strategy (Bui 2017), it is far from clear whether it could do the same in the future. In the economic domain, a comparable high-profile episode, though currently a rare event, would be China's use of deliberate measures to leverage Vietnam's economic vulnerability for its own foreign policy gains. Nonetheless, if Beijing imposes restrictions on the importation of agricultural products from Vietnam or export controls on capital and intermediate goods for Vietnam's critical industries as a form of economic coercion, it will certainly draw a backlash from the Vietnamese public. It remains to be seen how successful the Vietnamese government will be in managing anti-China nationalism in this new context.

Appendix

TABLE 5.A1
RCA Values for China and Vietnam, 2017

Code	Product	China	Vietnam	RCA (Vietnam) RCA (China)
751	Office machines	1.29	13.19	11.91
764	Telecommunication equipment, n.e.s.; & parts, n.e.s.	2.91	8.36	5.45
724	Textile & leather machinery, & parts thereof, n.e.s.	1.62	3.11	1.49
773	Equipment for distributing electricity, n.e.s.	1.41	2.38	0.97
811	Prefabricated buildings	1.36	1.51	0.14
763	Sound recorders or reproducers	2.53	2.66	0.13
792	Aircraft & associated equipment; spacecraft, etc.	0.14	0.16	0.02

Note: RCA values for electrical equipment, electronics, computers and components, and office Equipment (SITC 71–81, Rev3).
Source: UNCTAD (UNCTADstat).

FIGURE 5.A1
Chinese FDI in Vietnam, 2011–19 (million US$)

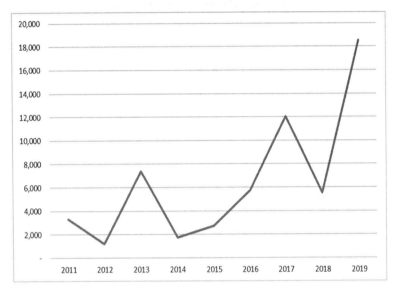

Source: CEIC

FIGURE 5.A2
Share of FDI in Vietnam by Country, 2011–19 (%)

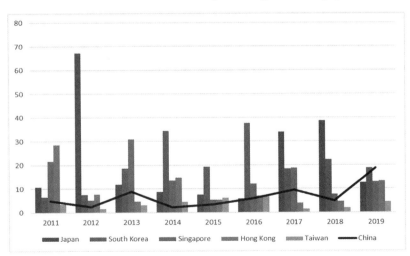

Source: CEIC.

FIGURE 5.A3
China's Development Aid and Financing to Vietnam, 2000–2014 (million US$)

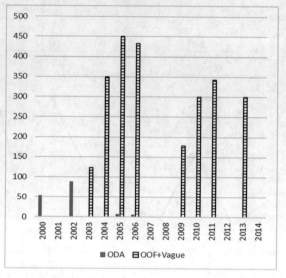

Source: AidData.

Figure 5.A4
China's Construction Contracts in Vietnam (million US$)

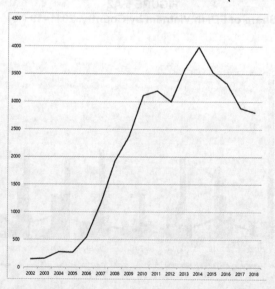

Source: CEIC.

Notes

1. China is a major investor in Vietnam but not a dominant one, although 2019 saw an upsurge in its investment. Chinese investment in Vietnam increased from US$3.4 billion in 2011 to 18.6 billion in 2019 (see Figure 5.A1 in Appendix). Traditionally, FDI in Vietnam has been dominated by East Asian countries. Japan, South Korea, Taiwan and China have been the top investors, along with Hong Kong and Singapore. In terms of share, China accounted for an average of 6.8 per cent of total inbound FDI in 2011–19, although it jumped to 19 per cent, the second largest, in 2019 (see Figure 5.A2 in Appendix). Although the expansion of bilateral trade between two counties and the rise of Chinese investment in Vietnam coincided in the past decade, it is unclear to what extent Chinese investment is linked to the global production network. In the absence of sectoral investment data it is difficult to answer this question. What is publicly available is China's sectoral investment in ASEAN countries as a whole. According to ASEANstats, about 50 per cent of Chinese investment in ASEAN in 2014–19 went into financial services (25 per cent) and real estate activities (23 per cent). Manufacturing comes in third place but only accounts for 14 per cent. Vietnam is not the top destination for Chinese investment in Southeast Asia. The official Chinese statistics indicate that in 2011–18 Vietnam received an average of 5 per cent of China's total FDI in the region, whilst over 70 per cent went to Singapore (45 per cent), Indonesia (14 per cent) and Malaysia (9 per cent) (CEIC). Beyond FDI, China's other economic activities in Vietnam, such as development financing and infrastructure development, are not expanding in the same manner. Data on China's development financing in Vietnam is limited, but AidData suggests it is not on the rise (Dreher et al. 2017) (Figure 5.A3 in Appendix). Chinese government data also indicate that, curiously, China's infrastructure contracts in Vietnam have been declining since 2014 (CEIC). See Figure 5.A4 in Appendix.

2. CAFTA was the first of its kind that ASEAN as a bloc signed with an external trading partner, and it has been the most important agreement that has governed China-ASEAN trade relations since then. It is true that ASEAN records a persistent trade deficit with China, but CAFTA's contribution is not straightforward. This is because for many member states of ASEAN trade deficits with China predate CAFTA.

3. Unless indicated otherwise, all trade statistics are from IMF DOTS.

4. ASEAN's trade deficit with China reached US$103 billion in 2019.

5. Table 5.A1 in the Appendix shows the RCA values for China and Vietnam in 2017 for electrical equipment, electronics, computers and components, and office equipment (SITC 71–81, Revision 3)

6. All the retaliations discussed above are "suspected" cases because there was no official announcement by the Chinse government. For the entire period, the Chinese government denied the existence of any official directive or instructions.

7. For the oil projects in the South China Sea, Vietnam had suspended development projects a number of times because of Chinese threats. The nature of the threats were "military", however, and not economic retaliation.

The most recent example is when PetroVietnam, the country's state-owned energy enterprise, halted its joint development of offshore oil and gas with Spanish energy firm Repsol (Hayton 2018).

References

ASEANstats. n.d. https://www.aseanstats.org (accessed 26 September 2020).

Balassa, Bela. 1965. "Trade Liberalisation and Revealed Comparative Advantage". *Manchester School of Economics and Social Studies* 33, no. 2 (May): 99–123.

Booth, Anne. 2020. "ASEAN-China Trade and Investment: Diversity versus Dependence". In *The Deer and the Dragon: Southeast Asia and China in the 21st Century*, edited by Donald K. Emmerson, pp. 65–87. Shorenstein Asia-Pacific Research Center/ISEAS – Yusof Ishak Institute.

CEIC. n.d. CEIC Database. https://www.ceicdata.com/en/indicators (accessed 16 August 2020).

Chheang, Vannarith. 2018. "China's Economic Statecraft in Southeast Asia". *ISEAS Perspective*, no. 2018/45, 15 August 2018.

Coxhead, Ian. 2007. "A New Resource Curse? Impacts of China's Boom on Comparative Advantage and Resource Dependence in Southeast Asia". *World Development* 35, no. 7 (July): 1099–119.

Desilver, Drew. 2015. "Growth from Asia Drives Surge in U.S. Foreign Students". Pew Research Center, June 2015. https://www.pew research.org/fact-tank/2015/06/18/growth-from-asia-drives-surge-in-u-s-foreign-students/.

Devadason, Evelyn S., and V.G.R. Chandran. 2019. "Unlocking the Trade Potential in China-ASEAN Relations: The China-Vietnam Context". *Journal of Southeast Asian Economies* 36, no. 3 (December): 380–99.

Dizioli, Allan, Jaime Guajardo, Vladmir Klyuev, Rui Mano, and Mehdi Raissi. 2016. "Spillovers from China's Growth Slowdown and Rebalancing to the ASEAN-5 Economies". International Monetary Fund.

Dollar, David, Bilal Khan, and Jiansuo Pei. 2019. "Chapter 7: Should High Domestic Value Added in Exports be an Objective of Policy?" In *Global Value Chain Development Report 2019: Technological Innovation, Supply Chain Trade, and Workers in a Globalized World*. Washington, DC: World Trade Organization.

Dreher, Axel, Andreas Fuchs, Bradley Parks, Austin Strange, and Michael J. Tierney. 2017. "Aid, China, and Growth: Evidence from a New Global Development Finance Dataset". AidData Working Paper 46. Williamsburg, VA: AidData.

Ernst, Dieter. 2015. "From Catching Up to Forging Ahead: China's Policies for Semiconductors". East-West Center Special Study. Honolulu: East-West Center.

Export-Import Bank of Korea. 2017. "Cheoguen Junggug Gyeongje Jejae Paguep Hyogua Chujeong" [Estimated economic effects of recent Chinese economic sanctions]. Issue Paper. No. 2017–05. Overseas Economic Research Institute.

Freund, Caroline, Aaditya Mattoo, Alen Mulabdic, and Michele Ruta. 2020. "The Supply Chain Shock from Covid-19: Risks and Opportunities". In *COVID-19 in Developing Economies*, edited by Simeon Djankov and Ugo Panizza, pp. 303–15. London: Centre for Economic Policy Research.

Harrell, Peter, Elizabeth Rosenberg, and Edoardo Saravalle. 2018. "China's Use of Coercive Economic Measures". 11 June 2018. Center for New American Security.

Hayton, Bill. 2018. "South China Sea: Vietnam 'Scraps New Oil Project'". BBC, 23 March 2018. https://www.bbc.com/news/world-asia-43507448.

Hsueh, Roselyn. 2016. "State Capitalism, Chinese-Style: Strategic Value of Sectors, Sectoral Characteristics, and Globalization". *Governance* 29, no. 1 (January): 85–102.

Hu, Huifeng. 2020. "Coronavirus: China's 'Cherry Freedom' Vanishes as Consumers Cut Discretionary Spending". *South China Morning Post*, 19 May 2020. https://www.scmp.com/economy/china-economy/article/3084926/coronavirus-chinas-cherry-freedom-vanishes-consumers-cut.

Hufbauer, Gary Clyde, and Euijin Jung. 2020. "What's New in Economic Sanctions?" *European Economic Review* 130: 103572. https://doi.org/10.1016/j.euroecorev.2020.103572.

Hufbauer, Gary Clyde, Jeffrey J. Schott, Kimberly Ann Elliott, and Barbara Oegg. 2009. *Economic Sanctions Reconsidered*. Washington, DC: Peterson Institute for International Economics.

Hyundai Research Institute (HRI). 2017. "Sad Baechie Daruen Juyo Ishuwa Jeonmang" [Major issues and prospects of the THADD deployment]. Issue Paper 17, no. 4.

Institute for Information and Communications Technology Promotion (IITP). 2017. "Sad Baechiro Inhan ICT Saneop Yeonghyang" [Impact of THAAD deployment on the ICT industry]. Daejeon, South Korea.

International Monetary Fund (IMF). 2019. "Chapter 4: The Drivers of Bilateral Trade and the Spillovers from Tariffs". In *World Economic Outlook: Growth Slowdown, Precarious Recovery.* Washington, DC: International Monetary Fund.

———. 2020. "Direction of Trade Statistics". https://data.imf.org (accessed 12 August 2020).

Klingler-Vidra, Robyn, and Robert Wade. 2020. "Science and Technology Policies and the Middle-Income Trap: Lessons from Vietnam". *Journal of Development Studies* 56, no. 4: 717–31.

Kolstad, Ivan. 2020. "Too Big to Fault? Effects of the 2010 Nobel Peace Prize on Norwegian Exports to China and Foreign Policy". *International Political Science Review* 41, no. 2 (March): 207–23.

Korwatanasakul, Upalat. n.d. "Global Value Chains and the Vietnamese Economic Development: A Path to Perils or Prosperity?"

Kwon, Jaebeom. 2020. "Taming Neighbors: Exploring China's Economic Statecraft to Change Neighboring Countries' Policies and Their Effects". *Asian Perspective* 44, no. 1: 103–38.

Lim, Darren, and Ferguson Victor. 2019. "Chinese Economic Coercion during the THAAD Dispute". The Asan Open Forum.

Meick, Ethan, and Nargiza Salidjanova. 2017. "China's Response to U.S.-South Korean Missile Defense System Deployment and its Implications". *Staff*

Research Report, 26 July 2017. Washington, DC: US-China Economic Security Review Commission.

Nakano, Takashi, and Takeshi Kawanami. 2019. "Vietnam and Singapore Face Pressure from US Currency Watchlist". *Nikkei Asia*, 30 May 2019.

Ngan Anh. 2014. "Vietnam has Trouble Escaping Dependence on China through FTAs". *Thanh Nien News*, 15 July 2014. https://www.bilaterals. org/?vietnam-has-trouble-escaping&lang=en.

Nguyen, Phuong, and Khanh Vu. 2020. "Vietnam Reports Supply Chain Issues from Virus, Says May Hit Samsung Output". Reuters, 21 February 2010. https://www.reuters.com/article/china-health-vietnam-trade/vietnam-reports-supply-chain-issues-from-virus-says-may-hit-samsung-output-idUSL4N2AL246.

Nitta, Yuchi, and Apornrath Phoonphongphiphat. 2020. "Coronavirus Leaves Tropical Fruit Rotting at China Border Crossings". *Nikkei Asian Review*, 6 February 2020. https://asia.nikkei.com/Spotlight/Coronavirus/ Coronavirus-leaves-tropical-fruit-rotting-at-China-border-crossings.

Oh, Yoon Ah, and Suyeon No. 2020. "The Patterns of State-firm Coordination in China's Private Sector Internationalization: China's Mergers and Acquisitions in Southeast Asia". *Pacific Review* 33, no. 6: 873–99.

Ohno, Kenichi. 2009. "Avoiding the Middle-Income Trap: Renovating Industrial Policy Formulation in Vietnam". *ASEAN Economic Bulletin* 26, no. 1: 25–43.

Paik, Wooyeal. 2020. "The Politics of Chinese Tourism in South Korea: Political Economy, State-Society Relations, and International Security". *Pacific Review* 33, no. 2: 331–55.

Politi, James, and Eva Szalay. 2020. "US Declares Switzerland and Vietnam Currency Manipulators". *Financial Times*, 16 December 2020. https:// www.ft.com/content/9bcd4d84-fdec-4f03-9560-dc58f2721899.

Reed, John, and Jung-A Song. 2020. "Samsung Flies Phone Parts to Vietnam after Coronavirus Hits Supply Chain". *Financial Times*, 17 February 2020. https://www.ft.com/content/0dc1c598-4f06-11ea-95a0-43d18ec715f5.

Reilly, James. 2013. "China's Economic Statecraft: Turning Wealth into Power". Lowy Institute Analyses Working Paper, 27 November 2013. http://www.lowyinstitute.org/publications/chinas-economic-statecraft-turning-wealth-power.

Seaman, John. 2012. "Rare Earths and the East China Sea: Why Hasn't China Embargoed Shipments to Japan?" Ifri-CIGS Op-Ed Series. IFRI.

———. 2019. "A Review of Changing Criticality in the New Economy". IFRI Center for Asian Studies. IFRI.

Shen, Yuzhou, Ruthann Moomy, and Roderick G. Eggert. 2020. "China's Public Policies toward Rare Earths, 1975–2018". *Mineral Economics* 33, nos. 1–2: 1–25.

Tham, Siew Yean, Andrew Jia Yi Kam, and Nor Izzatina Abdul Aziz. 2016. "Moving Up the Value Chain in ICT: ASEAN Trade with China". *Journal of Contemporary Asia* 46, no. 4: 680–99.

Tran, Hentry. 2019. "Vietnam Economy Heavily Depending on China". VietnamCredit, 29 November 2019. https://vietnamcredit.com.vn/news/ vietnam-economy-heavily-depending-on-china_13568.

Truong, Quang Hoan. n.d. "Vietnam's Participation in Global Value Chains: Achievements, Challenges and Policy Implication".

United Nations. UN COMTRADE. https://comtrade.un.org/ (accessed 15 September 2020).

United States Patent, Trademark Office (USPTO). n.d. "General Patent Statistics Reports". https://www.uspto.gov/web/offices/ac/ido/oeip/taf/reports.htm (accessed 8 October 2020).

Vũ, Quang Việt. n.d. "A Comparative Statistical View of The Vietnamese Economy under Reform Since 1985".

Vu, Truong-Minh. 2015. "The Politics of 'Struggling Co-evolution': Trade, Power, and Vision in Vietnam's Relations with China". Asan Open Forum, 13 August 2015. http://www.theasanforum.org/the-politics-of-struggling-co-evolution-trade-power-and-vision-in-vietnams-relations-with-china/.

Vu, Tuong. 2017. *Vietnam's Communist Revolution: The Power and Limits of Ideology*. Cambridge: Cambridge University Press.

White, Edward, Jong-a Song, Joe Miller, and Peter Campbell. 2020. "EU and US Carmakers Warn 'Weeks Away' from China Parts Shortage". *Financial Times*, 5 February 2020. https://www.ft.com/content/48bae4c0-472e-11ea-aeb3-955839e06441.

World Bank. "World Integrated Trade Solution (WITS)". https://wits.worldbank.org/ (accessed 9 October 2020).

World Bank and Ministry of Planning and Investment of Vietnam. 2016. *Vietnam 2035: Toward Prosperity, Creativity, Equity, and Democracy*. Hanoi: World Bank Vietnam.

World Tourism Organization (UNWTO). 2020. "Yearbook of Tourism Statistics: Data 2014–2018". World Tourism Organization.

Xian, Jiangnan. 2019. "Commentary: U.S. Risks Losing Rare Earth Supply in Trade War". *People's Daily*, 29 May 2019. http://en.people.cn/n3/2019/0529/c90000-9582572.html.

Yang, Florence W. 2019. "Asymmetrical Interdependence and Sanction: China's Economic Retaliation Over South Korea's THAAD Deployment". *Issues & Studies* 55, no. 4: 1940008.

YTN. 2017. *Yeonyeggyeeseo Gyeonggjekaji ... Jung Sad Bobok Ilji* [A chronology of China's THAAD retaliation: From entertainment to economy]. 3 March 2017.

Zhang, Keitan. 2018. "Calculating Bully: Explaining Chinese Coercion". Doctoral dissertation, Massachusetts Institute of Technology.

———. 2019. "Cautious Bully: Reputation, Resolve, and Beijing's Use of Coercion in the South China Sea". *International Security* 44, no. 1: 117–59.

Part II

Chapter 6

Who Owns and Leads Vietnam's Largest Firms? Evolving State-Business Relationships

Mai Fujita

As Vietnam strives to achieve productivity-driven growth, aiming to join the ranks of upper-middle-income countries with a modern industry by 2030 and becoming a high-income country by 2045—as set out at the 13th Communist Party Congress in 2021—the question of what shape the country's largest domestic firms will take is a major concern. In theory, large firms are better able to exploit economies of scale and are equipped with the resources to invest in capital- and technology-intensive sectors. In the foreseeable future, such firms are likely to take the lead in increasing the productivity of Vietnam's corporate sector, where small and micro enterprises dominate and robust medium-sized enterprises are largely absent—a phenomenon referred to as the "missing middle" (Le 2018; Dinh 2013).[1] Moreover, foreign-invested firms, which have come to comprise a sizeable share among Vietnam's largest firms over the past decade, have largely taken advantage of inexpensive labour and land to undertake processing production using imported materials (Le 2018). In this context, large domestic firms are of particular relevance for the country's ambitious medium- and long-term economic development strategy.

Cross-country experiences, however, demonstrate that large firms have not necessarily taken on positive roles in national economic development. Given their size and position in the economy, such firms are often capable of negotiating special favours from the government. Large firms, if properly supported, incentivized and disciplined to perform effectively, could become a driving force in the development of strategic industries and economic competitiveness (Amsden 1989; Wade 1990). But, where effective control mechanisms are absent, large firms may fall into unproductive rent-seeking and collusive activities.[2] Understanding who the large firms are and how they relate to the state therefore constitutes a crucial agenda in exploring Vietnam's economic development prospects.

To date, the discussion surrounding large domestic enterprises in Vietnam has centred primarily on state-led industrialization, and with wholly or majority state-owned conglomerates as the primary vehicle. In a country where one-party rule by the Communist Party has been sustained and the constitution assigns the state sector to play "a leading role of the economy", attempts have been made to maintain the state's ownership and control over the commanding heights of the economy. To this end, Vietnam established large-scale state-owned conglomerates in the mid-1990s and strengthened them further in the 2000s to lead the development of key economic sectors. Indeed, the dominance of state-owned conglomerates among large domestic firms came out clearly in a study conducted by Cheshier and Penrose (2007), which is the only study to date to have systematically examined Vietnam's largest firms. Using the data from the national enterprise survey in 2005, this study found that three quarters of the country's 200 largest domestic firms were SOEs, of which 120 belonged to state-owned conglomerates.

Developments over the following decade and a half suggest, however, that it might now be less relevant to equate large domestic firms solely with wholly or majority state-owned conglomerates. On the one hand, growing fiscal deficits, the failure and mismanagement of some of the largest state-owned conglomerates, and participation in international trade agreements have prompted Vietnam to launch new and significant attempts to accelerate the restructuring of SOEs. This is demonstrated by the extension of the restructuring programme to large SOEs, including major state-owned conglomerates in the late 2010s (Le 2017). On the other hand, large diversified business groups have emerged in the domestic private sector, which conventionally consisted largely of small enterprises. Notably, the rise of large private firms was observed even in regulated sectors that had hitherto been dominated by SOEs. In the aviation industry, which had long been monopolized by the flagship state carrier Vietnam Airlines (Vuving 2010; Vu-Thanh 2017), the new low-cost entrant Vietjet Airways, after starting operations in 2011, grew rapidly to compete head-to-head with Vietnam Airlines, gaining a 43 per cent share of the domestic air travel market by 2017 (Ho 2017). Vingroup, the country's largest private conglomerate, built on its success in real estate development to diversify into retail, healthcare and education, car production under its own brand name, and even artificial intelligence.

These developments raise a series of questions. How has the structure of the country's largest firms changed? Has the state's ownership in such firms in fact declined? What are the emerging patterns of state-business relationships in the new context? Would the divestment of state capital from SOEs and the rise of private companies translate into loosening of the state's grip over large businesses? This chapter explores these questions. The analysis draws on an original database of the top hundred firms listed on the Ho Chi Minh Stock Exchange constructed by the author. This sample constitutes a sizeable group of the country's largest firms pursuing aggressive growth strategies. It covers some of the leading companies among equitized SOEs, including subsidiaries of the country's largest state-owned conglomerates such as Vietnam Oil and Gas Group (PetroVietnam) and Vietnam Electricity (EVN), as well as some of the largest private companies such as Vingroup, Hoang Anh Gia Lai and Hoa Phat Group.

The remainder of the chapter is structured as follows. The next section briefly discusses the history of large firms in Vietnam and sets the research agenda. The third section sheds light on the transformation of large firms using national level statistics. The fourth section presents the analysis of the top hundred firms, focusing on various dimensions of state-business relationships. The last section summarizes the findings and discusses their implications and future research agenda.

Vietnam's Large Firms: Historical Background and New Developments in the 2010s

Historical Background

The history of building large industrial enterprises in Northern Vietnam dates back to the late 1950s. After rebuilding the plants and equipment left behind by the French and new investments carried out with Soviet and Chinese aid, the socialist industrialization drive was launched with a priority on building heavy industry operating under Soviet-type planning institutions (Beresford 1989; Beresford 2006). Progress was hampered, however, by shortages of capital and technology and by prolonged periods of war. Although the model of socialist industrialization was extended to the whole country following unification in 1976, the ensuing economic crisis resulting from mismanagement, failure of incentive mechanisms, and a shortage of inputs compelled the Vietnamese authorities to move towards partial reforms by the early 1980s.

Doi Moi, officially adopted at the 6th Communist Party Congress in 1986, marked a break from the old "heavy industry first" orientation by prioritizing the production of food, necessities and export products. With respect to the reforms of enterprises, restructuring of small-scale SOEs started in the late 1980s. Conversion of SOEs into joint stock companies, the process referred to as equitization, started on a pilot basis in 1992. Equitization was typically accompanied by the sale of a part of the shares to organizations or individuals inside or outside of the companies. In the meantime, the establishment of private firms was legalized in 1990,[3] but obstacles to the actual establishment and operation of private firms remains.

After the country successfully achieved economic stabilization in the early 1990s, heavy industrialization became a renewed focus. At the 8th Communist Party Congress in 1996, it was announced that Vietnam was moving to the new era of accelerating industrialization and modernization, setting the target of basically becoming an industrialized country by the year 2020. In practice, large corporate groups, called general corporations (GCs), started to be established under the management of central and local governments by consolidating SOEs operating in strategic sectors. The aim was to facilitate accumulation and concentration, improve competitiveness and improve the efficiency of the economy.[4]

The early 2000s changed the tide as Vietnam moved towards deregulation and international economic integration. New dynamics emerged among smaller firms and businesses in the private sector, which had hitherto been repressed and largely operated informally under uncertain circumstances. The promulgation of the Enterprise Law in 2000, which significantly streamlined the procedure for business registration, resulted in a rapid increase in private firms— mostly small enterprises. This reflected both formalization of pre-existing household businesses and the creation of new private firms. With respect to SOEs, the process of equitization, which had made only limited progress until the end of the 1990s, started to be accelerated from the early 2000s. Increasing numbers of smaller SOEs were equitized, and a part of them were listed on the stock market.

By the end of July 2008, more than ninety per cent of the companies listed on the Ho Chi Minh Stock Exchange were joint stock companies converted from SOEs (Hayashi 2013, p. 89).

The endeavour to nurture large state-owned conglomerates gained momentum again in the mid-2000s. Large and diversified state-owned conglomerates, called state economic groups (SEGs), started to be established, mostly by reorganizing some of the largest GCs. By around 2010, nearly a dozen SEGs operated as either monopolies or dominant players in sectors such as energy, mining, electricity and telecommunications. Their monopolies or dominant status stemmed primarily from a range of privileges provided by the state. But state-owned conglomerates, despite being the primary beneficiaries of generous subsidies, privileges and protection by the government, belied expectations (Vu-Thanh 2017). This is best demonstrated by the failure of Vietnam National Shipbuilding Group (Vinashin) in the aftermath of the global financial crisis in 2008, along with numerous other cases of financial failure, mismanagement and corruption related to major SOEs that came to the fore around that time (Leung 2015; Pincus 2015).

The failure of large SOEs, combined with the closely associated problems of the banking sector and public investment, was behind the macroeconomic imbalances and slowdown in economic growth that surfaced with the onset of the global financial crisis in 2008–9 and aggravated in the early 2010s (Karla 2015). These developments prompted Vietnam to focus on restructuring the economy—particularly, public investment, the financial sector and SOEs—in the five-year development plan for 2011–15.

New Developments in the 2010s

As a result of the historical background discussed above, Vietnam's domestic corporate sector came to exhibit a dual structure. On the one hand, the state sector was composed mainly of large enterprises operating primarily in strategic sectors. On the other hand, the private sector grew increasingly vibrant, yet it consisted overwhelmingly of small-scale businesses because of the state's control over the most lucrative segments and activities of the economy such as natural resource exploitation, domestic and international trading, transport, telecommunications and finance (Pincus 2017). Consequently, Vietnam had been referred to as a case of "near or complete absence of a private or even quasi-private enterprise sector" (London 2017, p. 410).

By the 2010s, however, new developments were under way. With respect to SOEs, restructuring gained further momentum by the late 2010s. First, the Party Central Committee adopted a series of resolutions in 2017 that sought to accelerate the restructuring of SOEs so they would be concentrated in essential sectors, ones important for national security, or ones that would not be invested in by other sectors, and at the same time assigned a proactive role to the private sector as an important engine of economic development.[5] Second, the scope of 100 per cent and majority state ownership was reduced (Prime Minister's Decision 58/2016/QD-TTg). While such attempts had been ongoing since the late 1990s (Cheshier, Penrose and Nguyen 2006), a notable development at this stage was that Decision No. 58 not only specified the sectors that would remain under 100 per cent, above 65 per cent, or above 50 per cent state ownership, but it also listed the names of companies that fell under each of the categories.[6] Moreover, subsequent road maps specified the names of SOEs planned for equitization or state capital divestment for each of the years from 2017 to 2020,[7] which included large SOEs and major state-owned conglomerates and their member enterprises.

Another notable development was the emergence of large privately owned business groups. While the study by Cheshier and Penrose (2007), discussed in the introduction, demonstrated the dominance of state-owned conglomerates among the largest domestic firms in the early 2000s, Vietnam Report's Top 500 Company rankings in the 2010s suggest changes in the structure of large domestic enterprises.[8] According to this ranking, the top twenty-five firms in 2011 included only one private company (Sacombank-SBJ), three foreign-invested companies (Honda Vietnam, Samsung Electronics Vietnam and Canon Vietnam) and one joint venture company (Vietsovpetro), while all the remaining firms were SOEs. The top twenty-five in 2020, by contrast, included a total of eight private companies: Vingroup, Digi World, Doji, Hoa Phat, Truong Hai Auto, VP Bank, Vinamilk and Vietjet Airways. Notably, many of the large private enterprises operate in regulated industries conventionally dominated by SOEs, such as transport, finance, real estate and trading.

Evolving State-Business Relationships

The above developments are likely to have crucial implications for what shape Vietnam's largest firms will take and how they will interact with the state. The direction and magnitude of the impact, however, are not entirely clear. Only limited systematic analysis of a sizeable cohort of Vietnam's largest firms has been conducted since Cheshier and Penrose (2007), and the limited availability of firm-level data is a major constraint. The following agendas derived from the previous literature deserve further scrutiny in particular.

First, with respect to SOEs, the consequences of SOE restructuring have not been examined thoroughly. Historically, SOEs were subject to various and sometimes competing interests within and outside of the enterprises (Gainsborough 2003b; Fforde 2004). Despite recurrent criticism about delays in equitization, more than 4,500 SOEs have been equitized between the start of the pilot programme in 1992 and the late 2010s (Phuong Dung 2017). Over time, the SOE equitization programme itself evolved, involving changes with respect to who the shares were sold to and the relationships between state shareholders and equitized enterprises, which means that SOEs equitized at different stages were subject to different procedures and requirements.[9] Furthermore, shares in many of the equitized firms, especially those listed on the stock exchange, have changed hands. Analysing the consequences of SOE equitization thus needs to consider the state's influence over SOEs not just in terms of state ownership ratios but also in terms of the different identities of actors having stakes in the firms before and after equitization. To date, little has been said about how the ownership structures of equitized enterprises have changed over time—not to mention other modes of influence exerted by various types of state actors.

Second, more than three decades after the start of Doi Moi, it remains a fact of life that political connections continue to be important in running businesses in Vietnam. But the *magnitude* and *types* of political connections cultivated by large businesses remain under-investigated. In the early years of Doi Moi, numerous central and local state cadres or SOE managers took advantage of their privileged positions to siphon off state funds or assets into newly established enterprises that operate as private firms (Greenfield 1994; Gainsborough 2003a). Previous studies measured the political connections of firm managers using indicators such as Communist Party membership, employment in the government, military service, and work or study abroad before 1991, and they analysed the impact of such connections on firm performance (Webster and Taussig 1999; Kim 2008; Taussig 2009). While the conclusions reached by these studies differed by the method and scope of analyses, such as the industry and location covered, and by the timing of the study, the recent rise of large private business groups deserves particular attention. It has been suggested that the newly emerging business groups, though privately owned, have in fact been established by individuals connected with the party state, and that such connections are likely to have been essential for their phenomenal growth in view of the fact that the strategic industries of many such firms are subject to regulations (Hayton 2010; Pincus 2015). Further scrutiny of these issues based on a systematic analysis covering a sizeable sample of large businesses and their owners would be highly worthwhile.

Third, the consequences of globalization of the Vietnamese economy on the growth of large domestic firms is another important agenda. On the one hand, the growing openness of the economy poses challenges to domestic firms as it increases competition. Nevertheless, the magnitude of the impact is likely to differ considerably across sectors, as suggested by the fact that strategic sectors remain protected even after Vietnam's participation in international trade agreements (Vu-Thanh 2017). On the other hand, globalization provides opportunities to domestic firms such as new alliances and access to new resources. Increasing numbers of foreign firms have acquired shares of Vietnamese firms, and some of such cases even involved strategic partnerships between foreign and Vietnamese firms. The amount of capital contributions and share purchases by foreign investors increased from US$6.2 billion in 2017 to US$15.5 billion in 2019.[10] Globalization also enabled Vietnamese firms to gain access to sophisticated managerial talent, which includes not only foreigners but also Vietnamese professionals who had studied or worked abroad or had been employed in foreign-invested companies in Vietnam.

Changing Structure of the Corporate Sector: Insights from Statistics

I begin the analysis of the evolving structure and role of large firms in Vietnam by examining the overall situation of Vietnam's corporate sector using the national-level enterprise survey published by the General Statistical Office. For statistical purposes, SOEs include enterprises with 100 per cent state capital and limited liability companies and joint stock companies in which the state holds more than 50 per cent of charter capital.[11] This means that, even after equitization, SOEs remain SOEs as long as the state owns more than 50 per cent of charter capital. As the state's ownership of charter capital falls to 50 per cent or below, the respective companies become domestic private companies.[12] Such enterprises are classified as "joint stock companies having state capital", which includes companies in which the state owns up to 50 per cent of charter capital. In case the state fully divests itself from the respective enterprise so that the state's ownership of charter capital falls to 0 per cent, the respective company becomes a "joint stock company without state capital". Interpretation of the statistical data thus requires some caution as the classification of "joint stock companies without state capital" includes companies that were originally established as privately owned entities as well as former SOEs in which the state no longer holds any stake.

Table 6.1 compares the number of enterprises by ownership in 2000 and 2018. The total number of enterprises increased by more than fifteen times over the period, primarily as a result of the dramatic increase in domestic private enterprises, while the number of SOEs declined by almost half. Of the remaining 2,260 SOEs in 2018, 1,097 were wholly state-owned, while 1,163 were more than 50 per cent owned by the state. It should be noted that the total number of SOEs that are more than 50 per cent owned by the state (1,163) and joint stock companies with state capital (1,125) only comes to 2,288, which is only about half the number of SOEs that had been equitized by the end of 2010, as discussed in the previous section (more than 4,500). No data is available to inform us what happened to the other half of the equitized SOEs. Some are likely to have been dissolved, have gone bankrupt or merged, while others are likely to have continued to operate either as joint stock companies without state capital in the case of companies owned by domestic private investors or as foreign-invested companies in the case of companies sold to foreign investors.

The table also points to crucial changes in the structure of large enterprises. In 2000, SOEs accounted for the overwhelming majority of large domestic enterprises, defined by both the number of employees and capital size. By 2018 the proportion of SOEs in large domestic enterprises had declined considerably, while a corresponding increase was observed in the share of domestic private enterprises. Among the various legal forms of domestic private enterprises, "joint stock companies without state capital", in particular, is highly represented among the largest domestic private enterprises. Whilst such companies only account for 20 per cent of all domestic private companies, they comprise 2,891 of 4,892 domestic private enterprises falling under the largest category of domestic private enterprises defined by capital size, which is equivalent of 59 per cent. Similarly, such companies account for 43 of 59 domestic private enterprises falling under the largest category of domestic private enterprises defined by the number of employees, equivalent to 73 per cent.

TABLE 6.1
Number of Enterprises

		Capital Size (billion VND)				Number of Employees				Total
		<10	10–49	50–499	500+	<50	50–299	300–4,999	5,000+	
2000	SOEs	2,382 43%	2,012 36%	1,115 20%	82 1%	1,124 20%	2,915 52%	1,529 27%	23 0%	5,591 100%
	Non-state enterprises	30,458 95%	1,241 4%	234 1%	17 0%	28,957 91%	2,581 8%	410 1%	2 0%	31,950 100%
	Foreign-invested enterprises	378 25%	582 38%	467 31%	101 7%	493 32%	723 47%	303 20%	9 1%	1,528 100%
	Total	33,218 85%	3,835 10%	1,816 5%	200 1%	30,574 78%	6,219 16%	2,242 6%	34 0%	39,069 100%
2018	SOEs	203 9%	456 20%	930 41%	671 30%	589 26%	969 43%	673 30%	29 1%	2,260 100%
	Non-state enterprises	442,060 75%	110,649 19%	33,928 6%	4,862 1%	567,650 96%	20,747 4%	3,043 1%	59 0%	591,499 100%
	Of which: JSCs with state capital	93 8%	249 22%	515 46%	268 24%	381 34%	514 46%	225 20%	5 0%	1,125 100%
	Of which: JSCs w/o state capital	70,986 60%	30,839 26%	13,922 12%	2,891 2%	109,257 92%	7,860 7%	1,478 1%	43 0%	118,638 100%
	Foreign-invested enterprises	5,193 31%	4,721 28%	5,305 31%	1,659 10%	9,770 58%	4,478 27%	2,500 15%	130 1%	16,878 100%
	Total	447,456 73%	115,826 19%	40,163 7%	7,192 1%	578,009 95%	26,194 4%	6,216 1%	218 0%	610,637 100%

Note: "JSC" denotes joint stock companies.
Sources: Tong cuc thong ke (2017); General Statistics Office (2019).

In order to examine the roles of SOEs and domestic private companies in the economy, Figure 6.1 compares the structure of enterprises in 2000 and 2018 with respect to three indicators: fixed assets and long-term investments, net turnover, and profits before tax. While declining shares of SOEs and increasing shares of domestic private companies are observed across all the indicators, the results for fixed assets and long-term investments and for profits before tax are particularly striking. Conventionally, the dominance of SOEs had been particularly salient when these indicators were used to assess their roles, which was consistent with the concentration of SOEs in capital-intensive industries and protected sectors shielded from competition (Wacker 2017; Vu-Thanh 2017; Pincus 2015). By 2018, the share of joint stock companies without state capital exceeded the respective shares of SOEs based on the two indicators. While the ratio of fixed assets to labour was still higher for SOEs than joint stock companies without state capital, the disparity between SOEs and joint stock companies without state capital had narrowed: the ratio for SOEs was 3.01 times that of joint stock companies without state capital in 2006 and had lowered to 2.00 by 2018.

The rapid decline in the role of SOEs in the economy, which seems to have been driven at least partly by SOE restructuring, raises the question of whether a corresponding expansion can be observed for joint stock companies having state capital. Given the small number of companies under this category, the share of these companies in the economy has remained limited (Figure 6.1). Nevertheless, these firms are particularly notable for their scale in terms of capital size (see Table 6.1). These firms also exhibit high capital intensity as demonstrated by the ratio of fixed assets to labour being only 1.79 times higher for SOEs than for joint stock companies having state capital in 2018[13]—a ratio lower than the ratio of joint stock companies without state capital mentioned above.

To sum up, the analysis of the statistical data has shown that, by the late 2010s, some types of domestic private companies—namely, joint stock companies with and without state capital—came to account for an increasing share of large domestic firms that operate in capital-intensive sectors and/or protected sectors, taking on part of the role that had previously been undertaken by SOEs. Interpretation requires caution, however, as the statistical classifications of firms do not necessarily provide clear indications of what types of companies are covered. The classification of "joint stock companies having state capital" may be expected to consist largely of companies that used to be state-owned and were equitized, yet the classification might also include companies that were established as private entities but subsequently received capital participation by state entities, typically SOEs. Likewise, "joint stock companies without state capital" includes companies established as private firms from inception as well as former SOEs whose state ownership has been reduced to zero. The implication is that historical analysis is critical in making sense of the changes that have taken place in the corporate sector.

FIGURE 6.1
Structure of Enterprises by Legal Form

Sources: General Statistics Office (2013); General Statistics Office (2019).

The Top Hundred Listed Firms: Analysis
of Companies and Top Leaders

Why Focus on Top-Listed Firms?

The analyses in the preceding section revealed that companies that are wholly or majority owned by the state (SOEs) account for a decreasing share of large enterprises and that their roles, to some extent, have been replaced by domestic private companies registered as joint stock companies. In order to shed further light on the emerging cohort of large enterprises, this section presents a detailed analysis of the top hundred firms listed on the Ho Chi Minh Stock Exchange. This choice of companies is appropriate for the following reasons. First, it is consistent with the purpose of analysing large firms because listing on stock markets is an attractive option for firms pursuing aggressive growth strategies, whilst it also requires firms to fulfil size and performance conditions. Second, this choice conforms to our interest in the consequences of SOE reforms and the rise of private business groups. By the 2010s, listed firms included some of the largest and best-performing equitized SOEs as well as many of the major private or quasi-private conglomerates such as Vingroup, Hoang Anh Gia Lai and Masan Group. Lastly, detailed and accurate firm-level data can be obtained with relative ease, without which detailed analyses of ownership and other forms of state-business connections would be difficult.

A potential constraint of using this sample of firms is that it excludes 100 per cent state-owned firms, which include Vietnam's largest firms. Nevertheless, many of the subsidiaries of the country's largest 100 per cent state-owned conglomerates have been equitized and listed on the stock exchange. As will be shown in the subsequent analysis, such firms in fact comprise the largest group among the top hundred listed firms. While I am aware of the limitations of excluding 100 per cent state-owned firms, focusing on top-listed firms provides a pragmatic approach in shedding light on the increasing diversity of large firms within the constraints of data availability.

Data Source

The analysis will utilize an original database constructed by the author.[14] The database covers the top hundred companies listed on the Ho Chi Minh Stock Exchange as at the end of 2016. The data were extracted in the following manner. First, a comprehensive list of listed firms, which contained 305 firms, was obtained from the website of the Ho Chi Minh Stock Exchange. Second, for these 305 companies, financial data were obtained from the website of VNdirect Securities

Corporation (www.vndirect.com.vn). Third, the 305 companies were ranked by the following two indicators: average net revenue and profits before tax during the five years from 2011 to 2015. For each company, the revenue and profit rankings, ranging from 1 (the top) to 305 (the bottom), were assigned, and the two figures were added to calculate the overall ranking. I then extracted the top hundred ranked companies.

For the top hundred companies, two types of database were constructed covering information up to the end of 2016. The firm-level database includes information on sector and ownership structure. The leader-level database covers basic profiles (e.g., year of birth and educational attainment) and detailed career histories of chairpersons and general directors of the hundred companies.

Company annual reports and websites were the main sources of data, but these were complemented by internet sources such as the CafeF website offered by the media company VCCorp Joint Stock Company (www.cafef.vn).

Company Ownership

Table 6.2 shows the structure of the top hundred firms by ownership and industry. The companies were categorized by ownership types according to the following rule, which considers not only the current state ownership ratios (as of the end of 2016) but also the historical background of the companies. SOEs are companies that are more than 50 per cent owned by the state. Former SOEs are companies that meet the following two criteria: (1) the companies were originally established as SOEs or their predecessor companies were SOEs; and (2) the state ownership ratio had been reduced to 50 per cent or below. All remaining companies that are not within the above two categories are private companies. State ownership ratios were calculated as the total percentage of shares held by state organizations or SOEs.

SOEs constitute the largest group, nearly 40 per cent of the top hundred companies, followed by former SOEs and private companies. A focus on the largest and most profitable of the top hundred companies, however, presents a somewhat different picture. Of the top twenty-five companies ranked by the combination of net turnover and profits before tax, eleven are SOEs, four are former SOEs and ten are private companies. While the dominance of SOEs among the ultra-large firms was expected, the share of private companies turned out to be strikingly high.[15] Former SOEs are concentrated among the smaller group of firms among the top hundred.

TABLE 6.2
Top Hundred Companies by Ownership and Industry

	SOEs	Former SOEs	Private Companies	Total
Industry and Construction				
Petroleum and natural gas exploration	5 (2)	0	0	5 (2)
Manufacturing				
Food and beverages	0	9 (1)	5 (3)	14 (4)
Textiles and garments	0	1	1	2
Chemicals	6 (2)	1	0	7 (2)
Pharmaceuticals	0	4	0	4
Rubber and plastics	5	2	0	7
Basic metals	0	0	4 (2)	4 (2)
Electric and electronic products	1	2	0	3
Other manufacturing	3	1	2	6
Electricity	4 (2)	0	0	4 (2)
Construction	1	2 (1)	2	5 (1)
Services				
Trade	3	3 (1)	5 (1)	11 (2)
Transport	4	2	1	7
Real estate	0	1	6 (2)	7 (2)
Finance	7 (5)	1	3 (2)	11 (7)
Other services	0	3 (1)	0	3 (1)
TOTAL	39 (11)	32 (4)	29 (10)	100 (25)

Note: Figures in parentheses denote the composition of the top twenty-five companies.
Source: Author's database.

With respect to the sectoral structure, SOEs are concentrated in such industries as resource exploitation, utilities, chemicals and transportation, many of which are sectors that have historically been reserved for firms with 100 per cent or majority state ownership because of their strategic importance for the national economy. Former SOEs are found in a wide range of industries, including non-strategic industries that are no longer reserved for majority state ownership. While many of the private companies are diversified, their main business lines are concentrated in food and beverages, metal, trade, and real estate.

Despite these differences, the top hundred firms share a number of common characteristics regardless of ownership. First, these firms predominantly target the domestic market, and this even applies to some of the companies operating in typically export-oriented industries such as electronics. In view of the pivotal role of export-oriented industries in the Vietnamese economy, the strong domestic market orientation of the top hundred listed firms is striking. Second, many of the former SOEs and private companies operate in so-called conditional businesses sectors, for which investors are required to meet specific conditions for reasons such as national defence, security and social order, and safety.[16] Typical examples include finance, transportation and real estate. Trading, one of the industries where many top companies including both private companies and former SOEs operate, has historically been subject to extensive regulations such as licensing. The top hundred companies include those that had been established as SOEs before or in the early years of Doi Moi and have continued to maintain dominant positions in these sectors up to the 2010s.

In an attempt to examine in detail the identities of the main shareholders and their ownership ratios, Table 6.3 shows the percentage of shares held by (a) the state, (b) foreign investors, and (c) the top leaders of the respective companies, including the chairperson of the management board and the general director. First, the table shows significant retreat of state ownership from SOEs and former SOEs. In more than half of the SOEs (21 of 39), the state ownership ratio was 60 per cent or less. In half of former SOEs (16 of 32), state ownership was 0 per cent, and in a further six companies, the ratio was 10 per cent or less. Second, the level of foreign ownership varied considerably, mostly within the 49 per cent cap for public companies, which was lifted only in September 2015.[17] Nevertheless, foreign ownership ratios were found to be particularly high for former SOEs, which include two companies whose foreign ownership ratios were 50 per cent or above, and a further ten companies in which the ratios were 47 per cent or above. Third, shareholding by top leaders was highly prevalent regardless of ownership types, even SOEs. In particular, all but one former SOE had a part of their shares owned by top leaders. Although the ratios were generally modest for the majority of SOEs and most former SOEs, much higher levels of shareholding by leaders were observed for private companies and some of the former SOEs. The ratios were 10 per cent or above for more than half of the private companies and four of the former SOEs, and 20 per cent or above for six private companies and one former SOE.

With respect to state ownership, we are interested not only in the level of state ownership but also in the type of state capital owners. Table 6.4 shows the types of the largest state capital owners for SOEs and former SOEs. The majority of SOEs are owned by state-owned conglomerates or their subsidiaries, demonstrating that the state's role as the controlling owner of large conglomerates via a pyramidal structure is intact. Some 25 of the 39 SOEs belong to five of the largest SEGs—namely, PetroVietnam, EVN, Vietnam National Chemical Group (Vinachem), Viettel Group, and Vietnam Rubber

TABLE 6.3
Ownership Structure of the Top Hundred Firms

(a) State ownership ratio	SOEs	Former SOEs	Private Companies	Total
0%	0	16	26	42
Above 0, 10% or less	0	6	3	9
Above 10, 30% or less	0	5	0	5
Above 30, 50% or less	0	5	0	5
Above 50, 60% or less	21	0	0	21
Above 60, 80% or less	15	0	0	15
Above 80%	3	0	0	3
TOTAL	39	32	29	100

(b) Foreign ownership ratio	SOEs	Former SOEs	Private Companies	Total
Less than 5%	8	5	1	14
5% or above, less than 10%	11	6	4	21
10% or above, less than 20%	6	1	8	15
20% or above, less than 30%	11	5	6	22
30% or above, less than 40%	2	2	5	9
40% or above, less than 50%	1	11	4	16
50% or above	0	2	1	3
TOTAL	39	32	29	100

(c) Top leaders' ownership ratio	SOEs	Former SOEs	Private Companies	Total
0%	13	1	5	19
Above 0%, less than 0.1%	13	2	0	15
0.1% or above, less than 1%	10	10	1	21
1% or above, less than 10%	3	15	7	25
10% or above, less than 20%	0	3	10	13
20% or above, less than 30%	0	0	3	3
30% or above, less than 40%	0	1	1	2
40% or above, less than 50%	0	0	2	2
TOTAL	39	32	29	100

Note: Top leaders' ownership ratio indicates the total of chairpersons and general directors.
Source: Author's database.

TABLE 6.4
Largest State Capital Owners

	SOE	Former SOE	Private Companies	Total
SEGs	25	2	1	28
GCs (Central)	9	8	0	17
of which: SCIC	2	7	0	9
GCs (Local)	2	1	1	4
SOE (Central)	0	0	1	1
SOE (Local)	0	3	0	3
Ministries/ministerial level organizations	3	1	0	4
Local party unit	0	1	0	1
None	0	16	26	43
TOTAL	39	32	29	100

Source: Author's database.

Group. PetroVietnam, in particular, was the state capital owner of six of the twenty-five ultra-large companies. Former SOEs present a very different picture. Apart from the state no longer holding shares in half of these companies, the only discernible type of state capital owners for these companies is State Capital Investment Corporation (SCIC), which was established in 2005 with the aim of representing state capital interests in SOEs.

To sum up the findings with respect to ownership, SOEs present the clearest pattern. Consistent with the literature, state-owned conglomerates remain the controlling owners of the majority of firms in this category. A sizeable group of private companies were owned by founding chairpersons. With respect to former SOEs and the remaining private firms, discernible patterns could not be identified. Particularly with respect to most former SOEs, state ownership had been reduced to negligible levels, while foreign shareholding increased significantly in some firms but not to the extent of holding controlling shares.

Leaders

The database of leaders includes a total of 173 individuals,[18] as shown in Table 6.5. The simultaneous appointment of chairperson and general director was common among former SOEs, accounting for about a quarter, and private companies, making up about a third. Although the Enterprise Law of 2014 stipulates that chairpersons of companies in which the state maintains more than 50 per cent of voting rights cannot concurrently serve as the general director (Article 152.2), there is one such case among the SOE sample.

TABLE 6.5
The Sample of Leaders

	SOE	Former SOE	Private companies	Total
Chairpersons (CP)	37	31	27	95
Chairpersons (CP) only	36	23	18	77
Chairpersons-cum-general directors	1	8	9	18
General directors (GD)	38	22	18	78
TOTAL	75	53	45	173

Source: Author's database.

Table 6.6 summarizes the basic profiles of the leaders. SOE leaders have an average age of fifty; chairpersons are slightly older than general directors. A relatively low standard deviation suggests the high level of homogeneity of this group of leaders. Former SOE leaders are on overage older than their SOE counterparts, but a high standard deviation suggests they are much more heterogenous. Private firm leaders constitute the youngest group of leaders. Eighty-seven per cent of the leaders are male, and the gender composition seems to be influenced more by sector than by ownership. Nearly three quarters of all female leaders (17 of 23) are found in the following four sectors: food and beverage (6 individuals; equivalent to 26.1 per cent of all the leaders in this sector), pharmaceuticals (4 individuals; equivalent to 50 per cent), real estate (3 individuals; equivalent to 27.3 per cent), and trading (4 individuals; equivalent to 25.3 per cent). The educational levels are high by national standards. This is particularly the case for leaders of SOEs and former SOEs as sizeable groups of high school graduates (i.e., leaders without a bachelor's degree) are found only among private companies. Three of the four private company chairpersons without bachelor's degrees had run workshops or factories registered as individual establishments (cơ sở cá thể), which were subsequently converted to companies.[19] Having studied abroad was found to be more common among former SOE and private company leaders than their SOE counterparts. Approximately 20 per cent of former SOE and private company leaders had studied in either former Eastern bloc or Western countries, or both. Having studied in a former Eastern bloc country before the start of Doi Moi—more common among former SOE leaders—is an indication the respective leader is likely to have political connections of some sort (Webster and Taussig 1999). On the other hand, studying in a Western country after Doi Moi signals the possession of advanced knowledge and skills. Typical examples were found among general directors of private companies who had studied business-related subjects such as management, finance and marketing in Europe, the United States or Japan before being posted to leadership positions in the Vietnamese companies.

The leaders' origins provide important clues about the background of companies (Webster and Taussig 1999). Table 6.7 shows the origins of the leaders based on their birthplace or, whenever such data were not available, the birthplace of their fathers (*nguyên quán*). Despite as many as 71 of the 100 companies being located in the South[20] and 45 in Ho Chi Minh City, the share of leaders with a Northern or Central origin, particularly those originating from the Red River Delta, turned out to be strikingly high. The proportion of leaders with a Northern or Central origin was higher for SOEs and former SOEs

TABLE 6.6
Leaders' Basic Attributes

	SOE			Former SOE			Private			Total
	CP	GD	Total	CP	GD	Total	CP	GD	Total	Total
(1) Age										
Average	52.6	49.1	50.9	58.4	51.0	55.3	51.9	47.0	50.0	52.0
Standard deviation	5.8	6.4	6.3	8.4	10.1	9.9	6.8	7.4	7.4	8.2
Maximum	61	62	62	79	73	79	65	68	68	79
Minimum	42	36	36	42	29	29	39	37	37	29
(2) Gender										
Female	2	0	2	9	4	13	3	5	8	23
Male	35	38	73	22	18	40	24	13	37	150
(3) Educational level										
High school graduate	0	0	0	0	1	1	4	3	7	8
Bachelor's degree	20	18	38	20	10	30	17	6	23	91
Master's degree	12	16	28	6	9	15	5	6	11	54
Doctoral degree	5	4	9	4	2	6	1	3	4	19
n/a	0	0	0	1	0	1	0	0	0	1
(4) Study abroad										
None	36	36	72	25	17	42	23	14	37	151
Western countries	0	2	2	2	2	4	2	4	6	12
Eastern bloc countries	1	0	1	3	2	5	2	0	2	8
Both	0	0	0	1	1	2	0	0	0	2
TOTAL	37	38	75	31	22	53	27	18	45	173

Note: CP and GD denote chairperson and general director, respectively.
Source: Author's database.

than for private companies, and within each of the ownership types it was higher for chairpersons than for general directors. Within SOEs, the share of leaders with a Northern or Central origin was found to be higher for leaders of companies belonging to the largest state-owned conglomerates. For firms belonging to the four SEGs headquartered in Hanoi—namely, PetroVietnam, EVN, Viettel and Vinachem[21]—the share of chairpersons with Northern or Central origins was as high as 93 per cent, while the corresponding figure for general directors was somewhat lower, at 78 per cent. This may be because, as we shall see, chairpersons of state-owned conglomerates tend to have developed

TABLE 6.7
Leaders' Origins

	SOE			Former SOE			Private			Total
	CP	GD	Total	CP	GD	Total	CP	GD	Total	
Leaders' Birthplace										
Northern Midlands and Mountain Areas	2	1	3	2	0	2	0	0	0	5
Red River Delta	12	10	22	10	9	19	9	5	14	55
North Central, Central Coast and Central Highlands	5	5	10	8	3	11	8	4	12	33
South East	2	5	7	1	1	2	6	3	9	18
Mekong River Delta	3	2	5	2	3	5	2	3	5	15
Foreign countries	1	0	1	0	1	1	1	0	1	3
Birthplace of leaders' fathers										
Northern Midlands and Mountain Areas	0	1	1	0	0	0	0	0	0	1
Red River Delta	1	4	5	2	0	2	0	1	1	8
North Central, Central Coast and Central Highlands	1	2	3	1	0	1	1	0	1	5
South East	0	3	3	1	1	2	0	0	0	5
Mekong River Delta	1	0	1	1	0	1	0	0	0	2
Data not available	9	5	14	3	4	7	0	2	2	23
TOTAL	37	38	75	31	22	53	27	18	45	173
Northern/Central-origin leaders (%)*	75	70	72	82	67	76	67	63	65	71

Notes: The share of Northern/Central-origin leader (%) was calculated by the total number of leaders whose birthplace or father's birthplace was in the Northern or Central regions, divided by the total number of leaders minus the number of leaders for whom data were not available. CP and GD denote chairperson and general director, respectively.

Source: Author's database.

their careers within corporate groups before being appointed to leadership positions in subsidiaries of the respective groups, while general directors, who manage the daily operations of the firms, tend to have spent most of their careers in the respective companies, many of which are located in the Southern part of the country. This leads us to ask why chairpersons of former SOEs, most of which do not belong to SEGs, exhibit an exceptionally high proportion of leaders with a Northern or Central origin, even exceeding that of SOE chairpersons. While the high average age is likely to be a part of the story, this issue will be brought up below in relation to the discussion of other crucial characteristics of this category of leaders.

The career history of leaders provides crucial information on the types of network resources they possess. A summary of these career histories is presented in Table 6.8. The first step of the analysis examines the percentage ratios of the number of years the respective leader had spent in the company (or corporate group, in case the company belonged to an SEG or GC) to the total number of years since he or she graduated from school (see [1] in Table 6.8). The high percentage ratios for SOE leaders and particularly for general directors suggests they spent a high proportion of their careers in the current company or corporate group. These leaders, who have largely been promoted internally after climbing the corporate ladder, are likely to have accumulated group-specific or firm-specific insider network resources. In contrast, former SOE and private company leaders spent on average higher proportions of their careers outside of their current companies, which raises the question of whether he or she had previously worked for the state sector.

The second step thus examines whether the leaders had cultivated experience in the state sector prior to joining their current companies or groups. Such experience is further classified into business-related experience in SOEs and other types of experience (see [2] in Table 6.8). Consistent with the findings from the first step discussed above, only a limited number of SOE leaders had state sector experience prior to joining their current companies. In contrast, a higher proportion of former SOE leaders, particularly chairpersons, had cultivated state sector experience, including non-business experience other than that in SOEs. Regarding private companies, approximately half of the leaders had cultivated state sector experience. Of the remaining half who did not have state sector experience, chairpersons were largely founding managers, whilst most general directors transferred into leadership positions in their current companies after developing their career elsewhere (Fujita 2020).

TABLE 6.8

Leaders' Career Histories

	SOE			Former SOE			Private			Total
	CP[d]	GD	Total	CP	GD	Total	CP	GD	Total	Total
(1) Percentage of period spent in the current company in the respective leader's career										
Average percentage[a]	77%	88%	83%	64%	64%	64%	57%	43%	52%	68%
(2) State sector experience prior to joining the current company/group										
None	20 / 54%	22 / 58%	42 / 56%	10 / 32%	9 / 41%	19 / 36%	16 / 59%	8 / 44%	24 / 53%	85 / 49%
Had experience with SOEs only	7 / 19%	13 / 34%	20 / 27%	5 / 16%	5 / 23%	10 / 19%	4 / 15%	7 / 39%	11 / 24%	41 / 24%
Had experience with organizations other than SOEs[b]	10 / 27%	3 / 8%	13 / 17%	16 / 52%	8 / 36%	24 / 45%	7 / 26%	3 / 17%	10 / 22%	47 / 27%
Total	37	38	75	31	22	53	27	18	45	173
(3) Types of experience with organizations other than SOEs										
Total number of leaders with experience other than SOEs of which (multiple answers):	10	3	13	16	8	24	7	3	10	47
Central government	4	0	4	4	3	7	1	0	1	12
Local government	3	1	4	4	1	5	3	2	5	14
Military	2	2	4	4	1	5	0	0	0	9
Academic	2	1	3	5	1	6	1	0	1	10
Studied/worked in former Eastern Bloc countries	1	0	1	4	4	8	2	0	2	11
Other	0	0	0	0	0	0	2	1	3	3
Average types of experience per leader	1.20	1.33	1.23	1.31	1.25	1.29	1.29	1.00	1.20	1.26
(4) Experience with state shareholders of current companies										
Had experience in state shareholders of current companies of which:										
GCs/SEGs	20	12	32	2	1	3	n/a	n/a	n/a	35
SCIC, HFIC, HIFU[c]	0	0	0	2	1	3	n/a	n/a	n/a	3
Ministries	1	0	1	2	1	3	n/a	n/a	n/a	4
Had experience in other types of government organizations	4	5	9	9	8	17	n/a	n/a	n/a	26
No experience in government organizations	12	21	33	16	11	27	n/a	n/a	n/a	60
TOTAL	37	38	75	31	22	53	n/a	n/a	n/a	128

Notes: (a) The percentage was calculated as the ratio (percentage) of the period the respective leader had spent in the company (or corporate group, in case the company belonged to an SEG or GC) in the period since he or she graduated from school. (b) These leaders might have had experience in SOEs in addition to non-SOE experience. (c) SCIC denotes State Capital Investment Corporation, HFIC denotes Ho Chi Minh City Finance and Investment State Owned Company, and HIFU denotes Ho Chi Minh City Fund for Urban Development. (d) CP and GD denote chairperson and general director, respectively.

Source: Author's database.

The third step of the analysis examines the types of non-business experience cultivated by the leaders (see [3] in Table 6.8). Some 47 individuals out of the total of 173 leaders, roughly a quarter, had varieties of non-business experience such as working in the government, the military, the party or academic organizations or studying or working in former Eastern bloc countries. These types of leaders are likely to have cultivated a broad range of non-business political connections and network resources. Such leaders turned out to be prevalent among former SOE chairpersons as well as private company leaders.

Some business leaders also hold positions in political, social or economic organizations outside of companies or organizations they

TABLE 6.9
Positions in Political and Socioeconomic Organizations

	SOE			Former SOE			Private			Total
	CP[c]	GD	Total	CP	GD	Total	CP	GD	Total	
Leaders who had not been in a political/ socioeconomic postion[a]	33	38	71	19	20	39	23	17	40	150
Leaders who had been in a political/ socioeconomic position[b]	4	0	4	12	2	14	4	1	5	23
in percentage	11%	0%	5%	39%	9%	26%	15%	6%	11%	13%
of which (multiple answers):										
Party	3	0	3	1	2	3	0	1	1	7
Central state organization	2	0	2	3	0	3	0	0	0	5
Business association	1	0	1	6	0	6	4	0	4	11
Mass organization	1	0	1	0	0	0	0	0	0	1
Military	1	0	1	2	0	2	0	0	0	3
National/local people's council	3	0	3	2	0	2	1	0	1	6
Average number of types of position per leader	2.8	0.0	2.8	1.2	1.0	1.1	1.3	1.0	1.2	1.4
TOTAL	37	38	75	31	22	53	27	18	45	173

Notes: (a) This includes leaders for whom no records of holding positions in political or social organizations outside of companies or organization they had worked for could be identified. (b) This includes leaders who were or had been holding such positions. Breakdown by the types of organizations (multiple answers) is shown below. (c) CP and GD denote chairperson and general director, respectively.

Source: Author's database.

worked for (Table 6.9).[22] The proportion of individuals who had positions in such organizations at any point in their career history turned out to be relatively high for chairpersons of former SOEs and private companies, suggesting a high incidence of political connections among these leaders. In particular, former SOE chairpersons held positions in varieties of organizations such as the party, the central government or the military, whereas the positions held by private company leaders were largely in business associations.

Discussion

The foregoing analysis provides crucial insights into evolving state-business relationships in Vietnam. With respect to the structure of the largest firms, this study found that the state's control over the largest domestic firms as the majority capital owner has narrowed considerably in comparison with the result of an earlier study by Cheshier and Penrose (2007). As at the end of 2016, SOEs, the majority of which belong to GCs or SEGs, only accounted for approximately 40 per cent of the top hundred listed firms, while more than half of the top hundred firms are either former SOEs—half of which no longer have any state capital participation—or firms established as private entities. Notably, the narrower group of twenty-five ultra-large firms included nearly as many private firms as SOEs, which confirms the growing role that private firms play in the economy. Nevertheless, the top hundred domestic firms, regardless of ownership type, primarily target the domestic market and are heavily concentrated in regulated sectors that are subject to entry barriers. This contrasts sharply with the "exceptionally globalized" status of the Vietnamese economy resulting from economic growth dependent on exports (Kopf 2018). What factors, then, allowed the largest firms, particularly privately owned ones, to succeed in regulated sectors?

This question was examined by analysing the backgrounds of the top leaders. With respect to SOEs, the story is relatively straightforward. SOE leaders constitute a homogenous group of highly educated individuals with Northern or Central origins who had spent most of their careers within the conglomerates. This suggests the state's control over subsidiaries of GCs and SEGs as majority owner is likely to be reinforced by the appointment of system insiders as the top leaders despite the frequent turnover of these leaders (Fujita 2020).

The analysis of former SOEs presented a very different picture. While state ownership in most of these companies has declined to nil or minimal levels, many of their leaders were found to be owners—albeit with relatively low ownership levels—who are equipped with ample state sector experience. Similar to the situation with SOE leaders discussed above, these individuals are highly educated and they largely originated from the Northern or Central regions. Differing from the case of the SOE leaders, however, who have developed insider network resources within corporate groups, these leaders had accumulated much wider varieties of non-business networks by working for the government, the party or the military, or by studying or working in former Eastern bloc countries, as well as working in political and socio-economic organizations outside of companies.

Notably, similar signs of political connections were identified for a sizeable cohort of private company leaders as well.[23] With respect to private firms, the findings of the present study suggest both continuity and change. More than half of private company leaders originated from the Northern or Central regions, and nearly half had cultivated state-sector employment or had studied or worked in an Eastern bloc country prior to establishing or joining their current company. Chairpersons in particular were found to have cultivated ample state-sector experience, including non-business experience, as was the case for former SOE leaders

Taken together, these profiles of former SOE and private company leaders suggest the persistence of state-business relationships in terms of personal ties rather than state-capital ownership. The analysis of leaders in our sample also points to a sizeable cohort of large business owners that have ample political connections, which is consistent with the rise of what Thuy Nguyen and Tuong Vu referred to as "red crony capitalism" in Chapter 1.

The prevalence of business owners with connections comes out clearly in Figure 6.2. It shows the composition of leaders in our sample in terms of two attributes—namely, ownership of the company's shares and possession of political connections—both of which are displayed as circles. With respect to the leaders of former SOEs, the majority (43 individuals out of 53; equivalent to 81 per cent) belong to the area where the two circles overlap. Apparently, equitization and divestment of state capital from SOEs has resulted in leaders equipped with political networks emerging as owners of major businesses that are already nominally private.

Turning to private company leaders, only 16 out of 45—equivalent to 36 per cent—belong to the same category. This has primarily to

FIGURE 6.2
Composition of Leaders by Possession of Political
Connections and Share Ownership

(a) Leaders of former SOEs (n=53)

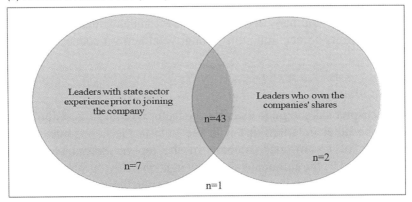

(b) Leaders of private companies (n=45)

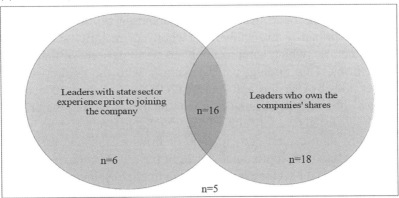

Source: Author's database.

do with the fact that half of the private company leaders did not have state sector experience before joining their current companies, which demonstrates the diversity of career pathways followed by private company leaders in our sample. They include, for example, old generation leaders who started as owner founders of household businesses as well as young and highly qualified professionals that had experience overseas before transferring into the leadership positions of major private businesses (Fujita 2020). Nevertheless, we need to be aware that the absence of a leader's experience in the state sector or political or socio-economic organizations, as analysed in our data, cannot rule out the possibility of other types of connections such as those possessed by a leader's close family members. Moreover, it is worth emphasizing that private company leaders generally exhibit higher levels of share ownership than those of SOEs or former SOEs—an indication of the degree of control that these private company leaders exert over management as well as their capacity to accumulate personal wealth from success in their business.

Conclusions

This chapter has sought to examine the features of the largest domestic firms and their relationships with the state in the new context. The analysis of an original database of the top hundred listed firms constructed by the author has shed new light on evolving state-business relationships not only in terms of state ownership ratios but also in terms of the identities of the state capital owners and the background of a firm's top leaders.

My analysis found that the largest domestic firms are no longer restricted primarily to members of wholly or majority state-owned conglomerates, which comprise only about 40 per cent of the largest listed firms. This finding, which contrasts with the findings of the earlier study by Cheshier and Penrose (2007) using data in 2005, albeit using a different type of sample, is new and important. The majority of the largest listed firms are either former SOEs, half of which no longer have any state capital participation, or firms established as private entities. Moreover, approximately half of the private company leaders did not have state-sector experience prior to establishing or joining the current companies.

My analysis identified various signs, however, that state-business collusion continues to prevail. Despite the ongoing globalization of the Vietnamese economy, the majority of the largest companies grew by focusing on sectors that are oriented towards the domestic market and are subject to entry barriers that limit competition. Many of the former SOEs and private companies are headed by owners equipped with ample political connections, whist younger professionals, many of whom studied and/or worked overseas, had been recruited into these enterprises. These findings seem to suggest that Vietnam has yet to witness the emergence of private firms that exploit new products, technologies or business plans without having to rely on transactions with government entities for access to the resources that permit them to operate, as has happened in China (Walder 2011), at least on any substantial scale. In short, after nearly three decades of gradual enterprise restructuring since the pilot equitization of SOEs and legalization of private enterprises, political connections remain an enduring feature of the largest domestic firms. An important point to note is that further divestment of state capital from SOEs or the promotion of private enterprises, which Vietnam is set to accelerate, is not likely to translate outright into diminishing state influence over large firms. Relationships are likely to persist in less visible modes, further blurring the boundary between the state and the private sector.

In exploring possible scenarios for the future, it is worth contemplating the implications of recent developments. One that deserves particular attention is the crackdown on corruption spearheaded by Communist Party General Secretary Nguyen Phu Trong, which intensified since his second term beginning in 2016. By targeting not only high-ranking party and government officials but also senior executives of large SOEs and banks, the campaign had a profound impact on the business community in general and business leaders in particular (Le 2019; Le, Levon and Nguyen 2019). A key question is whether the anti-corruption drive is to be followed by systematic reform of the legal systems, or whether the efforts will remain as simply punitive and selective (Le 2021). As far as the largest companies in our sample are concerned, the latter view seems more plausible as the impact thus far has been limited primarily to SOE leaders and in particular those who headed subsidiaries of PetroVietnam, which became one of the primary targets of the campaign.[24]

Another noteworthy development is the rise of privately owned conglomerates, some of which have already taken on leading roles in sectors of strategic significance. Vingroup is even preparing to extend its global reach by breaking into the US and European markets with electric vehicles under its own brand (Onishi 2021). While the Political Report adopted at the 13th Communist Party Congress expressed the party's intention of assisting the development of "strong private companies and economic groups with high levels of competitiveness", there is growing concern among the public about the undue influence of large private companies or special interest groups on government policies or decisions (Le, Levon and Nguyen 2019). While this study has shed light on the *existence* and *types* of relationships, further challenges lie in understanding how they function in practice and their implications for the development of those businesses as well as the economy as a whole.

Notes

1. The experiences of newly industrialized countries show it is not always large firms that take the leading roles in national economic development (Amsden 2003, pp. 194–95). While recent attempts by the Vietnamese government to improve the business environment for private firms by promoting the development of start-ups (Hồ 2019) deserves attention, the contribution of such firms to the overall economic transformation remains to be seen.

2. Cross-country experiences show that the relationship between rent-seeking and economic performance is complex and diverse (Khan 2000b). The outcomes may vary according to institutional structures and the political power of competing groups, which influences rent-seeking processes and their evolution (Khan 2000a).

3. Law on Private Enterprises and Company Law in 1990.

4. Prime Minister's Decisions 91-TTg and 90-TTg in 1994.

5. Resolution No. 10-NQ/TW dated 3 June 2017 of the Fifth Plenum of the 12th Party Central Committee on the development of private economy; Resolution No. 11-NQ/TW dated 3 June 2017 of the Fifth Plenum of the 12th Party Central Committee on perfecting the institution of a socialist-oriented market economy; and Resolution No. 12/NQ-TW dated 3 June 2017 of the Fifth Plenum of the 12th Party Central Committee on restructuring, renovation and increasing the efficiency of SOEs.

6. The decision provided classification for 240 wholly state-owned enterprises, not covering those in the fields of national defence and security and agriculture.

7. Official letter of the Prime Minister 991/TTg-ĐMDN in 2017; Prime Minister's Decision 1232/QD-TTg.

8. The rankings cover independent cost-accounting enterprises of all ownership types that have legal status and are established under Vietnamese law. Evaluation was based on sales data as of 31 December of the previous year, while profit, growth, total assets and the number of employees are also considered. For details, see https://vnr500.com.vn/.

9. In the early years, only Vietnamese investors were allowed to buy shares, and priority went to workers of the enterprises. Since the early 2000s, attempts have been made to diversify ownership by selling shares via auctions to external investors, including foreign investors. Concurrently, policies to separate the administrative functions of government organizations from ownership of SOEs were implemented, transforming the relationship between state organizations and SOEs into an investment-based one (Cheshier, Penrose and Nguyen 2006).

10. Data from the General Statistics Office. https://www.gso.gov.vn/default. aspx?tabid=621&ItemID=18668; https://www.gso.gov.vn/default.aspx?tabid =621&ItemID=19454.

11. This definition contrasts with the Enterprise Law of 2014, which defined SOEs as enterprises whose charter capital is 100 per cent owned by the state (Article 4.8). The legal definition was revised in the Enterprise Law of 2020 in which SOEs were defined to include enterprises with more than 50 per cent

of charter capital or the total number of voting shares held by the state (Article 88.1).

12. Enterprise statistics classify domestic private companies into private enterprises (*doanh nghiệp tư nhân*), partnership companies (*công ty hợp danh*), limited liability companies, joint stock companies without state capital, or joint stock companies with state capital. Limited liability companies include private limited liability companies and limited liability companies with less than 50 per cent of charter capital owned by the state (General Statistics Office 2019, p. 311). The statistics do not provide breakdowns for these two types of companies.

13. The corresponding ratio was 3.32 in 2006, suggesting that the decrease was faster than for joint stock companies without state capital.

14. Fujita (2020) presented the analysis of the origins and career pathways of leaders using the same database.

15. The ten private companies are as follows: Vingoup, Hoa Phat Group, Masan Group, Digi World, Hoa Sen Group, Hung Vung Corporation, Sacombank, Kido Group, Hoang Anh Gia Lai, and Eximbank.

16. The Investment Law of 2014 stipulates that investors have the right to invest in sectors and activities not prohibited by the law (Article 5.1). As an exception to this basic rule, investors wishing to invest in conditional business sectors or activities need to obtain separate certificates from the relevant authorities in addition to a general business registration certificate.

17. Government Decree No. 60/2015/ND-CP dated 26 June 2015, which came into effect on 1 September 2015. The following cases are stipulated as exceptions: (1) cases where international treaties in which Vietnam is a member contain provisions on foreign ownership ratio, and (2) cases of public companies operating in business lines and industries to which investment laws and relevant laws provide for a foreign ownership ratio.

18. Five companies were not included in the chairperson sample because of the post being vacant (1 company) and the simultaneous appointment as chairperson to two of the companies (4 companies). Twenty-two companies were excluded from the general director sample because of the simultaneous appointment of chairpersons as general directors (19 companies; only 18 of which were counted in the chairperson sample as the chairperson of the remaining companies simultaneously served as the chairperson of another one of the top hundred companies) and the post being taken by foreigners (3 companies).

19. Le Phuoc Vu (Hoa Sen Group), Doan Nguyen Duc (Hoang Anh Gia Lai), and Co Gia Tho (Thien Long Group).

20. The South includes the Southeast and the Mekong River Delta; the North includes the Northern Midlands and Mountain Areas and the Red River Delta; and the Centre includes the North Central, Central Coast and Central Highlands.

21. Vietnam Rubber Group is excluded as it is headquartered in Ho Chi Minh City.

22. This excludes party units, trade unions and the like within companies that the leaders had worked for.

23. The analysis found a lower incidence of leaders with an ample state background among general directors who are younger and more highly educated. Many of these individuals are likely to have been recruited into these companies relatively recently as professional managers (Fujita 2020).

24. Of the 173 leaders in our sample, 5 were found to have been dismissed from their positions by the end of 2020 as a result of disciplinary decisions. Of these, 4 were SOE leaders, including 3 at PetroVietnam subsidiaries, while 1 private bank executive was arrested for involvement in a fraud case. By 2017 at least 51 had been arrested across PetroVietnam and the banking sector on corruption-related charges (Reuters 2017).

References

Amsden, Alice. 1989. *Asia's Next Giant: South Korea and Late Industrialization*. New York: Oxford University Press.

———. 2003. *The Rise of "The Rest": Challenges to the West from Late-Industrializing Economies*. New York: Oxford University Press.

Beresford, Melanie. 1989. *National Unification and Economic Development in Vietnam*. London: Palgrave Macmillan.

———. 2006. "Vietnam: The Transition from Central Planning". In *The Political Economy of South-East Asia: Markets, Power and Contestation*, edited by Garry Rodan, Kevin Hewison, and Richard Robison, pp. 197–220. Melbourne: Oxford University Press.

Cheshier, Scott, and Jago Penrose. 2007. "The Top 200: Industrial Strategies of Vietnam's Largest Firms". United Nations Development Programme (UNDP) Policy Dialogue Paper 2007/4. Hanoi: UNDP.

Cheshier, Scott, Jago Penrose, and Nga Thi Thanh Nguyen. 2006. "The State as Investor: Equitisation, Privatisation and the Transformation of SOEs in Viet Nam". UNDP Viet Nam Policy Dialogue Paper. Hanoi: UNDP.

Dinh, Hinh Truong. 2013. "Light Manufacturing in Vietnam: Creating Jobs and Prosperity in a Middle-Income Economy". Washington, DC: The World Bank.

Fforde, Adam. 2004. "Vietnamese State-Owned Enterprises (SOEs) – 'Real Property', Commercial Performance and Political Economy". Working Paper Series no. 69. Hong Kong: SEARC City University of Hong Kong.

Fujita, Mai. 2020. "Top Corporate Leaders in Vietnam's Transitional Economy: Origins and Career Pathways". *Developing Economies* 58, no. 4: 301–31.

Gainsborough, Martin. 2003a. *Changing Political Economy of Vietnam: The Case of Ho Chi Minh City*. London: Routledge Curzon.

———. 2003b. "Slow, Quick, Quick: Assessing Equitization and Enterprise Performance Prospects in Vietnam". *Journal of Communist Studies and Transition Politics* 19, no. 11: 49–63.

General Statistics Office. 2013. *Development of Vietnam Enterprises in the Period of 2006–2011*. Hanoi: Statistical Publishing House.

———. 2019. *Statistical Yearbook*. Hanoi: Statistical Publishing House.

Greenfield, Gerard. 1994. "The Development of Capitalism in Vietnam | Socialist Register". *Socialist Register* 30: 203–34.

Hayashi, Yuko. 2013. "The Business Strategy of Vietnamese Enterprises Listed in the Stock Exchange: Change in the Business Strategy of REE after Listing". In *Vietnam's Economic Entities in Transition*, edited by Shozo Sakata, pp. 88–117. Basingstoke: Palgrave Macmillan.

Hayton, Bill. 2010. *Vietnam: Rising Dragon*. New Haven: Yale University Press.

Ho, Andy. 2017. "Vietnam's Domestic Airline Industry Takes off". *Financial Times*, 11 October 2017. https://www.ft.com/content/00baba5e-adc2-11e7-aab9-abaa44b1e130.

Hồ Thị Thu Hiền. 2019. "Cơ Chế, Chính Sách Hỗ Trợ Phát Triển Doanh Nghiệp Khởi Nghiệp Việt Nam". *Tạp Chí Tài Chính*, January 2019. http://tapchitaichinh.vn/tai-chinh-kinh-doanh/co-che-chinh-sach-ho-tro-phat-trien-doanh-nghiep-khoi-nghiep-viet-nam-311305.html.

Karla, Sanjay. 2015. "Vietnam: The Global Economy and Macroeconomic Outlook". *Journal of Southeast Asian Economies* 32, no. 1: 11–25.

Khan, Mushtaq H. 2000a. "Rent-Seeking as Process". In *Rents, Rent-Seeking and Economic Development*, edited by Mushtaq H. Khan, pp. 70–144. Cambridge: Cambridge University Press.

———. 2000b. "Rents, Efficiency and Growth". In *Rents, Rent-Seeking and Economic Development*, edited by Mushtaq H. Khan, pp. 21–69. Cambridge: Cambridge University Press.

Kim, Annette Miae. 2008. *Learning to Be Capitalists: Entrepreneurs in Vietnam's Transition Economy*. Oxford: Oxford University Press.

Kopf, Dan. 2018. "Vietnam Is the Most Globalized Populous Country in Modern History". World Economic Forum. https://www.weforum.org/agenda/2018/10/vietnam-is-the-most-globalized-populous-country-in-modern-history/.

Le Duy Binh. 2018. "Vietnam Nam Private Sector Productivity and Prosperity". Hanoi: Economica Vietnam.

Le Hong Hiep. 2017. "Vietnam's New Wave of SOE Equitization: Drivers and Implications". *ISEAS Perspective*, no. 2017/57. Singapore: ISEAS – Yusof Ishak Institute.

———. 2019. "The Impact of Vietnam's Anti-Corruption Campaign on the Real Estate Sector". *ISEAS Perspective*, no. 2019/19. Singapore: ISEAS – Yusof Ishak Institute.

Le Huong Thu. 2021. "Vietnam's Coming Leadership Change". *The Diplomat* 74 (January 2021). https://magazine.thediplomat.com/#/issues/-MP3bG9zf0K8NVsEkcVl/read.

Leung, Suiwah. 2015. "The Vietnamese Economy: Seven Years after the Global Financial Crisis". *Journal of Southeast Asian Economies* 32, no. 1: 1–10.

London, Jonathan. 2017. "Varieties of States, Varieties of Political Economy". In *Asia after the Developmental State*, edited by Toby Carroll and Darryl S.L. Jarvis, pp. 388–428. Cambridge: Cambridge University Press.

Onishi, Tomoya. 2021. "Vingroup Charges into Asian EV Brand Race in U.S. and Europe". *Nikkei Asia*, 28 October 2021. https://asia.nikkei.com/Business/Automobiles/Vingroup-charges-into-Asian-EV-brand-race-in-U.S.-and-Europe.

Phuong Dung. 2017. Cổ phần hoá DNNN: Chuyên gia chỉ ra chiêu lách "khe hở nhà đất". *Thanh tra*, 22 August 2017. https://thanhtra.com.vn/kinh-te/thi-truong/Co-phan-hoa-DNNN-Chuyen-gia-chi-ra-chieu-lach-khe-ho-nha-dat-123395.html.

Pincus, Jonathan. 2015. "Why Doesn't Vietnam Grow Faster? State Fragmentation and the Limits of Vent for Surplus Growth". *Journal of Southeast Asian Economies* 32 no. 1: 26–51.

———. 2017. "Vietnam: In Search of a New Growth Model". In *Southeast Asian Affairs 2016*, edited by Malcolm Cook and Daljit Singh, pp. 379–97. Singapore: ISEAS – Yusof Ishak Institute.

Le Quang Canh, Christian Levon, and Nguyen Thi Kieu Vien. 2019. "Vietnam Corruption Barometer 2019". Hanoi: Towards Transparency. https://towardstransparency.vn/wp-content/uploads/2018/11/VCB-2019_EN.pdf.

Reuters. 2017. "What's behind Vietnam's Corruption Crackdown?" 11 December 2017. https://www.reuters.com/article/us-vietnam-security-crackdown-explainer-idUSKBN1E51AO.

Taussig, Markus. 2009. "Business Strategy during Radical Economic Transition: Vietnam's First Generation of Larger Private Manufacturers and a Decade of Intensifying Opportunities and Competition". A Policy Discussion Paper. United Nations Development Programme Viet Nam. Hanoi: UNDP Viet Nam.

Tong cuc thong ke. 2017. *Doanh Nghiep Viet Nam 15 Nam Dau the Ky 21 (2000–2014)*. NXB thong ke. Hanoi.

Vu-Thanh, Tu Anh. 2017. "Does WTO Accession Help Domestic Reform? The Political Economy of SOE Reform Backsliding in Vietnam". *World Trade Review* 16, no. 1: 85–109.

Vuving, Alexander L. 2010. "Vietnam: A Tale of Four Players". In *Southeast Asian Affairs 2010*, edited by Daljit Singh, pp. 367–91. Singapore: Institute of Southeast Asian Studies.

Wacker, Konstantin M. 2017. "Restructuring the SOE Sector in Vietnam". *Journal of Southeast Asian Economies* 34 no. 2: 283–301.

Wade, Robert. 1990. *Governing the Market: Economic Theory and the Role of Government in East Asian Industrialization*. Princeton: Princeton University Press.

Walder, Andrew G. 2011. "From Control to Ownership: China's Managerial Revolution". *Management and Organization Review* 7, no. 1: 19–38.

Webster, Leila, and Markus Taussig. 1999. "Vietnam's Under-sized Engine: A Survey of 95 Larger Private Manufacturers". Private Sector Discussions no. 8. Hanoi. Mekong Development Project Facility. http://documents.worldbank.org/curated/pt/906791468339061996/Vietnams-under-sized-engine-a-survey-of-95-larger-private-manufacturers.

Chapter 7

The Vietnamese Communist Party's Leadership in Public Higher Education

Quang Chau and Mai Van Tinh

Higher Education Governance and Political Regimes

Probably nobody would deny that higher education cannot be isolated from politics. The politics of higher education has been addressed by many higher education researchers, especially those in the United States (see McLendon 2003). For instance, a significant number of studies, including a seminal work by Burton Clark (1983), have critically analysed how higher education is governed by the state, and how such a relationship has been fundamentally restructured in the era of neoliberalism. But apart from notable exceptions such as Levy (1980; 1981) and Jungblut (2015), most higher education scholars tend to treat the state quite homogeneously. In other words, these scholars do not usually differentiate state models in their analyses of higher education governance.

In fact, higher education is governed by different logics in democratic and authoritarian regimes. In multi-party democracies the state cannot easily twist the arms of universities, although through financial policies, for instance, it is possible to exert indirect influence. In contrast, although authoritarian regimes generally have the power to dictate the internal affairs of universities, they are deeply perplexed when making policies.[1] The logic, in its simplest form, runs like this: since universities usually nourish the democratic spirit (Bueno de Mesquita and Downs 2005; Sanborn and Thyne 2014), authoritarian regimes normally try to abolish the higher education system entirely (as illustrated by the Chinese Cultural Revolution), hamper the expansion of higher education, or adopt preferential admission and funding schemes to channel most higher education benefits into the regime's loyal constituencies (Hanson and Sokhey 2020). But when it comes to the largely unquestionable contribution of higher education to economic development (Lane and Johnstone 2012), authoritarian regimes seem to be left considerably bewildered. Simply put, economic development could be a double-edged sword for these regimes. It contributes to social stability, a primary source of legitimacy for the regime's resilience, but at the same time produces the middle class that will normally demand more autonomy from the state. Recent empirical evidence, however, tends to challenge this simplistic prediction of modernization theory, and shows that authoritarian regimes are markedly adept in reaping the benefits while significantly reducing the threats of economic development (see Wright 2010 for the case of China). In the case of China, the Chinese Communist Party (CCP) chooses to rapidly expand and greatly invest in the higher education system (Wan 2006; Wang 2014; Song 2018) to maintain social and economic stability, while tactically skimming much of higher education's democratic values through a sophisticated system of on-campus cultural and political surveillance (Perry 2020; 2017).

Most current studies—as a result of their focus on military-authoritarian rule, especially those looking at Latin America—do not sufficiently highlight the partisanship of the governance of higher education in one-party authoritarian regimes. Intriguingly, such partisanship has likewise been overlooked even in studies on communist higher education. Some of these studies have only mentioned in passing that communist party committees play a key role in university governance (see Katz 1956; Rudma 1964 for the Soviet case). At best, a handful of studies on the Chinese case elaborate that Chinese universities are governed by two agencies, i.e., the party committee and the board of rectors; the former uses party resolutions to guide the latter (see Yitao and Hua 2019; Huang 2017; Jiang and Li 2012). In addition, these studies note that almost all of the board of rectors are de facto CCP members. In the case of Vietnam, although it is generally accepted that the Vietnamese Communist Party (VCP) plays a predominant role in public universities, we still know very little about how the party keeps the system of higher education in check, how the system is organized and how the party maintains its influence on campus.

This chapter depicts and analyses the VCP's hard power (i.e., structure and control mechanism) rather than its soft power (i.e., ideology and ideological constraints) in higher education governance. Our analyses are at both the national and institutional levels, but more focus is placed on the latter. We especially concentrate on the VCP's role in personnel planning for the leadership positions of public universities. Our data have been gathered from archived documents stored at the National Archives III in Hanoi, as well as correspondence and in-depth interviews with over forty informants of diverse backgrounds—namely, cadres at various state agencies, including VCP ones, public university leaders (presidents, board chairs, deans and department chairs), and leaders of the Ho Chi Minh Communist Youth Union and Vietnam Union of Students. It should be further noted that this study is exploratory, given the remarkable variations among universities. In fact, one of the conclusions that almost all the informants emphasized when asked to comment on the VCP's influence on the institutional personnel planning was: "It all depends!"

Following this introductory section, the chapter will proceed with four main parts. We first briefly lay out the structure of Vietnam's higher education. We then describe the overall national structure of the VCP's leadership in governing Vietnam's higher education before looking closer at the VCP's structure at the university, school and department levels. Our focus is on how the VCP becomes involved in key personnel planning and selection. Afterwards, we examine how the two VCP-affiliated youth organizations operate on campus. In the conclusion, we tie together the key findings, comment on how the ongoing public administration reform might affect the VCP's leadership role in the public higher education sector and then propose several avenues for future study.

Vietnam's Higher Education System

Throughout its history of nearly ten centuries, higher education in Vietnam has practically never been autonomous from the government. Elsewhere, while most medieval universities pursued religious and social missions (Perkin 2007), Vietnamese Imperial colleges, the first of which was founded in 1076, explicitly set missions to train the literati class for the imperial courts (Nguyen 2011). The University of Indochina (UI)—the foundation of Vietnamese contemporary higher education, established in 1907 by the French Colonial Administration—brought with it the Napoleonic model of state-controlled higher education (Duong 1978). After the 1954 Geneva Accords, higher education in the Democratic Republic of Vietnam (North Vietnam) and the Republic of Vietnam (South Vietnam) followed two contrasting patterns. The UI model of state interventionism emigrated from Hanoi to Saigon, thriving in the First Republic (1955–63) before the US model of greater autonomy arrived in the Second Republic (1967–75) (Hoang 2015). Contemporaneously, in the North, the UI model remained, strengthened and expanded during the Sovietization period. In the Soviet model, higher education was essentially a political tool whereby the communist party intervened deeply into all key aspects from admission, curriculum and funding to personnel. After 1975, the Soviet model stretched nationwide until the summit of university and college presidents in Nha Trang in 1987, when a road map for higher education autonomy was drafted and eventually, although slowly, implemented (St. George 2003). Nevertheless, institutional autonomy has since remained a highly contested realm in higher education policies, and in general, Vietnamese public universities are still subject to substantial state control (Hayden and Thiep 2007).

A major Soviet legacy that persists in contemporary Vietnam's higher education is its extensive segmentation. In the command economy, higher education institutions were tasked to annually supply a specific number of workforce members for specific sectors and industries. These institutions were largely mono-disciplinary and under the jurisdiction of dozens of central ministries (Tran 1998). After Doi Moi, despite the relative success of departing from the command economy, the state's repeated pledges and resolutions to restructure the higher education system, especially to abolish the line ministry mechanism (*co che bo chu quan*), have met with little success. Indeed, in many respects the system, which now consists of approximately five hundred institutions, has become increasingly uncoordinated. With the rise of local politics, dozens of provincial universities have been established since the late 1990s. They have been funded entirely and governed substantially—including in terms of personnel aspects—by provincial governments (Nguyen 2016; Natali 2001). But many of these universities have lately proposed to be merged with centrally governed universities. Probably the most remarkable example of incoordination is the recent transfer of all short-cycle higher education institutions (*truong cao dang*) from the Ministry of Education and Training (MOET) to the Ministry of Labour, Invalids and Social Affairs (MOLISA). The transfer, which was persistently and strongly lobbied for by MOLISA's ministers, was considered a highly political decision that also involved nepotism.

In terms of governance, although MOET regulates the academic matters of all higher education institutions, it directly governs fewer than a third of them. Generally, universities under other ministries are considered a part of that ministry's bureaucracy, and thus subject to tighter control. Presidentship at these universities can aid instant legitimacy for one to elevate their rank in the bureaucracy. Two notable examples are Tran Tuan Anh, head of the VCP's Central Economic Commission and former minister of industry and trade, and Nguyen Thanh Nghi, minister of construction. Both had been president and vice president, respectively, of the two universities governed by the ministries they would later become the minister of. In addition, as an unwritten rule, the president of the University of Law is almost guaranteed the position of deputy minister of justice.

Given the significant diversity in the governance of Vietnam's higher education, it seems nearly impossible for us to investigate all types of public universities. Some colleagues and informants kindly suggested we examine a particular university as a case study. But for accessibility and feasibility matters, and especially because of the exploratory nature of this chapter, we decided to focus primarily on universities under the governance of MOET. Our choice is obviously not without problems. Compared with the majority of universities governed by other ministries, those governed by MOET tend to be more academically focused, and consequently their personnel planning is not excessively partisan. These features might not hold true for other types of public university.

The VCP's Governance Structure in Higher Education

Although the higher education system looks highly fragmented and considerably uncoordinated, the VCP has developed its own sophisticated structure to keep the entire system in check. In principle, all civil universities are now subject to specialized agencies under the VCP, the government, and the National Assembly. The VCP's Central Propaganda and Training Commission (*ban Tuyen giao*; CPTC) proposes, consults on and drafts education resolutions for the Central Committee as well as overseeing the implementation of these resolutions. This commission was established in 2007 from the amalgamation of the two central commissions: Science and Education (*ban Khoa giao*), and Ideology and Culture (*ban Tu tuong, Van hoa*). In the legislative branch, the Committee for Culture, Education, Youth, Adolescents and Children (*Uy ban Van hoa, Giao duc, Thanh thieu nien, Nhi dong*; CCEYAC) proposes and drafts education policies as well as oversees the implementation of these policies. Most committee members—as with the National Assembly in general—have VCP membership. Additionally, the head of the CCEYAC is a member of the National Assembly's Party Union (*Dang doan Quoc Hoi*)—a special party cell under the direct supervision of the Politburo. In the executive branch, the Ministry of Education and Training (*Bo Giao duc & Dao tao*; MOET)—especially its Higher Education Department (*Vu Giao duc Dai hoc*)—has the most expertise in making higher education policies. MOET's regulations on degrees, curriculum, and criteria for leadership appointments must (in theory) be followed by all civil universities, although the majority of universities in Vietnam do not depend on the MOET for funding or personnel appointments. The VCP leads the MOET through the MOET's Party Committee (*Dang uy Bo Giao duc & Dao tao*) and Civil Affairs Committee (*Ban can su dang Bo Giao duc & Dao tao*); the latter outweighs the former when it comes to making higher education policies, although there are a significant number of members that overlap between the two committees. The MOET's Party Committee is subordinate to the Party Committee of Central Agencies (*Dang uy khoi cac co quan Trung uong*), which is in turn is under the direct supervision of the Central Committee (see Figure 7.1).

Although the heads of all three aforementioned specialized agencies (CPTC, CCEYAC and MOET) are Central Committee members, the CPTC's head is de facto a higher rank than his two peers, and is usually a Politburo ex-officio member. In principle, when making higher education laws and policies, CCEYAC and MOET must closely

FIGURE 7.1
VCP's Overall Structure of Higher Education Governance

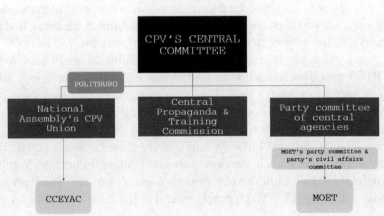

refer to the education resolutions passed by the Central Committee upon the CPTC's endorsement, as well as consult constantly with the CPTC itself.

In reality, since its establishment in 2007 from the amalgamation of the Central Commission of Science and Education, CPTC's influence over higher education has eroded. When it comes to proportional power between the three agencies, other than the endowed political capital of the agency head, his or her educational credentials, expertise and seniority do matter significantly. In general, while heads of the CCEYAC and MOET are normally professors and former directors of the national universities, or at least former presidents of major universities, the head and deputy head of CPTC responsible for education are younger, have no prior experience in university leadership positions, and have lower educational qualifications. Summed into a brief statement, CPTC's control of higher education has recently been increasingly loosened.

Elite Dualism in the Governance of Vietnam's Public Universities

The VCP's deep intervention in higher education, as elaborated above, leads naturally to such questions as "how closely will public universities be linked to the party?" and "to what extent will these universities become political organizations?" Intriguingly, although they are subject to the tight control of the party, Vietnam's public universities still have plenty of space for intellectual development. This conclusion is drawn primarily from elite dualism—a theory that postulates that communist states have been governed by both political and intellectual elites.

Elite Dualism

Much has been written about the relationship between intellectuals and politicians in communist states. In the 1950s, Milovan Djilas, a senior communist leader in the former Yugoslavia,[2] posited that communist leaders contradicted their claims of a classless society when these leaders had already become a new class (Djilas 1983). Scholars after Milovan Djilas have examined this emerging class more thoroughly. For example, in 1979, based on their observations in Hungary, novelist George Konrád and sociologist Ivan Szelényi pointed to the ongoing "self-evolution" among Eastern European communist leaders. These leading groups consisted both of politicians who were being intellectualized and of intellectuals who were eager to join politics in the hope of replacing politicians to contribute to the positive development of society (Konrád and Szelényi 1979). Approximately a decade later, after being deported from Hungary, Ivan Szelényi, then professor at the University of Wisconsin–Madison, slightly modified his stance because of unforeseeable incidents occurring throughout Hungary and Eastern Europe (Szelényi 1987). He concluded that intellectuals tended to retreat because politicians were more stubbornly resistant to sharing power than he had expected. Besides, pressed by economic hardship, communist leaders had to legalize the private economy, and they indirectly facilitated the emergence of a leadership alliance between politicians and entrepreneurs. Once allowed to return to Hungary, Ivan Szelényi witnessed the rise of numerous villas in the countryside, and the owners of the villas were state cadres and entrepreneurs.

In the case of China, the relationship between intellectuals and politicians, as well as the question of which attribute (political or educational capital) is more important for one to climb the leadership ladder, has remained largely inconclusive. Many writers—such as Li (2016); Bian, Shu and Logan (2001); and Landry (2008)—posit that the CCP in the Mao period usually preferred "reds" over "experts" in leadership planning and appointments, while in the post-Mao era expertise was considered to have more weight as a factor in leadership selection. Based on statistical data, Xiaowei Zang argues that there exist two separate tracks within the state's bureaucracy in contemporary China: government and politics. Party seniority is more important for promotion within politics, whereas those with respected educational credentials are more likely to move up the ranks in government. And for someone possessing neither of these qualities, it is extremely challenging for them to enter into leadership (Zang 2004; 2001b). Xiaowei Zang succinctly concludes that "party cadres and technocrats need each other to stay in office" (Zang 2001a, p. 73). Although similarly separating the CCP's leadership into two tracks—i.e., administrative and professional—Andrew G. Walder argues that the administrative track requires both educational credentials and political capital, whereas professional leaders need *only* the former to succeed (Walder 1995; Walder, Li and Treiman 2000). Joel Andreas discovered that many Chinese leaders were trained as engineers and technological experts at elite public universities, especially Tsinghua, the leading Chinese university of technology. The implication of Andreas's findings—slightly different from the conclusions mentioned above—is that Chinese leaders are a rather homogeneous group who have *both* political and educational capital (Andreas 2009). This conclusion is shared by Eddy U, whose recent book points to the CCP's resilient and strategic mobilization attempts to incorporate intellectuals into its bureaucracy (U 2019).

In most of the aforementioned studies on elite dualism, formal education levels appear to be the predominant qualifier for one to be classified as an intellectual. This is a rather deficient approach, however, especially for communist states, where the party can basically force a university's hand. For example, research tends to overlook the mode of study or the subject major of those considered intellectuals or intellectualized politicians. In the case of China, although over seventy-five per cent of all members of the Eighteenth Central Committee obtained postgraduate degrees, seventy-five per cent of these members participated in part-time programmes (Li 2016), which are normally of dubious quality. Furthermore, many members of the same Central Committee graduated from military or Marxist-Leninist philosophy programmes at party-affiliated education institutions, and these programmes are often ambiguously placed under "Law" majors. A number of politicians graduated from full-time programmes at prestigious Chinese universities. Still, we cannot simply assume that they underwent as equally rigorous training as their peers. Instead, we need to examine more closely whether these people had any state/party affiliation or held senior positions before admission into or graduation from universities. In the end, universities, prestigious or not, are still governed by the Chinese state and its CCP. Simply put, degrees do not seem to strongly indicate which intellectuals are in communist societies. Consequently, when collecting data for this paper, we also asked whether an academic elite was *well-recognized* in their field.

To the best of our knowledge, there is no study on elite dualism in Vietnam to date. Reds versus Experts debates, while constituting an important part in the CCP's developmental policies, did not play out significantly nor explicitly in the case of Vietnam. Only in Ho Chi Minh's Testament were Reds and Experts mentioned officially as expectations: Ho hoped that members of the Ho Chi Minh Communist Youth Union and youth in general would be interested in both socialist/ communist values and being well-trained in their professional fields.

It is tremendously challenging to conduct empirical studies on Vietnam's elite dualism. Available anecdotal evidence is also inconclusive. For instance, the vast majority of the current Politburo members have postgraduate degrees, but most of their degrees have been awarded by party-affiliated education institutions, especially Ho

Chi Minh National Academy of Politics (*Hoc vien Chinh tri Quoc gia Ho Chi Minh*). Nguyen Dinh Quyen, deputy head of the National Assembly Committee for Justice (*Uy ban Tu phap Quoc Hoi*), publicly raised the incapability of many high and middle-ranking officials in the executive branch (Anh 2015). In a recent commentary on VietnamNet, Nguyen Si Dung, former deputy head of the National Assembly Office, an outspoken and well-noted social critic, reiterated the significance of recruiting talent and concluded that, "Whenever the party still wishes to remain [*sic*] its leadership, then to attract talents into the party is not simply a goodwill gesture; it is indeed a prerequisite" (Nguyen 2020).

There is vast evidence that the VCP has tried to collaborate with people whose academic and cultural capital and expertise are widely recognized, but this collaboration has not necessarily been equal. For example, on the one hand, activist intellectuals constituted a substantial part of the VCP during its formative years (see Marr 1984), and many of those eventually assumed state leadership roles. On the other hand, many intellectuals did not survive the repeated expulsion campaigns such as the Land Reform (Vu 2010) and Nhan Van Giai Pham (Zinoman 2011). Outspoken intellectuals are often charged as political dissidents and usually repressed, especially when they become involved in organized activities (Abuza 2001). More contemporary examples are the party's endeavours, when critically pressed by the sociopolitical crises around Doi Moi, to seek consultation from overseas Vietnamese experts who had previously been labelled as traitors because of their affiliation with the former Republic of Vietnam (for instance, see Le 2015), and foreign—even US—experts (Perkins, Dapice and Haughton 1994). Succinctly, the VCP did not entirely turn its back on intellectuals, including those whose "Red" side is by far outweighed by their "Expert" side, but it seems to do so opportunistically, and only if such collaboration benefits the regime.

Dual Elitism in Vietnam's Public Universities

The "four pillars" of public universities include the president, party secretary, trade union chairman, and secretary of the Ho Chi Minh Communist Youth Union (HCYU). All of them are de facto party members. For a long time, the posts of university president and party committee secretary were separate; the former had relatively more power than the latter. Since the 2000s, the two posts have been merged, first on an institution-level pilot basis, then system-wide. Consequently, the four-pillar model has essentially become a triangle of three considerably unequal power centres: the president, concurrently

FIGURE 7.2
Public Universities' Internal Management Structure

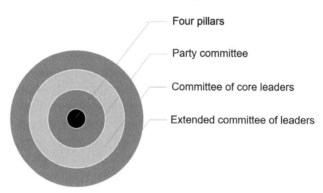

Four pillars

Party committee

Committee of core leaders

Extended committee of leaders

the party secretary, sits at the top of the hierarchy, while the remaining two figures hold only nominal power. Some universities, however, resist this power convergence model and retain the four-pillar one.

In general, the party committee is now the most powerful agency within public universities. Apart from the aforementioned four pillars, it includes vice-presidents, heads of academic affairs and organization, heads of human resources, and the deans of several key schools. There are at most fifteen members in the party committee, between three and five of whom constitute the standing committee (*Ban Thuong vu Dang uy*).[3] Among the committee's five main responsibilities stipulated in Regulation 97-QĐ/TW issued by the Party Central Committee's Secretariat on 22 March 2004, personnel planning is considered the most important. There are in addition two other important committees that are outside the structure of the VCP but which are heavily involved in key personnel decisions. The first is the committee of core leaders (*Tap the lanh dao chu chot*), which consists of the president, all vice-presidents, the party committee, and chairman of the university board. The other, called the extended committee of leaders (*Tap the lanh dao mo rong*), includes the above committee of core leaders plus all deans, office heads and directors of university-affiliated research institutes (see Figure 7.2).

Institutional Leaders

Current regulations stipulate, although not explicitly, that university presidents and vice presidents must have both political and academic qualities—the latter specifically means a doctoral degree—and at least five years of previous leadership experience as a dean or head of an administrative office. In reality, all university presidents and almost all vice-presidents are party members and have obtained doctoral degrees from respected universities in either Vietnam or overseas. At major universities, presidents are often prominent scholars in their field of expertise. Although HCYU leadership has become an increasingly common pathway for future leadership positions in the party's and state's bureaucracy, it is hardly a sufficient foundation to secure a top position at public universities (HCYU structures will be discussed in the following section). In other words, academic credentials are a must-have for those who aspire to become university leaders, and they are not entirely interchangeable with political capital. In most cases, the members of the board of rectors have worked for a long time at the university, except for a few cases in which internal conflicts urge governing agencies (usually a central ministry) to appoint external people into the university's leadership positions. In short, although a university president is often the most political figure on campus, they are also predominantly an academic.

While the board of rectors is largely responsible for academic affairs, the party committee is in principle tasked to ensure party leadership in universities. The convergence of these two leadership groups was institutionalized in the 2000s, although it has remained an open question as to what caused the VCP to pursue such a convergence. In any case, through a sophisticated procedure of both appointment and orchestrated election, the secretary of the party committee is normally the president of the university. The convergence of power tends to be followed more strictly at universities that are under the jurisdiction of other agencies and ministries other than the MOET. In general, the president will not take the secretary role under the following two scenarios. First, although the terms for both the president and secretary are five years, the president's tenure starts from the appointment date, whilst that of the secretary is fixed after the VCP's National Congress. Consequently, in the case that the president is removed prematurely or appointed to another position, there will be a gap between the terms of the president and the secretary. In this case the position of secretary will be temporarily vacant until the next party committee congress of the university, when the incoming president will likely be elected the secretary. The second scenario, which is much less likely to occur, is when the president's political qualities are by far outweighed by their academic qualities, and thus they are not elected to be the secretary. After all, party secretary is an elected position, and sometimes the "democratic" element in the "democratic centralism" principle prevails. Furthermore, there are usually "black sheep" or factions, either veiled or disclosed, within the party committee. Some informants revealed that opposing voices are more likely to come from deans than administrators, and these voices cannot be easily ignored.

Personnel is a central aspect that is controlled predominantly by the university party committee. The committee usually works on and finalizes its personnel plan in the second half of its term, detailing who will be nominated for each position. At the university party committee's congress, all party members or their representatives use their votes to select the incoming party committee from among the nominated candidates. The incoming committee will then elect the secretary and one or two deputy-secretaries. For the presidency, the current party committee, either outgoing or incoming, nominates candidate(s) for the extended committee of leaders to give their vote of confidence.[4] This committee includes several deans, who have more academic than political capital (as elaborated on below), and it therefore tends to prefer candidates with good academic records. The result of the vote is known only to the committee of core leaders, who will then finalize their appointment decisions. Although the decision needs to be approved by some agencies at the local and central levels, such approval is rather a formality.

There are usually very few surprises between whom the party committee nominates, whom the extended committee of leaders votes for, and whom the committee of core leaders appoints. In the majority of cases there is only one candidate nominated by the party committee, and self-nomination is essentially not allowed. The outgoing president is asked by the party committee to nominate their successor, and normally the party committee agrees to that nomination. Aspiring presidents therefore often seek support from their predecessors. This often causes rent-seeking and nepotism, which easily leads to factional infighting at several major universities. Occasionally, the party committee nominates more than one candidate. But it is quite obvious for almost everyone to recognize which is the preselected candidate: normally, they are a deputy secretary. No matter how many presidential candidates there are, however, the preselected candidate must have good academic credentials; otherwise, they will have a low chance of receiving enough votes of confidence.

In reality there exist "beautification" campaigns for preselected candidates who are slightly academically underqualified. For instance, they will be appointed to serve in various academic committees to network with key persons in order to increase the chance of gaining

FIGURE 7.3
VCP's Structure at Public Universities

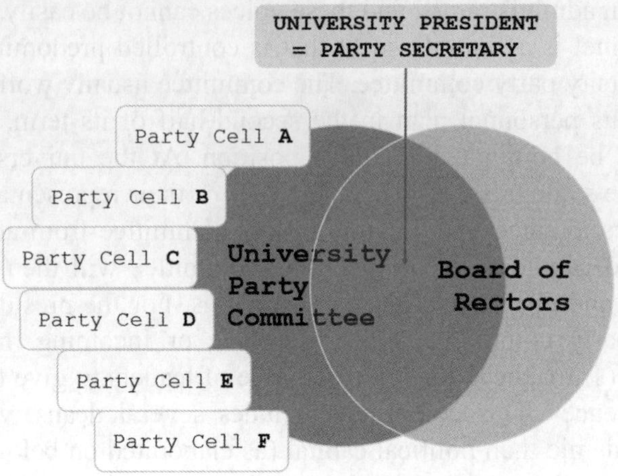

more votes. In addition, with tremendous support from the campaign team, the preselected candidate will often win research grants that should theoretically be awarded on a competitive basis. Currently, as an unwritten rule, the university president must at least hold an associate professorship. But the professorial appointment procedure has many loopholes that a candidate with the endorsement of the party committee, a good campaign team and excellent networking skills can easily utilize.

Deans and Department Chairs

While the members of most boards of rectors are party members, some sub-institutional leaders, especially the deans and directors of research institutes, do not have party membership. The minimum academic requirement for deans and directors is a doctoral degree. Office heads, apart from those who lead academic affairs or research management offices, only need a bachelor's degree to qualify for the position. In many cases deans do *not* have the strongest academic background or record within the school, but at the same time they *almost never* stand near the bottom of the school's academic spectrum. In other words, political capital cannot compensate completely for deficiencies of academic capital in the appointments of deans. In reality, party membership is only a formality in many cases. Many candidates for dean or office head are encouraged to join the party after they have already been shortlisted by the party committee for such a position.

And some of those who reject the offer of party membership are still appointed.

Although the president has the full authority, after consulting with the party committee, to appoint deans and office heads, appointment decisions usually combine both top-down and bottom-up approaches. Office heads are usually straightforwardly appointed by the president (top-down). The appointment of deans is more complex and varies between universities. A full process begins with tenured faculty nominating candidates, whom will be shortlisted by the party committee based on MOET's criteria for deanship. Tenured faculty then give qualified candidates a vote of confidence, and the vote result theoretically gives preferences for the president to finalize appointment decisions. Vote results are usually not released, but voters normally discuss with one another and thus can be certain of who actually obtained more votes. There are, however, various tactics that are commonly applied to ensure the preselected candidate is appointed legitimately. First, like in the case of elections for the president, the preselected candidate will be clearly signalled through the beautification process. Alternatively, the president can transfer a competing candidate that seems to be gaining more votes to another position. Another tactic, confirmed by one informant, is to verbally command a loyal vote-counting staff to falsify the vote result. As the last resort, it is still legitimate for the president to override the vote result and appoint the preselected candidate anyway. This is sometimes a strategic decision. For instance, in some schools the candidate from the largest department will almost always get the most votes, and thus would easily be elected the dean. This can lead to nepotism and rent-seeking behaviour, which the president can crack down on strategically by appointing his or her own alliance instead. But this is usually considered a very risky decision. Our informants tend to agree that a high vote of confidence is essential for a candidate to perform their duties after the appointment. Moreover, internal conflicts easily arise when a candidate with a low vote is chosen over a highly trusted one. These conflicts can cause chaos for the school or even for the whole university, and for the institutional leaders in particular. In short, during the appointment process for deans, the president does not completely ignore the preferences of tenured faculty, although they could legally do so, and they are more likely to do so with office heads. All in all, deanship is comparatively closer to that of an academic than a political position.

While a requisite for the board of rectors, and a preferred quality for deans and office heads, party membership is far dwarfed by academic credentials in the appointment of department chairs. At the departmental level, the chair is selected rather democratically: usually by a vote of confidence, and occasionally by popular vote. Even in the case of the former, deans and the president do not usually reverse the vote result, although legitimately they could.

Most informants agree that there remains some extent of academic autonomy at the departmental level. There are no explicit rules for censorship. Instead, self-censorship is the norm: faculty members prefer to use books licensed and printed in Vietnam, ignore politically sensitive topics, and avoid critiquing issues that have been firmly asserted by the state. Courses with the potential to give rise to political debate will hardly be offered. Other than that, department chairs can propose to open new programmes, add new courses to current programmes, or adopt new textbooks in existing courses. Such proposals are usually approved, although they need to go through several bureaucratic steps. All the interviewees who are faculty members seem satisfied with their academic autonomy, although they are fully aware of the self-censorship practice. Even the content and teaching methods of Marxist-Leninist courses have been continuously and substantially reformed by the Central Commission of Science and Education (currently the CPTC) to accommodate students' interest.

In conclusion, although political capital and academic credentials are both essential in appointment decisions, the role of the former is more important at the university leader level, but steeply declines at the school and departmental levels. That said, academic credentials tend to carry more weight in personnel planning and appointment, even for the position of president. Furthermore, appointment decisions at any level tend to tactically combine both coercion and consent, which resemble the tactics adopted by the VCP at the national level to maintain the regime's resilience (Nguyen 2019), and the latter prevails at lower leadership levels.

There are at least two reasons why faculty members, unlike state bureaucrats, enjoy more professional autonomy. First, tenured faculty do not work nine to five, and thus have the time to earn an additional legal income and can become fairly financially independent from the university. It is not uncommon for faculty members to refuse leadership roles—extra duties are often more time-consuming and less financially rewarding than what they would be able to earn from a secondary job. Second, as a result of inbreeding recruitment, many people eventually become leaders at the same university they had attended as a student. Therefore, their backgrounds—both their achievements and any scandals—are more or less known by their professors. Some professors whose students are now university leaders are still teaching at the same university. This student-professor relationship will give professors substantially more protection and autonomy.

Between a Rock and a Hard Place: Vietnamese Youth Organizations in Public Universities

Our understanding of political parties would be incomplete without an examination of their extended arms. In communist states, social realms are supervised through a network of party-affiliated mass organizations. In the case of China, university campuses have remained an important component of the CCP's power structure since the foundation of the party (see, for example, Kuo-tai 1989). The Communist Youth League, now an integral part of the governance of Chinese universities (Liu 2017), screens and nominates qualified candidates for party membership. Most high-achieving students are offered party membership, and the majority of them accept. Consequently, the number of party members recruited on campuses has significantly increased since the late 1980s (Koss 2018). The motivations of these individuals to join the party, however, are less ideological and more pragmatic: to secure career promotions (Guo 2005).

In the case of Vietnam, the Ho Chi Minh Communist Youth Union (*Doan Thanh nien Cong san Ho Chi Minh*; HCYU) and the Vietnam National Union of Students (Hoi Sinh vien Viet Nam; VNUS) are the two most important youth organizations. Whilst the HCYU is the official recruitment pipeline for the VCP, the relationships it has with other mass organisations are considerably ambiguous. On the one hand, it is a core member of the Vietnam Youth Federation (*Hoi Lien hiep Thanh nien Viet Nam*; VYF), which is in turn a member of the VCP-led sociopolitical coalition called the Vietnam Father Front (*Mat tran To Quoc Viet Nam*; VFF). On the other hand, HCYU is also listed as a direct member of VFF, which is not under the VYF.

Both HCYU and VNUS are well-grounded in the higher education system. HCYU's secretary is an ex-officio member of the university party committee. HCYU's cells are present at all schools and departments, including those where party cells are absent. The class-level HCYU cell (*chi Doan*)[5] is the smallest unit, many of which constitute the school-level HCYU cell (*Doan khoa*). The structure of VNUS runs in parallel with that of HCYU. In fact, according to some informants, VNUS is considered inferior to HCYU. The establishment of VNUS cells was in fact orchestrated by HCYU. For the last several terms, at the national as well as university levels, the VNUS chairman has usually held the position of HCYU deputy-secretary. In general, only elite students (approximately 13 per cent of all students, according to statistics cited by Ngo 2004) are admitted to the HCYU, whereas the rest are offered VNUS membership. The leaders of both HCYU and VNUS are not usually academically excellent, although they must meet certain minimum academic requirements to maintain their leadership roles. For instance, a report in the early 2000s showed that only 20 per cent of all HCYU's leaders in Hanoian universities had "good" (*gioi*) academic records, while the majority had either "fair" (*kha*) or "poor" (*yeu*) results (Dinh 2000).

Except for the secretary of the HCYU (university level), the leadership roles of both youth organizations at school and departmental levels are elected rather democratically. At the class level, the secretary is normally elected by popular vote. In reality, not many students are interested in the position, and thus the secretary often remains unchanged during the whole programme. At the school level, leaders are selected either by popular vote or based on the result of the confidence vote. Even the secretary of the HCYU committee has lately been elected by popular vote at some universities.

In late 2017, VCP general secretary Nguyen Phu Trong warned that students had become "ideologically indifferent, uninterested in HCYU, and politically distant" (*nhat Dang, kho Doan, xa roi chinh tri*) (Duong 2017). Two years later, *Sai Gon Giai Phong*, one of the largest newspapers in Vietnam, affiliated with Ho Chi Minh City's Party Committee, published a special issue commentary that elucidated these issues. It revealed that the number of students recruited to the party has declined since 2017, and students had become increasingly pragmatic: they are more interested in opportunities to practice speaking English, and to volunteer in social projects abroad. While the HCYU and VNUS do not currently offer these opportunities, international non-governmental organizations do. Additionally, more and more students are seeking employment abroad or in the domestic private sector with foreign investments, and thus party membership and its required regular meetings and reports are more burdensome than helpful. In fact, all of these issues had already been pointed out more than two decades ago, in the second plenum of the 8th National Congress in 1996 (Ngo 2004).

HCYU and VNUS now find it increasingly challenging to manage their student members. Under the recently adopted credit system, students disperse (instead of studying together for the entire programme) and consequently the class-level officials of HCYU and VNUS cannot closely supervise their members. In response, HCYU and VNUS initiated a new approach to manage their students. On the one hand, they encourage students to form and actively participate in clubs and organizations of various kinds. On the other hand, all clubs and organizations are required to register with either HCYU or VNUS in order to operate on campus. But these clubs and organizations are connected rather loosely, and only as a formality with the two mainstream youth organizations.

There is some "division of labour" between HCYU and VNUS. While the former is tasked with ideological campaigns, the latter is responsible for volunteering and extracurricular activities; all of the activities of VNUS must be vetted by HCYU. In reality, students are generally more interested in volunteer work and extracurricular activities organized by VNUS than in ideological campaigns organized by HCYU. This usually leaves HCYU with a sense of unease, and could be the reason for lingering conflicts between the two organizations, although their logos are almost always displayed side by side in any student activities on campus to signal their unity. Most leaders of both HCYU and VNUS that we interviewed agreed that there has been a veiled yet uninterrupted desire within VNUS for it to become more autonomous from HCYU.

Overall, these findings tend to confirm those of previous studies on youth activities in Vietnam. For example, although the Vietnamese state, like the Chinese case, has spent enormous efforts and resources on managing Vietnamese youth ideologically, and directing them to political correctness, these projects have not reaped any considerable success (Marr and Rosen 1998). Likewise, as Karen Valentin encountered in her fieldwork, many of HCYU's elite members revealed that "it's no big deal to become a member" (Valentin 2007).

Conclusion

This chapter has described and analysed the leadership of the VCP in Vietnam's higher education, at both the national and institutional levels. On the one hand, the party and party-led youth organizations control and supervise most key aspects of higher education. At the national level, education resolutions produced by the CPTC provide legitimacy for the CCEYAC to pass relevant laws, and for MOET to enact subsequent policies. At the institutional level, the party committee dictates personnel planning and appointments, especially for leadership roles such as the board of rectors, deans, office heads and directors of institutes. At the student level, HCYU is the party's representative to supervise students.

On the other hand, the party's control is not without some counterbalance at both the national and institutional levels. Although the CPTC is in principle more powerful than CCEYAC and MOET, in reality, each of these three agencies needs to keep the other two in the loop. CPTC consults with CCEYAC and MOET while drafting education resolutions. CCEYAC and MOET, in turn, have to keep the CPTC fully informed during the lawmaking and policymaking processes. In a similar vein, at the university level, although the party committee has traditionally been the most powerful agency on campus, its members are not fully politicians; most of them do have substantial academic credentials. At the sub-institutional level, office heads are more likely to be party members, while deans and department chairs are more likely to be academics. Despite the legal right to dictate who will be appointed as deans, office heads and department chairs, the president usually does not go against the preferences made by tenured faculty and staff members.

Overall, the chapter points out the elite dualism leadership in Vietnam's higher education. *Both* political and academic capital are essential indicators for leaders—as high as CPTC heads, and as grass-roots as department chairs—to get appointed. At the institutional level, the party secretary (who is usually concurrently the president) must also acquire significant academic achievements. Substantial political capital cannot completely compensate for insufficient educational credentials, and this explains why the HCYU secretary can hardly become a university president. At the school and department levels, "Expertise" tends to outweigh "Red": some deans and many department chairs are non-party members. Succinctly, the closer to the grass-roots, the more significantly that expertise prevails.

This elite dualism leadership style is likely to be hindering the development of Vietnamese higher education. Top leaders are expected to obtain both expertise and political capital. One could optimistically conclude that experts eventually gain their footing in communist states like Vietnam. But this leadership style tends to exclude potential leaders that have sharp and reformist mindsets but are politically uncompromised. In other words, most of Vietnam's public university leaders are only "good enough", but rarely are they exceptional. And this makes breakthroughs hard to come by.

Some hopes for greater university autonomy have emerged lately. Amidst the exhaustion of its traditional sources of legitimacy, and the increasing pressure to operate more efficiently and to deliver sustainable economic growth (Le 2012), the VCP has since the early 2000s urged public service delivery units (*don vi hanh chinh su nghiep*), including public universities, to become increasingly autonomous, first and furthermost in financial respects (Vo 2018; Vo and Laking 2019; Vo and Lofgren 2019). According to Government Resolution #77 issued in 2014, if a public university guarantees to receive a lower annual appropriation—or even none—it will be granted greater autonomy in its curriculum, programme offerings and even personnel. The authority of central ministries over public universities will be transferred to the board of trustees (BoT), which will soon be established. The BoT, as stipulated in the 2018 Higher Education Amended Law, is a rather open, democratic and representative entity that in principle includes non-party members outside the university. It is also charged with the appointment of the board of rectors.

It is still too early to hope, however, for substantial autonomy. In fact, since it was first legislated in 2003, the BoT model has been continuously delayed or detrimentally modified, largely as a result of its conflict with the roles of the party committee, especially in respect to key personnel planning and appointments. When the 2018 Higher Education Amended Law was being drafted, the subject of the BoT—and particularly its relationship to the party committee—led to heated debate. In general, three main policy options were considered by policymakers (Association of Vietnam Universities and Colleges 2017). First was the division of labour between the board and party committee. The former is responsible for personnel decisions, while the latter ensures the decisions of the board are in line with the party's resolutions. The second option was to invite an individual—preferably a local government leader, superior to the secretary of the university party committee—to chair the BoT. Such an arrangement would ensure the party could maintain its leadership of the board and that the board would hold the ultimate authority on campus. In the last option, the secretary of the party committee would chair the board. The first option tends to transfer personnel decisions from the party committee to the board, and thus would weaken the party committee's power. The second option was considered risky because it places the supreme leadership of the university in the hands of someone outside of the university and unfamiliar with the management of academic institutions. The VCP Central Committee ultimately decided, in Resolution 19-NQ/TW issued on 25 November 2017, to endorse the third option. As a result, the university party committee is expected to

FIGURE 7.4
VCP's Reformed Structure in Public Universities

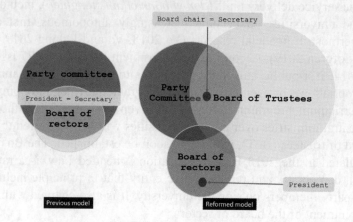

become increasingly separate from the board of rectors since by law the president must not concurrently chair the board (see Figure 7.4).

As of early 2021, almost all universities have already established their BoT. The formation of the board has tended to follow one of four main patterns. First, there is still little room for non-party members to sit on the board. Although the 2018 Higher Education Amended Law stipulates there must be external members on the board, these members are nominated by the president and party committee, and, understandably, party members are preferred. Currently, many elected external members are representatives of state-owned enterprises and local governments. Second, at several major universities the party secretary has refused to give up their president position, although this contrasts with the resolution by the VCP's Central Committee. Third, the current party secretary (concurrently the president) can tactically elevate someone politically junior, such as the dean or even the vice-dean, to the position of secretary to serve as a proxy. Some informants call this scenario "escaping secretary": one is more willing to sacrifice their party position to remain the president, the post of which allows key decisions, particularly financial ones, to be made. Fourth, at several universities the separation of power is real, but the road has been bumpy and not without resistance. The separation creates a powerful post (board chair) for rival groups to compete for, and one can hope such competition might increase democracy. For instance, at a major university in Hanoi, two vice-presidents openly competed for the position of president. After losing in the presidential vote, the losing vice-president was successfully elected to the position of secretary, and thus also chairs the board.

In the future, and if party resolution is followed strictly, one can expect that Vietnamese public universities will likely resemble their Chinese counterparts in terms of the governance model. There will be two relatively separate power blocs, although both will be dominated by party members. In Vietnam, the university board will counterbalance the board of rectors, whereas in Chinese universities, counterbalances are between the party committee and the board of rectors. In any case, the common pathway for an aspiring university leader in Vietnam is to first become the president and then the party secretary (who is concurrently the board chair). This arrangement might help intellectualize and professionalize the party secretary. But there remains one question that VCP theorists have not yet resolved: where will the party committee be situated in the new governance model, given that most of the members have joined the university board and carried out similar duties?

Notes

1. For comparative higher education studies in Latin American authoritarian regimes, see Salto (2020) and Levy (1981).
2. Milovan Djilas later became a political prisoner under charges of ideological contamination.
3. The standing committee exists only at large universities with populous party members.
4. Decision 3268/QĐ-BGDĐT (dated 29 August 2018), Charter of appointment, re-appointment, extension, dismissal, resignation, and rotation of cadres and officials in managerial and leadership positions at the Ministry of Education & Training (Quyet đinh ban hanh quy che bo nhiem, bo nhiem lai, keo dai thoi gian giu chuc vu, thoi giu chuc vu, tu nhiem, mien nhiem, luan chuyen cong chuc, vien chuc giu chuc vu lanh dao, quan ly ua Bo Giao duc va Dao tao).
5. Vietnam has traditionally followed the year-based class: students of the same cohort and same major will usually study together until graduation.

References

Abuza, Zachary. 2001. *Renovating Politics in Contemporary Vietnam*. Boulder, CO: Rienner.

Andreas, Joel. 2009. *Rise of the Red Engineers: The Cultural Revolution and the Origins of China's New Class*. Stanford, CA: Stanford University Press.

Anh, Vu. 2015. "Nhiều vụ Trưởng, Giám Đốc Sở Trình Độ Yếu Kém, Thiếu Tự Trọng". *Thanh Nien* (blog), 11 May 2015. https://thanhnien.vn/thoi-su/ nhieu-vu-truong-giam-doc-so-trinh-do-yeu-kem-thieu-tu-trong-561074.

html?fbclid=IwAR19TxohGy0amxdFn76DYGQjt9X5YCrDY0lPe9p-byua1JFc_lkz2OJDG69o.

Association of Vietnam Universities and Colleges. 2017. "Hội Đồng Trường – Khâu Đột Phá Trong Việc Thực Hiện Tự Chủ Đại Học". Hai Duong: Association of Vietnam Universities and Colleges.

Bian, Yanjie, Xiaoling Shu, and John Logan. 2001. "Communist Party Membership and Regime Dynamics in China". *Social Forces* 79, no. 3: 805–41.

Bueno de Mesquita, Bruce, and George W. Downs. 2005. "Development and Democracy". *Foreign Affairs* 84, no. 5: 77–86.

Clark, Burton R. 1983. *The Higher Education System: Academic Organization in Cross-national Perspective*. Berkeley, CA: University of California Press.

Dinh, Song Linh. 2000. "Party Developing among Students" [Phat Trien Dang Trong Sinh Vien]. *Nhan Dan*, 16393 edition.

Djilas, Milovan. 1983. *The New Class: An Analysis of the Communist System*. San Diego: Harcourt Brace Jovanovich.

Duong, Duc Nhu. 1978. "Education in Vietnam under the French Domination 1862–1945". Doctoral dissertation, Southern Illinois University at Carbondale.

Duong, Tam. 2017. "Tổng Bí Thư: 'Tránh Nhạt Đảng, Khô Đoàn, Xa Rời Chính Trị'". *VNExpress* (blog). 11 December 2017. https://vnexpress.net/tong-bi-thu-tranh-nhat-dang-kho-doan-xa-roi-chinh-tri-3682756.html.

Guo, Gang. 2005. "Party Recruitment of College Students in China". *Journal of Contemporary China* 14, no. 43: 371–93. https://doi.org/10.1080/10670560500065504.

Hanson, Margaret, and Sarah Wilson Sokhey. 2020. "Higher Education as an Authoritarian Tool for Regime Survival: Evidence from Kazakhstan and around the World". *Problems of Post-Communism* 68, no. 3. https://doi.org/10.1080/10758216.2020.1734839.

Hayden, Martin, and Lam Quang Thiep. 2007. "Institutional Autonomy for Higher Education in Vietnam". *Higher Education Research & Development* 26, no. 1: 73–85. https://doi.org/10.1080/07294360601166828.

Hoang, Thi Hong Nga. 2015. "Giáo Dục Đại Học Dưới Chế Độ Việt Nam Cộng Hòa (1956–1975)". Doctoral dissertation, Vietnam National University, Hanoi.

Huang, Futao. 2017. "Who Leads China's Leading Universities?" *Studies in Higher Education* 42, no. 1: 79–96. https://doi.org/10.1080/03075079.2015.1034265.

Jiang, Hua, and Xiaobin Li. 2012. "Party Secretaries in Chinese Higher Education Institutions, Who Are They?" *Journal of International Education and Leadership* 2, no. 2: 1–13.

Jungblut, Jens. 2015. "Bringing Political Parties into the Picture: A Two-Dimensional Analytical Framework for Higher Education Policy". *Higher Education* 69, no. 5: 867–82. https://doi.org/10.1007/s10734-014-9810-5.

Katz, Zev. 1956. "Party-Political Education in Soviet Russia 1918–1935". *Soviet Studies* 7, no. 3: 237–47.

Konrád, György, and Iván Szelényi. 1979. *The Intellectuals on the Road to Class Power*. New York: Harcourt Brace Jovanovich.

Koss, Daniel. 2018. *Where the Party Rules: The Rank and File of China's Communist State*. Cambridge: Cambridge University Press.

Kuo-tai, Hu. 1989. "The Struggle between the Kuomintang and the Chinese Communist Party on Campus during the War of Resistance, 1937–45". *China Quarterly* 118: 300–23.

Landry, Pierre F. 2008. *Decentralized Authoritarianism in China: The Communist Party's Control of Local Elites in the Post-Mao Era*. Cambridge: Cambridge University Press.

Lane, Jason E., and D. Bruce Johnstone, eds. 2012. *Universities and Colleges as Economic Drivers: Measuring Higher Education's Role in Economic Development*. Albany: State University of New York Press.

Le, Hong Hiep. 2012. "Performance-Based Legitimacy: The Case of the Communist Party of Vietnam and Doi Moi". *Contemporary Southeast Asia* 34, no. 2: 145. https://doi.org/10.1355/cs34-2a.

Le, Xuan Khoa. 2015. *Bùi Kiến Thành - Người Mở Khóa Lãng Du*. Hanoi: Thai Ha.

Levy, Daniel C. 1980. *University and Government in Mexico: Autonomy in an Authoritarian System*. New York: Praeger.

———. 1981. "Comparing Authoritarian Regimes in Latin America: Insights from Higher Education Policy". *Comparative Politics* 14, no. 1: 31–52.

Li, Cheng. 2016. *Chinese Politics in the Xi Jinping Era: Reassessing Collective Leadership*. Washington, DC: Brookings Institution Press.

Liu, Xu. 2017. "The Governance in the Development of Public Universities in China". *Journal of Higher Education Policy and Management* 39, no. 3: 266–81. https://doi.org/10.1080/1360080X.2017.1300122.

Marr, David G. 1984. *Vietnamese Tradition on Trial, 1920–1945*. Berkeley: University of California Press.

Marr, David, and Stanley Rosen. 1998. "Chinese and Vietnamese Youth in the 1990s". *China Journal* 40 (July): 145–72. https://doi.org/10.2307/2667457.

McLendon, Michael K. 2003. "The Politics of Higher Education – Toward an Expanded Research Agenda". *Educational Policy* 17, no. 1: 165–91.

Natali, Jeanne Beth. 2001. "Post Doi Moi Urban Higher Education in the Socialist Republic of Vietnam – The Case of Hong Duc University". Doctoral dissertation, Old Dominion University.

Ngo, Bich Ngoc. 2004. "Sự Lãnh Đạo Của Tổ Chức Cơ Sở Đảng Đối Với Đoàn Thanh Niên Cộng Sản Hồ Chí Minh Trong Các Trường Đại Học & Cao Đẳng ở Hà Nội Giai Đoạn Hiện Nay" [Party's leadership of Ho Chi Minh Communist Youth Unions at universities and colleges in Hanoi in the contemporary era]. PhD dissertation, Ho Chi Minh National Academy of Politics.

Nguyen, Cong Ly. 2011. *Giáo Dục Khoa Cử và Quan Chế ở Việt Nam Thời Phong Kiến, Thời Pháp Thuộc*. Ho Chi Minh City: Vietnam National University Ho Chi Minh.

Nguyen, Hai Hong. 2019. "The Persistence of a Non-responsive Political Regime in Vietnam". *Asian Politics & Policy* 11, no. 4: 527–43. https://doi.org/10.1111/aspp.12492.

Nguyen, Huy Vi. 2016. *Trường Cộng Đồng Bậc Đại Học ở Việt Nam – Hiện Tại và Tương Lai* [Vietnam's community colleges: Current situation and prospects]. Hanoi: Vietnam National University Hanoi.

Nguyen, Si Dung. 2020. "Lựa Chọn Người Tài" [Talent Selection]. *VNExpress* (blog), 27 December 2020. https://vnexpress.net/lua-chon-nguoi-tai-4212607.html.

Perkin, Harold. 2007. "History of Universities". In *International Handbook of Higher Education*, edited by James J.F. Forest and Philip G. Altbach, pp. 159–205. Dordrecht: Springer.

Perkins, Dwight, David Dapice, and Jonathan Haughton, eds. 1994. *Việt Nam Cải Cách Kinh Tế Theo Hướng Rồng Bay*. Hanoi: Chinh tri Quoc gia.

Perry, Elizabeth J. 2017. "Cultural Governance in Contemporary China: 'Reorienting' Party Propaganda". In *To Govern China*, edited by Vivienne Shue and Patricia M. Thornton, pp. 29–55. Cambridge University Press. https://doi.org/10.1017/9781108131858.002.

———. 2020. "Educated Acquiescence: How Academia Sustains Authoritarianism in China". *Theory and Society* 49, no. 1: 1–22. https://doi.org/10.1007/s11186-019-09373-1.

Rudma, Herbert C. 1964. *Structure and Decision-Making in Soviet Education*. Washington, DC: US Department of Health, Education, and Welfare.

Salto, Dante J. 2020. "Comparative Higher Education Policy under Nondemocratic Regimes in Argentina and Chile: Similar Paths, Different Policy Choices". *Higher Education Policy* (May). https://doi.org/10.1057/s41307-020-00194-x.

Sanborn, Howard, and Clayton L. Thyne. 2014. "Learning Democracy: Education and the Fall of Authoritarian Regimes". *British Journal of Political Science* 44, no. 4: 773–97. https://doi.org/10.1017/S0007123413000082.

Song, Jia. 2018. "Creating World-Class Universities in China: Strategies and Impacts at a Renowned Research University". *Higher Education* 75, no. 4: 729–42. https://doi.org/10.1007/s10734-017-0167-4.

St. George, Elizabeth. 2003. "Government Policy and Changes to Higher Education in Vietnam, 1986–1998: Education in Transition for Development?" PhD dissertation, Australian National University.

Szelényi, Ivan. 1987. "The Prospects and Limits of the East European New Class Project: An Auto-Critical Reflection on the Intellectuals on the Road to Class Power". *Politics & Society* 15, no. 2: 103–44. https://doi.org/10.1177/003232928701500201.

Tran, Phương-Hoa. 1998. "Vietnamese Higher Education at the Intersection of French and Soviet Influences". PhD dissertation, State University of New York at Buffalo.

U, Eddy. 2019. *Creating the Intellectual: Chinese Communism and the Rise of a Classification*. Oakland: University of California Press.

Valentin, Karen. 2007. "Mass Mobilization and the Struggle over the Youth: The Role of Ho Chi Minh Communist Youth Union in Urban Vietnam". *YOUNG* 15, no. 3: 299–315. https://doi.org/10.1177/110330880701500305.

Vo, Minh Thi Hai. 2018. "Autonomy of Public Service Delivery Units in Vietnam: An Institutional Perspective". PhD dissertation, University of Wellington.

Vo, Minh Thị Hải, and Rob Laking. 2019. "An Institutional Study of Autonomisation of Public Universities in Vietnam". *Higher Education* (October). https://doi.org/10.1007/s10734-019-00457-6.

Vo, Minh Thị Hải, and Karl Lofgren. 2019. "An Institutional Analysis of the Fiscal Autonomy of Public Hospitals in Vietnam". *Asia & the Pacific Policy Studies* 6, no. 1: 90–107. https://doi.org/10.1002/app5.268.

Vu, Tuong. 2010. *Paths to Development in Asia: South Korea, Vietnam, China, and Indonesia*. New York: Cambridge University Press.

Walder, Andrew G. 1995. "Career Mobility and the Communist Political Order". *American Sociological Review* 60, no. 3: 309. https://doi.org/10.2307/2096416.

Walder, Andrew G., Bobai Li, and Donald J. Treiman. 2000. "Politics and Life Chances in a State Socialist Regime: Dual Career Paths into the Urban Chinese Elite, 1949 to 1996". *American Sociological Review* 65, no. 2: 191. https://doi.org/10.2307/2657437.

Wan, Yinmei. 2006. "Expansion of Chinese Higher Education since 1998: Its Causes and Outcomes". *Asia Pacific Education Review* 7, no. 1: 19–32. https://doi.org/10.1007/BF03036781.

Wang, Qinghua. 2014. "Crisis Management, Regime Survival and 'Guerrilla-Style' Policy-Making: The June 1999 Decision to Radically Expand Higher Education in China". *China Journal* 71: 132–52.

Wright, Teresa. 2010. *Accepting Authoritarianism: State-Society Relations in China's Reform Era*. Stanford: Stanford University Press.

Yitao, Wang, and Wang Hua. 2019. "Party Secretaries at Private Institutions of Higher Education: Group Characteristics, Channels for Selection, and Policy Recommendations". *Chinese Education & Society* 52, nos. 1–2: 76–89. https://doi.org/10.1080/10611932.2019.1608756.

Zang, Xiaowei. 2001a. "University Education, Party Seniority, and Elite Recruitment in China". *Social Science Research* 30, no. 1: 62–75. https://doi.org/10.1006/ssre.2000.0688.

———. 2001b. "Educational Credentials, Elite Dualism, and Elite Stratification in China". *Sociological Perspectives* 44, no. 2: 189–205. https://doi.org/10.2307/1389610.

———. 2004. *Elite Dualism and Leadership Selection in China*. London: RoutledgeCurzon.

Zinoman, Peter. 2011. "Nhân Văn—Giai Phẩm and Vietnamese 'Reform Communism' in the 1950s: A Revisionist Interpretation". *Journal of Cold War Studies* 13, no. 1: 60–100. https://doi.org/10.1162/JCWS_a_00071.

Chapter 8

Mediatized Infrapolitics and Government Accountability in Vietnam

Nguyen Thuc Cuong and Hoang Cam Thanh

In 2017, the Vietnamese government began drafting eighty-five articles of a regulatory bill to open three special economic zones (SEZs) in Phu Quoc, Van Don and Bac Van Phong that offered foreign investors fewer regulations and greater fiscal incentives. The SEZ project first appeared in Quang Ninh province's proposal for the establishment of Van Don in 2014 after Pham Minh Chinh's meeting in 2013 with Chinese SEZ researchers from the China Center for Special Economic Zone Research (CCSEZR) of Shenzhen University. The initiative was then expanded into Bac Van Phong's and Phu Quoc's economic zones of Khanh Hoa and Kien Giang provinces, respectively, at the "International Science EEZ development – Experience and Opportunities" conference, which was co-organized by the Quang Ninh government and CCSEZR on 20 March 2014. The seminar brought together more than four hundred provincial government and private industry leaders, policy experts and academic professors to discuss "the mechanisms and specific policies for the special economic zones" (Tuan Anh 2015).

In October 2017, the SEZ draft bill was proposed and submitted for revision at the fourth session of the 14th National Assembly (NA), and then re-submitted at the fifth session. On 23 May 2018, Nguyen Khac Dinh, chairman of the 14th NA's legal committee, announced that the majority of NA delegates agreed on the necessity to open public discussions on the bill's regulatory scope and potential benefits of

SEZs for the Vietnamese economy (Lawsoft 2018). According to the Politburo's Conclusion No. 21, the reasons for opening these economic zones include "taking advantage of the regional potential; attracting strong investment capital, advanced technology, new management methods; generating more resources and motivations; and helping accelerate the process of economic development and restructuring of provinces, regions and the country as a whole" (Le Kien 2017). The draft law contains a controversial provision permitting the foreign lease of land in SEZs for up to ninety-nine years, and this sparked numerous waves of demonstrations and riots between June and September of 2018. At the sixth session, the NA conclusively approved the withdrawal of the SEZ bill. Out of 483 delegates, 423 of them voted in favour of the postponement, only 8 voted against it, and 55 abstained. The first wave of anti-SEZ demonstrations occurred nationwide on 10 June despite the decision by the NA's Standing Committee to postpone the passage of the bill until the sixth session. The delay, violent police crackdowns and arrests of protesters could not halt the second wave of large-scale protests on 17 June and other episodic demonstrations from June to the end of August. In Binh Thuan, Binh Duong, Long An and Dong Nai provinces, protesters were arrested and detained for engaging in what government officials described as reactionary, extremist and hostile actions that caused public disorder and damaged government assets. In late August, the general secretary of the NA, Nguyen Hanh Phuc, announced the deferral of the bill to a future session. The draft law has currently been put on hold.

From the official narrative, the bill was withdrawn because of a need for further research and a reconsideration of the implications for the SEZs. Nonetheless, we argue that the postponement and withdrawal of the bill *partly* resulted from anti-SEZs protests by civilians and the emergence and politicization of discourses on SEZs on social media, which began in early 2011 and effectively transformed this into an issue of national salience in the period between May and September 2018. The lease duration of ninety-nine years and economically unbeneficial investment privileges drew national attention from NA delegates and the local epistemic community (e.g., political pundits, government policy advisors, academic professors), human rights activists, local citizens and the Vietnamese diaspora. It was such objections that provided protesters with justifications to become involved in public anti-SEZs demonstrations. Our chapter traces the public discourse on the SEZ law between 2014 and 2018, focusing on two primary subjects. First, we look at how public policy discussions, criticisms, debates and commentaries for and against the SEZ laws were represented in mainstream local and foreign-based newspapers and at the discursive strategies employed by journalists, critics and proponents of the bill to either defend or undermine it. Second, we also examine the politicizing and framing effect of the anti-SEZ discourse on local protests and demonstrations against the policy's implementation during 2018.

Existing Theoretical Frameworks for Analysing State-Society Relations in Vietnam

State-society relations have increasingly gained greater traction in the study of contemporary Vietnamese politics. Empirical scholarship of state-society relations in contemporary Vietnam is dominated by three theoretical interpretations (Kerkvliet 2001, pp. 238–78; Kerkvliet 2019). First, the "dominant state thesis" posits that the Vietnamese party-state is an overly powerful totalitarian system capable of forestalling alternative independent social organizations and groups that seek to challenge it at both the national and grass-root levels (Kerkvliet 2014, pp. 100–34). The second interpretation, the mobilizational corporatism thesis, emphasizes the mediating role of organizations within which the state dominates. Though political institutions serve to transmit social forces to policymaking domains, state officials utilize these organizations to mobilize public support for their programmes and policies, facilitate communication between authorities and citizens, and coordinate and manage social and economic groups. Third, the state-in-society thesis shifts focus away from formal organizations and state authorities to the complex webs of local actors, their everyday practices of resistance, and state-citizen relations at a grass-root level. Because of the lack of resources, and administrative decentralization, the power of the state is more restrained than what the dominating state and mobilizational corporatism theses would lead one to believe. Policy formulation involves piecemeal negotiations between local and central authorities and between state and societal interests. Since the mid-1990s, the power of the Vietnamese party-state has been challenged from the bottom up. There have been increasing incidences of public criticism and collective action against government policies, including condemning corrupt local authorities, resisting land confiscations, speaking out against the state repression of religious freedom, calling for a multiparty political system, organizing labour strikes for improved working conditions in factories, and challenging the state's pro-China foreign policies that undermine national interests (Wells-Dang 2014, pp. 162–83).

An important arena where state-society relations and their social boundaries are contested is the mass media. From the dominant state perspective, the VCP-led government tolerates no political dissent or opposition and holds a total grip on the institutions of mass media (Kerkvliet 2001, pp. 251–52). All printing presses, newspaper outlets and publishing houses are owned, controlled and regulated by government ministries and party organizations. While article 23 of the September 2013 constitution permits freedom of the press and freedom of association, articles 14.2 and 15.4 enable the government to overrule these rights should they violate "unambiguously defined national security interests" (Abuza 2015, p. 10). The insertion of such a vague and arbitrary "national security threat" discourse into the constitution enables the state to criminalize speech that it deems threatening to "the unity of the socialist fatherland" or national security, or that is associated with activities aimed at overthrowing the government (article 253), abusing democratic freedoms or disseminating anti-state propaganda. To stifle dissent in cyberspace the party regularly instructs thousands of state cybersecurity personnel to impose tight internet censorship and restrictions—for example, installing internet firewalls, monitoring online discussion forums and hacking into personal blogs and websites—to prevent the leakage of any potential anti-government issues (Cain 2014, pp. 85–107; Human Rights Watch 2010). According to the mobilizational corporatism hypothesis, mass media is a political device for state mobilization of public support. The state uses mass media institutions to promulgate the official position on a wide array of international and domestic issues. For authoritarian regimes, media propaganda is an effective tool for non-coercive social control to shape public perceptions of state authorities and sustain political stability and harmony in the long run. For instance, in 2014 the party instructed newspaper outlets to promote a moderate anti-China rhetoric, which served to divert public attention from the economic crisis by channelling anti-Sino sentiment and animosity into a more positive modality of pro-government nationalism (Bui 2017)

Nevertheless, in concurring with the state-in-society thesis, we argue that despite draconian measures to control social media platforms and punish political dissent the latter has continued to empower the mobilizational and participatory capacities of citizens in shaping state policymaking by producing a virtual space for criticism of government policies (Wells-Dang 2010, pp. 93–112; Bui 2016, pp. 89–111). Against the second school's emphasis on formal organizations, our framework zeroes in on political discourses and the deliberative processes whereby a policy is discussed, criticized and defended on mass media platforms. Such virtual political spaces, which exist outside formal economic and political institutions, often fall beyond the analytical purview of the first and second approaches. With the aid of discourse analysis, this chapter seeks to capture the dynamic discursive space of state-society relations that are empirically underemphasized and undertheorized by most Vietnamese studies of the state-in-society thesis. If the state-in-society thesis tends to concentrate on how political non-state actors, their acts of resistance and their organizational capacities contribute to policy change, we devote our analytical commitment to understanding how social and political discourses give meaning and ideas to actors' practices of and motivations for resistance. While the internet and social media have been understood in the traditional institutionalist perspective to provide alternative sources of information, reduce the cost of political participation and strengthen the mobilizational capacity of opposition forces (Chang, Chu and Welsh 2013, pp. 150–64), we argue that they also serve to sustain the continuity and development of everyday political discourses on a wide range of public policies, and more importantly, enable the politicization of policy issues into problems of national salience.

Our Model of Mediatized Infrapolitics

In this chapter, we seek to capture an increasingly salient dimension of contemporary Vietnamese civil society called *mediatized infrapolitics*— an unobtrusive realm of everyday state-society discursive struggle on mass media platforms (Scott 2012, pp. 112–17). Unlike noisy, headline-grabbing protests and demonstrations, *mediatized infrapolitics*, albeit seemingly innocuous to political stability, quietly and effectively sets the scene for collective political action to spread in moments of external crisis. The notion of infrapolitics was first coined by political scientist James C. Scott to refer to an obtrusive realm of "informal leadership and nonelites, of conversation and oral discourse, and of surreptitious resistance" (Scott 1990, p. 200). Infrapolitics in its original meaning refers to political action in "the forms that are designed to obscure their intention and take cover behind an apparent meaning" (Scott 1990, p. 199). But the kinds of "malicious gossips, character assassination, nicknames, and rumors" that constitute Scott's notion of infrapolitics have found a new home. In the internet age, infrapolitics has been mediatized: social media has increasingly become an effective breeding ground for anonymous and underground symbolic resistance, and grievances towards state authorities (Soriano and Sreekumar 2012, pp. 1028–39; Yang, Tang and Wang 2015, pp. 197–214). The domain of both offline and online news is our selected area of investigation into mediatized infrapolitics in Vietnam.

We argue that mediatized infrapolitics has increasingly influenced government policymaking in a three-stage communicative process. First, news outlets publish competing narratives about a particular policy decision. Second, government justifications for the decision are critically evaluated, defended and debunked by various social actors and groups. Third, the government's deliberative failure to justify the policy decision could politicize the policy decision into a problem of national salience, thus providing an ideational context for the mobilization of civilian protests and demonstrations against its implementation. Mounting public political criticism and the threat of protests pressure policy change. The mechanism can be summarized by Figures 8.1 and 8.2. Figure 8.2 shows the application of the theoretical model in Figure 8.1 to analyse the deferral of the draft bill on SEZs.

FIGURE 8.1
Mediatized Infrapolitics, Contentious Politics and Policy Change

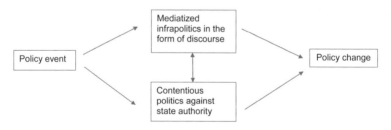

FIGURE 8.2
Mediatized Infrapolitics and the Deferral of SEZs Draft Law

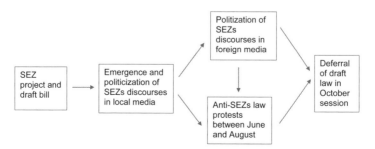

It has been the conventional wisdom that local newspaper outlets in authoritarian systems are heavily censored and controlled to the degree that they lack agency for policy change. On the contrary, we wish to emphasize that the role of state-owned media in this deliberative process is by no means minimal. In contrast to foreign newspapers, local media in Vietnam have the tendency to avoid discussing and assessing policy issues in a politically sensitive fashion that could undermine the VCP's legitimacy. This only goes so far in suggesting potential differences in their discursive strategies and styles. One should not infer from such a fact to conclude that local news is either devoid of political criticism of governmental policy or lacks any evaluative power. As Scott argues, even what appears to be a trivial act of symbolic defiance can give credence to "an enlarged political space" and touch off "a flurry of bold assertions and claims" (Scott 1990, p. 20). Our model of mediatized infrapolitics posits that state-owned official newspaper outlets in Vietnam also supply readers with a repertoire of infrapolitical criticism of government policy and raise public attention about policy problems. Opinions from journalists of state-owned media and commentaries by non-government policy experts enable readers to assess the government's policy claims. We do not reject the premise that authorities can monitor media content. In lieu of dismissing the role of state-owned newspapers, this chapter examines the stage(s) of the SEZs discourse at which the politicizing effect of local news is predominant. We also maintain that once news becomes widely circulated it is beyond the power of the state to control and restrict how readers interpret such content. The meanings of social media texts may be context-bound, but their discursive context is boundless. A written text decontextualizes itself from particular sociocultural circumstances and recontextualizes itself differently through the act of reading in light of contingent events (Ricoeur 1981, p. 51). Discourses are reproducible and yet their originality becomes compromised, if not lost, in the process of reproduction: their meanings and interpretations alter even if their words and sentences and the medium of transmission remain the same.

Discourse Analysis

We conducted a discourse analysis to explore the discursive state-society interaction at the time of the proposal of the draft law on SEZs in late October 2017. This case was selected for three analytical reasons. First, it highlights the combined effect of public criticism of and mass contentious politics towards government policy change.

Second, the case shows that both foreign and state-owned newspapers play an important role in the development and politicization of anti-SEZs discourse, though the timing of their influence may differ. This could be a deviational case given that the state holds a tight grip over what local media outlets can report. Once we traced and compared the dates of when local and foreign newspapers began to cover the issue, the contribution of local newspapers to the development and politization could be seen to precede that of foreign news articles. On 17 January 2015, one news article from BBC Vietnam reported that former prime minister Nguyen Tan Dung "gave the green light" to the opening of a casino project in Phu Quoc, but it did not provide any details about the special economic zones. On 18 November 2017, BBC Vietnam released a critical evaluation of special economic zones by lawyer Ngo Ngoc Trai. RFA and VOA only began to cover the issue frequently a month (or less) prior to the protests of 10 June. We employ discourse analysis of 402 news articles (published both online and offline between 2011 and 2018) on the issue.[1] Our data comes from major national newspapers (*Thanh Nien* and *Tuoi Tre*) and foreign-owned media outlets that are considered credible and have large Vietnamese readerships—the BBC, Voice of America (VOA) and Radio Free Asia (RFA).[2] Out of 402 articles, 73 are from BBC Tieng Viet, 15 from VOA, 85 from RFA, 125 from *Tuoi Tre*, and 103 from *Thanh Nien*.

This chapter relies on two mainstream traditions of discourse analysis. We employ a variant of critical discourse analysis (CDA) developed by British sociolinguist Norman Fairclough and his collaborators (Fairclough and Fairclough 2012). The framework consists of five analytical categories employed to collect and evaluate arguments made by government officials to defend a specific policy. First, researchers need to identify policymakers' claims for action. Second, researchers need to examine the situational setting under which the policy is being discussed, justified and formulated. Third, for effective evaluation of the policy, it is imperative to ask what social and economic benefits and values its implementation would bring about and the specific goals it seeks to achieve. Fourth, critical discourse analysts investigate the means for achieving these goals that government officials present to the public and evaluate whether these means are sound. Fifth, researchers also pay attention to discursive exchange between the opponents and proponents of the policy.

The CDA framework is combined with a genealogical analysis developed by the Foucauldian sociologist Jean Carabine (2001).

Her discourse model adds two analytical techniques that we find relevant for data collection and analysis. First, we pay attention to the interrelationship (or discursive intertextuality) between discourses in local and foreign media and among social and state actors. Second, we identify and analyse discursive strategies used for representing ideas within the discourses. A discursive strategy refers to a means through which knowledge about the objects and subjects of a particular discourse is produced and developed (Carabine 2001, p. 288). In this research, our task entailed constantly looking out for and analysing the discursive strategies through which ideas about the SEZs initiative and draft bill have been put into the discourse. We ascertained the ways discourse and counter-discourse (resistance), as well as certain themes, were deployed by the proponents and critics of SEZs. The news content of *Thanh Nien*, *Tuoi Tre* and BBC Tieng Viet were found to consist of a mixture of pro- and anti-SEZs commentaries, whereas the reports by RFA and VOA were mainly anti-SEZs. Finally, we identify the effects of these discourses on anti-SEZs demonstrations and protests.

Analysis of State-Owned Media Discourse

The first news articles about the SEZs from *Tuoi Tre* appeared on 29 April 2014. Four years later, an article from *Thanh Nien News*, on 23 May 2018, was entitled "Economic zones must make breakthroughs" and "Economic Zones must be special to make breakthroughs" (Phuong, Phong and Van 2018). Between April 2014 and May 2018, the content and tone of media discourses on SEZs from these national media outlets had been relatively consistent and neutral vis-à-vis the narratives after the first protest on 10 June 2018 broke out. We argue that local newspapers in this period contributed to the emergence and politicization of the SEZs initiative and draft law into an issue of national salience in mid-2018. The analysis of local media discourse on the SEZs consists of two sections. We first examine the pro-SEZs discourse in the *Tuoi Tre* and *Thanh Nien* newspapers in which the proponents of the draft law put forward their arguments for the necessity of these SEZs. Our focus is on the social and economic context under which the bill was discussed as well as the discursive strategies employed by the government in seeking to justify the policy. Our goal was to understand how the official narrative had been constructed to draw public support. In the second section we examine the extent to which the state's deliberative efforts failed by analysing key objections to the initiative and draft bill and the politicizing effect of these objections.

Pro-SEZs Discourse

News articles consisting of discussions of the context for developing special economic zones have appeared since early 2014. In an interview conducted by *Tuoi Tre News* with Dr Tran Dinh Thien, the director of the Vietnam Economic Institute, it was recommended that the SEZs initiative be launched in 2014. He reasoned that establishment of the SEZs would solve institutional problems, bring about administrative reform and improve the business environment. The SEZs would create fresh momentum for Vietnam. He cited examples of successful SEZs in Shenzhen in China, Incheon in South Korea and Dubai in the UAE from which Vietnam could learn. Dr Tran Dinh Thien likened the SEZs to "a nest for phoenixes to hatch their eggs". Other experts also used the nest metaphor to describe SEZs as a new organizational model for new services such as casinos (Nguyen Nga and Mai Phuong 2017).

The Politburo of the VCP advocated building three special units in Van Dong, Bac Van Phong and Phu Quoc to "unlock the potential in the region, and attract strong investment capital, high technology and new management". As a result, SEZs would create more resources to accelerate the development and economic restructuring of these provinces, the regions and the nation as a whole. Minister of planning and investment Nguyen Chi Dung, one of the most passionate advocates for the bill, underscored the necessity of the SEZs as "an institutional laboratory" to stimulate growth and lure investment. Minister Dung affirmed that the opening of the SEZs represented a national effort and aspiration, and was testament to the institutional reform effort in upgrading national competitiveness (*Tuoi Tre News* 2018a).[3] State officers have reiterated this concept of an "institutional laboratory" as a context for SEZs. The head of the Central Organization Committee, Phạm Minh Chính, at a seminar on the draft law on SEZs of Quang Ninh described them as "the laboratory of the institution" and concluded that "it is necessary to take the foreign economic model as a development target" (Tien Thang 2018).

Another discursive strategy by proponents of the SEZs plan was constructing the narrative of the project as a must-have policy for improving Vietnam's economy. They argued that although for the past twenty-five years of development, industrial and export processing zones, hi-tech parks and economic zones had made positive contributions to socio-economic development, these economic models showed signs of decreased competitiveness and faced various limitations. Therefore, according to Minister Nguyen Chi Dung's response to *Tuoi Tre News* in August 2017, the development of a SEZ model with special administrative and economic mechanisms would create a "new competitive force" and beneficial spillover effects for Vietnam (Ngoc An 2017). *Thanh Nien News* also reported the minister's comments that foreign investment in Vietnam had remained level and that the draft bill would attract more investors. Vietnam can also learn from the experience of Shenzhen's successful model for building SEZs (Mai Phuong and Nguyen Nga 2017). Another proponent of the plan, associate professor Vu Minh Khuong of the Lee Yuan Yew School of Public Policy, stressed that the SEZs would serve three major goals. First, the draft bill would be a sign of developmental commitments. Second, SEZs would serve as incubators to accelerate state reform and development through deep integration with the global economy and to pilot innovative governance models. Third, they are places to accumulate human talent and give rise to institutional breakthroughs. They will be the most effective sites to utilize, attract and train human resources for Vietnam, especially in the fields of management, leadership and international integration. The bigger ambition is to transform Vietnam into a developed centre of SEZs for Asia and the world. This is "a manifesto of the Vietnamese generation nowadays", Dr Khuong concluded (Vu 2018).

Another argument from a number of Vietnamese economic experts is that the SEZs will serve as "the magnet for foreign capital and investments" (Mai Phuong 2018). Thus, as Minister Dung advised, Vietnam needs to proactively design a new arena and new rules with outstanding policy institutions to compete for and lure domestic and foreign investment. The SEZs would be expected to increase government revenue, GDP growth, and income per capita after 2020. Specific policies and regulatory mechanisms would serve as guidelines for developing each region to its fullest potential and contributing to the country's prosperity as a whole. The draft bill is thus necessary (Phuong, Phong and Van 2018).

Outspoken advocates of the SEZs draft bill also hypothesize the "scenarios" for Vietnam's economic development in the absence of the SEZs. Minister Dung stated that Vietnam ought to "give what investors truly need". Without establishing SEZs and understanding what investors really want, "institutional breakthroughs" would not occur. Building a special zone that lacks effective institutional mechanisms (e.g., tax incentives, land leases and specific organizational models) would hardly attract investment (Le Kien 2018a, p. 6). The proposed land lease of ninety-nine years—compared to the current limit of fifty or seventy-five years for certain exclusive cases—Dung continued, would be an appealing feature of the SEZs, without which investors would not "come in". It is an open and flexible policy mechanism for SEZs that has been used widely around the world. Vietnam does not have to be too concerned about the long term because the foreign infrastructural assets stay in Vietnam. If an investor uses a loan project, it is even more encouraging. Significantly, Vietnam "does not have ample time" to become a "prosperous country" because it is nearing the end of the golden population structure. This signals the need for innovative breakthroughs and a less-thinking-and-more-doing mentality to implement the provisions of the draft law (Le Kien 2018c). That Vietnam has lagged behind other SEZs around the globe explains why Vietnam's SEZs must have exceptional mechanisms to be able to compete.

At a state meeting in May 2017, in response to public perceptions that the draft bill could undermine national security and that too many relaxed regulations could risk becoming unconstitutional, Mr Pham Minh Chinh, the head of the Central Organization Commission, emphasized that the SEZs initiative had been discussed under different nomenclature twenty years previously and that the party's position on the establishment of SEZs remained consistent. Additionally, National Assembly chairwoman Nguyen Thi Kim Ngan affirmed that the establishment of a special economic administrative zone did not violate the constitution and was under the authority of the National Assembly. The National Assembly would make appropriate amendments to SEZ regulations that conflict with local laws. Dr Luu Bich Ho, former director of the Institute of Development Strategies, did not consider the issues of national security and defence to be of concern, for even if SEZ administrative committees enjoyed too much institutional power, their authority is limited to within the SEZ and may be under the supervision of national authorities (Nguyen Nga 2017).

The pro-SEZs discourse also underscored the comparative advantages of the SEZs and the readiness on the part of local governments for their implementation. Phu Quoc is the largest island in the Gulf of Thailand and it holds a prominent position enriched with marine ecosystems and rainforests. Since 2011, Phu Quoc has upgraded important infrastructure and facilities, including roads, aviation and electricity. Many investment projects on tourism and services have been deployed. Phu Quoc has also prepared a land fund for investors to quickly develop planned projects (Minh Khoa

2016). By the same token, Van Don island is known for its marine life and a forest ecosystem suitable for developing a high-class eco-tourism industry (Nguyen 2017). In addition, Van Don made some investments in advance for building its infrastructural projects, such as an international airport, a system of highways, a seaport, and a casino for the upcoming proposed special zone plan. The proposed SEZ plans demonstrate the ambitious drive and determination of senior leaders. Van Don's efforts for social and economic growth has boosted the confidence of those paying attention to the SEZ plans (Moc Lan 2018). The answer to the advanced and greater constitutions of the special economic units lies in the unprecedented policies such as ninety-nine-year land leases, use of US dollars in parallel with Vietnamese dong, sales tax exemptions for special goods, and gambling operations (Khoa Nam and Dung 2017).

With a total area of 150,000 hectares, including 70,000 hectares of land and 80,000 hectares of water surface, Van Phong is located at the North of Khanh Hoa province of the Southern-Central coastal region of Vietnam. The Van Phong SEZ plan was approved by Prime Minister Nguyen Tuan Dung under Decision 380/QD-TTg in March 2014. The plan would include Nam (Southern) Van Phong in Ninh Hoa town and Bac (Northern) Van Phong in Van Ninh district (Van Phong EZ website). Bac Van Phong is a large and deep bay with a total area of 66,000 hectares (19,000 hectares of land and 47,000 of water surface). Hoang Dinh Phi, head of Van Phong Economic Zone Management Board, described Bac Van Phong as a potential international transit hub. The provincial government would promote investments in logistics, financial services, hi-tech healthcare and education services, and marine information technology under the guidance of the central government. Meanwhile, Mr Hoang Dinh Phi, head of Van Phong Economic Zone Management Board, revealed that the local authorities in Bac Van Phong had rejected many investors over the past five years because they anticipated the ratification of the SEZ law. Since 2012, Khanh Hoa province has reserved the entire Bac Van Phong for the SEZ project, although there had been many requests from large corporations to invest in the area. Khanh Hoa estimates infrastructure expenses for the whole area to come to 400,000 billion dong. The further development of the province is currently on temporary hold in order for its institutional framework to be completed (Nhu Binh 2017). Aiming to placate growing public anxiety over the ninety-nine-year term in early June 2018, the minister of planning and investment, Nguyen Chi Dung, asserted that "history will tell us who is responsible for the country's mission at the most important moment. Easier said than done! If we are afraid of everything, we cannot do anything." He went on to say that the first rule when drafting the bill was that it must be neither above the constitution nor pose any threat to national security, sovereignty, the environment or the people (Vu Han 2018).

The Politicization of the Ninety-Nine-Year Land Lease

While reporting on the SEZs draft bill, *Tuoi Tre* and *Thanh Nien* newspapers have published criticism and news of negative consequences resulting from the proposal, especially the provision of the ninety-nine-year land lease. And critics have pointed out the adverse consequences of the plan for territorial sovereignty. We argue that the publication of these objections to the official narrative have helped to politicize the ninety-nine-year land lease into an issue of national salience, although critics of the bill have avoided making politically sensitive comments that could undermine the party's legitimacy. Anti-SEZs discourses centred on the provision of ninety-nine-year land leases by linking it to a matter of national security. Since the end of 2017, most news articles brought up this challenging question: "Should land be allocated for 99 years?" *Tuoi Tre News* ran a front-page headline on 24 May 2018 titled, "Land allocation in the special zone up to 99 years" (Thai and Nhu Binh 2018; Le Kien 2018b, 2018c). There was a series of op-eds from writers that focused their criticism on the "special 99-year lease" of SEZs. Criticism of the ninety-nine-year lease centred on the meaning of the number ninety-nine. A ninety-nine-year period exceeds the lifetime of a person. It legally implies a territorial concession. Ninety-nine years was too long for the cycle of capital recovery in production and business activities, and is detrimental to the state. The question concerned what the government defines to be a "strategic investor" entitled to such privileges. Given that a party looking to invest in a casino project with 44,000 billion dong can qualify for the ninety-nine-year land lease, will the government reacquire the land if the project fails after thirty years (Chi Hieu 2017)? Many writers regarded the idea of a ninety-nine-year land lease as a territorial concession.

Phan Nguyen Nhu Khue, deputy head of Ho Chi Minh City's National Assembly delegation, stated that if the land use rights were allocated for ninety-nine years, "how would our children and grandchildren deal with national security and defence problems in the future?" If we did not trade the environment for economic development,[4] we will not trade sovereignty for economic development. Delegate Le Thanh Van asked for the opinions of policy experts on the strategic implications of building the SEZs for national security and defence (Le Hiep 2018a). In permitting investors to mortgage their land-attached assets at foreign credit institutions or to transfer land-use rights to other organizations, the draft bill could result in divergence from an investor's initial investment goals and commitments. Only poorly developed economies rely on land lease as a comparative advantage. Critics pointed out that some countries want simply to extract resources from other countries and that they sought not so much economic benefits as territorial claims. They would simply move to favourable regions and find a way to stay and try to influence domestic politics and security. This was the primary concern about the ninety-nine-year land lease shared by the National Assembly's delegates Duong Trung Quoc, Le Thu Ha and Truong Trong Nghia. Delegate Truong Trong Nghia further articulated,

> Our laws and policies must be designed so that they only welcome friends and do not invite bandits to our house. If bandits pretend to be our good friends, we need punitive measures to deter them. Since the draft bill offers too many investment privileges and too much power in the special zones, it is necessary to set strict criteria, procedures and supervision for strategic investors. Will high-tech investors choose to invest in the special economic zones, or will the SEZs merely attract investment in casinos, tourism and real estate?

He suggested choosing one SEZ as a test case before applying the policy to the others. He likens the current public tension over the SEZs to a "hot furnace" (Anh Vu 2018a). Delegate Duong Trung Quoc expressed that SEZs would become places for immigrants, and that interest groups were likely to exploit the investment and tax privileges of SEZs (Anh Vu 2018c). Associate professor Huynh Ngoc Giao, director of the Institute of Legal Policy and Development Studies, was concerned with how the law could ensure that the administrative committees of the SEZs would not abuse their power and run the regions like autonomous territorial units.

Depicted as "outstanding" or "superior" institutions, in theory the SEZs are the engine for regional economic development with their relaxed, flexible and investor-friendly regulations. The official narrative, however, seemed to fail to convince the public that the project would be successful. The long period of the land leases would only be beneficial to real estate, resort and casino businesses. The prospects of the SEZs were not realistic and would not contribute to the long-term development of high-tech industries (*Tuoi Tre News* 2018b, 2018c). Nguyen Anh Tri questioned Deputy Prime Minister Vuong Dinh Hue on the degree to which SEZs would contribute to development. The government needs to consider any national security and sovereignty problems over the next ten to a hundred years or even more when analysing the economic development of the SEZs (*Tuoi Tre News* 2018d; Anh Vu 2018b).

Dr Vu Thanh Tu Anh, an economics professor at Fulbright University, listed four reasons that the SEZ model was not feasible. First, the SEZ policy lacked a practical basis if the primary goal was to test new governance models and improve the organizational structure of the political system. The three selected provinces will not be able to make any significant breakthroughs and will only become industrial centres in the next ten to twenty years if the rest of the country stagnates. Lessons learned from the open economic zone model in Chu Lai in 2003 showed that without systematic change at the national level local initiatives would surely be stifled by the networks of cumbersome bureaucratic institutions and regulations that are incompatible with those of the SEZs. The possibility of replicating these innovative SEZ models is low because of the large gaps in investment incentives and institutional structures between the SEZs and the rest of the country. Thus, any hope of an institutional and policy diffusion from the SEZs to other parts of the nation is far-fetched. Second, while the SEZs are intended to catch up with the 4.0 Industry (the 4th Industrial Revolution), the regulations are still stuck with the 1.0 Industry in the sense that they try to attract more FDI by relying on traditional comparative advantages. This is indicated by the intention to open casinos for Vietnamese in the SEZs. Third, given the proposed plans for SEZs, there is no guarantee these zones would be economically sustainable and produce positive externalities for the nation (e.g., economic restructuring and upgrading of the national economy). Subsequently, Vietnam's economy would keep being dependent on FDI, resulting in the domination of foreign enterprises over the domestic private sector. This goes against successful stories of development in which the key to economic growth lies in institutional and policy structures that promote the expansion of local businesses. Dr Vu's fourth concern was that given their vital and strategic positions, are Phu Quoc, Bac Van Phong and Van Don suitable sites for policy testing? (Vu Anh 2018).

Analysis of Anti-SEZs Discourse on
RFA, VOA and BBC Tieng Viet

In the early morning of 9 June 2018, amid calls from citizens for public protest against the draft law, the government issued a notice that the passage of the controversial Special Zone Law would be postponed to the next meeting (the 6th session of the 14th National Assembly). After tracing public discourse on the SEZs issue, we argue that the impact of foreign newspapers began to play out in the month leading up to the first protests on 10 June, after which articles by *Thanh Nien* and *Tuoi Tre* increasingly reported the state's narrative on the anti-SEZs demonstrations and riots. Local mediatized infrapolitical resistance to the establishment of SEZs moved to foreign social media platforms.[5] Two shared discursive strategies were employed in RFA, VOA and BBC Vietnam in their news articles to politicize the SEZs initiative. First, in comparison with state-owned media, they were filled with commentaries aimed at debunking the SEZ bill in a politically sensitive language that undermined the VCP's legitimacy. Second, they constructed narratives on the democratic and patriotic characteristics of anti-SEZs protests that counterposed the dismissive caricatures of protesters painted by the official discourse.

The Politicization of the China Threat

The coverage of anti-SEZs discourses by RFA, the BBC and VOA news centred around the bill's detrimental consequences to Vietnamese territorial sovereignty and national security. In particular, these articles trace a direct link between the establishment of the three SEZs and China's threat to national security and sovereignty. Anti-Sino sentiment is not unusual in Vietnam, yet Vietnamese animosity towards China has intensified since the *Hai Yang Shi You 981* standoff in 2014. Anti-SEZ discourses reported by RFA and VOA continued to tap into the existing Chinese threat narrative. Dr Nguyen Trung Truc, a former head of the government border committee, dubbed Van Don the "second Crimea" under the passage of the draft law. Dr Truc and VOA journalist Le Anh Hung raised the concern that a similar scenario to the one that unfolded in the Crimea would occur in Van Don. Like Russian-backed Ukrainian separatists in the Crimea, Chinese immigrants in Van Don could pressure the local government for the island's integration into mainland China.

This could be a serious threat to Vietnamese security because of Van Don's close proximity to China and its strategic importance for the defence of Vietnam's northeastern shore (VOA Tieng Viet

2018a; Le Anh Hung 2018). RFA journalist Cat Linh wrote a two-part article, "Pham Minh Chinh and Van Don Special Economic Zone", tracing the SEZs initiative to a low-profile meeting of secretary of the Party Committee of Quang Ninh province Pham Minh Chinh with a group of five Chinese SEZ specialists from the China Center for Special Economic Zone Research (CCSEZR) of Shenzhen University on 19 January 2013. The group was led by Dr Tao Yitao, the head of CCSEZR and the chief architect of China's One Belt One Road Initiative (Cat Linh 2018b). Later, on 20 March 2014, the Quang Ninh government and CCSEZR co-organized a conference called "International Science EEZ development – Experience and Opportunities" under the chairmanship of Pham Minh Chinh to discuss "the mechanisms and specific policies for the special economic zones" (Tuan Anh 2015). The seminar brought together National Assembly spokeswoman Nguyen Thi Kim Ngan and nearly four hundred leaders of industry, experts and top speakers in the field of domestic and international economics. The president of the Independent Journalists' Association, Pham Chi Dung, and journalist Nguyen Dan An gave two bold interpretations of this visit and of Chinh's initial idea. According to Dung, in the initial proposal by Quang Ninh province to the national government, the duration of the land leases was for up to "120 years".

This fact makes it difficult not to believe that the "ulterior motive" of Pham Minh Chinh and Quang Ninh province behind the "too preferential and special policy recommendation" was that of "selling the nation" to China. From a geopolitical perspective, journalist An points out that as the northeastern gateway overlooking the Tonkin Gulf and situated only two hundred nautical miles from Hainan, Van Dong is more strategically significant to China than Van Phong and Phu Quoc. According to professor Tuong Lai, Van Don is a strategic location at the northeastern gateway where Ngo Quyen fought against the Han army, Ly Thuong Kiet the Song invaders, and King Tran Hung Dao the Yuan (Cat Linh 2018a). Bac Van Phong would be a vital entry point for China's One Belt One Road into Vietnam. In a commentary titled "Three Special Economic Zones, Three Great Catastrophes", journalist Le Anh Hung continued to extend the "Chinese threat hypothesis" to Van Phong and Phu Quoc (Le Anh Hung 2018). Hung lists three security problems if Van Phong were to be subject to foreign control. First, Bac Van Phong is only 130 kilometres from the Highlands and encompasses Highway 1A as the only north–south highway. Van Phong Bay is considered the second Cam Ranh because of their similar geographical and political features, and it is located only

60 kilometres from Cam Ranh. The seizure of Van Phong would result in a north–south division and the loss of control over the Highlands region. If China were to control Van Phong, it could threaten freedom of navigation and security on the water surrounding Cam Ranh Bay and neutralize Vietnam's military bases and alliances in the area.

In Phu Quoc, besides the separatist strategy that Chinese separatists could employ against Vietnam as in the case of Van Don, Beijing could back Cambodian annexation of Phu Quoc, over which Phnom Penh has claimed controversial ownership rights (Mudrick 2014). According to Nguyen Xuan Nghia, an economic consultant of RFA, "it is mistakenly believed that tourists are in these zones for gambling but when the Chinese are there they will use military intelligence systems for espionage and controlling the island" (Nguyen 2018). A former economic advisor to the prime minister, Pham Chi Lan, voices the same concern that "China has not concealed its territorial ambitions for Vietnam for many years: the 1979 border war, the occupation of Gac Ma island and other islands.... [T]he introduction of this Special Law, especially with ninety-nine years, can turn three special economic zones into real territories of the neighbouring country" (Cat Linh 2018a).

Conflicting Representations of Anti-SEZs Demonstrations

The news items of RFA, the VOA and to some extent the BBC construct counter-discourses to the official narrative on anti-SEZs demonstrations and riots. The narratives of these news outlets underscore the democratic awareness and patriotism of the Vietnamese people in contrast to the depiction of the protesters' behaviour in the official media as "reactionary" and "obstructive to public order". Prime Minister Nguyen Xuan Phuc explained to the public that the decision-making process of the National Assembly is "communicative, transparent, sincere and accountable for the collective good, and the government always listens to public opinions" (Le Tan 2018). But he continued that "there have been some bad, reactionary groups that deliberately dragged and instigated citizens into riots and created misunderstandings". The minister of security, To Lam, responded at an inquiry session of the Standing Committee of the National Assembly in the afternoon of 13 August 2018 that recent protesters were paid between 200,000 and 400,000 Vietnam Dong to protest (RFA 2018b). He claimed his recent investigation found that most of the protesters who received the money were drug addicts and HIV-infected people from "the oppositional and exiled forces against the Vietnamese government". The chairwoman of the National Assembly,

Nguyen Thi Kim Ngan, decried that the public demonstrations are "extremist acts [*hanh dong qua khich*] affecting people's lives" and that "Vietnamese patriotism [*long yeu nuoc*] has been exploited to stir up social unrest" (Le Hiep 2018b). In her closing remarks at the fifth session of the National Assembly on the morning of 15 June 2018, Mrs Ngan asserted that "the National Assembly condemns any act of abusing democracy, misrepresenting facts, or inciting and provoking extremism" (Le Hiep 2018b). If state-owned media outlets were instructed by the party to portray public demonstrations and protests as "reactionary" and "extremist", foreign media newspapers interpreted the protests in a much more positive light. Foreign news articles highlighted Vietnamese patriotism, their constitutional right to demonstrate, and cases of abuse of power by the police in attacking and detaining protesters. *Tuoi Tre* and *Thanh Nien* news depicted anti-SEZ protesters in Bình Thuận province as mobs of reactionary extremists, criminals and drug addicts, describing how thousands of protesters on 10 and 17 June burned and hurled stones at local government premises and assets. In contrast, RFA, VOA and the BBC covered stories about victims of violent police crackdowns, physical assaults and arrests. These counter-narratives may have kept the anti-SEZ discourse and public opposition alive and reinvigorated throughout June and July.

In his interview with RFA, Mr Phan Huu Hien, who was born and raised in Binh Thuan, opined that

> Binh Thuan people are very good-natured, and they rarely behave aggressively. So, their feelings must have been repressed for years. The power plants destroyed the environment, and the fishermen have lost their regular fishing grounds. But this time was the straw that broke the camel's back and it surprisingly brings about catastrophic consequences. (RFA 2018a)

Nguyen Van Thuan was sentenced to between three and five years in prison by Binh Thuan Court for throwing stones at the local government headquarters. Mr Nguyen Cu, Thuan's father, told RFA that his son was a kind, hard-working man and a father of two kids who was saving money for his father's medical treatment. Activist Nguyen Thuy Hanh added that the Binh Thuan police indirectly threatened the families of those detained. The police interrogated the protestors and tried to coerce them into revealing the identities of any groups or individuals they had received money from by offering to reduce the charges against them (Hoa Ai 2018).

VOA news reported that numerous protesters have expressed on Facebook that they had been wrongly accused by the government of burning public vehicles and injuring policemen (VOA Tieng Viet 2018b). Many bystanders were arrested without warrant. For instance, BBC Vietnam interviewed Mrs Nguyen Ngoc Lua who had been collared by four strangers in front of the Notre-Dame de Paris statue and taken to a sports complex where at least three hundred people were detained. According to Mrs Lua, the police assaulted a Catholic couple with batons, who were later taken to hospital by ambulance (BBC Tieng Viet 2018a). A Vietnamese photographer, Mrs Khanh Mai, was abruptly arrested by a group of policemen, who yelled "What are you taking photos for? Arrest her!" while she was shooting a model on Nguyen Van Binh street. She had not attended the 17 June protest.

The police detainment and physical assault of Will Nguyen, a Vietnamese American graduate student at the National University of Singapore, was among the headlines that went viral on online social media. The official media described Will's behaviour as "disrupting public order" (*gay roi trat tu cong cong*) and causing serious traffic obstruction (Phan Thuong 2018; *Tuoi Tre News* 2018e). Foreign ministry spokeswoman Nguyen Thi Thu Hang publicly stated that the Vietnamese security forces did not resort to the use of force against William Nguyen. At his trial on 20 July 2018, a state-owned newspaper reported that "William acknowledged his behaviour, expressed his remorse and regret, and hoped to receive leniency from the Court" (Dang Quan 2018). Contrary to what had been portrayed by the local media, on 27 July 2018, RFA released Will's Facebook and Twitter comments that he "never regretted helping Vietnamese people exercise democracy and will help Vietnam develop" for the rest of his life. On 4 October 2018, RFA uploaded a video and script of their interview with Will Nguyen. At odds with what was presented by the official media, Will responded that he was aware of the draft bill and why people protested, that he was severely injured during the arrest, and that what he did during the protest was misrepresented by the official news (Chan Nhu 2018).

Legal experts and political pundits have characterized the act of protesting as a sign of increasing awareness among the Vietnamese people of their constitutionally protected democratic rights. Increasing concern has been expressed among government officials, activists and policy experts that violent riots and the vandalism of government assets are a result of a lack of public demonstration laws in Vietnam, which have been proposed since 2011 and continue to be delayed from passing into law. Many activists, lawyers and policy experts joined a roundtable discussion hosted by BBC Vietnam on YouTube to talk about the legality and constitutionality of the protests. According to Pham Duc Bao, deputy director of the Institute for Policy, Law and Development, "without public demonstration laws, citizens who exercise that constitutional right do not know how to comply with the law, and when protests occur the authorities are also very difficult to handle" (BBC Tieng Viet 2018b). Lawyer Le Cong Dinh argued that the "official media's portrayal of protests as illegal behaviour is unwarranted" (BBC Tieng Viet 2018b). He went on to say that protesting is a constitutional right. If someone organizes a protest, they are simply exercising their constitutional right and should not be charged under criminal or administrative law. Freelance journalist and blogger Truong Duy Nhat added that "just because there is no public demonstration law this does not mean that people do not have the right to protest, which is a constitutional one". The passage of the demonstration law was delayed for legislative reasons, but that does not mean that people do not have the right to protest.

Conclusion

This chapter contributes to the discursive dimension of civil society in Vietnam, which has been underemphasized in mainstream interpretations of contemporary Vietnamese politics. We do not deny the impact of the public demonstrations against the SEZs law and protests over the deferral of the draft bill in the National Assembly's October session. We suggest, however, that the mobilization of these collective actions was made possible partly because public media discourses on the SEZs project and draft law exposed the government's deliberative failure in justifying its decision making and provided citizens with the motivation to protest. Our discourse analysis of news articles by *Thanh Nien*, *Tuoi Tre*, VOA, BBC Tieng Viet and RFA published between 2014 and 2018 traces the emergence of the SEZ project and draft law as a "promising" grand economic strategy of the VCP in early 2014 to the radical transformation of its status into a "hidden pedestal" for China's potential annexation of Vietnam's geopolitically and strategically vital regions, and as a critical threat to the security and sovereignty of the nation. Since the protests, the government has been more vigilant with regard to official announcements on the future implementation of SEZs bill and SEZs-related investment projects. Since 2019, local authorities have manged to keep the issue under the radar.[6] In fact, the government issued pilot Resolution no. 102/NQ-CP on the establishment of Van Don Economic Zone management board under the management of the People's Committee of Quang

Ninh province on 14 November 2019. Six months later, on 15 May 2020, the People's Committee of Quang Ninh province announced the chairman, Cao Tuong Huy, and vice chairman, Le Huu Phuc, of the Van Don Economic Zone management board (Ministry of Planning and Investment 2020). The official government reports only released a few brief details about the current plan.

Notes

1. We sourced the online news articles by searching for key words via Google (e.g., *99 nam, kinh te dac khu*). For print newspapers, we traced the case back to 2011 when the issue was first mentioned and then moved forward to 2018.

2. Discourse analysis is often criticized for lacking a systematic scientific method to test whether a particular discourse or group of discourses represents the viewpoint of a population and does not marginalize the minority's voice. One way of reducing selection bias is by selecting newspapers that have large readerships. We assume daily newspapers with large readerships, both online and offline versions, will influence people's understanding and perceptions of an event. Because of time constraints, we limited our analysis to discourses in mass social media, and newspapers were selected to represent this genre.

3. Minister Dung calls institutional competitiveness a dynamic determinant of growth, in contrast to static determinants such as natural resources, natural advantages and cheap labour.

4. The delegate might have alluded to the Formosa spill incident.

5. Not being subject to state censorship, RFA, VOA and the BBC are more critical of the Vietnamese authorities and the SEZs draft bill than their local counterparts. These foreign media outlets tended to "politicize" the SEZs draft bill and associate it with China—a standard strategy for attracting more readership by media institutions in democratic societies.

6. We conducted Google searches from 1 November 2019 to the present and found that no mainstream local newspapers such as *Tuoi Tre* and *Thanh Nien* have discussed the opening of Van Don EZ. Readers of the local news since early 2020 will not have been able to find any further information about controversial issues such as the land lease provision or other benefits for foreign investors. In a BBC article in 2020, prominent local economists Dr Pham Chi Lan and Dr Nguyen Chi Hieu said they were neither "aware" of nor were "consulted" about the establishment of Van Don (My Hang 2020)

References

Abuza, Zachary. 2015. *Stifling the Public Sphere: Media and Civil Society in Vietnam*. National Endowment for Democracy. https://www.ned.org/wp-content/uploads/2015/10/Stifling-the-Public-Sphere-Media-Civil-Society-Vietnam-Forum-NED.pdf.

Anh Vu. 2018a. "Lo da nong roi, khong ai muon co them cui sau khi dac khu ra doi". *Thanh Nien News*, 23 May 2018. https://thanhnien.vn/thoi-su/

lo-da-nong-roi-khong-ai-muon-co-them-cui-sau-khi-dac-khu-ra-doi-965730.html.

———. 2018b. "Co xe 'tam ma dac khu' can tu duy dot pha". *Thanh Nien News*, 24 May 2018. https://thanhnien.vn/thoi-su/co-xe-tam-ma-dac-khu-can-tu-duy-dot-pha-965953.html.

———. 2018c. "Dai bieu quoc hoi de nghi Pho thu tuong lam ro hieu qua kinh te khi phat trien dac khu". *Thanh Nien News*, 6 June 2018. https://thanhnien.vn/thoi-su/dbqh-de-nghi-pho-thu-tuong-lam-ro-hieu-qua-kinh-te-khi-phat-trien-dac-khu-970451.html.

BBC Tieng Viet. 2018a. "TPHCM: Hai phu nu ke chuyen bi bat hom 17/6". 18 June 2018. https://www.bbc.com/vietnamese/vietnam-44518485.

———. 2018b. "Ly do bieu tinh: "Chong Trung Quoc va mong moi dan chu". 22 June 2018. https://www.bbc.com/vietnamese/vietnam-44571729.

Bui, Hai Thiem. 2016. "The Influence of Social Media in Vietnam's Elite Politics". *Journal of Current Southeast Asian Affairs* 35, no. 2: 89–111.

Bui, Nhung T. 2017. "Managing Anti-China Nationalism in Vietnam: Evidence from the Media during the 2014 Oil Rig Crisis". *Pacific Review* 30, no. 2: 169–87.

Cain, Geoffrey. 2014. "Kill One to Warn One Hundred: The Politics of Press Censorship in Vietnam". *International Journal of Press/Politics* 19, no. 1: 85–107. https://doi.org/10.1177/1940161213508814.

Carabine, Jean. 2001. "Unmarried Motherhood 1830–1990: A Genealogical Analysis". In *Discourse as Data*, edited by Margaret Wetherell, Stephanie Taylor, and Simeon Yates. London: Sage.

Cat Linh. 2018a. "Dac khu 99 nam va con ac mong mang ten Trung Quoc". RFA, 6 May 2018. https://www.rfa.org/vietnamese/in_depth/Sez-99-years-and-the-nightmare-named-china-06052018143807.html?searchterm:utf8:ustring=%20thu%C3%AA%20%C4%91%E1%BA%A5t%2099%20n%C4%83m.

———. 2018b. "Pham Minh Chinh va Dac khu Van Don (Phan 1)". RFA, 19 June 2018. https://www.rfa.org/vietnamese/in_depth/pham-minh-chinh-and-van-don-sez-part1-06192018143537.html?searchterm:utf8:ustring=%20thu%C3%AA%20%C4%91%E1%BA%A5t%2099%20n%C4%83m.

Chan Nhu. 2018. "William Nguyen: 'vi sao toi phai tham gia bieu tinh?'" RFA, 4 October 2018. https://www.rfa.org/vietnamese/in_depth/A-conversation-with-William-Nguyen-10042018080459.html?searchterm:utf8:ustring=%20%C4%91%E1%BA%B7c%20khu%202018.

Chang, Alex, Yun-Han Chu, and Bridget Welsh. 2013. "Southeast Asia: Sources of Regime Support". *Journal of Democracy* 24, no. 2: 150–64. https://ink.library.smu.edu.sg/soss_research/1170.

Chi Hieu. 2017. "Nhieu lo ngai ve chinh sach cho dac khu". *Thanh Nien News*, 23 November 2017. https://thanhnien.vn/thoi-su/nhieu-lo-ngai-ve-chinh-sach-cho-dac-khu-902849.html.

Dang Quan. 2018. "Truc xuat William Nguyen vi toi gay roi trat tu cong cong". *Nhân Dân News*, 20 July 2018. https://nhandan.com.vn/thoi-su-phap-luat/truc-xuat-william-nguyen-vi-toi-gay-roi-trat-tu-cong-cong-330249/.

Fairclough, Isabela, and Norman Fairclough. 2012. *Political Discourse Analysis: A Method for Advanced Students*. London: Routledge.

Hoa Ai. 2018. "Viet Nam tiep tuc bo tu nhung nguoi tham gia cac cuoc bieu tinh hoi thang 6/2018". RFA, 17 October 2018. https://www.rfa.org/vietnamese/in_depth/vn-continues-to-imprison-the-people-participated-in-the-last-june-protests-10172018140443.html.

Human Rights Watch. 2010. *"Vietnam: Stop Cyber Attacks against Online Critics: Government Crackdowns on Bloggers and Websites"*. 26 May 2010. https://www.hrw.org/news/2010/05/26/vietnam-stop-cyber-attacks-against-online-critics.

Kerkvliet, Benedict J. Tria. 2001. "An Approach for Analysing State-Society Relations in Vietnam". *SOJOURN: Journal of Social Issues in Southeast Asia* 16, no. 2: 238–78.

———. 2014. "Government Repression and Toleration of Dissidents in Contemporary Vietnam". In *Politics in Contemporary Vietnam: Party, State, and Authority Relations*, edited by Jonathan D. London, pp. 100–134. London: Palgrave Macmillan.

———. 2019. *Speaking Out in Vietnam: Public Political Criticism in a Communist Party–Ruled Nation*. Ithaca: Cornell University Press.

Khoa Nam and H.T. Dung. 2017. "Uu dai chua tung co de thuc day dac khu Phu Quoc cat canh". *Tuoi Tre News*, 18 September 2017. https://tuoitre.vn/chuan-bi-tot-nhat-cho-dac-khu-phu-quoc-20170918084343442.htm.

Lawsoft. 2018. "The Special Economic Zones Bill". https://thuvienphapluat.vn/tintuc/vn/thoi-su-phap-luat/thoi-su/20379/toan-van-du-thao-luat-dac-khu.

Le, Anh Hung. 2018. "Ba dac khu, ba dai hiem hoa". *VOA Tieng Viet*, 9 June 2018. https://www.voatiengviet.com/a/dac-khu-phu-quoc-van-don-bac-van-phong/4430518.html.

Le Hiep. 2018a. "Lo giao dat dac khu toi 99 nam anh huong toi chu quyen quoc gia". *Thanh Nien News*, 4 April 2018. https://thanhnien.vn/thoi-su/lo-gi-ao-dat-dac-khu-toi-99-nam-anh-huong-toi-chu-quyen-quoc-gia-948983.html.

———. 2018b. "Chu tich Quoc hoi: Nghiem khac len an hanh dong loi dung dan chu, kich dong, qua khich". *Thanh Nien News*, 15 June 2018. https://thanhnien.vn/thoi-su/chu-tich-quoc-hoi-nghiem-khac-len-an-hanh-dong-loi-dung-dan-chu-kich-dong-qua-khich-973615.html.

Le Kien. 2017. "Dac khu kinh te can mot the che vuot troi". *Tuoi Tre News*, 13 November 2017. https://tuoitre.vn/dac-khu-kinh-te-can-mot-the-che-vuot-troi-20171113095005461.htm.

Le Kien. 2018a. "Van ban khoan co che cho dac khu". *Tuoi Tre News*, 12 January 2018, p. 6.

———. 2018b. "Dac khu rat nhay cam, co nen giao dat den 99 nam?" *Tuoi Tre News*, 23 May 2018. https://tuoitre.vn/dac-khu-rat-nhay-cam-co-nen-giao-dat-den-99-nam-20180523143353428.htm.

———. 2018c. "Co nen giao dat dac khu vuot qua doi nguoi?" *Tuoi Tre News*, 24 May 2018. https://tuoitre.vn/co-nen-giao-dat-dac-khu-vuot-qua-doi-nguoi-20180524081907318.htm.

Le Tan. 2018. "Thu tuong: Nguoi dan can binh tinh, tinh tao de khong bi ke xau loi keo, xui giuc". *Thanh Nien News*, 18 June 2018. https://thanhnien.vn/thoi-su/thu-tuong-nguoi-dan-can-binh-tinh-tinh-tao-de-khong-bi-ke-xau-loi-keo-xui-giuc-974453.html.

Mai Phuong. 2018. "Dac khu se la 'nam cham' thu hut von". *Thanh Nien News*, 16 April 2018. https://thanhnien.vn/tai-chinh-kinh-doanh/dac-khu-se-la-nam-cham-thu-hut-von-953038.html.

Mai Phuong and Nguyen Nga. 2017. "Can chinh sach dot pha cho dac khu kinh te". *Thanh Nien News*, 31 August 2017. https://thanhnien.vn/tai-chinh-kinh-doanh/can-chinh-sach-dot-pha-cho-dac-khu-kinh-te-870906.html.

Minh Khoa. 2016. "Trien vong dac khu kinh te Phu Quoc". *Thanh Nien News*, 25 February 2016. https://thanhnien.vn/tai-chinh-kinh-doanh/trien-vong-dac-khu-kinh-te-phu-quoc-670885.html.

Moc Lan. 2018. "Hoi tu kinh te xanh – tri thuc o dac khu Van Don". *Thanh Nien News*, 7 February 2018. https://thanhnien.vn/tai-chinh-kinh-doanh/hoi-tu-kinh-te-xanh-tri-thuc-o-dac-khu-van-don-931880.html.

Mudrick, Jeff. 2014. "Cambodia's Impossible Dream: Koh Tral." *The Diplomat*, 17 June 2014. https://thediplomat.com/2014/06/cambodias-impossible-dream-koh-tral/.

Ngoc An. 2017. "Dac khu duoc danh co che vuot troi thue dat 99 nam". *Tuoi Tre News*, 24 August 2017. https://tuoitre.vn/dac-khu-duoc-danh-co-che-vuot-troi-thue-dat-99-nam-1374013.htm.

Nguyen Nga. 2017. "Dac khu phai giup dot pha kinh te". *Thanh Nien News*, 26 October 2017. https://thanhnien.vn/tai-chinh-kinh-doanh/dac-khu-phai-giup-dot-pha-kinh-te-893702.html.

Nguyen Nga and Mai Phuong. 2017. "Dac khu phai giup dot pha kinh te: Lo ap mo hinh the che moi". *Thanh Nien News*, 27 October 2017. https://thanhnien.vn/tai-chinh-kinh-doanh/dac-khu-phai-giup-dot-pha-kinh-te-lo-ap-mo-hinh-the-che-moi-894048.html.

Nguyen, Thu Tra. 2017. "Mo hinh nao de Van Don thanh dac khu kinh te?" *Tuoi Tre News*, 9 November 2017. https://tuoitre.vn/mo-hinh-nao-de-van-don-thanh-dac-khu-kinh-te-20171109094919686.htm.

Nguyen, Xuan Nghia. 2018. "Moi nguy cua Dac Khu Tu Tri". RFA, 5 June 2018. https://www.rfa.org/vietnamese/news/programs/high-risks-of-special-economic-zone-06052018073913.html?searchterm:utf8:ustring=%20thu%C3%AA%20%C4%91%E1%BA%A5t%2099%20n%C4%83m.

Nhu Binh. 2018. "Dac khu Bac Van Phong khong chi co casino va tien". *Tuoi Tre News*, 22 November 2017. https://tuoitre.vn/dac-khu-bac-van-phong-khong-chi-co-casino-va-tien-do-20171122140812134.htm.

Phan Thuong. 2018. "Xet xu bi cao nguoi My goc Viet William Anh toi gay roi trat tu cong cong". *Thanh Nien News*, 20 July 2018. https://thanhnien.vn/thoi-su/xet-xu-bi-cao-nguoi-my-goc-viet-william-anh-toi-gay-roi-trat-tu-cong-cong-984973.html.

Phuong, M., T. Phong, and V. Van. 2018. "Dac khu phai dac biet de dot pha". *Thanh Nien News*, 23 May 2018. https://thanhnien.vn/tai-chinh-kinh-doanh/dac-khu-phai-dac-biet-de-dot-pha-965530.html.

Ricoeur, Paul. 1981. *Hermeneutics and the Human Sciences: Essays on Language, Action and Interpretation*, edited by John B. Thompson. Cambridge: Cambridge University Press.

RFA. 2018a. "Bao dong tai Binh Thuan nhu giot nuoc tran ly". 11 June 2018. https://www.rfa.org/vietnamese/in_depth/binh-thuan-violence-the-water-drop-06112018125210.html.

———. 2018b. "Bo truong To Lam lap lai cao buoc nguoi bieu tinh nhan tien". 13 August 2018. https://www.rfa.org/vietnamese/news/vietnamnews/tolam-accuses-200-400-dong-08132018082342.html?searchterm:utf8:ustring=%20thu%C3%AA%20%C4%91%E1%BA%A5t%2099%20n%C4%83m.

Scott, James C. 1990. *Domination and the Arts of Resistance: Hidden Transcripts*. Yale: University Press.

Scott, James. 2012. "Infrapolitics and Mobilizations: A Response by James C. Scott". *Revue française de'études américaines* 131, no. 1: 112–17.

Soriano, Cheryll Ruth, and T.T. Sreekumar. 2012. "Multiple Transcripts as Political Strategy: Social Media and Conflicting Identities of the Moro Liberation Movement in the Philippines". *Media, Culture & Society* 34, no. 8: 1028–39. https://doi.org/10.1177/0163443712454262.

Thai Ba Dung and Nhu Bình. 2018. "Dac khu co nen cho nha dau tu thue dat 99 nam?" *Tuoi Tre News*, 3 June 2018. https://tuoitre.vn/dac-khu-co-nen-cho-nha-dau-tu-thue-dat-99-nam-2018060309491778.htm.

Tien Thang. 2018. "Dac khu kinh te la lo thi nghiem cua the che". *Tuoi Tre News*, 15 May 2018, https://tuoitre.vn/dac-khu-kinh-te-la-lo-thi-nghiem-cua-the-che-20180515202032455.htm.

Tran, Van Tho. 2018. "Ba dac khu can tra loi 3 cau hoi". *Tuoi Tre News*, 6 August 2018, p. 6.

Tuan Anh. 2015. "Mechanisms and Specific Policies for Special Economic Zones". Permanent Mission of Vietnam to the United Nations, 27 December 2015. https://vnmission-newyork.mofa.gov.vn/enus/About%20Vietnam/General%20Information/Economic/Pages/Mechanisms-and-specific-policies-for-special-economic-zones.aspx.

Tuoi Tre News. 2018a. "Khat vong quoc gia thinh vuong". 25 February 2018, p. 2.

———. 2018b. "Co nen giao dat vuot qua doi nguoi?" 24 May 2018. https://tuoitre.vn/co-nen-giao-dat-dac-khu-vuot-qua-doi-nguoi-20180524081907318.htm.

———. 2018c. "Dac khu co nen cho nha dau tu thue dat 99 nam?" 3 June 2018. https://tuoitre.vn/dac-khu-co-nen-cho-nha-dau-tu-thue-dat-99-nam-2018060309491778.htm.

———. "Pho thu tuong: Co 3 dac khu, Ha Noi va TP.HCM van la dau tau kinh te". 6 June 2018. https://tuoitre.vn/pho-thu-tuong-co-3-dac-khu-ha-noi-va-tp-hcm-van-la-dau-tau-kinh-te-20180606130629246.htm.

———. "Bat tam giam mot Viet kieu gay roi tai trung tam TP. HCM". 15 June 2018. https://tuoitre.vn/bat-tam-giam-mot-viet-kieu-gay-roi-tai-trung-tam-tp-hcm-20180615220316817.htm.

VOA Tieng Viet. 2018a. "Lo ngai Van Don thanh Criemea thu hai neu giao dat 99 nam". 29 May 2018. https://www.voatiengviet.com/a/lo-ngai-van-don-thanh-crimea-thu-hai-neu-giao-dat-99-nam/4414571.html.

———. 2018b. "Bung no bieu tinh chong luat dac khu, nhieu nguoi bi bat". 6 August 2018. https://www.voatiengviet.com/a/n%E1%BB%95-ra-bi%E1%BB%83u-t%C3%ACnh-ch%E1%BB%91ng-lu%E1%BA%ADt-%C4%91%E1%BA%B7c-khu-nhi%E1%BB%81u-ng%C6%B0%E1%BB%9Di-b%E1%BB%8B-b%E1%BA%AFt/4432357.html.

Vu Han. 2018. "Bo truong KH-DT: Khong co mot chu 'Trung Quoc' nao trong du thao luat 'Dac khu'". *Thanh Nien News*, 6 June 2018. https://thanhnien.

vn/thoi-su/bo-truong-kh-dt-khong-co-mot-chu-trung-quoc-nao-trong-du-thao-luat-dac-khu-970303.html.

Vu, Minh Khuong. 2018. "Tao dot pha tu dac khu kinh te". *Tuoi Tre News*, 7 April 2018. https://tuoitre.vn/tao-dot-pha-tu-dac-khu-kinh-te-20180407 102040659.htm.

Vu, Thanh Tu Anh. 2018. "Vi sao dac khu van chi la 'loi cu ta ve?'?" *Tuoi Tre News*, 4 June 2018. https://tuoitre.vn/vi-sao-dac-khu-van-chi-la-loi-cu-ta-ve-20180604100413464.htm.

Wells-Dang, Andew. 2010. "Political Space in Vietnam: A View from the 'Rice Roots'". *Pacific Review* 23, no. 1: 93–112.

———. 2014. "The Political Influence of Civil Society in Vietnam". In *Politics in Contemporary Vietnam: Party, State, and Authority Relations*, edited by Jonathan D. London, pp. 162–83. London: Palgrave Macmillan.

Yang, Peidong, Lijun Tang, and Xuan Wang. 2015. "Diaosi as Infrapolitics: Scatological Tropes, Identity-Making and Cultural Intimacy on China's Internet". *Media, Culture & Society* 37, no. 2: 197–214. https://doi.org/10.1177/0163443714557980.

Chapter 9

Freedom of and Workers' Participation in Trade Unions in Vietnam

Thinh-Van Vu

Throughout its history, the Vietnamese Trade Union has accompanied the ruling Vietnamese Communist Party (VCP) at the national and sub-national levels (Collin 2020; Schweisshelm and Do 2018). In the global economic crisis of the 1930s, the working environment in Vietnam under French rule was tough. Trade unions were illegal as strikes were repressed and activists were stifled by the colonial power (Pringle and Clarke 2010). In 1929, the VCP established the Red Federation of Trade Unions (*Tong Cong Hoi Do*), its first trade union federation, to call workers to fight for national independence (Collin 2020). From the beginning, the trade unions not only prioritized protecting the interests of members and combating exploitation by employers, but also liberating the country from foreign invaders. In 1946, a year after the formation of the Democratic Republic of Vietnam in the North, the Red Federation of Trade Unions was renamed the Vietnam General Confederation of Labour (VGCL). Leaders of the VGCL were members of the VCP. During the subsequent war against the United States, the union became an essential wing of the VCP to gather workers for war-oriented production in order to build a socialist economy in the North and to assist the national revolution in the South. In contrast, labour associations emerged in the South along with an explosion of strikes (Schweisshelm and Do 2018). This included organizing thousands of strikes with the Trade Union of Southern Liberation Vietnam (*Lien hiep Cong doan giai phong mien Nam Viet*

Nam) during the 1960–1970s (Kerkvliet 2010; Schweisshelm and Do 2018).

After the war ended, when private enterprises were confiscated and became state-owned, the two unions merged. Trade unions continued to serve as the "transmission belt" of the government and the extended personnel department of state-owned enterprises in order to achieve economic targets and social stability (Collin 2020; Zhu and Fahey 2000). Before Doi Moi, the legitimacy of Vietnamese trade unions depended on their alliance with the Communist Party at the national and sub-national levels, and with managers in the state-owned enterprises and community-owned enterprises—the only form of enterprise at that time. The VCP controlled all aspects of labour relations, while the unions mostly played an administrative role rather than a representative function (Zhu et al. 2008). The management boards of the companies were staffed by VCP members employed by the government, which followed the model of "Concentrated Democratic Socialism" (*Tap Trung Dan Chu Xa Hoi Chu Nghia*), including representatives from the VCP leadership, management, union representatives and youth (Collins, Ren and Warner 2019). Since Doi Moi in late 1986 until now, and despite the development of a socialist market economy in Vietnam (*nen kinh te thi truong dinh huong xa hoi chu nghia*) in which a rights-based system for the regulation of industrial relations has been established, trade unions have maintained the same function as they had under the centrally planned economy in order to retain their political power (Arnold 2013; Clarke, Lee and Do 2007; Collins, Ren and Warner 2019).

According to the International Labour Organization (ILO 1994), the earliest ILO Convention to address the right to organize was the Right of Association Convention, 1921 (No. 11), followed by the Right of Association Convention in 1947 (No. 84). But the project to regulate the freedom of association on an international scale only really materialized with the adoption of the Freedom of Association and Protection of the Right to Organize Convention (No. 87) in 1948, and the Right to Organize and Collective Bargaining Convention (No. 98) the following year. Together, these constitute the basic instruments that govern freedom of association.

Vietnam was a member of the ILO from 1950 to 1976 and from 1980 to 1985; it rejoined again in 1992. The main aims of the ILO in Vietnam are to promote workers' rights and decent employment opportunities. It is also involved in measures to enhance social protection and to strengthen dialogues on work-related issues. By

July 2020, Vietnam had ratified seven out of the eight fundamental ILO conventions (see Appendix Table 9.A1). There remains one fundamental convention—that is, Freedom of Association and Protection of the Right to Organize Convention (No. 87)[1]—which Vietnam has not yet ratified but purportedly intends to in 2023.[2]

This chapter explores the role, function and organizational structure of the VGCL in contemporary Vietnam's industrial context. It explains why the VGCL functions inefficiently and how it depends on the VCP. The chapter also explores the issue of trade union freedom in Vietnam, the processes of their formation and development, and the existence of illegal trade unions in the country. The study found that during the operation of Vietnamese trade unions freedom of association has in some periods been practised or has at least been intended for implementation. In addition, some illegal independent trade unions have been established and have existed for many years. This chapter seeks to explain why the government and the VCP have promoted trade union freedom in the new context. The findings show that provisions of the law have until now been vague and do not specify how to establish and manage new workers representative organizations (WROs) in the workplace. Moreover, union subservience to the VCP and managerially dependent unions still hinder trade union reform. Many workers doubt the protection and representation of their current unions and consider leaving them to join new WROs.

This research is based on documentation analysis and interviews. In collaboration with other researchers in Vietnam, I conducted in-depth, group and semi-structured interviews with workers and union officials working in industrial and export processing zones in Hanoi, Hung Yen, Ha Nam, Ho Chi Minh City and Binh Duong in 2018, 2019 and 2020 (see Appendix Table 9.A2). Together, we also conducted interviews with five union officials in the executive board of trade unions of industrial zones.

The Function and Role of Trade Unions in Vietnam

The 2013 constitution of the Socialist Republic of Vietnam stipulates in Article 10 as follows:

> The Trade Union is the sociopolitical organization of the working class and labourers, established on a voluntary basis that represents the workers, looks after and protects the legitimate and legal rights and interests of the workers; participates in state administration and socio-economic management; participates in the control, inspection, and supervision of the activity of state bodies,

organizations, units and enterprises with respects to the matters concerning the rights and duties of the workers; propagandizes, mobilizes learning, development of abilities and professional skills, conformity of law, and construction and defense of the Fatherland among the workers.

The 2013 constitution supplemented regulations on the participation of trade unions in the inspection of agencies, organizations, units and enterprises on issues related to workers' rights and obligations. This constitution also clarifies the rights and responsibilities of trade unions to workers and includes provisions on union responsibilities in propagating and mobilizing workers to study and improve their qualifications, occupational skills and compliance with the law.

The 1994 Labour Code defines the duties of trade unions as to join with state agencies, organize socio-economic development, protect and take care of the rights of workers, participate in checking and supervising the enforcement of provisions of the labour law (Chapter 1, Article 12), participate in making the collective labour agreement (Chapter 5), the salary regime (Chapter 6), and the work of occupational safety and sanitation.

Trade unions have focused on organizing patriotic emulation movements (*phong trao thi dua yeu nuoc*), good labour/creative labour emulation movements (*phong trao thi dua lao dong gioi, lao dong sang tao*), anti-corruption activities, helping to reduce poverty, and providing social welfare service (VGCL 2016). In the 2012 Labour Code, there are more detailed provisions on the role of trade unions in labour relations; the procedure to establish, join and operate trade unions in enterprises, agencies and organizations; prohibited conduct for employers related to the establishment, accession and functioning of trade unions; and the rights of grass-roots trade union officials in labour relations. This law states that the immediate upper-level trade union (*cong doan cap tren co so*) could represent and safeguard the legitimate rights and interests of workers in non-unionized companies.

By 2012 the Trade Union Law had been amended. This new law consists of six chapters and thirty-three articles. This is an increase of two chapters and fourteen articles over the 1990 Trade Union Law.[3] Among the many issues covered by this law is a major change that obliges all companies to pay a mandatory union fee of two per cent of total payroll as a social insurance contribution, even if the company has no trade union. This budget is to be used for union activities at all levels of the VGCL. The Vietnamese legal system also has decrees related to trade unions. For instance, Decree No. 43/2013/ND-CP detailed the implementation of Article 10 of the Trade Union Law regarding the rights and responsibilities of unions in representing and protecting the legitimate rights and interests of workers. Others include Decree No. 191/2013/ND-CP on trade union finance,[4] Decree No. 200/2013/ND-CP on the implementation of Article 11 of the Trade Union Law on the rights and responsibilities of trade unions in participating in state management[5] and socio-economic management, and Decree No. 60/2013/ND-CP on implementing democratic regulations in the workplace.[6]

The VGCL has pursued the goal of "employment, life, democracy and social justice" (*viec lam, cuoc song, dan chu va cong bang xa hoi*) by improving workers' living conditions, ensuring labour discipline and improving production, organizing social activities for workers, protecting labour rights, improving the living conditions of union members, and assisting management to achieve economic targets. The VGCL has made attempts to improve the living standards of workers and their working environment by paying attention to the workers' daily lives and providing social welfare. This is in addition to assisting management in achieving production targets (Schweisshelm and Do 2018; Tran and Bales, 2017). At the same time, the VGCL continues to face problems with bureaucracy, authoritarianism, corruption and low labour standards (Dong 2016; Nguyen 2016). An industrial zone trade union official described the situation as follows:

> The industrial zone trade unions are under the management of the industrial zone authority and are a level within the VGCL system. Our union was established to support grass-roots operations, focusing on negotiation, dialogue, representation and the protection of workers' interests in industrial zones. We have organized a lot of cultural activities, gymnastics and sports programmes to support poor workers, such as the annual workers' song contest, annual women's and men's soccer and badminton tournaments, an annual elegant worker contest, flower arrangement contests, and a cooking contest on Women's Day. In addition, we have given Tet gifts and provided bus tickets to remote workers returning home to celebrate Tet. We have organized some training courses for grass-roots trade union officials and workers in enterprises in the industrial zones. We also consult the grass-roots trade union executive committee to negotiate an annual salary increase for workers, to raise the quality of meals, and so on. The industrial zone trade unions also handle labour disputes and letters of complaint from workers, and we consult on any problems related to industrial relations for the enterprises and workers (personal interview, October 2019).

Evidently, the activities of VGCL units at many levels are still heavily administrative and lack innovation and creativity. Despite this, VGCL union membership has steadily increased over time. Total union membership of the VGCL was 7.3 million in 2011, 8.6 million in 2014, and 9.7 million in 2017 (Nina 2018; VGCL 2017). The unionization rate was about 45 per cent from 2008 to 2010, peaked at 50.25 per cent in 2011, and slightly decreased to 43.8 per cent in 2016 (see Figure 9.1).

After Doi Moi, although the VGCL was confronted with a new system with multiple ownership, including state-owned enterprises (SOEs), multinational companies (wholly owned foreign-invested companies), joint ventures (between foreign investors and local SOEs), and privately owned enterprises (Clarke 2006; Zhu et al. 2008), the VGCL has not substantively changed its policy or practices to redefine its role as the representative of workers (Schweisshelm and Do 2018; Tran and Bales, 2017). There have been approximately six thousand labour strikes in Vietnam since 2005 (see Figure 9.2). But none of the so-called "wildcat strikes" followed the prescribed legal procedure and none of them were led by trade unions (Collin 2020; Do 2017; Nguyen 2017; Trinh 2014). Despite the wildcat strikes having become the most important instrument for workers to bargain for higher wages and better working conditions, trade unions only exercise a role in

FIGURE 9.1
Unionization Rate and Collective Bargaining Coverage, 2012–16

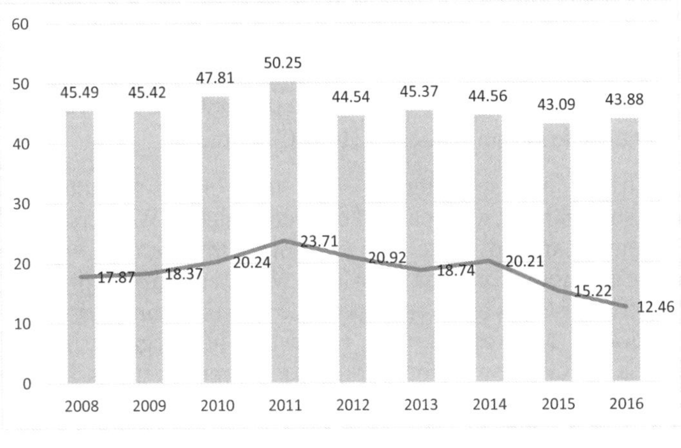

Source: VGCL's database 2017, cited from Do (2019).

FIGURE 9.2
Number of Labour Strikes in Vietnam since 2005

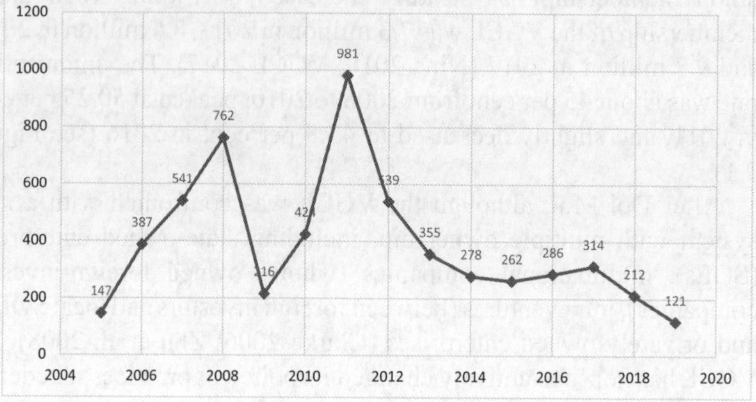

Source: Adapted from Collin (2019) and laodong.vn (2020),

settling the strikes. According to Do (2017), about seventy per cent of labour strikes took place in unionized companies, suggesting that unions at enterprises have been unsuccessful in negotiations with employers.

According to Do (2017) and Tran (2007), enterprise unions have played no role in organizing strikes, whereas upper-level unions have been the most active in settling disputes through strike task forces. The upper-level unions usually rely on their political power to pressure employers to accept the demands of workers rather than using the strikes as opportunities to negotiate with employers on behalf of the workers. Strikes are usually settled by a strike task force composed of the local labour administration and the upper-level union, which collects the workers' demands and then persuades employers to accept them. As a trade union leader in HCMC shared,

> All strikes are spontaneous and take place without union leadership. Strikes were carried out very quickly. Workers transmit information and advocate with each other in their own way. With such a method, it can be seen that when employees proceed to collectively stop work it is imperative that the employer sit down to negotiate and resolve their requests. The illegal strikes have become the fastest way for workers to claim their rights. (personal interview, March 2019)

Some researcher found there are cases of "covert collaboration between the informal leaders and the official trade union leaders, and the official union leaders can exploit threats of unofficial action to negotiate with management" (Anner and Liu 2016; Clarke, Lee and Do 2007; Do 2017).

Organizational Structure of the Vietnam General Confederation of Labour (VGCL)

According to current regulations, the organizational structure of the Vietnam Trade Union has four levels (VGCL 2020). These are (1) the VGCL (*Tong Lien doan lao dong Viet Nam*); (2) the provincial labour confederation (*Lien doan lao dong tinh, thanh pho*), trade union of the national industry (*Cong doan nganh trung uong*) and trade unions of corporations belonging to the VGCL (*Cong doan Tong cong ty thuoc Tong Lien doan*); (3) immediate upper-level trade unions *(Cong doan cap tren co s*o); and (4) grass-roots trade unions (*Cong doan co so*).

The current law stipulates that organizations operate on the principle of democratic centralism, which has created unity through top-down decisions and the actions of the various union levels (Do and Broek 2013). But this approach limits the activeness and accountability of these union levels. Local trade unions in some businesses are under the direction of many intermediaries, which creates "multi-leadership" and entails heavy administration. The upper-level trade union must represent and protect the interests of employees at enterprises that do not have a trade union, while union officials at this level are few and of limited capacity. As a trade union official of the District Labour Confederation in HCMC stated,

> The number of trade union officials under the District Labour Confederation is too small, but the workload is very large. With the union-style jobs (*lam dau tram ho*) of the union, we cannot represent all workers in unorganized enterprises. We also cannot help, share difficulties or protect the rights of all workers. (interview, November 2019)

Figure 9.3 shows the dual management of both the VGCL and the state (through its ministries) over what used to be primarily state-owned factories and corporations. At the national level, the VGCL is a mass organization affiliated to the VCP that represents the working population of Vietnam. It comprises an umbrella organization under which all local levels and primary unions operate. All unions must be recognized by the local offices of the VGCL, which functions as the country's umbrella labour organization. The VGCL is a unified organization at the national level, and there is a matrix of smaller unions under it that are organized geographically into provinces,

FIGURE 9.3
Organizational Structure of Vietnamese Trade Unions
in Relation to the State Agency System and the VCP

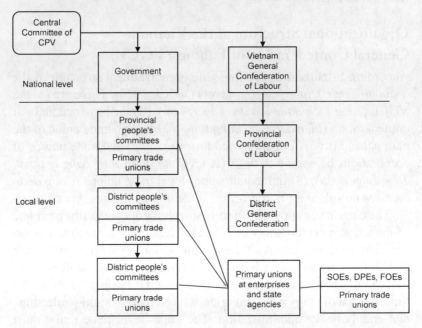

Source: Nguyen (2016, p. 26).

cities, counties or districts and within enterprises and state agencies at provincial, district and ward levels (Nguyen 2016). While the three broad branches are under the overarching umbrella of the VGCL, the industrial union (*cong doan nganh*) is under the direct management of different ministries (notably the Ministry of Industry and Trade), which, in principle, should coordinate with the VGCL.

Trade Union Freedom in Vietnam

In the process of the formation and development of Vietnamese trade unions, the issue of trade union freedom was implemented and mentioned in the following three periods. According to Chan (1998), between the 1960s and 1970s in southern Vietnam, unions were not part of the state system. Prior to 1975, there was no ideology requiring workers to sacrifice their interests for the state. Instead, workers and unions in the south of Vietnam occasionally took a combative position against capitalism and the Saigon government. Frequent strikes occurred, and labour organizers and trade unionists were beaten, murdered, or imprisoned. Some researchers have suggested that the practice of freedom of association and union-led strike activities before 1975 in southern Vietnam is not yet a distant memory (Kerkvliet 2010).

During the economic reforms of Doi Moi in the late 1980s, the government considered giving workers the freedom of union participation, but eventually chose not to. Indeed, in this period there were voices within the party leadership, led by the then party secretary-general Nguyen Van Linh, calling for a transformation of the trade union system in line with the economic revolution. According to Schweisshelm and Do (2018), during the Sixth Union Congress in 1988, Nguyen Van Linh, who used to be chairman of the VGCL before he became party secretary-general, called for the "institutional independence of the VGCL from the government and the party, the extension of union membership to non-traditional areas and making the grass-roots level and workers central to union activities". Although he did not specifically call for the separation of the VGCL from the VCP, he nevertheless believed that both the state and the working class represented by the VGCL would benefit from a trade union that had an independent voice in national policymaking and monitoring the activities of state-owned enterprises. The 1989 Tiananmen Square incident in China, however, served as a warning to Vietnam's leadership about how reform could hurt the stability of the regime. As a result, the newborn sense of democracy and independence ushered by the union system did not last long.

The period of participation in the new generation of free-trade agreements (FTAs) required member states to continue efforts towards ratifying all the basic conventions to ensure that free trade contributed to the protection of workers' rights, prevented a race to the bottom, and saw a fairer division of the economic gains from the process. According to Tran, Bair and Werner (2017), with the stagnation of the WTO's Doha Round, a substantial number of regional trade agreements (RTAs) have been negotiated between industrialized and developing nations. In this scenario, developed countries are more likely to have leverage over their low-income partners than they would in a multilateral arrangement, allowing them to demand higher labor standards in exchange for greater trade liberalization. The United Nations' Sustainable Development Goals and the ILO's Declaration on Fundamental Principles and Rights at Work (1998 ILO Declaration) are cited more frequently in RTAs' labor chapters. According to the ILO (2016), as of 2015, seventy-six trade agreements included some form of labour provision, and half of these were undertaken after 2008. A key factor in the expansion of labour provisions in trade agreements has been the recent adoption of agreement frameworks by the United States and the European Union. These nations have been particularly enthusiastic in their pursuit of RTAs, and both require that labour provisions be included in the body of their bilateral and regional agreements.

According to Do (2017), labour strikes, along with a prolonged slump in economic activity in Vietnam since 2008 and Chinese aggression in the South China Sea, all contributed to Vietnam's decision to sign the Trans-Pacific Partnership Agreement (TPP), which included a "consistency plan" that contains a bilateral agreement signed with the United States on the advancement of industrial relations. According to Pham (2017), as a developing country competing on cheap, labour-insensitive products,

> Vietnam used to oppose the inclusion of labour provisions in free trade agreements, particularly the TPP. From the beginning, Vietnam protested against the inclusion of a chapter on labour in the TPP, then opposed the application of a binding dispute settlement mechanism on labour commitments. However, Vietnam has signed the TPP which contains the strongest labour provisions of all existing FTAs. For Vietnam, the TPP is the first FTA containing a chapter on labour commitments.

Vietnam's strong labour commitments in the TPP have even been noted as "surprising for a communist, one-party system" (Pham 2017; Schweisshelm 2015). In January 2017, newly elected US president Donald Trump withdrew the United States from the TPP, possibly marking the end of the partnership. But in the wake of this the remaining member nations formed the Comprehensive and Progressive Agreement for Trans-Pacific Partnership (CPTPP), which also contains a clause on freedom of association. Chapter 19 on labour in the CPTTP is based on the 1998 ILO Declaration. It also establishes links between the implementation of the declaration and trade conditions within a specific time frame. Accordingly, each party to the agreement shall adopt and maintain in its statutes and practices the following rights as stated in the ILO on Fundamental Principles and Rights at Work and its follow-up (1998): (a) freedom of association and the effective recognition of the right to collective bargaining; (b) the elimination of all forms of forced or compulsory labour; (c) the effective abolition of child labour; and (d) the elimination of discrimination in respect of employment and occupation. Each party shall adopt and maintain statutes and regulations, and practices thereunder, governing acceptable conditions of work with respect to minimum wages, hours of work and occupational safety and health.

According to the ILO (2019), together with the CPTPP, the European Union–Vietnam Free Trade Agreement (EVFTA) emphasizes provisions on labour and the environment to ensure that free trade contributes to sustainable development. At the heart of both the CPTPP and the EVFTA is the 1998 ILO Declaration on Fundamental Principles and Rights at Work. Do (2017) argues that the Politburo (Ban Chap hanh Trung uong Dang) issued Resolution 06 (So 06-NQ/ TW) just a few days before President Trump's decision in order to recognize "worker organizations" (or independent unions) along with the VGCL (see Politburo 2016). This suggests that the decision to recognize independent unions did not result from external pressure through the TPP or the United States, but rather resulted from internal demands for reforms within Vietnam. The recognition by the VCP of independent unions also shows the impact of non-conventional labour activism in the global supply chains in Vietnam on the country's institutional settings (Collin 2020; Do 2017).

In December 2019, the National Assembly of Vietnam passed a new Labour Code that came into effect in January 2021. In the 2019 Labour Code (National Assembly of Vietnam 2019), union-related provisions are presented in Chapter I (Article 3.5.7) and Chapter XIII, from Article 170 to 178. This amended law makes a clear distinction between "trade union" (*cong doan*) and the term "workers representative organization" (WRO; *to chuc dai dien nguoi lao dong*) or "workers' organization" (*to chuc cua nguoi lao dong*)—the term "union" refers to unit levels under the VGCL, whilst "WRO" includes both trade unions and workers' organizations.

Despite this distinction, the VGCL still remains state-sponsored and has many advantages over other WRCs (Buckley 2021). Article 3 states that

> a WRO at the grass-roots level is an organization established on the voluntary basis of workers in an undertaking to protect the lawful rights and legitimate interests of workers in labour relations via collective bargaining or other forms as stipulated by labour laws. WROs at the grass-roots level include the grass-roots trade union and the workers' organization at the enterprise.

Article 5 states that employees have the right to establish a WRO, to join a WRO at the grass-roots level, to participate in the activities and occupational associations of a WRO and of other organizations in accordance with the law; to request and participate in dialogue; to implement democratic regulations; to conduct collective bargaining with the employer; to engage in consultation at the workplace to protect their lawful rights and interests; and to participate in the management in accordance with the employer's regulations. However, Article 7 (building labour relations) provides that only the "trade union (*cong doan*) may cooperate with competent authorities in assisting the development of progressive, harmonious and stable labour relations; supervising the implementation of labour laws; and protecting the legitimate rights and interests of workers". Chapter XIII of the 2019 Labour Code further sets out various rules about WROs at the grass-roots level.[7] The most prominent feature of these stipulations is that they allow workers to form independent unions at the workplace. But these regulations are not clear and are left open to interpretation. For example, Article 172 only states that the government shall provide for documents and procedures for registration; the competence to grant and cancel the registration, state management of finance and assets of internal employee organizations; division, amalgamation, merger, dissolution thereof; and the right to association of workers in enterprises. Moreover, Articles 172, 173, 174 only stipulate the workers' organization in the enterprise, but not other types of organizations like public organizations or non-governmental organizations. A trade union leader in an enterprise in Ha Nam remarked:

> I am a grass-roots trade union leader, so I am very interested in the law on freedom of association and the grass-roots WROs. At present, however, the regulations are still unclear, and we need to wait for the government's decree to guide us. While we need to know the rules early enough to prepare our plans for the future, the company management will often ask us about our plans as they are also worried if there is no plan. It's easy to get upset when there are too many WROs in the company. (personal interview, May 2020)

This vague situation has left trade union officers and worker highly puzzled.

Up until October 2022, the government had not issued any legal provisions for the WROs defined in Chapter XIII of the 2019 Labour Code, although this code has been in effect since January 2021. Several regulations related to WROs, however, were issued in Decree No. 145/2020/ND-CP[8] on 14 December 2020 and have been in effect since 1 February 2021. This Decree elaborates on and guides the implementation of several articles of the Labour Code on regulations of the organization of dialogue at the workplace and implementation regulations on grass-roots democracy at the workplace. In this decree, Article 37 states that "the employer shall cooperate with the internal WRO (if any) in organizing dialogue at the workplace.... In case of workers that are not members of any internal WRO, the employer shall cooperate with the internal WRO (if any) in instructing and enabling these workers to choose their representatives (representative group) who will participate in the dialogue". Additionally, the internal WRO and the representative group have the responsibility of assigning representatives to participate in the dialogue at the workplace. Article 38 specifies that the internal WRO and the representative group shall appoint a number of participants in the dialogue based on the proportion of their members to the total number of workers employed by the employer. At least once every two years, a list of participants in the dialogue at workplace discourses should be produced and made public at the workplace. Article 48 states that the employer is responsible for promulgating internal workplace democracy regulations. When the workplace democracy regulations are formulated or revised, the employer must consult with the internal WRO (if any) and the representative group (if any) before promulgating them. It can be seen that this framework could favour the establishment and operations of new WROs or representative groups in the enterprises, thereby encouraging workers' participation in labour union activities at the grass-roots level. But according to Article 68 in the 2019 Labour Code, only the WRO with the largest membership in the enterprise shall have the right to request collective bargaining. Considering that grass-roots trade unions under the VGCL have more advantages than other new WROs, they have greater opportunities to participate in collective bargaining. Moreover, given that the government has not yet issued detailed regulations on the establishment and operations of WROs and collective bargaining, the implementation of dialogue, grass-roots democracy and collective bargaining at the workplace seem to have stagnated.

Moreover, Articles 172, 173 and 174 of the 2019 Labour Code only stipulate the workers' organization in the enterprise, but not other types of organizations such as public organizations or non-governmental organizations. Although regulations on the organization, operation and management of associations in Decree No. 45/2010/ND-CP[9] and the operation of foreign non-governmental organizations in Decree No. 12/2012/ND-CP[10] were released, these frameworks have many shortcomings and limitations (Khanh Linh 2018; VVH 2021). It has therefore been essential that the Law on Associations be issued.

The Law on Associations has actually been drafted and submitted twice to the National Assembly, but has so far not been approved (VVH 2021). This could make it difficult for public organizations or non-governmental organizations to support WROs and workers' participation at the grass-roots level.

On 12 June 2021, party general secretary Nguyen Phu Trong approved the Politburo's Resolution No. 02-NQ/TW on renewing the organization and operation of the Vietnam Trade Union (i.e., the VGCL) in the new context (Nhan dan online 2021). It has the general aim of building a strong and comprehensive trade union for Vietnam that will be capable of adapting to and solving problems, performing its functions and tasks well in the new situation, and serving as a solid sociopolitical foundation for the party and the state as well as a bridge to maintain the close relationship between the party, the state and the workers. It also aims to build the VGCL to be worthy as the largest representative organization of workers nationwide.[11] This stated objective of the resolution demonstrates that the VCP will continue to support the organization and operations of VGCL in the future. This is a substantial advantage for the VGCL compared to other WROs.

At present the National Assembly has not enacted a new law on WROs but has only amended the 2012 Trade Union Law. The Trade Union Law only regulates matters relating to the operation of the VGCL and its members (Thuvienphapluat 2020), and it does not cover issues relating to other workers' organizations. The amended union law has not been enacted yet, although the 2019 Labour Code was scheduled to come into effect in 2021. On 30 May 2019, at the tentative discussion session of the 2019 Law and Ordinance Building Program, Pham Minh Chinh, the head of the committee, suggested it would be necessary to amend the Trade Union Law (Luan Dung 2019).

However, the VGCL would like to delay such a revision for a number of reasons. According to Bui Van Cuong, chairman of the VGCL, and Ngo Duy Hieu, the head of VGCL's Labour Relations Department, the reasons are as follows. First, the National Assembly's Party Committee and Legal Committee want the VGCL to focus on the organizational structure. Currently there is only the four-level organizational system of trade unions prescribed in Article 7 of the law. Issues pertaining to the union's apparatus and payroll are covered in the party's document and the VGCL's charter. Second, the VGCL needs time to study the regulations on freedom of association in the CPTTP. Third, the VGCL has at the same time been busy focusing on the implementation of Directive 09 of the secretariat on organizing the Trade Union Congress at all levels and the 12th VGCL. Many deputies argued, however, that the reason of being busy organizing the congress was not convincing (Luan Dung 2019; Vo Hai 2018).

In October 2019, at the 15th plenary session of the National Assembly's Committee on Social Affairs, after the Vietnam Trade Union Congress, Nguyen Dinh Khang, the new president of the VGCL, continued to postpone submitting an amendment of the Law on Trade Unions until 2020 (Thanh Trung 2019). On 26 June 2020, at the conference to gather the opinions of members of the Legal Policy Advisory Council and experts on the Trade Union Law, Ngo Duy Hieu noted that the draft law was expected to be commented on by the National Assembly in Session 10 (October 2020) and adopted at the last session of the XIV National Assembly in 2021 (Minh Ngoc 2020). There are, however, still many controversies about unclear and unreasonable financial revenues and expenditures by the VGCL and other workers' organizations. One trade union official of an industrial zone had this to say: "We have commented on the revised trade union law, especially on trade union finances and grass-roots association rights, since May 2020. But so far no new draft of this law has been issued" (personal interview, July 2020). Thus, some two years after Vietnam ratified the CPTPP, the VGCL remains confused and afraid and has not found a way out of the challenges of union freedom in the new context.

Illegal Independent Unions in Vietnam

Before the 2019 Labour Code was passed in December, Vietnamese law recognized only the VGCL as the sole union confederation and only allowed the establishment of union organizations under it. Despite this restriction some individuals established illegal trade unions that claimed to be independent union organizations. For example, according to Kerkvliet (2010), in 2006 the country's first independent trade union was formed, called the Independent Labour Union of Vietnam (ITUV; *Cong doan doc lap Vietnam*). In October 2006, two workers established the United Workers-Farmers Association (UWFA; *Hiep hoi doan ket Cong-Nong Viet Nam*), which publicly claimed to be an independent organization representing the interests of oppressed labourers and peasants. But, given that these were deemed illegal unions founded by reactionary groups to disrupt social and political security, the founders were swiftly arrested and their unions closed down (Cong an nhan dan 2007; Hutt 2019). In 2008, Tran Ngoc Thanh established the Free Viet

Labour Federation (*Lien doan Lao dong Viet tu do*) by merging the Committee of Vietnamese Workers with Vietnam's Union, Vietnam's Association, and Vietnamese Labour in Poland. According to Nhan Dan online (2015), however, this organization actually deceives and entices workers into engaging in illegal activities, violating the laws of both Vietnam and the host country. The organization is still active, both domestically and internationally, and affirms that it has helped many workers by filing complaints and organizing strikes to fight for their rights and interests (Free Viet Labour Federation 2015).

In addition, on 1 July 2020 a union organization called the Vietnamese Independent Union (VIU; *Nghiep doan doc lap Viet nam*) was born. This organization claims the following:

> VIU is an organization of people from many different professions, with the goal of establishing free trade unions. We hope to accompany the VGCL in the mission of protecting the rights and legitimate interests of workers effectively, improving the lives of workers in order to have fair competition between businesses, and help Vietnamese workers enjoy the same benefits as workers in other countries in the CPPP and the EVFTA. (Vietnamese Independent Union 2020)

Since its inception, this organization has regularly provided news related to labour and workers through a professional-looking website.[12]

Workers' Participation in Unions

Research results show that workers are not yet fully aware of the role of trade unions and the benefits of trade union membership. In fact, many workers think that a union is a company-owned department. Workers may consider joining a union "for fun", given its low monthly premium and some additional marginal company benefits, but they do not regard the role of unions as particularly significant. As a worker in Binh Duong reported, "In my old companies, I found that joining a union did not have many benefits. Most of my co-workers' opinions on the union were ambivalent, so I did not participate in the union there. But in my current company, only about 2–3 per cent of the workers have not joined the union, and the company has about a thousand workers. So, I decided to join the same trade union as the others. Moreover, the monthly fee is not much, but I can receive Tet gifts, birthday gifts, women's day gifts, and so on from the union" (personal interview, November 2019). This view was echoed by a worker in Hanoi: "In fact, I have joined the union with my colleagues for fun. I found that the union did not help much in protecting our rights and interests. The trade union department in my company is the employer's right hand" (personal interview, December 2019).

Evidence from interviews further suggests that workers engage mainly in "movement activities"[13] but without engaging in other activities such as union personnel decisions, union meetings, agreements of the trade union with employers, and union training activities. In particular, the highest participation rate is 69.86 per cent for movement activities, and the lowest is only 5.48 per cent for participating in the agreements of the trade union with employers. In addition, members do not regularly attend the meetings or training activities conducted by grass-roots trade unions. For example, a worker in Hung Yen noted, "I like to participate in community activities of the union to interact with people. But my job is very busy; I have to work extra hours, so I don't have time to participate in more activities that are organized outside working hours or on holidays. I have to spend time with my family after working days" (personal interview, October 2019). Another worker commented, "If we have any ideas, we will discuss with a leader, so there is no union meeting. Last month, the union in my company organized sports competitions among factories. I participated and found it interesting" (personal interview, November 2019). A similar sentiment is echoed by another worker:

> I heard my colleagues who had been working for a long time in my company said that, in the past, many workers also used to ask for a raise in salary, bonus, or improved meals with the trade union. However, most requests are not resolved, so people have fewer ideas. If they cannot tolerate those low wages and working conditions, they quit their job. We mainly attend union movement activities for fun and do not expect any protection or assistance. (personal interview, December 2019)

While workers are ambivalent about the role of trade unions, they are notably willing to participate in collective work stoppages and wildcat strikes. According to the survey results, 47.9 per cent of respondents said they would participate in a strike even if they knew it was an illegal one. This is for two main reasons. First, if a union leads workers on a strike, the procedures for strikes are complicated and time-consuming, leading workers to feel frustrated when they want their employers to solve the problem immediately. Second, workers do not really believe in the ability of union officials, who are paid by employers to settle strikes. As a worker in Ha Nam put it, "When the company announced the Tet bonus policy, we found it inappropriate, and then felt very frustrated. The workers in the production team discussed closely with each other and then invited more people to collectively stop work and gather in front of the company gate. We asked the company director to change the method of paying Tet bonuses and we stayed there until the company representatives came to have a dialogue. We said we would not return to the factory to continue working until the results of the negotiations were favourable" (personal interview, December 2020).

Simply put, many workers do not trust the protection and representation roles of trade unions because they view unions as largely more beneficial to employers than to workers. They therefore do not actively participate in trade union activities and only exchange ideas with the head of the department rather than grass-roots trade union leaders. A worker in HCMC had this to say:

> In my company, all union leaders are part-time union officials (*can bo cong doan kiem nhiem*). They are also human resources or managerial staff so they do not take the side of the workers; they do not represent the workers. They are afraid to protect workers or be on the side of workers because they will be repressed, and they are not foolish enough to do that. They also have to worry about money and their future career in this company. If we have any ideas, we just tell the team leaders so that the team leader can reflect them to the supervisor. (personal interview, October 2019)

In fact, factory workers are often linked together by networks of compatriots, temporary residents in boarding houses, those working together, or perhaps even those of the same religion. These channels of communication will greatly influence their perceptions, attitudes and behaviours on issues, including those related to union operations. Therefore, when they share negative opinions about a trade union by word of mouth it will influence the decisions of others about joining it. This view was expressed in a comment by a trade union official of an industrial zone, that "the union is little more than a yes-man—a puppet in the hands of the government and enterprises (*Cong doan an theo, noi leo*)" (personal interview, November 2019). As a result of these influences, many workers are not interested in trade union activities because they do not know what the union can do for them, while the owner of the enterprise considers the trade union as his right-hand man. Because the company pays their wages, they "eat the king's meal, dance all day (*an com Chua, mua toi ngay*), so they must stand on the side of the enterprise and help them take care of the workers' lives in the company" (personal interview, November 2019).

Workers would increase their participation in trade union activities when their employers have an "open attitude and support trade unions". We found that support by the company's leadership for union activities is one of the most important factors to affect workers' participation in unions. When the board of directors of the company encourages and creates good conditions for workers to join union activities, workers will be more proactive in their participation. In addition, when the company leadership has a strong relationship with the union leadership it will also make workers more active in union activities. For instance, a union leader in an enterprise in Hanoi stated:

> My company director supports the union's activities because he believes the union can help better understand the needs and wants of the workers. Enterprise unions set up feedback boxes for workers to report problems in their workplace. Every week, the trade union executive committee will open the mailbox to solve the problems of employees. The major issues will be resolved at the regular monthly dialogue meeting between company leaders and the trade union executive committee. Therefore, workers in my company trust in the union and enthusiastically participate in union activities. (interview, December 2019)

When the company management clearly recognizes the role of the trade union, it not only helps the development of grass-roots trade unions but also promotes the union participation of workers.

Workers' participation in the union is not only reflected in their decision to join trade unions or their attitudes when participating in union activities, but also through their commitment to their organizations. The survey results show that 86.3 per cent of workers would consider leaving their current trade union and joining a new WRO if such an organization would bring them greater benefits. A worker in Binh Duong expressed, "I have never heard that workers can set up or join another trade union in the enterprise, but if my co-workers join this new organization and that union helps to improve my income and working conditions I will be ready to leave the current union and join a new one" (personal interview, October 2019). This analysis thus suggests that the VGCL could indeed face many challenges in maintaining its membership levels in the future.

Conclusion

This chapter contributes to a rich and growing literature on industrial relations and freedom of trade union association in one-party socialist states that have economies in transition. Since its inception, the Vietnamese trade union movement has maintained a close relationship with the Vietnamese government through the VCP, including the leaders of the VGCL being members of the VCP. Although freedom of association has been practiced and planned for implementation in some periods during the operation of a Vietnamese trade union, as of 2022 the VGCL still retains its *monopoly* in Vietnam. From their inception, trade unions in Vietnam prioritized not only members' interests and combating exploitation by employers but also national liberation from colonization. After the war ended, trade unions continued to serve as the "transmission belt" of the government and the extended personnel department of state-owned enterprises in order to achieve economic targets and social stability. Since Doi Moi, despite the country's socialist market economy and the forces of globalization, Vietnamese unions have maintained the same role they had under the centrally planned economy. The VGCL still pursues the goal of "employment, life, democracy and social justice", including improving workers' living conditions, ensuring labour discipline, improving production, organizing social activities for workers, protecting labour rights, improving the living conditions of union members, and assisting management in obtaining economic targets. The enterprise unions have, however, played no role in organizing strikes; the upper-level unions have been active in settling disputes through the strike task forces, and all strikes in Vietnam are wildcat strikes. Moreover, Vietnam's union system has a complex, overlapping organizational structure, and union levels are tightly controlled by the party and the government. The activities of VGCL units at many levels are still heavily administrative and lack innovation or creativity.

Under the pressure of economic recession, labour instability, international integration and the advantages of FTAs, Vietnam decided to join the CPTPP and EVFTA. But Vietnam must accept amendments to its laws in order to comply with labour commitments based on the 1998 ILO Declaration on Fundamental Principles and Rights at Work, including provisions on freedom of association. In December 2019, the Vietnamese National Assembly passed a new labour code that came into effect in January 2021. One of the most prominent features of the amended law is that workers are permitted to form independent unions at the workplace, but these regulations remain ambiguous and undefined. Moreover, to date the National Assembly has not enacted a new law on WROs but has only amended the 2012 Trade Union Law, which just regulates matters relating to the operation of the VGCL and does not cover issues relating to other workers' organizations. Hitherto, several regulations related to WROs have been issued. This framework could favour the establishment and operations of new WROs or representative groups in enterprises, and so encourage workers' participation in labour union activities at the grass-roots level. But as the government has not yet released more detailed regulations on the establishment and operations of WROs and collective bargaining, the implementation of dialogue, grass-roots democracy and collective bargaining at the workplace seems to have stalled. In fact, around four years after Vietnam's ratification of the CPTPP, the VGCL remains largely confused over how to face new challenges and demands for union freedom in Vietnam, and it continues to postpone the formulation of its own legislation in the interest of preserving its position against competition from new WROs.

Meanwhile, freedom of association has been applied in the form of illegal independent trade unions. Although Vietnamese law recognizes only the VGCL as the sole union confederation and only permits the establishment of union organizations under the VGCL, some individuals have established illegal trade unions that they claim are independent union organizations. These organizations have created other challenges for both the VGCL and for the VCP.

As to workers' participation in trade unions, evidence from extensive interviews with them suggests that workers are not fully aware of the role of trade unions and their benefits. Although workers may willingly participate in collective work stoppages and wildcat strikes, they are reluctant to participate in trade union activities beyond some "movement activities". Many workers in fact do not trust the protection and representation offered by trade unions and see them as offering greater benefits to employers than to workers. Workers therefore do not actively participate in trade union activities, and they only exchange opinions with their heads of department rather than grass-roots trade union leaders. The survey results show that most workers would consider leaving their current trade union and joining a new WRO if such an organization would bring them greater benefits. This indicates that the VGCL will face many challenges in maintaining its membership in the future. At the same time, the VCP needs to be vigilant with measures to ensure security and stability and to avoid confusion at the workplace should there become too many independent union organizations, such as in Cambodia and Indonesia.

Appendix

TABLE 9.A1
List of Fundamental ILO Conventions Ratified by Vietnam

No.	Name of ILO fundamental convention	Year of ratification
1	C100 – Equal Remuneration Convention	1997
2	C111 – Discrimination (Employment and Occupation) Convention	1997
3	C182 – Worst Forms of Child Labour Convention	2000
4	C138 – Minimum Age Convention	2003
5	C029 – Forced Labour Convention	2007
6	C098 – Right to Organize and Collective Bargaaining Convention	2019
7	C105 – Abolition of Forced Labour Convention	2020

TABLE 9.A2
Number of Interviews

Object	Number of workers	Number of trade union officers in enterprises	Total	%
City/Province	**73**	**20**	**93**	**100**
Ha Nam	18	9	27	29
Ha Noi	15	5	20	22
Hung Yen	9	2	11	12
Ho Chi Minh City	9	3	12	13
Binh Duong	22	1	23	2
Age	**73**	**20**	**93**	**100**
Under 25	31	6	37	40
25–35	27	8	35	38
36–45	12	4	16	17
Above 45	3	2	5	5
Industry	**73**	**20**	**93**	**100**
Textiles	21	6	27	29
Footwear	16	4	20	22
Electronics	17	4	21	23
Wood processing	11	4	15	16
Warehousing and logistics	8	2	10	11

Notes

1. See the Freedom of Association and Protection of the Right to Organize Convention, https://www.ilo.org/dyn/normlex/en/f?p=NORMLEXPUB:121 00:0::NO:12100:P12100_INSTRUMENT_ID:312232:NO.

2. See http://ilo.ch/hanoi/Areasofwork/international-labour-standards/lang--en/index.htm.

3. This law provides the right to form, join and operate labour unions; the functions, rights and responsibilities of the trade union; the rights and responsibilities of trade unionists; and the responsibilities of the state, state agencies, organizations, units and enterprises in employing labourers with respect to trade unions. It also details ensuring the operation of trade unions and the handling of dispute settlements and violations.

4. Available online at https://thuvienphapluat.vn/van-ban/Lao-dong-Tien-luong/Decree-No-191-2013-ND-CP-on-trade-union-finance-215722.aspx.

5. Available online at https https://vanbanphapluat.co/decree-no-200-2013-nd-cp-trade-unions-in-state-management-and-socio-economic-management.

6. Available online at https://www.ilo.org/dyn/natlex/natlex4.detail?p_lang=en&p_isn=94441.

7. Specifically, these include the following articles: Article 170 (right to establish, join and participate in activities of a WRO at the grass-roots level); Article 171 (the grass-roots trade union belongs to the Vietnam Trade Unions organization system); Article 172 (establishment and joining in workers' organization at enterprises); Article 173 (board of leaders, head and members of workers' organization at enterprises); Article 174 (constitution of workers' organization at enterprises); Article 175 (prohibited acts of employers related to the establishment, accession and operation of workers' organizations at enterprises); Article 176 (rights of members of the leadership team of WROs at the grass-roots level); Article 177 (obligations of the employer to WROs at the grass-roots level); Article 178 (rights and obligations of WROs at the grass-roots level in the labour relations).

8. Available online at https://vanbanphapluat.co/decree-145-2020-nd-cp-elaboration-of-the-labor-code-on-working-conditions-and-labor-relations.

9. Available online at http://ilo.org/dyn/natlex/docs/ELECTRONIC/84259/935 33/F1158441545/VNM84259.pdf.

10. Available online at https://english.luatvietnam.vn/decree-no-12-2012-nd-cp-dated-march-01-2012-of-the-government-on-registration-and-management-of-activities-of-non-governmental-organizations-in-viet-68514-Doc1.html.

11. Available online at https://tulieuvankien.dangcongsan.vn/he-thong-van-ban/van-ban-cua-dang/nghi-quyet-so-02-nqtw-ngay-1262021-cua-bo-chinh-tri-ve-doi-moi-to-chuc-va-hoat-dong-cua-cong-doan-viet-nam-trong-tinh-7519.

12. See http://mail01.tinyletterapp.com/joebuckley/vietnam-labour-update-67/17 482050-nghiepdoandoclapvn.org/?c=723155b9-39fd-47ee-a428-bb424c4c0aa5.

13. "Movement activities" or "*hoat dong phong trao*" refers to activities organized by a trade union, including cultural activities, recreational activities, gymnastics, sports programmes, beauty contests, community activities, etc.

References

Anner, Mark, and Xiangmin Liu. 2016. "Harmonious Unions and Rebellious Workers: A Study of Wildcat Strikes in Vietnam". *ILR Review* 69, no. 1: 3–28.

Arnold, Dennis. 2013. "Social Margins and Precarious Work in Vietnam". *American Behavioral Scientist* 57, no. 4: 468–87.

Buckley, J. 2021. "Freedom of Association in Vietnam: A Heretical View". *Global Labour Journal* 12, no. 2: 79–94.

Chan, Anita, and Irene Norlund. 1998. "Vietnamese and Chinese Labour Regimes: On the Road to Divergence". *China Journal* 40: 173–97.

Clarke, Simon. 2006. "The Changing Character of Strikes in Vietnam". *Post-Communist Economies* 18, no. 3: 345–61.

Clarke, Simon, Chang-Hee Lee, and Do Quynh Chi. 2007. "From Rights to Interests: The Challenge of Industrial Relations in Vietnam". *Journal of Industrial Relations* 49, no. 4: 545–68.

Collins, Ngan. 2020. "The Reform of Vietnam Trade Union and the Government's Role since Doi Moi". In *Trade Unions and Labour Movements in the Asia-Pacific Region*, edited by Byoung-Hoon Lee, Sek-Hong Ng, and Russell D. Lansbury, pp. 273–92. Routledge.

Collins, Ngan, Shuang Ren, and Malcolm Warner. 2019. "The Changing Role of the State in Industrial Relations since Vietnam's Reform". *Asia Pacific Journal of Human Resources* 58, no. 3: 450–68.

Cong an nhan dan. 2007. "To Chuc 'Bach Dang Giang' và 'Hiep Hoi Doan Ket Cong Nong'". Cong an Nhan Dan Online, 4 October 2007. http://cand.com.vn/Su-kien-Binh-luan-thoi-su/To-chuc-Bach-Dang-Giang-va-Hiep-hoi-doan-ket-cong-nong-115694/.

Do, Quynh Chi. 2017. "The Regional Coordination of Strikes and the Challenge for Union Reform in Vietnam". *Development and Change* 48, no. 5: 1052–68. https://doi.org/10.1111/dech.12326.

Do, Quynh Chi, and Di van den Broek. 2013. "Wildcat Strikes: A Catalyst for Union Reform in Vietnam?" *Journal of Industrial Relations* 55, no. 5: 783–99.

Dong, Thi Thuong Hien. 2016. "Developing Industrial Relations: The Role of Vietnam Trade Union". In *Labour Market and Industrial Relations in Vietnam*, edited by Ingrid Artus, Judith Holland, Uwe Blien, and Van Phan thi Hong, pp. 263–82. Bloomsbury.

Free Viet Labour Federation. 2015. "Tai Lieu ve LDV". https://laodongviet. org/tai-lieu-ve-ldv-%e2%80%a2%e2%80%a2-briefing-paper-on-viet-labour/. (accessed 3 June 2020).

Hutt, David. 2019. "Workers of Vietnam, Unite?" *The Diplomat*, 29 November 2019. https://thediplomat.com/2019/11/workers-of-vietnam-unite/.

ILO. 1994. "Freedom of Association and Collective Bargaining". http://white. lim.ilo.org/qvilis_world/english/infobd/l_intro.html (accessed 15 April 2020).

———. 2016. "Assessment of Labour Provisions in Trade and Investment Arrangements". https://www.ilo.org/wcmsp5/groups/public/---dgreports/---inst/documents/publication/wcms_498944.pdf.

————. 2019. "Labour Chapter Important to EU-Viet Nam Free Trade Deal". 16 May 2019. https://www.ilo.org/hanoi/Informationresources/Publicinformation/newsitems/WCMS_702194/lang--en/index.htm.

Kerkvliet, Benedict J. Tria. 2010. "Workers' Protests in Contemporary Vietnam (with Some Comparisons to Those in the Pre-1975 South)". *Journal of Vietnamese Studies* 5, no. 1: 162–204.

Khanh Linh. 2018. "De nghi sua doi quy dinh ve to chuc phi chinh phu nuoc ngoai tai Viet Nam". *Bao Chinh Phu*, 25 January 2018. http://baochinhphu.vn/Chinh-sach-moi/De-nghi-sua-doi-quy-dinh-ve-to-chuc-phi-chinh-phu-nuoc-ngoai-tai-Viet-Nam/328255.vgp.

Luan Dung. 2019. "Truong Ban to Chuc Truong Uong de Nghi Sua Luat Cong Doan". *Tien Phong*, June 2019. https://www.tienphong.vn/xa-hoi/truong-ban-to-chuc-tu-de-nghi-sua-luat-cong-doan-1278921.tpo.

Minh Ngoc. 2020. "Hoi Nghi Lay y Kien ve Du an Luat Sua Doi, Bo Sung Mot so Dieu Cua Luat Cong Doan". VGCL, June 2020. http://www.congdoan.vn/tin-tuc/chinh-sach-phap-luat-quan-he-lao-dong-509/hoi-nghi-lay-y-kien-ve-du-an-luat-sua-doi-bo-sung-mot-so-dieu-cua-luat-cong-doan-512096.tld.

National Assembly of Vietnam. 2019. "Labour Code 2019".

Nguyen, Phuong Bac. 2016. "The Strategy of Trade Union Revitalisation in Vietnam". PhD dissertation, RMIT University.

Nguyen, Tu Phuong. 2017. "Workers' Strikes in Vietnam from a Regulatory Perspective". *Asian Studies Review* 41, no. 2: 263–80.

Nhan dan online. 2015. "Ve Cai Goi La 'Lien Doan Lao Dong Viet Tu Do'". 28 May 2015. https://nhandan.com.vn/binh-luan-phe-phan/ve-cai-goi-la-lien-doan-lao-dong-viet-tu-do-233590.

————. 2021. "Politburo Issues Resolution on Reforming Vietnam Trade Union". 15 June 2021. https://en.nhandan.vn/politics/domestic/item/10002402-politburo-issues-resolution-on-reforming-vietnam-trade-union.html.

Nina, Torm. 2018. "Does Union Membership Pay off? Evidence from Vietnamese SMEs". World Institute for Development Economic Research (UNU-WIDER).

Pham, Nghia Trong. 2017. "Trade and Labour Rights: The Case of the TPP". GEG Working Paper.

Politburo. 2016. "Nghi Quyet So 06-NQ/TW Hoi Nghi Lan Thu Tu Ban Chap Hanh Trung Uong Dang Khoa XI". https://thuvienphapluat.vn/van-ban/bo-may-hanh-chinh/Nghi-quyet-06-NQ-TW-thuc-hien-tien-trinh-hoi-nhap-kinh-te-quoc-te-giu-vung-on-dinh-chinh-tri-xa-hoi-2016-332532.aspx.

Pringle, Tim, and Simon Clarke. 2010. *The Challenge of Transition: Trade Unions in Russia, China and Vietnam*. Springer.

Schweisshelm, Erwin. 2015. *Vietnam's Trade Agreements with the EU and the US*. FES Vietnam.

Schweisshelm, Erwin, and Quynh Chi Do. 2018. "From Harmony to Conflict: Vietnamese Trade Unions on the Threshold of Reform". In *Trade Unions in Transition: From Command to Market Economies*, edited by R. Traub-Merz and T. Pringle, pp. 110–47. Friedrich-Ebert-Stiftung.

Thanh Trung. 2019. "Xin Lui Thoi Diem Trinh Du an Luat Cong Doan (Sua Doi) Sang Nam 2020". *Bao Lao Dong*, 2 October 2019. https://laodong.

vn/thoi-su/xin-lui-thoi-diem-trinh-du-an-luat-cong-doan-sua-doi-sang-nam-2020-757911.ldo.

Thuvienphapluat. 2020. "Du Thao Luat Sua Doi, Bo sung Mot So Dieu Cua Luat Cong Doan". https://Thuvienphapluat.vn/van-Ban/Doanh-Nghiep/Luat-Cong-Doan-Sua-Doi-445264.Aspx (accessed 17 April 2020).

Tran, Angie Ngoc. 2007. "Alternatives to the 'Race to the Bottom' in Vietnam: Minimum Wage Strikes and Their Aftermath". *Labour Studies Journal* 32, no. 4: 430–51.

Tran, Angie N., Jennifer Bair, and Marion Werner. 2017. "Forcing Change from the Outside? The Role of Trade-Labour Linkages in Transforming Vietnam's Labour Regime". *Competition & Change* 21, no. 5: 397–416.

Tran, T.K.T., and R. Bales. 2017. "On the Precipice: Prospects for Free Labor Unions in Vietnam". *San Diego International Law Journal* 19, no. 1: 71–94

Trinh, Ly. 2014. "Trade Union Organizing Free from Employers' Interference: Evidence from Vietnam". *Southeast Asian Studies* 3, no. 3: 589–609.

VGCL. 2016. "Summary of the Process of Formation and Development of the Working Class and Vietnam Trade Union Organization" [Tom Tat qua Trinh Hinh Thanh va Phat Trin Cua Giai Cap Cong Nhan và to Chuc Cong Doan Viet Nam]. 22 April 2016. http://www.congdoan.vn/gioi-thieu/lich-su-cdvn-489/tom-tat-qua-trinh-hinh-thanh-va-phat-trien-cua-giai-cap-cong-nhan-va-to-chuc-cong-doan-viet-nam-(phan-6)-32021.tld.

———. 2017. ""Phat Trien Doan Vien, Xay Dung To Chuc Cong Doan". 14 July 2017. congdoan.vn/tin-tuc/phat-trien-doan-vien-xay-dung-to-chuc-cong-doan-508/ca-nuoc-co-tren-97-trieu-doan-vien-cong-doan-267923.tld.

———. 2020. "Charter of Vietnam Trade Union". http://www.congdoan.vn/tra-cuu-van-ban/chi-tiet-2173.tld (accessed 28 April 2020).

Vietnamese Independent Union. 2020. "Thong cao: Nghiep doan doc lap Viet Nam ra mat". Nghiep doan doc lap Viet Nam, 1 July 2020. https://nghiepdoandoclapvn.org/thong-cao/nghiep-doan-doc-lap-viet-nam-ra-mat/144-799-1674.nddl.

Vo Hai. 2018. "Tong Lien Doan Xin Lui Sua Luat Cong Doan de Dap Ung Quy Dinh Cua CPTPP". *Vnexpress*, 30 May 2018. https://vnexpress.net/tong-lien-doan-xin-lui-sua-luat-cong-doan-de-dap-ung-quy-dinh-cua-cptpp-3756811.html.

VVH. 2021. "Nghien cuu hoan thien quan ly nha nuoc ve hoi va to chuc phi chinh phu". *Vietnam Journal of Science, Technology and Engineering*, 1 June 2021. http://vjst.vn/vn/tin-tuc/4703/nghien-cuu-hoan-thien-quan-ly-nha-nuoc-ve-hoi-va-to-chuc-phi-chinh-phu.aspx.

Zhu, Ying, Ngan Collins, Michael Webber, and John Benson. 2008. "New Forms of Ownership and Human Resource Practices in Vietnam". *Human Resource Management: Published in Cooperation with the School of Business Administration, The University of Michigan and in Alliance with the Society of Human Resources Management* 47, no. 1: 157–75.

Zhu, Ying, and Stephanie Fahey. 2000. "The Challenges and Opportunities for the Trade Union Movement in the Transition Era: Two Socialist Market Economies–China and Vietnam". *Asia Pacific Business Review* 6, nos. 3–4: 282–99.

Chapter 10

Rising Inequality and Exploitation of Workers in Vietnam: Labour Export and Human Smuggling from Vietnam to Europe

Trinh Khanh Ly

Despite significant economic achievements, Vietnam continues to see a rising number of illegal Vietnamese immigrants to Europe. In October 2019, for example, British police found thirty-nine illegal Vietnamese immigrants dead inside a lorry trailer in Essex (BBC 2020). The trailer arrived by sea from Zeebrugge in Belgium. The story has drawn worldwide attention to the plight of illegal Vietnamese immigrants in Europe and the criminal networks of human smuggling from Vietnam. While the story reveals a tragic aspect of Vietnam's integration into the global economy, it is important to note that thousands of Vietnamese workers travel to foreign countries every year to work legally under government-sponsored programmes. In fact, the Vietnamese government has long promoted labour export as part of its strategy to reduce poverty while earning remittances from overseas workers. In spite of such programmes, to cope with persistent poverty and insufficient opportunities for training and higher-paid jobs, young Vietnamese in poor areas, such as those ill-fated immigrants above, have sought work opportunities abroad by relying on networks of human smugglers.

This chapter addresses the related phenomena of labour export and human smuggling from Vietnam to Europe. Both groups of workers, including those exported legally and illegally smuggled workers, have contributed significantly to the Vietnamese economy through remittances. But both forms of labour migration have encountered problems. On the one hand, the legal labour export programmes operated by state-owned agencies engage in the exploitative practice of charging excessive labour service fees. Another problem is visa overstaying as workers refuse to return after the end of their contracts. On the other hand, associated with smuggled workers are problems of human trafficking, money laundering, labour exploitation and risks of death.

The plight of both groups of workers points to a larger issue—namely, that Vietnam has achieved rapid economic growth but this growth has created rising inequality, and workers especially are exploited through low wages. Vietnam has a large workforce of 55.5 million, which remains one of its advantages in attracting foreign investment. While non-skilled labour is abundant, skilled workers are in great shortage, and training opportunities for workers are insufficient. The Vietnamese government has recently reformed the relevant laws, but it is doubtful whether the problems in its labour export programmes and human smuggling activities have effectively been solved. As a result, the above-mentioned incident in the United Kingdom is likely to be repeated in the future.

This chapter draws from documents on the relevant Vietnamese policies and laws and from other published reports and documents. It also benefits from my personal observations garnered over years of working experience in the Vietnam General Confederation of Labour (VGCL) and the International Labour Organization (ILO) in Vietnam. In addition, I have conducted interviews with many illegal Vietnamese immigrants who live and work in Belgium.

Economic Growth and Rising Income Inequality

In the socio-economic development strategy for the period 2011 to 2020, the Vietnamese Communist Party (VCP) set the goal for the country's GDP growth rate to be between 7 and 8 per cent per year. Industry and services were set to account for approximately 85 per cent of GDP. Another goal was to increase the percentage of skilled labour by more than 70 per cent, of which workers with vocational training certificates should account for 55 per cent of the total labour force. The VCP also set a goal to reduce the income gap between localities and local groups.

The strategy can be considered to have succeeded in some measures. Vietnam's GDP growth rate was 7 per cent in 2019, numbering it among the twenty countries with the highest GDP growth (ADB 2020; Statista 2020). Foreign direct investment (FDI) into the country has continuously increased. By the end of 2019, total registered capital had reached US$211.78 billion (MPI 2020). Together, FDI in Vietnam accounts for approximately 20 per cent of the country's GDP (*Thoi Bao Tai Chinh* 2020).

It appears that the country is taking the right steps to integrate into the regional and global economy and to become a centre in the global supply chain for trade and production (Choe 2019). Many foreign investors consider Vietnam their new long-term investment destination. For example, Samsung opened its first factory in Vietnam in 2008 with initial capital of US$670 million. The amount of its total investment increased by US$17.3 billion in 2018 (Ngoc Thuy 2020). Similarly, Vietnam is consistently considered a preferred alternative destination for Japanese investors. In 2020, the Japanese government announced subsidies to thirty Japanese companies to invest in Southeast Asian countries. Of those thirty, fifteen have planned to move their factories from China to Vietnam (Bloomberg 2020).

Vietnam currently has trade relationships with over two hundred countries and territories. Asian countries remain its biggest trade partners, accounting for 49.2 per cent of its total exported products (Vinanet 2020). The United States and the European Union (EU) are also becoming important export markets for Vietnam. In 2019 the EU signed the Free Trade Agreement and Investment Protection Agreement with Vietnam. By the end of 2019 Vietnam had received more than US$38 billion from EU investors, an increase of 7.2 per cent compared with 2018. With an average investment capital of approximately US$3 billion per month, the EU has become one of the top four foreign investors in Vietnam (Quang Dan 2020). The domestic private sector has also developed significantly in the country. According to official statistics, this sector contributes about 40 per cent of GDP and employs approximately 85 per cent of the total workforce (Duc Trieu 2020). In 2019, for example, the sector obtained a total investment capital of US$40.7 billion, accounting for 46 per cent of the total investment capital (GSO 2020).

As the chapters by Korwatanasakul, Truong Quang Hoan and Vu Quang Viet in this volume point out, Vietnam's impressive growth has not been based on a high position in the global value chain. Rather, foreign enterprises in Vietnam mainly aim at exploiting the low-paid, unskilled Vietnamese labour. Success in attracting foreign investment has not helped Vietnam to improve the overall productivity of the country. Its labour productivity still lags far behind the top six ASEAN countries. In 2019 it was only the equivalent of 7.6 per cent of

Singapore's, 19.5 per cent of Malaysia's, 37.9 per cent of Thailand's, 45.6 per cent of Indonesia's, 56.9 per cent of the Philippines', and 68.9 per cent of Brunei's (An Nguyen 2020). One of the major reasons for this is the low rate of workers who obtain vocational training. Only 22.8 per cent of the total workforce obtains vocational training qualifications (GSO 2019).

Decades of sustained economic growth built on low-skilled labour has turned Vietnam into one of the fastest growing wealth markets in the world. In 2014, for example, there were 142 super-rich Vietnamese individuals with assets of over US$30 million. This number increased to 458 individuals in 2019 and is expected to be 753 in 2024—an increase of 64 per cent (Knight Frank 2020). While Vietnam's economic growth has mainly benefited the richest ten per cent of the population, young Vietnamese today have fewer opportunities to earn a higher income than they had ten years ago (Wells-Dang and Vu 2019).

In European countries, the top twenty per cent of the population received 5.2 times as much income as the bottom twenty per cent (Eurostat 2018). In Vietnam, unfortunately, the situation is much worse; the top twenty per cent of the population received 21 times as much income as the bottom twenty per cent.

One often reads about how the country is one of the most successful stories of poverty reduction in the world, with the number of the extreme poor being reduced from 49 per cent of the total population in 1992 to 2 per cent in 2016 (Pham Thanh Huong 2019). By the end of 2019, the average poverty rate was below 4 per cent (MOLISA 2020a). While such statistics are impressive, the lives of certain groups of Vietnamese have not significantly improved. For example, the poverty rate among ethnic minority groups accounted for 55 per cent of the whole country's poor in the same year. The poorest localities are Central Coast provinces such as Thanh Hoa, Nghe An, Binh Dinh, Quang Nam and Quang Ngai (Saigoneer 2019).

In Hanoi, there is a big gap between the highest-paid employees and other employees in different types of enterprises. The highest actual wage in the joint stock companies under state ownership was VND 185 million per month (US$8,020)—approximately 38 times higher than the lowest actual wage of VND 4.9 million per month (US$212).[1] Similarly, in FDI enterprises the highest actual wage was VND 180 million (US$7,787) and the lowest actual wage was VND 4.73 million per month (US$205). In private local enterprises, the highest actual wage was VND 180 million (US$7,787) and the lowest actual wage was VND 4.75 million per month (US$206) in 2020 (ibid.).

Income inequality has created another barrier in terms of finding good employment opportunities. Wealthy households have better connections to find highly paid jobs for their members. Poor households, including those who obtain academic diplomas, are facing more difficulties in finding employment opportunities with high pay (Oxfam 2018a, pp. 43–45).

Income inequality has also prevented the poor from accessing adequate housing, especially in big cities such as Hanoi and Ho Chi Minh City where housing prices continuously increase. According to survey findings, within the span of a few years, the average price of properties increases by 50 per cent. In certain locations, the price increases between 100 and 200 per cent. It is reported that the average housing price in Vietnam is approximately 20 to 25 times higher than the average income (Hong Khanh 2020).

In addition, income inequality has negatively affected children's education. For the age group of 5–10, the rate of children not attending school or dropping out of school is three times higher for the poorest group than for the richest group. This gap increases to ten times for children between the ages of 11 and 14 (UNICEF 2016, pp. 20, 104). The increase of income inequality in Vietnam is an important factor contributing to the increased number of Vietnamese leaving the country. Many Vietnamese migrate for better job opportunities with better pay (IOM 2021).

Low Wages Insufficient for Workers' Basic Needs

Wages are paid to workers in accordance with their employment contracts, provided they are not lower than the minimum wage specified by the government. Minimum wages are paid to workers who perform the simplest work in normal working conditions. These wages are supposed to cover the minimum living needs of their families and themselves.[2] The regional minimum wages, which are applied equally for enterprises in different sectors, have been steadily increased in Vietnam. But the lowest wages on average are only between 8 and 12 per cent higher than the regional minimum wage (Thanh An 2019).

Despite the constant increase in minimum wages over the years, the majority of Vietnamese workers are still struggling in order to make ends meet. The garment and textile sector, for example, is one of the key industrial sectors; the total amount of exported products reached US$38.9 billion in 2019 (Custom Office 2020). The sector employs approximately three million workers, 83 per cent of which are non-skilled (Ta Van Canh 2019). In general, the basic wages of garment

TABLE 10.1
Regional Minimum Wages and Lowest Average Wages (million VND)

	Region I	Region II	Region III	Region IV
Regional miniumum monthly wage (2015)	3.1 (US$134)	2.75 (US$119)	2.4 (US$104	2.15 (US$93)
Regional minimum monthly wage (2020)*	4.42 (US$191)	3.92 (US$170)	3.43 (US$148)	3.07 (US$133)
Lowest average monthly wage (1Q 2019)	4.67 (US$202)	4.01 (US$173)	3.59 (US$155)	3.23 (US$140)

Note: * Article 3 of Decree No. 90/2019/NĐ-CP promulgated by the government on 15 November 2019. Because of the pandemic, it was announced that minimum regional wages would remain unchanged in 2021.
Source: Trinh (2015).

workers are equal to the minimum regional wage plus 7 per cent for training allowances and 5 per cent for hazard allowances. The actual wages of garment workers who are under the time-based pay system (accounting for between 15 and 25 per cent of the total workforce in the sector) are a little higher than the minimum wage (Oxfam 2018b, pp. 9, 19).

In other sectors it is reported that the average actual wage of workers in 2020 was VND 6.7 million per month (US$290)—a decrease of 8.6 per cent compared to the previous year as a result of the pandemic (Duc Binh 2021). In Hanoi City the average wage in 2020 was VND 6.1 million per month (US$264) in private local enterprises and VND 6.3 million (US$273) in FDI enterprises (Hoang Manh 2021).

In general, the low wages of Vietnamese workers are insufficient to meet their basic living needs. Nearly 70 per cent of garment workers were unable to cover their living expenses. About 30 per cent of them had no savings, and 37 per cent borrowed money on a regular basis to pay for their living expenses. As many as 65 per cent of workers had to regularly work additional hours in order to compensate for their low wages. At the same time, 53 per cent of them could not pay for medical expenses (Hai Duong and Pham Thi Thu Lan 2019). Enterprises in Industrial Zones and Processing Zones in Hanoi City are paying their workers higher than the regional minimum wages. Their wages are insufficient, however, to cover their decent living needs. Most of the workers are migrants from other localities, and rent (excluding utility costs) accounts for a third of their wages. Similarly, in Ho Chi Minh City the minimum wage is insufficient to cover the minimum living needs of workers. They therefore need to work additional hours to earn extra income (Thu Hang 2019).

Labour Export Practices

Labour export had been a policy of the Vietnamese government even prior to Doi Moi. On 9 November 1991, Decree No 370-HDBT on Vietnamese guest workers was promulgated.[3] Accordingly, Articles 1 and 2 of the decree were aimed at sending Vietnamese workers abroad temporarily as a solution to unemployment while contributing to generating income for the workers and revenues in foreign currencies for the country. In recent years, labour export targeting poor households and ethnic minorities has been one of the main policies of the government in order to sustainably eliminate poverty. On 29 April 2009, the prime minister promulgated Decision No 71/2009/QD-TTg on supporting poor districts to accelerate labour export, contributing to sustainable poverty reduction for the period 2009–20. Its aim was to improve the quality and increase the quantity of labour exports from poor districts, thereby contributing to employment creation, increasing incomes and creating sustainable poverty reduction.

As mentioned in Item 1 of this decision, the government set a goal of sending ten thousand workers from the target districts to work overseas between 2009 and 2010. In the period from 2011 to 2015, the government aimed to increase this number by fifty thousand workers. And from 2016 to 2020, the number of workers in poor districts sent to work overseas should have been increased by 15 per cent compared to the previous period, contributing to a decline of poor households by 19 per cent in sixty-one poor districts in Vietnam. MOLISA set a specific goal for the period 2017–20 for which the number of Vietnamese guest workers was to be somewhere between 100,000 and 120,000 per year (MOLISA 2019).

As a result of this, the number of Vietnamese guest workers continues to grow at a steady rate. There are currently more than a million Vietnamese guest workers in more than forty countries and territories, including European countries (Lan Anh 2020). Since 2014, more than 102,000 Vietnamese guest workers have been sent to work abroad each year, and they account for 7 per cent of the total employment creation for the whole country (Dung Hieu 2019). In 2019 there were 152,530 guest workers in total, of which female workers accounted for approximately 36 per cent (MOLISA 2020b). In the first eleven months of 2020, this number was 54,307 workers, of which 20,170 were female, accounting for 37.1 per cent. This number represented a decrease of 40.9 per cent because of the pandemic. The traditional destinations such as Japan, Taiwan and South Korea account for approximately 96 per cent of the total number of Vietnamese guest workers (VAMAS 2021).

According to MOLISA deputy minister Nguyen Thi Ha, labour export contributes to approximately 10 per cent of job creation for the whole country. In addition, the lives of the returned Vietnamese guest workers are improved (Kim Thanh 2019). In general, the average wages of the Vietnamese guest workers are higher than those of the same occupations who are working in Vietnam (ibid.). For example, the average monthly wage of a Vietnamese guest worker is between US$1,000 and 1,200 in Japan and South Korea; between US$700 and 800 in Taiwan; and between US$400 and 600 in Saudi Arabia (ibid.), which is much higher than the average monthly wages paid in Vietnam, as detailed above.

However, high labour service fees, a shortage of skilled guest workers, and the problem of Vietnamese guest workers disappearing to live and work illegally in the receiving countries after the termination of their contracts are among some significant problems with the arrangements. For example, despite the efforts of the Vietnamese and South Korean authorities, the number of Vietnamese workers that disappear in South Korea after the termination of their contracts remains high (Kim Thanh 2019). There are currently 363 licensed labour-sending companies, and approximately half a million Vietnamese workers working abroad (ibid.).[4] Studies show that the Vietnamese guest workers need to pay twice the official service fees (Nhat Duong 2019). In order to work temporarily in countries such as Japan, Taiwan and China, Vietnamese guest workers have to pay service fees of between US$7,000 and 16,000 (ibid.).

Remittances as an Important Source of Revenue and Income

Remittances play a significant role in the Vietnamese economy. According to official statistics, the total personal remittances received in Vietnam between 1993 and 2019 came to more than US$167 billion (Minh Nhung 2020). The amount of annual remittances was US$1.34 billion in 2000. It increased by US$17 billion in 2019 and accounted for approximately 6.5 per cent of the country's GDP (World Bank 2019).

The remittances received in Ho Chi Minh City, for example, increase between 8 and 10 per cent annually. In 2019, Ho Chi Minh City was the destination of US$5.3 billion in remittances. This amount increased by US$5.5 billion in 2020 despite the pandemic (Tran Le 2020). Remittances not only contribute to economic growth in large cities but also play a significant role in other localities, and they are especially conspicuous in the poor provinces. According to MOLISA deputy minister Nguyen Thi Ha, the economies and infrastructures of localities and rural areas that have a high density of Vietnamese guest workers have been significantly improved thanks to billions of US dollar remittances received annually (ibid.). Ha Tinh, for example, is one of the poorest provinces of Vietnam. According to 2019 data, the province received over VND 4,000 billion (US$173 million) in remittances, accounting for approximately 50 per cent of the total revenue of the province (ibid.).

Vietnam ranks among the top ten countries in the world in terms of the value of remittances received, accounting for approximately 2.5 per cent of global remittances in 2017 (UNDP 2018, pp. 54–56). Vietnamese abroad send home US$735 per month on average, which is ten times the average monthly household income. To many Vietnamese families, the remittances from their families working abroad is a major source of the whole family's income. The received remittances have helped their families to pay household costs and the costs of other necessities such as loans, medical care, education and savings (UniTeller 2019, pp. 5–7).

Despite the increased amount of remittances, the laws and policies on anti-money laundering are still underdeveloped in Vietnam. The use of cash is still common in the country. The Vietnamese government acknowledges a medium level of risk in terms of money-laundering crimes with respect to remittances through the official banking system and a high level of risk for such crimes for remittances sent via informal transfer systems (ibid.). State management over remittances, however, remains weak. A person may receive cash remittances through the banking system without any limit on the amount of money received. Receivers are not required by law to prove the source of such remittances. In practice, the banks are competing with one another for remittance commissions. And as a result the control by banks over the sources of remittances remains very weak. This situation has created room for money laundering.

Among the reasons many Vietnamese abroad prefer using informal channels rather than formal ones to send money home are the simpler procedures, the attractive commission fees, and the lack of requirements to prove the purpose for sending the money home (State Bank of Vietnam 2019, pp. 25–28). According to official statistics, Vietnam continues to receive remittances via informal channels other than the banking system, which accounts for 27.4 per cent of the total (Nhung Nguyen 2019).

Case 1. Labour Export in Nghe An Province

Nghe An is one of the poorest provinces in Vietnam; it has 51,949 poor households.[5] Manual workers account for a majority of Nghe An's workforce. Only 32.7 per cent of the employed population have obtained any vocational skills. On average, the monthly wage of an enterprise employee is VND 5.5 million (GSO 2020, pp. 378–83).[6] The average monthly wage of a garment worker in Nghe An in 2020 was between VND 6 and 7 million (Hoang Trinh 2020).[7]

On 30 July 2013, the Politburo of the Vietnamese Communist Party issued Resolution No. 26-NQ/TW on the development orientation and tasks for Nghe An Province by the year 2020. Item 3 of the resolution mandates the continuous implementation of policies for Vietnamese guest workers, prioritizing the poor and ethnic minorities in poor and extremely poor districts and communes.

In the period 2010–15, there were between 12,000 and 13,000 guest workers abroad from Nghe An (ibid.). This number increased to 60,898 workers by the end of 2018—the highest number of all provinces and localities in Vietnam. The three provinces with the largest number of guest workers are Nghe An, Thanh Hoa and Ha Tinh (ibid.). In Nghe An, guest workers accounted for 35 per cent of the total workforce for the province. The major markets for guest workers from Nghe An are Taiwan, Malaysia, South Korea and Japan (Nghe An DOLISA 2019).

With the increased number of guest workers from Nghe An, mainly to East Asian countries, young people in this area have sought work opportunities in Europe by relying on a network of human smugglers. This network offer an attractive package that entails simple procedures and a lower price than the service fees required to be paid to regulated labour export companies (ibid.). According to my interview findings, individuals using the informal network of human smugglers may not need to borrow money to cover the cost of the trip. Instead they would only need to pay the loan back to the human smuggling network gradually after they arrive in the target country.[8]

Similarly, most of the local people from Ha Tinh province that are working abroad are in European countries illegally. They send money home via informal money sending services because it is difficult for them to access the formal remittance services of the countries where they are residing illegally (Nguyen Oanh 2019).

The Vietnamese guest workers contribute to the reduction of the unemployment rate in their home provinces, as mentioned above. In addition, they remit a large amount of money home to their families. According to official statistics, the income of a Nghe An guest worker is between two and six times higher than the income of workers with the same qualifications and ten times higher than a worker in the province who does not have a regular job. Annually, Nghe An received US$255 million in remittances. In practice, the real amount their families receive is much higher because the workers, particularly those who are working illegally abroad, often send home money via a non-official system (Nguyen Khac Thuan 2017, pp. 16–17). Currently, more than fifteen thousand guest workers from Yen Thanh district, Nghe An province, are working abroad. In 2018, for example, Yen Thanh district received remittances totalling US$30 million. This amount increased to US$35 million in 2019 (Xuan Hoang 2019).

Case 2: Son Thanh Commune, Yen Thanh District, Nghe An Province

In the 1990s, Son Thanh was the poorest commune of Yen Thanh district. Labour export has been a major goal of the local authorities in order to eliminate poverty. Now, after almost thirty years, Son Thanh has become one of the richest communes. There are now between 1,500 and 1,800 Son Thanh residents working in Europe. This number, which is about 50 per cent of the total local workforce, includes those who are living and working illegally there (Nguyen Son-Nguyen Thu 2019). On average, at least one member from every household of the commune is working abroad (Xuan Hoang 2021). Annually, the commune receives remittances of more than US$13 million sent through the official banking system (Duc Hau 2018). According to Nguyen Huu Sau, the president of Son Thanh People's Committee, the commune receives more than US$16 million annually. The pandemic had greatly affected the amount of remittances received by Son Thanh commune in 2020, which amounted to approximately US$8 million, a decrease of approximately 50 per cent compared to previous years (ibid.).

Case 3: Do Thanh Commune, Yen Thanh District, Nghe An Province

Do Thanh was a poor commune fifteen years ago. Today it is still a rural commune where agriculture is the major economic activity. But the lives of the local residents have changed as a result of labour export. According to Nguyen Van Ha, president of Do Thanh People's Committee, the major destinations for Do Thanh residents used to be South Korea and Taiwan. In recent years the target countries have been the member states of the European Union and the United Kingdom (ibid.). These destinations account for a total of 1,500 workers, both legally and illegally (approximately 17 per cent of the total workforce) (Viet Anh 2019). Today, Do Thanh has become one of the richest communes in Vietnam; it has over 300 billionaires, approximately 2,000 villas and over 200 registered cars, thanks mainly to the received remittances (Ba Nam 2019).

The interview findings show that local residents of Do Thanh commune may first obtain residence permits to operate small businesses in the Czech Republic. From there they travel illegally to other European countries such as Spain, Portugal, Sweden, France, Germany, Belgium and the United Kingdom. Many of them were aged between 16 and 17 years old. After earning a considerable amount of money in Europe they would often come back to Vietnam to get married and then would travel again illegally to Europe to earn more income until the age of approximately 40 years old.[9]

The above examples show that labour export has long been an important strategy of the Vietnamese government to reduce poverty and unemployment. Many Nghe An households have transitioned from being poor to being more affluent, contributing significantly to improving the living standards of the local people. The Nghe An cases also show that many local people have chosen to travel and work abroad illegally, especially in European countries and the United Kingdom because they find that there are opportunities there of earning higher incomes compared to other traditional labour markets in Asian countries.

Human Smuggling from Vietnam to Europe—The Case of Belgium

Belgium is located in Western Europe, bordering the North Sea between France and the Netherlands. The country had 11,492,641 inhabitants as of January 2020 and a GDP per capita of US$54,545 (Statbel 2020; OECD 2020). Belgium is not only a preferred destination among Western European countries for illegal migrants but it is also a transit country for migrants and people smugglers because of its proximity to the United Kingdom.

The total number of illegal Vietnamese living in Belgium is not yet known. But it has been reported that over the last three years thousands of illegal Vietnamese arrived in Western European countries, of which hundreds of them arrived illegally in Belgium, including many adolescents (De Standaard 2019). Between 2017 and 2019, around a hundred illegal Vietnamese were arrested there. Most of them were on their way to the United Kingdom. It is very common, both in the Netherlands and Belgium, for illegal Vietnamese immigrants declared to be adolescents to disappear within a short space of time from reception centres for asylum seekers. For example, forty-four such Vietnamese disappeared within twenty-four hours of being brought to asylum reception centres in Belgium over the same period (De Morgen 2019). By 12 June 2020, the rate of such persons disappearing quickly after being brought to the Asylum reception centres was nine in twelve (De Standaard 2020a).

In the wake of the deaths of thirty-nine illegal Vietnamese migrants in Essex, the United Kingdom, in October 2019, many Vietnamese still continue to risk their lives in order to reach the United Kingdom illegally. Belgium has continued to be used as one of the main routes to the United Kingdom. For example, on 6 March 2020, the police arrested ten illegal Vietnamese who were on their way to the United Kingdom (De Standaard 2020b). According to the public prosecutor, the human smuggling network must have transported tens of illegal migrants per day for months. Most of the migrants are Vietnamese (De Morgen 2020).

Vietnamese wishing to travel to the United Kingdom illegally have to pay up to 40,000 euros for the whole trip (ibid.). They may receive a tourist visa to fly from Vietnam to Russia or the Ukraine and from there travel to Eastern European countries such as Poland, the Czech Republic or Romania. From those countries they will continue their journeys to Germany, the Netherlands, France or Belgium in order to reach the United Kingdom.[10]

According to the interview findings, Belgium is not only a transit country for many Vietnamese attempting to reach the United Kingdom but is also a final destination for the illegal Vietnamese migrants. Nail salons and restaurants are two popular businesses for residents of Vietnamese origins. In recent years the number of nail salons owned by Vietnamese in Belgium has increased considerably. In 2008 there were 12,738 Vietnamese nail salons in Belgium. This number had increased to 24,450 by 2019 (Bruzz 2019). Inspections conducted by the Belgian authorities on 34 nail salons in Brussels, Vilvoorde, and Oostende in 2019 showed that 15 out of 34 inspected nail salons used illegal workers, mostly Vietnamese (ibid.).

According to survey findings, sixty per cent of workers at such businesses worked between 9 and 12 hours a day for 7 days a week, or for 15 hours a day for 6 days a week (Myria 2018, p. 169). These findings are comparable with the results of interviews conducted by this author. A Vietnamese without legitimate documentation working in a nail salon in Belgium would often have to work 12 hours a day. A working day often starts at 8 a.m. and lasts until 8 p.m., and a worker would typically work 7 day a week.[11] According to one inspection report, young female Vietnamese working illegally in a nail salon in the city of Vilvoorde, Belgium, had to endure poor working conditions. They had to spend their nights between the chemical products in the nail salon (Dierickx and Berlanger 2019).

The interview findings revealed that Vietnamese illegal migrants often have relatives or friends in the target countries who can offer them help such as with accommodation or jobs upon arrival. A Vietnamese working illegally in a nail salon in Belgium with good skills, for example, may receive 40 per cent of the profit, whilst the salon owner nets the balance. His or her monthly income could reach more than 2,000 euros (around US$2,320). An illegal Vietnamese migrant who works as a kitchen assistant could receive a monthly wage of 1,800 euros per month (around US$2,088); a skilled chief, meanwhile, might receive up to 2,500 euros a month (around US$2,900). In addition, these workers would pay no taxes or social security contributions to the Belgian government (ibid.). These amounts are more than ten times higher than the average monthly income of a non-skilled worker in Vietnam.

The information gained from the interviews aligns with the figures cited above, showing large amounts of remittances sent to Vietnam. The interviews revealed that the reasons for these individuals to leave Vietnam was to secure higher incomes. According to Le Xuan Duong, deputy president of the People's Committee, Do Thanh Commune, Yen Thanh district, Nghe An province, many local residents had lost their lives while working illegally in Europe. Others risked being deported to Vietnam as they had not obtained the necessary papers to legitimize their stay. He also thought, however, that they had no other choice.[12]

Case 1. Illegal Female Migrant in Belgium from Ha Tinh Province
Ms T. obtained a valid Vietnamese passport and travelled from Vietnam to Romania with a tourist visa. She then travelled to Germany, and her final destination was Belgium. In Vietnam, Ms T had finished high school but had obtained no vocational skills and did not speak any other languages than Vietnamese. She was pregnant upon her arrival in Belgium in the summer of 2019. She gave birth to a baby girl with the help of Belgian social services, which paid for her maternity costs. It has now been more than a year and she has neither a job nor has she been able to obtain a legal residence permit. Ms T. has no intention, however, of returning to Vietnam because if she did so it would be

impossible for her to travel to Europe again. Ms T. expressed the strong hope that she would be able to find a job in Belgium.[13]

Because of the pandemic, the federal government of Belgium decided to close all non-essential stores and offices, including nail salons, restaurants and coffee houses, for almost two months—from 18 March to 8 June 2020. A second lockdown was announced from 19 October until 13 December 2020.[14] Many migrants, including Vietnamese, work in the hospitality industry. Those who have obtained legal residence permits and jobs receive unemployment benefits and other financial support from the Belgian government. But illegal migrants who have lost their jobs because of the pandemic have received no such help during the lockdown periods.

Case 2. Asylum Seeker from Ha Tinh Province

Mr D., who obtained a bachelor's diploma in Vietnam, arrived in Belgium in May 2019 on a Belgian tourist visa. He then initiated procedures to be recognized as an asylee. In May 2020 he received a decision from the Belgium authorities, who officially refused to grant him asylum status. Mr D. told this author that if he was deported to Vietnam he would not return to Ha Tinh province because there would be no job opportunities for him there. Shortly after the interview, Mr D. disappeared from the reception centre for asylum seekers.[15]

Case 3. Illegal Male Migrant from Yen Thanh District, Nghe An Province

Mr H. is a thirty-year-old illegal migrant from Yen Thanh district, Nghe An province. He worked at different jobs in Belgium in order to earn money to send home to support his family. Because of the pandemic, he could not find any work and had no income for months. He was later arrested by the Belgian authorities. Mr H. volunteered to work in the prison. He received a monthly compensation of 160 euros (US$197) and decided to send all of the amounts he received to his family in Vietnam.[16]

Will the New Legal Framework Reduce Human Smuggling to Europe?

On 13 November 2020, the Law on Vietnamese Guest Workers No. 69/2020/QH14 was promulgated by Vietnam's National Assembly. It was scheduled to come into force on 1 January 2022, replacing Law No. 72/2006/QH11, which had been enforced for more than thirteen years. Article 44 of the new law provides conditions for workers to work abroad under employment contracts. There is no change between the two laws in terms of requirements of foreign language skills, technical skills, other professional qualifications, and any other conditions of the receiving countries.

According to information gathered by this author, however, those Vietnamese in Europe illegally do not speak any other language than Vietnamese. In addition, most of them are non-skilled workers. It would be difficult for such people to meet the above-mentioned requirements. In practice, as mentioned above, those wishing to travel from Vietnam to Europe to work often have to pay a large service fee to labour export companies before departure. Meanwhile, the human smuggling networks may accept that their clients will gradually pay back the debt once they arrive and begin working illegally in the target countries.

Fortunately, Law No. 69/2020/QH14 sets for the first time a ceiling on the rate of service charges levied by labour export companies on Vietnamese workers. Accordingly, the service charge must not be higher than the monthly wage of a worker under a 12-month contract, or not higher than three months' wages of a worker under a contract of 36 months or longer. The service charge rate applied for guest workers in merchant vessels must not be higher than 1.5 times the monthly wage of a worker under a 12-month contract (Article 23, Item 4). Moreover, guest workers will no longer need to refund to service enterprises any brokerage commissions paid by the enterprise to brokers in order to sign and perform a labour supply contract (Article 7, Item 8 and Article 22).

As a result of weak enforcement mechanisms in the Vietnamese legal system, however, it is still doubtful whether the new law will aid in eliminating human smuggling through its attempt to eliminate service fees of labour export companies. Because of rising income inequality, it is difficult for the poor to find good employment opportunities in their localities. This has meant children in these poor communities have been unable to access adequate education. And as a result it is likely that many Vietnamese, particularly the poor, will continue to attempt to leave the country in search of better work opportunities abroad, and Europe will continue to be a preferred destination for this.

Conclusion

Income inequality has become a considerable challenge facing Vietnam. Many Vietnamese, especially the poor, do not fully benefit from the opportunities created by economic growth. The Vietnamese government has considered labour export to be a major solution to eliminate poverty and unemployment. But a more sustainable approach is necessary in order to gradually improve the qualifications and skills of the local workforce so as to be able develop the local economy rather than depend on labour export and remittances. Efficient intervention is needed from the state to enable the poor to benefit from economic growth and reduce income inequality.

With fewer administrative requirements, improved access to more favourable credit, low-cost courses on foreign languages, and practical vocational training, the new legal framework on Vietnamese guest workers should create more opportunities, especially for the poor, to be able to access official labour export services. Moreover, the Vietnamese authorities should issue specific strategies to guide and encourage local people to use the received remittances efficiently to develop the local economy. Finally, sufficient legal mechanisms to police remittances is needed to contribute effectively to preventing human smuggling.

Notes

1. For this chapter, I use the exchange rate of US$1 to VND 23,113.
2. The 2019 Labour Code, Article 90, clause 1; Article 90, clauses 1 and 2; Article 91 clause 1.
3. Decree No. 370-HDBT was replaced by Decree No. 07/CP dated 20 January 1995; Decree No. 152/1999/ND-CP dated 20 September 1999; Decree No. 81/2003/ND-CP dated 17 July 2003; and Decree 126/2007/ND-CP dated 1 August 2007.
4. Enterprises of different types of ownerships that obtain licences granted by the Department of Overseas Labour (DOLAB) are entitled to provide labour export services.
5. Decision No. 1052/QĐ-LĐTBXH.
6. Around US$240.
7. Between US$261 and US$304.
8. Interview on 8 April 2020 in Belgium.
9. Interview on 4 June 2020 in Belgium.
10. Interviews on 8 January 2020 in Belgium.
11. Interview on 25 July 2020 in Belgium.
12. Interviews on 15 May and 8 July 2020 in Belgium.
13. Interview on 30 April 2020 in Belgium.
14. During the second lockdown, restaurants were only allowed to accept take-away orders.
15. Interview on 4 August 2020 in Belgium.
16. Interview on 24 December 2020 in Belgium.

References

Asian Development Bank. 2019. "Economic Indicators for Vietnam". https://www.adb.org/vi/countries/viet-nam/economy.

Ba Nam. 2019. "Thu vi ve nhung ngoi lang ty phu giau nhat tai Viet Nam". *An Ninh Thu Do*, 19 March 2019. https://anninhthudo.vn/doi-song/thu-vi-ve-nhung-ngoi-lang-ty-phu-giau-nhat-tai-viet-nam/803402.antd.

BBC. 2020. "Essex Lorry Deaths: Two Found Guilty of Killing 39 Migrants". 21 December 2020. https://www.bbc.com/news/uk-england-55399004.

Belgian Statistical Office. 2020. "Structure of the Population". https://statbel.fgov.be/en/themes/population/structure-population.

Blomberg. 2020. "Japan Starts Paying Firms to Cut Reliance on Chinese Factories". 21 July 2020. https://www.bloombergquint.com/global-economics/japan-to-pay-at-least-536-million-for-companies-to-leave-china.

Bruzz. 2019. "Vietnamese jongeren ook in Brussel uitgebuit in nagelsalons". 3 July 2019. https://www.bruzz.be/samenleving/vietnamese-jongeren-ook-brussel-uitgebuit-nagelsalons-2019-07-03.

Choe, Nam-suk. 2019. "Vietnam – An Attractive Investment Destination in 2019". *Korea IT Times*, 25 January 2019. http://www.koreaittimes.com/news/articleView.html?idxno=88884.

Custom Office. 2020. "Tinh hinh xuat khau, nhap khau hang hoa cua Viet Nam thang 12 va nam 2019". 31 January 2020. https://www.customs.gov.vn/Lists/ThongKeHaiQuan/ViewDetails.aspx?ID=1734&Category=PhpercentC3percentA2npercent20tpercentC3percentADchpercent20percentC4percent91percentE1percentBBpercent8Bnhpercent20kpercentE-1percentBBpercentB3&Group=PhpercentC3percentA2npercent20tpercentC3percentADch.

De Morgen. 2019. "In 2,5 jaar tijd 44 Vietnamese minderjarigen verdwenen in België". 2 July 2019. https://www.demorgen.be/nieuws/in-2-5-jaar-tijd-44-vietnamese-minderjarigen-verdwenen-in-belgie~b05ad124.

―――. 2020. "Dertien verdachten opgepakt in ons land voor gestikte migranten in koelwagen". 27 May 2020. https://www.demorgen.be/nieuws/dertien-verdachten-opgepakt-in-ons-land-voor-gestikte-migranten-in-koelwagen~bed10cf0.

De Standaard. 2020a. "Acht kinderen werden gered van mensenhandelaars, dag later is België hen alweer kwijt". 12 March 202. https://www.standaard.be/cnt/dmf20200312_04886711.

―――. 2020b. "Tien migranten gered uit vrachtwagen nabij Gent, vier verdachten opgepakt". 27 June 2020. https://www.standaard.be/cnt/dmf20200306_04879198.

Dierickx, Robby, and Dimitri Berlanger. 2019. "Jonge Vietnamese meisjes leven en werken in slechte omstandigheden: Hans Bonte sluit nagelstudio?" 23 May 2019. https://www.hln.be/in-de-buurt/vilvoorde/jonge-vietnamese-meisjes-leven-en-werken-in-slechte-omstandigheden-hans-bonte-sluit-nagelstudio~a6ff6559.

Duc Binh. 2021. "Thu nhap cua nguoi lao dong dat 6,7 trieu dong/thang, giam gan 9%". *Tuoi Tre*, 8 January 2021. https://tuoitre.vn/thu-nhap-cua-nguoi-lao-dong-dat-67-trieu-dong-thang-giam-gan-9-20210108112731002.htm.

Duc Chieu. 2020. "Kinh te tu nhan Viet Nam: Dong luc phat trien van nhung ky vong moi". *Tai Chinh*, 26 January 2020. http://tapchitaichinh.vn/

su-kien-noi-bat/kinh-te-tu-nhan-viet-nam-dong-luc-phat-trien-va-nhung-ky-vong-moi-318178.html.

Duc Hau. 2018. "Son Thanh-dien mao moi". *Nong Nghiep*, 1 November 2018. https://nongnghiep.vn/son-thanh---dien-mao-moi-d229829.html.

Dung Hieu. 2019."Trien vong tu xuat khau lao dong". *Nhan Dan*, 2 March 2019. https://nhandan.com.vn/doi-song-xa-hoi/trien-vong-tu-xuat-khau-lao-dong-351164.

EUROSTAT. 2018. "Income Inequality in the EU". 26 April 2018. https://ec.europa.eu/eurostat/web/products-eurostat-news/-/EDN-20180426-1.

Hai Duong and Thi Thu Lan Pham. 2019. "Tien luong khong du song va he luy-nhin tu cac doanh nghiep may?" *Cuoc Song An Toan*, 28 July 2019. https://cuocsongantoan.vn/tien-luong-khong-du-song-va-he-luy-nhin-tu-cac-doanh-nghiep-may-1528.html.

Hoang Manh. 2021. "Ha Noi: Muc tra luong cao nhat duoc thong ke la 185 trieu dong/thang". *Dan Tri*, 4 January 2021. https://dantri.com.vn/lao-dong-viec-lam/ha-noi-muc-tra-luong-cao-nhat-duoc-thong-ke-la-185-trieu-dongthang-20210104063805422.htm.

Hoang Trinh. 2020. "Nghe An: Kho tuyen lao dong pho thong". *Nghe An 24h*, 20 February 2020. http://nghean24h.vn/nghe-an-kho-tuyen-lao-dong-pho-thong-a599391.html.

Hong Khanh. 2020. "Gia bat dong san tang soc 200%, nghin nguoi mua nha tai mat?". *Vietnamnet*, 7 January 2020. https://vietnamnet.vn/vn/bat-dong-san/thi-truong/gia-bat-dong-san-tang-soc-200-nghin-nguoi-mua-nha-tai-mat-606815.html#inner-article.

IOM. 2021. "General Country Information: Vietnam". https://www.iom.int/countries/viet-nam.

Kim Thanh. 2019. "Lao dong xuat khau cua Viet Nam dang o dau so voi cac nuoc?" *Dang Cong San Viet Nam*, 4 October 2019. https://dangcongsan.vn/xa-hoi/lao-dong-xuat-khau-cua-viet-nam-dang-o-dau-so-voi-cac-nuoc-538257.html.

Knight Frank. 2020. "The Wealth Report". https://content.knightfrank.com/content/pdfs/global/the-wealth-report-2020.pdf.

Minh Nhung. 2020. "Luong kieu hoi ve Viet Nam lien tuc tang". *Dau tu*, 9 January 2020. https://baodautu.vn/luong-kieu-hoi-ve-viet-nam-lien-tuc-tang-d114228.html.

MOLISA. 2019. "Nang cao chat luong lao dong xuat khau". 1 January 2019. http://www.molisa.gov.vn/Pages/tintuc/chitiet.aspx?tintucID=219367.

―――. 2020a. "Muc tieu nam 2020: Giam ty le ho ngheo ca nuoc binh quan 1-1,5 %". 11 March 2020. http://www.molisa.gov.vn/Pages/tintuc/chitiet.aspx?tintucID=222333.

―――. 2020b. "Bo truong Dao Ngoc Dung: Hinh thanh thi truong lao dong lanh manh, dong bo va hien dai". 9 January 2020. http://www.molisa.gov.vn/Pages/tintuc/chitiet.aspx?tintucID=222208.

MPI. 2020. "Tinh hinh thu hut dau tu nuoc ngoai nam 2019?". *FIA Vietnam*, 7 January 2020. https://dautunuocngoai.gov.vn/tinbai/6318/Tinh-hinh-thu-hut-dau-tu-nuoc-ngoai-nam-2019.

MYRIA. 2019. "Annual Evaluation Report 2019: Trafficking and Smuggling of Human Beings". https://www.myria.be/files/19-JVMH-Statistieken.pdf.

Nhat Duong. 2019. "Lao dong Viet Nam di lam viec o nuoc ngoai phai tra phi qua cao". *VnEconomy*, 14 November 2019. http://vneconomy.vn/lao-dong-viet-nam-di-lam-viec-o-nuoc-ngoai-phai-tra-phi-qua-cao-20191114185522586.htm.

Ngoc Thuy. 2020. "Samsung Vietnam Earns US\$4.3 Billion in Profit in 2019". *Hanoi Times*, 4 March 2020. http://hanoitimes.vn/samsung-vietnam-generates-us43-billion-in-profits-in-2019-311239.html.

Nguyen, An. 2020. "Nang suat lao dong cua Viet Nam dung o dau so voi cac nuoc ASEAN-6". *Dau Tu*, 10 October 2020. https://baodautu.vn/nang-suat-lao-dong-cua-viet-nam-dung-o-dau-so-voi-cac-nuoc-asean-6-d131091.html.

Nguyen, Khac Thuan. 2017. "Xuat khau lao dong o Nghe An va nhung van de dat ra". http://ngheandost.gov.vn/documents/10190/781841/KHCNpercent20THANGpercent209_04.pdf.

Nguyen, Nhung. 2019."Khoi dong kieu hoi". *Saigon Giai Phong*, 20 November 2019. https://saigondautu.com.vn/tai-chinh/khoi-dong-kieu-hoi-74325.html.

Nguyen Oanh. 2019. "'Suc nong' nao se 'ra dong' thi truong kieu hoi o Ha Tinh?". *Bao Ha Tinh*, 29 December 2019. https://baohatinh.vn/dau-tu/suc-nong-nao-se-ra-dong-thi-truong-kieu-hoi-o-ha-tinh/184669.htm.

Nguyen, Son, and Thu Nguyen. 2019. "Son Thanh-Yen Thanh: Diem sang trong phong trao xay dung nong thon moi". *Anh Sang Va Cuoc Song*, 16 June 2019. https://anhsangvacuocsong.vn/son-thanh-yen-thanh-diem-sang-trong-phong-trao-xay-dung-nong-thon-moi.

OECD. 2020. "Selected Indicators for Belgium". https://data.oecd.org/belgium.htm.

Oxfam. 2018a. "Dich chuyen xa hoi va binh dang co hoi tai Viet Nam: xu huong va cac yeu to tac dong". https://oi-files-cng-rod.s3.amazonaws.com/vietnam.oxfam.org/s3fs-public/file_attachments/Oxfam_Socialpercent20mobilitypercent20andpercent20equalitypercent20ofpercent20opportunitypercent20inpercent20Vietnam_VIE.pdf.

———. 2018b. "Tien luong khong du song va he luy: nghien cuu mot so doanh nghiep may xuat khau o Viet Nam". https://cng-cdn.oxfam.org/vietnam.oxfam.org/s3fs-public/file_attachments/Tienpercent20luongpercent20khongpercent20dupercent20songpercent20vapercent20hepercent20luyper cent20-percent20Nghienpercent20cuupercent20motpercent20sopercent-20doanhpercent20nghieppercent20maypercent20xuatpercent20khauper-cent20opercent20Vietpercent20Nampercent20(screen)_0.pdf.

Pham, Thanh Huong. 2019. "Phat trien ben vung: Nen tang cua niem tin – Bai 2: Ky tich xoa doi, giam ngheo". *Tin Tuc*, 4 December 2019. https://baotintuc.vn/kinh-te/phat-trien-ben-vung-nen-tang-cua-niem-tin-bai-2-ky-tich-xoa-doi-giam-ngheo-20191204153629285.htm.

Quang Dan. 2020."Von FDI tu EU se do manh vao Viet Nam nho EVFTA?". *Nha Dau Tu*, 23 February 2020. https://nhadautu.vn/von-fdi-tu-eu-se-do-manh-vao-viet-nam-nho-evfta-d34039.html.

Saigoneer. 2019. "As Vietnam Gets Wealthier, Economic Inequality Also Gets Worse". *Saigoneer*, 26 July 2019. https://saigoneer.com/vietnam-news/17029-as-vietnam-gets-wealthier,-economic-inequality-also-gets-worse.

State Bank of Vietnam. 2018. "National Risk Assessment Report on Money Laundering and Terrorism Financing in the Period of 2012–2017". 30 October 2018. https://www.ssi.com.vn/tin-tuc/tin-tuc-chung/cong-bo-ket-qua-danh-gia-rui-ro-quoc-gia-ve-rua-tien-tai-tro-khung-bo-cua-viet-nam.

Statista. 2020. "The 20 Countries with the Highest Growth of the Gross Domestic Product (GDP) In 2019?" https://www.statista.com/statistics/273977/countries-with-the-highest-growth-of-the-gross-domestic-product-gdp.

Ta Van Canh. 2019. "Thach thuc doi voi nguon nhan luc det may Viet Nam trong boi canh cuoc Cach mang Cong nghiep 4.0". *Khoa Hoc va Cong Nghe*, 14 March 2019. https://khcncongthuong.vn/tin-tuc/t3311/thach-thuc-doi-voi-nguon-nhan-luc-det-may-viet-nam-trong-boi-canh-cuoc-cach-mang-cong-nghiep-4-0.html.

Termote, Roeland. 2019. "Nagels lakken om smokkelaars terug te betalen". 3 July 2019. https://www.standaard.be/cnt/dmf20190702_04491440?&articlehash=24EACA78B7FC2D72A2A7790804BFD1C48697CCCAB7 7D1BC31CCD63E719BDA14103EFE9B618930E19AE68056F7ED-513EF784C87C3FF3F540DE3E87D8A3EDF68D2.

Thanh An. 2019. "Doanh nghiep dang tra cao hon muc luong toi thieu vung". *Dan Sinh*, 11 October 2019. https://baodansinh.vn/doanh-nghiep-dang-tra-cao-hon-muc-luong-toi-thieu-vung-20191011102216138.htm.

Thien Thanh. 2020. "Xuat ngoai, kieu hoi va chuyen lao dong di cu". *Cong an Nghe An*, 5 January 2020. https://congannghean.vn/kinh-te-xa-hoi/202001/xuat-ngoai-kieu-hoi-va-chuyen-lao-dong-di-cu-888672.

Thoi bao Tai chinh Viet Nam. 2020. "Thay gi qua co cau nguon von FDI do vao Viet Nam nam 2019?" 15 January 2020. http://thoibaotaichinhvietnam.vn/pages/kinh-doanh/2020-01-15/thay-gi-qua-co-cau-nguon-von-fdi-do-vao-viet-nam-nam-2019-81572.aspx.

Thu Hang. 2019. "Ban luong toi thieu the nao khi nhieu cong nhan cuoi thang chi an com chan canh suong?". *Thanh Nien*, 11 July 2019. https://thanhnien.vn/thoi-su/ban-luong-toi-thieu-the-nao-khi-nhieu-cong-nhan-cuoi-thang-chi-an-com-chan-canh-suong-1102073.html.

Tran, Le. 2020. "Kieu hoi chuyen ve TP. HCM nam 2020 uoc dat 5,5 ty". *Vietnam Finance*, 23 December 2020. https://vietnamfinance.vn/kieu-hoi-chuyen-ve-tp-hcm-nam-2020-uoc-dat-55-ty-usd-20180504224247519.htm.

Trinh, Ly Khanh. 2015. "The Right to Strike in Vietnam's Private Sector". *Asian Journal of Law and Society*, no. 2: 115–35. https://doi.org/10.1017/als.2015.2.

UNDP. 2018. "Financing Sustainable Development in Viet Nam". https://www.vn.undp.org/content/vietnam/en/home/library/poverty/DFA.html.

UNICEF. 2016. "Sang kien toan cau ve Tre em ngoai nha truong". https://www.unicef.org/vietnam/media/2496/file/B%C3%A1o%20c%C3%A1o%20tr%E1%BA%BB%20em%20ngo%C3%A0i%20nh%C3%A0%20tr%C6%B0%E1%BB%9Dng%202016.pdf.

Unitelleer. 2019. "Both Sides of the Coin: The Receiver's Story". 20 December 2019. http://bizhub.vn/news/low-income-households-benefit-enormously-from-remittances-study_312017.html.

V. Đinh, D. Hoa, Q. Nam, and B. Dung. 2019. "Đuong day 'co' dua 'lao dong chui' sang chau Au ra sao?". *Tuoi Tre*, 3 November 2019. https://tuoitre.vn/du-ong-day-co-dua-lao-dong-chui-sang-chau-au-ra-sao-2019110308343231.htm.

VAMAS. 2021. "So lieu lao dong di lam viec o nuoc ngoai 11 thang nam 2020".

4 January 2021. http://vamas.com.vn/so-lieu-lao-dong-di-lam-viec-o-nuoc-ngoai-11-thang-nam-2020_t221c655n44836.

Viet Anh. 2019. "Ngoi lang 'toan ty phu' nho xuat khau lao dong tai Nghe An len bao nuoc ngoai". *24h*, 1 November 2019. https://www.24h.com.vn/tin-tuc-quoc-te/ngoi-lang-toan-ty-phu-nho-xuatkhau-lao-dong-tai-nghe-an-len-bao-nuoc-ngoai-c415a1096441.html.

Vinanet. 2020. "Châu Mỹ, EU chưa phải khu vực xuất khẩu lớn nhất của Việt Nam". 20 March 2020. http://vinanet.vn/kinhte-taichinh/chau-my-eu-chua-phai-khu-vuc-xuat-khau-lon-nhat-cua-viet-nam-726643.html.

Worldbank. 2019. "Personal Remittances, Received (current US$) – Vietnam". https://data.worldbank.org/indicator/BX.TRF.PWKR.CD.DT?locations=VN

―――. 2018. "Climbing the Ladder: Poverty Reduction and Shared Prosperity in Vietnam". http://documents1.worldbank.org/curated/en/206981522843253122/pdf/124916-WP-PULIC-P161323-VietnamPovertyUpdateReportENG.pdf.

Wells-Dang, Andrew, and Thi Quynh Hoa Vu. 2019. "Shrinking Opportunities: Social Mobility and Widening Inequality in Vietnam". UNRISD, 20 May 2019. https://www.unrisd.org/UNRISD/website/newsview.nsf/(httpNews)/C0838EC429923FAAC125840000323191?OpenDocument.

Xuan Hoang. 2019. "Huyen Yen Thanh-Nghe An nhan 35 trieu USD kieu hoi gui ve dip Tet". *Nghe An*, 30 January 2019. https://baonghean.vn/mot-huyen-o-nghe-an-co-35-trieu-usd-kieu-hoi-gui-ve-dip-tet-232474.html.

―――. 2021. "Mot xa cua Nghe An co luong kieu hoi gan 8 trieu USD". *Nghe An*, 3 January 2021. https://baonghean.vn/mot-xa-cua-nghe-an-co-luong-kieu-hoi-gan-8-trieu-usd-279999.html.

Zingnews. 2019. "Biet thu, xe sang o xa co 1.500 nguoi xuat khau lao dong". 1 November 2019. https://zingnews.vn/biet-thu-xe-sang-o-xa-co-1500-nguoi-xuat-khau-lao-dong-post1008115.html.

Part III

Chapter 11

Why Accountability Differs in Vietnam and China? A Nested Game Explanation

Nguyen Khac Giang

In the early summer of 2018, a rare wave of protests rocked Vietnam. Believing the draft law on Special Economic Zones (SEZs) would give China the right to occupy strategic geopolitical positions across the country, many thousands of angry citizens poured out on to the streets demanding it be withdrawn. In Binh Thuan province, protesters burned police cars, vandalized the provincial government office and attacked members of the police force (Duc Trong 2018). In response the National Assembly voted to withdraw the SEZ law, although this was seen by the Vietnamese Communist Party (VCP) as a priority to boost economic development. This was not the first time the regime had to back down because of popular pressure. In 1997 a revolt by farmers against corruption in Thai Binh province ended with a government concession. The then permanent member of the VCP's Secretariat, Pham The Duyet, holding the fifth most powerful position in the party, was sent to discuss matters with the enraged farmers. In the aftermath of the Thai Binh revolt, the VCP issued the grass-roots democracy directive, which aimed to prevent such incidents from happening in the future. Mr Duyet stayed on in his position until the end of his term.

It is striking to compare responses to similar incidents in China. In early 1989, a series of protests broke out across the country, most prominently at Beijing's Tiananmen Square. The then general secretary of the Chinese Communist Party (CCP), Zhao Ziyang, visited the site and talked with the protesters, urging them to end their hunger strikes. He was among the CCP faction that wanted to seek a peaceful solution. The ultimate result, however, was the opposite: On 4 June 1989, tanks and soldiers from the People's Liberation Army (PLA) invaded the square and massacred hundreds—if not thousands—of protesters. Mr Zhao was himself a victim: he was stripped of the party chief's position and placed under house arrest until his death. The Tiananmen incident created a path dependence for the CCP to solve popular tensions: coercive actions are preferred over making concessions, particularly for incidents that are deemed threatening to the regime. In one dataset, of 1,418 mass events recorded from 2001 to 2012, 41 per cent were repressed by the police, although only 5 per cent of them could be considered as voicing radical political claims (Li 2019). Repression has been even worse under the rule of Xi Jinping, which further marginalizes the already limited space for activism (Fu and Distelhorst 2017).

The above observations challenge the conventional wisdom that Vietnam shares identical characteristics of political accountability with China, based on which most prominent classification strategies put the two countries into the same category, as civilian, communist or single-party regimes. In fact, as shown in a pathbreaking paper by Malesky, Abrami and Zheng (2011), the Vietnamese political system has a higher level of intra-party democracy and has been more responsive to popular demand than China has. Access to the global internet is a vivid example: while there are around sixty million Facebook and Google accounts each in the country of ninety-six million people (Reuters 2019), China has set up the "Great Firewall" and blocked major social media platforms since 2008.

Vietnam, as such, has the characteristics of a high-accountability regime, where the rulers are less repressive and more accommodative to popular demands. China, on the other hand, is a low-accountability regime that focuses on control capacity and administrative effectiveness. To explain this divergence of accountability, I argue that both regimes are involved in a nested game of three sub-games in which different payoff expectations affect the regimes' choices towards accountability during market reforms.

The games have four players: the ruler (R), the selectorate (S), the population (P), and foreign powers (F). The regime's policy towards the population and foreign powers is the unified response by the ruler and the selectorate. The three sub-games are the internal accountability game (between the ruler and the selectorate), the external accountability game (regime–population), and foreign pressure game (regime–foreign powers).

FIGURE 11.1
The Authoritarian Regime's Nested Games

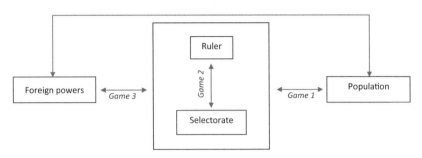

Rulers

Personal leaders retained the key role in the policymaking process in Vietnam and China. The highest-ranked leader in a communist regime is usually the party's general secretary, although the real power might stay elsewhere in some cases (during the 1980s, Deng Xiaoping did not hold an official party position except chairing the Central Military Commission, but he maintained supreme power over the policymaking process). The opinions of the party chief are not always conclusive under a system of collective leadership; his choice can be overruled by the selectorate, which is described below.

The Selectorate

The selectorate can be defined as "the set of people whose endowments include the qualities or characteristics institutionally required to choose the government's leadership" (De Mesquita et al. 2003, p. 42). In an electoral democracy, the selectorate consists of anyone with the right to vote. In authoritarian regimes, the de facto right to choose the regime's leadership is limited to a very small group of people; they have different characteristics depending on the regime type. Most communist regimes formally assign this right to the central committee. But the power of the central committee varies. In the post-Stalin Soviet Union, the Central Committee of the Communist Party of the Soviet Union (CPSU) had the power to decide the fate of the supreme leader: while it protected Nikita Khrushchev from an anti-party plot in 1957, it removed him from power in 1964 after viewing his actions as being increasingly dictatorial (Svolik 2012, p. 90). Meanwhile, central committees have failed to constrain the power of personal rulers in Romania (Tismaneanu 1989, p. 185) or China (Svolik 2012, p. 60).

The Population

The populations in both countries are disenfranchised and have no voice in deciding the leadership of the regimes. They could, however, threaten the survival of the regimes through mass uprisings. Although empirical evidence shows that coups account for most regime changes (Geddes, Frantz and Wright 2018), events in Eastern Europe have made communist rulers in Vietnam and China worry about "colour revolutions" staged by the population (Chen 2010; Duong 2020).

There are two assumptions about the population. First, the population as a whole does not intentionally seek to overthrow the regime. When demanding greater accountability, they are simply asking for an improvement of their living conditions. The population is much less likely to support regime change when the country has a higher level of economic development as their interests are also vested in the system (Kennedy 2010). Mass uprisings and regime change, when they happen, are unexpected results rather than a rational calculation by the population. This non-revolutionary perspective is sensible in light of the inherent problems of organizing collective action in a large and diverse population (Olson 1971) and considering the repressive nature of the Vietnamese and Chinese regimes. Second, this research assumes that the population considers more accountability to be better than less. Anyone would want to hold the regime more accountable, regardless of their stance vis-à-vis the regime. The population in this sense represents the majority of the public and is considered as a unitary actor.

Foreign Powers

As in the case of the Eastern bloc, foreign powers (i.e., the West)[1] want to influence the process of democratization in Vietnam and China. While the most preferred result would be regime change, the West is generally satisfied if there is progress in political reform that makes the governments more accountable to their populations. In this they can use both carrots and sticks to pressure the authoritarian regimes into adopting more liberal reforms. It should also be noted that democratic powers have to consider their domestic public, which makes them choose their fights carefully. In the words of De Mesquita et al. (2003, p. 225), they "only engage in fights they anticipate winning". This explains why Western countries have relatively strong bargaining power with Vietnam (against which they are in a winning position), but do not have similar leverage in dealing with China (against which they do not have a certain probability of winning).

The Nested Game Analysis

In the games described below, each number represents the priority order of the players (1>2>3>4) instead of an exact payoff value. The outcome depends on the combination of choices made by the players as an ordered pair (x, y). Each player aims to obtain the greatest return, which is to have an optimized x or y in each game. The interaction between two players produces a Nash-equilibrium outcome in which each player's strategy is the best response to that of the other. However, players participate in multiple arenas that are nested within each other. Consequently, a player's specific choice might appear irrational in one sub-game but will be optimal in the nested game's final outcome.

Game 1: The Regime and the Population

In the external accountability game, the regime can either become more accountable or maintain the status quo; the population can apply either strong or weak pressure for more accountability.

The game has three stages, each with different payoff expectations, which are as follows: the first stage of authoritarian stability (late 1970s to early 1980s); the second stage of authoritarian crisis (late 1980s to early 1990s), and the third stage of authoritarian consolidation (from the early 1990s to the present). The first stage refers to the period when both regimes found stable (although temporary) conditions of domestic and external accountability after years of chaos. In the second stage, both regimes reached a critical juncture where existential crises unfolded. The "breaking points" were the Tiananmen incident in China in 1989 and the socio-economic crisis preceding the 6th Party Congress in Vietnam in 1986. In the third stage, the two regimes recovered from the crises and consolidated their power.

TABLE 11.1
Three Stages of Political Accountability
Development in Vietnam and China

	Stability	Authoritarian crisis	Consolidation
Vietnam	1976–85	1986–89	1990 to present
China	1976–85	1986–89	1990 to present

Note: One could argue that the entire period from 1976 to 1989 can be considered a period of crisis for Vietnam. This is certainly true if we consider the country's dismal economic and social performances. But from the perspective of state-society relations the legitimacy crisis can be seen to begin around the mid-1980s. On the periodization of Vietnam's reform process, see Chapter 1 of this volume.

Stage 1: Authoritarian Stability – The Baseline Model

In this stage, the regime's monopolistic power has already been consolidated, which means it does not face the chaotic and fragile period of an early dictatorship (Geddes, Frantz and Wright 2018), and either no existential crises have arrived or, if they have, they have been temporarily put under control.

After the death of Mao Zedong, the subsequent purge of the Gang of Four and the ouster of the then CCP chief Hua Guofeng, Deng Xiaoping and his supporters quickly consolidated power and by 1978 they possessed the essential political capital to launch the "Open door" policy (Shirk 1993; Baum 1994). The 1979 war against Vietnam helped Deng reassert control over the military and establish himself as the paramount leader (Zhang 2010).

In Vietnam, the turbulent five years after the Vietnam War—which saw the Cambodian invasion and the 1979 war with China—devastated its already shattered economy and isolated the country from the world. But external threats helped sustain the regime's legitimacy as the nation's protector. In addition, the million-strong police force and the 2.6 million members of the armed forces—accounting at the time for up 47 per cent of the country's budget expenditure–prevented any possibility of an uprising (Vo 1990). Similar to how events transpired for Deng in China, Le Duan amassed unrivalled power within the VCP after the death of Ho Chi Minh in 1969 (Huy Duc 2012).

The Regime's Payoff Order

The first and second preferences for both regimes were to keep low accountability (1;3), and to allow accountability (2;2) without popular demand. The latter is known as the "controlled opening" and can be seen in several authoritarian regimes in Latin America and Southern Europe (O'Donnell, Schmitter and Whitehead 1986). In this case, the regime faced some risk from being more politically open but had a positional advantage to dictate the country's path of development. Under pressure from the population, the second-worst outcome (3;4) was to maintain the status quo, which led to greater repression and nurtured underlying tensions for future discontent. The worst outcome was to allow accountability under pressure. In this case, the regime would be in a reactive position for any reform agenda and thus risked being overthrown by the population.

The Population's Payoff Order

Prior to market reforms, the populations in both countries were tightly controlled. The household registration systems (*hukou* in China, and *hộ khẩu* in Vietnam) severely restricted domestic movements, making it nearly impossible to organize any kind of collective action. The rationing system of essential goods provided an efficient tool to control the population. Strong repressive capacity—including both the security and military forces—also suppressed any potential mass uprisings. Furthermore, hostile relations with the West during this period prevented any meaningful support for pro-democracy movements. Consequently, the populations under both regimes prior to reforms were fragmented and had little chance of raising the kind of collective action that might threaten regime survival. A Vietnamese minister commenting on the frustrating situation for the masses in 1980 on account of the economic mismanagement said that "in another country, the government would have changed" (Womack 1987, p. 503).

The population also had two choices: they could apply strong pressure for accountability or accept the status quo. In choosing the former, the population would have had the best outcome if the regime acquiesced. But they would risk receiving the worst outcome if the regime refused.

Outcome

At this time, both regimes had a dominant strategy to maintain the status quo. The outcome of the game, as a result, was the lower-right cell (1;3). The preference of both players is contextual. The historical contexts provided the Vietnamese and Chinese regimes leverage to maintain the status quo in terms of political control. This choice was also sensible because, after years of turmoil, both regimes preferred stability to moving into the uncertain terrain of political reform. The populations—in addition to their fragmentation

Table 11.2
External Accountability in Stable
Authoritarian Regimes – Priority Order

		Population	
		Strong pressure for accountablity	Weak pressure for accountablity
Regime	Reform	4;1	2;2
	Do not reform	3;4	1;3

Priority order: 1>2>3>4.

and powerlessness—had been indoctrinated with the ruling ideology for decades and lacked guiding ideas for their demands. The rapid changes in Vietnam and China in the early 1980s, however, had a huge impact on both players, and thus changed their preferences.

Stage 2: Authoritarian Crisis

The rise of Deng Xiaoping to supremacy was accompanied by a brief period of limited liberalization, including the rehabilitation of millions of intellectuals, a more tolerant view on cultural products and a general relaxation of control over society. In a much-cited speech delivered to the Political Bureau of the Central Committee on 18 August 1980, Deng noted the mission to "practise people's democracy to the full" as one of three main objectives of the modernization process (Deng 1984). Activists from the Democracy Movement could compete in a grass-roots election, where they stimulated political debate and even won in some local areas (Nathan 1986, pp. 193–223). This period is regarded as the second blooming of "the Hundred Flowers", during which different segments of the population were able to express their opinions more freely. One scholar noted that during this time the Chinese "enjoyed much greater access to information from and about the outside world than at any period since 1949" (Huan 1986, p. 8). Meanwhile, after a promising start, the economic reforms were not as rosy as had been expected. The regime faced periodic economic crises in the 1980s, and by the end of that decade the economic situation had become much worse. Frustrated with economic stagnation and delayed political reforms, there were occasional demonstrations across China in the period 1985–87. Most notably, more than fifty thousand protesters took to the streets of Shanghai in mid-December 1986, sending shock waves to the core of the leadership (Meisner 1996, p. 362). By the time the democracy movement intensified in 1989, the pressure for greater accountability was already immense.

In Vietnam, the VCP realized the disastrousness of its economic mismanagement and attempted to reform the economy in late 1979. The subsequent success of economic liberalization proved, however, to be short-lived and the economy stagnated by the mid-1980s. The failure of the price-wage-currency reforms of 1985—which caused the inflation rate to shoot up to 700 per cent in 1986—caused further deterioration in the country's situation (Harvie and Hoa 1997). Despite being an agricultural country, Vietnam failed to have food self-sufficiency and had to depend on food imports to feed its population (Dang Phong 2008). Vietnam became increasingly dependent on foreign aid, which made circumstances more difficult on account of the unfolding crisis within the Soviet Union (Horn 1987). In 1985, Vietnamese prime minister Pham Van Dong admitted that the country's per capita national income had not increased much since 1976 (Vo 1990, p. 160). The official political report of the 6th Congress admitted that the ongoing malaise "significantly reduces the faith among the people in the party's leadership" and that the party has "failed to stabilize the socio-economic situations as well as the people's living conditions" (Vietnam Communist Party 1986). As such, both regimes faced existential crises at the end of the 1980s. Maintaining the status quo had become costlier, while the population's preference for payoff orders had changed.

The Regime's Payoff Order

The preference for payoff order of the regimes had not changed from the first stage. As economic reforms stagnated, both the VCP and CCP preferred to have less bottom-up pressure. In addition, the internal accountability game in both countries at this stage—with the omnipresence of supreme leaders Deng Xiaoping and Le Duan—produced an outcome of low accountability equilibrium (see Game 2 for details). As such, although the stakes were high, their formidable repressive capacity, relatively unified internal stance and a lack of credible external threats convinced both regimes to stay firm in their hard-line approach.

In the various internal documents of the VCP from 1979 to 1986, keeping "social and political stability" was emphasized as one of its most important tasks. For example, in the VCP's tenth plenum in 1986, just months before the 6th Party Congress, the Central Committee concluded that the next five-year plan should "fundamentally stabilize the social and economic situations, of which the most important are to stabilize and make progress in economic production; stabilize the market, price, finance and monetary circulation; and stabilize and improve the living conditions of the working class" (Vietnam Communist Party 2006, p. 144).

In China, the regime began clamping down on the democracy movement a few months after Deng Xiaoping formally took power in 1979 (Meisner 1996). In his remarks at the sixth plenum of the CCP in 1986, Deng admitted that there was "a trend of thought ... in favour of liberalization" among the young population, and that if no action had been taken "it would have undermined our political stability and unity" (Deng 1994, pp. 123–24).

The Population's Payoff Order

It is important to note that both the VCP and CCP in the early 1980s wanted to carry out economic modernization without political reforms—or, in the words of Barrington Moore, "conservative modernization" (Moore 1993). This explains the rationale of keeping low accountability while pushing for economic reforms in both countries. The unexpected social results of the market reform, however, gradually dismantled the existing structure of the communist societies in both Vietnam and China. The egalitarian principle was set aside for the motto of "someone must get rich first"; there were sharp increases in income inequality, widespread corruption fuelled the appearance of the "bureaucratic class", the de-collectivization of the rural economy created an army of farmers flocking to urban areas in search of jobs and markets (Zweig 1997), and liberal ideas equipped the population—particularly the youth and intelligentsia—with ideological weapons in their negotiations with the state. Under the new circumstance, the payoff order of the population changed.

The first and second preferences of the population were similar to those in the first stage; both saw the regime carry out reforms with either strong pressure from the population (1) or with weak pressure from them (2). But the payoff order of the third and fourth preferences shifted. The population was more willing to take risks to put forward their demands as their living standards had deteriorated significantly. In Vietnam, before the market reform policy was officially announced in 1986, the risk of famine was visible (Vo 1990).

Table 11.3
External Accountability in Authoritarian
Regimes in Crisis – Priority Order

		Population	
		Strong pressure for accountablity	Weak pressure for accountablity
Regime	Reform	4;1	2;2
	Do not reform	3;3	1;4

Priority order: 1>2>3>4.

Outcome

While the regime preferred strictly to keep low accountability, the population had now shifted their preference to high accountability. Consequently, we have the most likely outcome of 3;3. In this scenario the ruling powers have maintained their positions but face greater risks of mass uprisings in the future. In addition, in order to keep low accountability, further investments into repressive capacity were needed. The population faced the risk of being repressed but pressed for change in the hope of changing the status quo.

Stage 3: Authoritarian Consolidation

The outcome of the game in Stage 2 is not sustainable as it would entail increasing the levels of repression and thereby adding fuel to the fire of future uprisings.

In China, social tensions ran high in the late 1980s. Economic conditions continued to worsen and inflation reached a point where the CCP admitted "the masses cannot bear it, enterprises cannot bear it, and the country cannot bear it" (Chinese Communist Party 2011, p. 257). Social discontent translated into widespread protests across the country. They first started in Beijing and then broke out in Shanghai, Xian, Nanjing and other big municipalities (Ash 1989). In a rare study of public opinions of working urban residents in China just three months before the Tiananmen incident, Zhu and Rosen proposed that attitude towards reform was the strongest predictor of dissatisfaction, and thus the 1989 pro-democracy protesters were concerned about the direction the country was heading under the CCP (Zhu and Rosen 1993).

In Vietnam, there were far fewer cases of outright social unrest during the same period. The biggest known incident was a mass protest of more than three hundred farmers in Ho Chi Minh City in 1988. A small student protest in Hanoi in June 1989 (coinciding with the Tiananmen protest in Beijing) was quickly resolved as the authorities made concessions to the protesters by giving larger stipends and guaranteeing better living conditions (Cima 1990). In total, there were thirteen recorded student mass protests nationwide by the summer of 1989 (Huy Duc 2012). The atmosphere in the country, however, was no less precarious for the VCP, particularly as its social and economic problems persisted after 1986 (Duiker 1989; Schellhorn 1992).

At this stage, the regimes in both Vietnam and China had two choices: either accommodate the dissatisfied population or implement repressive actions to stifle the risk of mass uprisings. And it was at this juncture that the preferences of the two diverged.

The Regime's Payoff Order

In Vietnam, as the needs for reform increased, having higher accountability was preferred. The regime already faced too many serious problems—from its quagmire in Cambodia, the lingering standoff with China over its northern border, the severe economic and food crises, and decreasing aid from the Soviet Union—to be able to allocate more resources into repressing dissent. Furthermore, as the market reforms stagnated, the party needed popular support rather than risk further alienation from the country's citizens.

It is important to note that the regime did not automatically have a unified response to the calls from the population. The response also depended on how the internal accountability game played out. At the beginning of the reform era, the dynamics of Vietnamese politics were similar to those of China, with the balance of power tilting towards a supreme leader—Le Duan. Duan was known to be a follower of the Soviet Union's conservative economic model and he hesitated to carry out market reforms (Vu 2016). His health, however, had deteriorated by the mid-1980s and he died just months before the historic 6th Congress started. This changed the power balance within the VCP: while the "old guard" conservatives still maintained influence, the "reformist" faction of younger and more open-minded leaders was gaining ground. At the 6th Congress, Nguyen Van Linh, who had been ejected from the Politburo six years previously—presumably by Le Duan (Huy Duc 2012)—was elected as the new general secretary. Linh was famous as a market promoter during his time working in Ho Chi Minh City.

The reformers were more tolerant of the demands from the population for accountability. More importantly, in order to push through market reforms, they needed to use popular support as another channel of pressure on the conservatives. This explains why Linh was calling for more openness right after being elected (called *Coi mo* policy in Vietnamese), in a move similar to the *Glasnost* of the Soviet Union. The period 1986—89 was considered the Vietnamese equivalent of the "hundred flowers", during which many cultural products critical of the government and party policies were published. On one occasion Linh even came to the conference of a national writers' association and encouraged those present to "untie yourself" (Huy Duc 2012, p. 10). He also wrote a regular column called *"Nhung viec can lam ngay"* (Things must be done immediately) in *Nhan dan* (People's Daily), the party's mouthpiece, urging the system to become more transparent. This dissatisfied some of his conservative comrades (Quang and Duong 2015).

Table 11.4
External Accountability in Reforming
Vietnam – Priority Order

		Population	
		Strong pressure for accountablity	Weak pressure for accountablity
Regime	Reform	3;1	1;2
	Do not reform	4;3	2;4

Priority order: 1>2>3>4.

Placing these developments into the game matrix, the best and second-best scenarios, respectively, for the regime were to reform (1;2) or to maintain the status quo (2;4) under weak pressure from the population. As the reformist faction took control, the regime believed being more open was inevitable because accountability and market reforms had to come together (Vietnam Communist Party 1986).

In China, the political landscape in the late 1980s was different. Deng Xiaoping started to warn about the risk of liberalization in the early 1980s (Deng 1984). Regarding internal politics, Deng remained the paramount leader without holding any formal position in either the state or the party. Accordingly, his views were decisive in determining the CCP's approach in dealing with the population. Furthermore, the relationship between the regime and the population in China was much more intense than in Vietnam. There was never any public gathering with more than a thousand people in Vietnamese cities in the 1980s, while public protests in China drew huge turnouts. The string of protests in early 1989 that led to the Tiananmen incident on 4 June are estimated to have involved more than a million protesters across more than a hundred Chinese cities (Zhu and Rosen 1993). Understandably, the perceived threat to regime survival from mass uprisings was greater among the Chinese ruling elites than their Vietnamese counterparts. After the Tiananmen incident, the hardliners cemented their positions and maintained their preference for low accountability because they perceived that a soft approach to popular demands would be fatal to regime survival (Shambaugh 1994). The outcome of the internal accountability game makes it difficult for any "reformist" faction to prevail in the manner they did in Vietnam.

Table 11.5
External Accountability in Reforming
China – Priority Order

		Population	
		Strong pressure for accountablity	Weak pressure for accountablity
Regime	Reform	4;1	2;2
	Do not reform	3;4	1;3

Priority order: 1>2>3>4.

Applying the above contexts to the game matrix, the best and second-best scenarios, respectively, for the regime would be to maintain the status quo (1;3) or to reform (2;2) without pressure from the population. With such pressure, the third-best scenario would be to keep to low accountability, while the worst result would be to be made accountable.

The Population's Payoff Order

The first and second preferences for the populations in both countries were similar to those in the previous stage, which were for the regimes to reform following either strong pressure from the population (1) or weak pressure (2). The third and fourth preferences, however, were different in each country depending on how the respective regimes responded to the popular demand in the critical junctures of Stage 2.

In Vietnam, the slight preference of the VCP for political reform opened the space for the population to demand accountability. Consequently, the third and fourth preferences of the population, respectively, were to exert strong pressure for accountability or, in the case of the regime insisting on maintaining the status quo, to apply weak pressure. In China, because the CCP was determined to keep low accountability, pushing for high accountability was the least desirable scenario (3;4).

Outcome

In Vietnam, the regime strictly preferred initiating political reforms, while the population's dominant strategy was to demand accountability. As such, the most likely outcome was 3;1. In this scenario the regime was at risk of mass uprisings, but it had the opportunity to carry out the reforms from a position of strength.

In China, the regime strictly preferred keeping low accountability, while the population did not have a dominant strategy. But, given the regime's choice, the most likely outcome was 1;3, wherein the regime maintains the status quo and there is only weak pressure from the population.

The outcomes of the external accountability game in Stage 3 show how the relationship between the regimes and the population has diverged in Vietnam and China during market reforms. This game alone, however, cannot explain why the payoff perception of regimes changed in the late 1980s. We need to look at other factors that influenced the decisions of the regimes—those of their internal politics and external pressure.

Game 2: The Internal Game between the Ruler and Selectorate

This game determines the characteristics of internal accountability between the ruler and the selectorate. Specifically, the ruler can either opt for a more personalized or a collective power-sharing regime (which makes them more accountable to the selectorate). The selectorate can choose either to demand for accountability or to accept the ruler's power personalization.

Both countries shared rather similar political dynamics in the first stage of market reforms. But the death of Le Duan changed the balance of power in favour of the reformists (Esterline 1987; Irvin 1995). The lack of a paramount leader shaped the internal accountability game in Vietnam differently from in China, where Deng Xiaoping wielded his influence over the system. For simplicity, the games analysed below start in Stage 3 (Authoritarian consolidation).

Vietnam

After the death of Le Duan, the Vietnamese political structure changed into a "diffused troika"—power was shared between the general secretary of the VCP, the prime minister and the president. The power of the chair of the National Assembly was also increasing (Dang Phong and Beresford 1998). The reform policy itself was driven by various internal players, from pro-market reformists and state sector leaders to southern liberals (Fforde and Vylder 1996). As argued by Thayer (1993, p. 179), rather than being controlled by top leaders, the Central Committee members represented diverse interests from different sectoral and regional constituencies.

During the 1990s, the regime continued the process of "de-Stalinization", whereby the VCP gradually delegated executive and legislative roles to the government and the National Assembly. Within the party, the Central Committee effectively became the most powerful organ, although the Politburo maintained its supreme position. When first elected as the general secretary in 1986, Nguyen Van Linh told the Central Committee that while previous general secretaries were a head taller than other Politburo members, "for now we are just a hair different" (Huy Duc 2012, p. 10).

The new arrangement allowed the Vietnamese selectorate to have strong bargaining power vis-à-vis the ruler. Consequently, they are more able to push for accountability with less risk of being punished. The ruler's first and second preferences, respectively, are to either personalize power (1;4) or to allow high accountability (2;3) without pressure from the selectorate.

The third preference for the ruler (3;1) would be to accept high accountability under pressure from the selectorate. In this scenario the regime moves towards a collective leadership system. The political developments in Vietnam since 1986 resemble this arrangement, as has been analysed above.

The worst outcome for the ruler (4;2) would be trying to personalize power while the selectorate kept pressuring for accountability. In this scenario the ruler risks being overthrown. There are two historical examples for this case. In 2001 the then general secretary Le Kha Phieu was not considered for re-election and forced to retire from both the Politburo and the Central Committee. Phieu was seen as a compromise candidate in 1997 but had grown too ambitious to the point he intended

Table 11.6
Payoff Perception in Internal Accountability
Game in Reformed Vietnam

		Selectorate	
		Strong pressure for accountablity	Weak pressure for accountablity
Ruler	Allow high accountability	3;1	2;3
	Personalize power	4;2	1;4

Priority order: 1>2>3>4.

to "unify" the post of general secretary and the presidency, spied on his Politburo counterparts and abolished the Advisory Committee, which was instrumental in choosing the leadership (Koh 2001; Abuza 2002). The same happened with Prime Minister Nguyen Tan Dung before the 12th Congress; he was not considered for the party chief post as the Central Committee worried about his overwhelming power within the system (Vuving 2017).

From Table 11.6 it can be seen that the dominant strategy for the selectorate is to push for high accountability. Given the power of the selectorate (the Central Committee) vis-à-vis the general secretary, the risk associated with challenging the ruler is reasonably small. This explains the surprisingly high level of intra-party democracy in Vietnam compared with China (Malesky, Abrami and Zheng 2011). Indeed, the collective leadership mechanism has been maintained for the most part after Doi Moi, despite several efforts from ambitious leaders (Abrami, Malesky and Zheng 2013). In contrast with the complete monopoly of the VCP over Vietnamese society, internal politics have become increasingly competitive from the grass-roots level to the top post. Certainly, this mechanism only works if the push for high accountability stays within party affairs rather than spilling over to society. The expulsion of Politburo member Tran Xuan Bach, who was accused of supporting political liberalization and pluralism, serves as an example for those who cross the line (Thayer 2010).

China

After the disastrous Cultural Revolution, the CCP under Deng Xiaoping initiated in 1978 the policy of "Reform and Opening-up". In terms of economic achievements, it was immediately successful (McMillan and Naughton 1992). But despite endeavours to restore the norms of "democratic centralism", and Deng Xiaoping's own efforts to tackle over-centralization, the intra-party democratic reforms that had been called for failed to materialize (White 1993). The Central Committee, which in other communist regimes is seen as the most powerful institution, was weak and submissive to top party leaders (Shirk 1993). The Chinese political system remained heavily centralized, with the Politburo Standing Committee (PBSC) as the most powerful policymaking organ (Unger 2016). In 1993, Deng's successor Jiang Zemin was elected state president, effectively unifying the three most important posts (CCP general secretary, chairman of the Central Military Commission, and state president). During the 1990s and 2000s, the process of institutionalization was enhanced, leading analysts to consider the China model as "resilient" (Nathan 2003). This

Table 11.7
Payoff Perception in Internal Accountability
Game in Reformed China

		Selectorate	
		Strong pressure for accountablity	Weak pressure for accountablity
Ruler	Allow high accountability	4;2	3;1
	Personalize power	2;4	1;3

Priority order: 1>2>3>4.

was proved in the smooth leadership transition to the fourth generation of leaders in 2002 and to a lesser extent the fifth generation in 2012. During the sixth transition, however, power has become increasingly concentrated with President Xi Jinping (Economy 2018; Shirk 2018).

Centralization of power significantly weakens the collective leadership arrangement and the role of the selectorate. Although the Central Committee is formally authorized to select the CCP leadership, Deng Xiaoping handpicked three out of four party chiefs after 1978 (Hu Yaobang, Zhao Ziyang and Jiang Zemin), while Hu Jintao was also personally endorsed by Deng (Ewing 2003). The influence of party elders over the leadership selection further undermines the Central Committee. As such, the internal politics in China is characterized by a strong leader and a weak selectorate.

The best case for the ruler (1;3) is to personalize power while the selectorate does not pressure for accountability. This is the third-best scenario for the selectorate: although they are much restricted in power, a low accountability system allows the regime to deal with risks from the population. The second-best case (2;4) for the ruler is to personalize power while the selectorate pushes for high accountability. As analysed above, the political developments in China after the Tiananmen incident resulted in heavy centralization, with a strong leader and a weak selectorate. Any challenge to the ruler would therefore be risky and the cost of failure high. The second-worst and worst scenarios for the ruler, respectively, would be to accept high accountability while the selectorate did not pressure for it (3;1) or to do so under pressure for it (4;2).

From Table 11.7 it can be seen that both the ruler and selectorate in China have dominant strategies; the former strictly prefers personalizing power, while the latter strictly prefers maintaining weak pressure for accountability. This is because the Chinese political system—particularly after the Tiananmen incident—tends to emphasize political stability, which requires the presence of a strong leader. The demand for order triumphs over the demand for higher accountability within the system. On several occasions Chinese leaders have even criticized the Vietnamese collective leadership system for being too radical (Abrami, Malesky and Zheng 2013).

Game 3: Foreign Pressure Game

Pressures from the West are among the major drivers of democratization in authoritarian regimes (Huntington 1993; Levitsky and Way 2010). Democratic powers, most notably the United States and the European Union, are incentivized to demand authoritarian regimes be more open and accountable and that they be moving towards democracy. Since the "third wave of democratization", there have been active efforts to democratize China and Vietnam. For example, the inclusion of Beijing and Hanoi within the global liberal order—such as their membership of the WTO and other international institutions—reflects the belief that greater integration will lead to faster democratization. The West can also use economic sanctions to pressure authoritarian regimes on specific issues. But such a strategy depends on specific circumstances. The sanctions against China in the wake of the Tiananmen incident only lasted a few years (Mann 1991) and did not do enough to push Beijing towards a more open democratic path (Liu 2019).

To theorize, foreign powers might choose to apply strong or weak pressure for democratic practices from the regime—which is external accountability. Such powers will be criticized by their domestic publics if they apply only weak pressure on autocracies, while strong pressure might be harmful to their relations with authoritarian regimes, and consequently entail economic loss.

This is obviously a very simplified illustration of the overall dynamics of this game because the amount of pressure levelled by the West depends on a wide range of things, including the particularity of cases, domestic politics, the international context, and so on. It aims, however, to reflect the tendency of the regimes when dealing with foreign pressure for accountability. In the case of Vietnam, threats of punishment might be seen as credible, while this is not the case for China.

Vietnam

As a middle power with a high dependence on trade, Hanoi is more susceptible to foreign pressure. The economic malaise of the pre-reform period, though mainly the result of mismanagement by the regime, was partly caused by international sanctions and the isolation imposed on Vietnam in the wake of its invasion of Cambodia in 1978. When the VCP announced the Doi Moi policy in 1986, exports were considered one of the three most important economic programmes (1986–91) (Vietnam Communist Party 1986). As the aid money from its main donor, the Soviet Union, was greatly reduced in the late 1980s and had totally vanished by the early 1990s (Dang Phong 2009), Vietnam had to integrate itself into the liberal world order. Consequently, the regime made a series of significant concessions, including its withdrawal from Cambodia in 1989, its policy reforms in the normalization process with the United States (Manyin 2005), and initiating the process to join such international institutions as the WTO, Asia-Pacific Economic Cooperation (APEC) and ASEAN.

As the economy continues to grow, the regime is becoming increasingly dependent on trade. Vietnam's trade volume reached 188 per cent of GDP in 2018, up from just 23 per cent in 1986 (World Bank 2019). This rate is among the highest in the world, which shows the remarkable degree of the country's economic openness. In the words of Levitsky and Way, the linkage between Vietnam and the West is high, and the latter has a decent level of leverage on the former (Levitsky and Way 2010, pp. 40–43). Translating this into the game matrix, the foreign pressure game on Vietnam during the reform era can be described in Table 11.8.

Table 11.8
Foreign Pressure Game in Reformed Vietnam

		Foreign powers	
		Strong pressure for accountablity	Weak pressure for accountablity
Regime	Reform	3;2	2;1
	Do not reform	4;3	1;4

Priority order: 1>2>3>4.

The regime can choose either to reform—or give specific political concessions to foreign demand—or to reject demands to do so. The foreign powers—or the West—can either apply strong or weak pressure for accountability.

The best case (1;4) for the regime is to reject demands for reform when foreign powers apply weak pressure. This implies Hanoi can maintain its economic benefits with the West without needing to accept any demands for accountability. The second-best choice (2;1) would be reforming under weak pressure from foreign influences. In this scenario the regime has more room to initiate its own reform plans with only little external pressure. As adopting higher accountability might imply a higher risk of mass uprisings, this scenario is less preferred. For the West, this is the best scenario because the regime democratizes without the need for intervention.

The third-best case (3;2) would be when the regime is put under strong pressure and consequently gives in. This makes the regime look weak to its domestic audience but helps it avoid economic consequences. A vivid example of this was when the Vietnamese government unofficially blocked access to Facebook in the early 2010s in an attempt to build its own social media ecology, in a similar way to how China had (Gray 2015). Under pressure from the United States and the European Union, however, this effort failed. By 2019 Vietnam had 58 million Facebook users and 68 million Google accounts—roughly equal to two-thirds of the country's population (Reuters 2019). A more recent example was the agreement by the regime to ratify Convention 87 of the International Labor Organization as a condition for signing the European Union–Vietnam Free Trade Agreement (EVFTA). Convention 87 would in effect allow the establishment of independent associations in Vietnam, which has not been possible since the VCP came to power.

The least preferred choice is 4;3, where the regime keeps low accountability despite strong pressure from foreign powers. This will incur sanctions and isolation, pushing the regime into the risk of spiralling economic crises. Performance-based legitimacy can hardly be achieved in such circumstances, forcing the regime to become increasingly dependent on repression for survival. This will negatively affect the outcomes of the internal accountability game (the risk of internal coups increases when power is concentrated with coercive force) and the external accountability game (tensions with the population increase with deteriorating economic conditions).

China

The nature of the game is different in China given its status as a global power. With its vast economic resources and domestic market, the regime will not be too vulnerable to external threats of sanctions. Enforcing sanctions on China would in fact also be costly for the West. This was the case with the short-lived sanctions on China following the Tiananmen incident, which lasted for just three years (Shambaugh 1994). When the United States threatened to revoke China's MFN (Most-favoured nation) status in the 1990s in an attempt to improve China's human rights situation, it only led to increasing hostility (Li and Drury 2004). Putting these contexts into the game matrix, the preferences of the two players will be as follows.

Beijing has a dominant strategy to keep low accountability, both without pressure from foreign powers (1;3) and with pressure from them (2;4). In the former, inaction by the West would be seen as failure by their domestic publics, but in exchange it would allow them to maintain economic links with China. In the latter, the economic size and bargaining power of China would allow the regime to endure sanctions. In addition, strong foreign pressure can also be used by the regime as propaganda to boost nationalism among the population and retain their monopolistic power. This was the case after the Tiananmen incident, where Beijing's leaders were defiant in protecting their actions, accusing the United States of "unwarranted interference in its domestic affairs" while also warning of "deleterious consequences to the Sino-American relationship" (Ang and Peksen 2007, p. 135). This is the worst scenario for foreign powers as they must pay the high cost of applying strong pressure and at the same time are unable to effect any favourable outcomes.

Table 11.9
Foreign Pressure Game in Reformed China

		Foreign powers	
		Strong pressure for accountablity	Weak pressure for accountablity
Regime	Reform	4;2	3;1
	Do not reform	2;4	1;3

Priority order: 1>2>3>4.

As analysed in Game 1, the Tiananmen incident made Beijing see any political reforms linked to democratization as being harmful to the regime's existence and leading the country to chaos (Shambaugh 1996). As such, all choices that involve political reforms would be undesirable. In contrast, such choices will be those preferred by the West. Given that Beijing's dominant strategy is to reject any such demands, the choice of the West will be to apply weak pressure, and thus the outcome of the game is 1;3.

The Nested Game and its Implications

In conclusion, the different outcomes of the three games played in China and Vietnam over the reform period—(1) the external accountability game, (2) internal accountability game, and (3) foreign pressure game—define the characteristics of accountability in their respective rules. For both regimes, Game 1 is the main arena. The most desired outcome for them in this game is to retain low accountability, meaning they would not bow to pressure from the population. While Game 2 defines the dynamics of internal politics, Game 3 relates to external accountability as both players (the regimes and the West) vie for opposing outcomes (the regimes prefer to keep low accountability, while foreign powers push for higher accountability). Borrowing from the design of Jesse, Heo and DeRouen, Jr. (2002, p. 413) for the South Korean democratization model, the nested game of accountability in Vietnam and China can be simplified as follows:

$$PO = kPO(1) + lPO(2) + (1-k-l)PO(3)$$

Where PO equals the total payoff to the regime, PO(1), PO(2) and PO(3) are the respective payoffs of Games 1, 2 and 3. The parameters k and l represent the preferences the regime puts on each game, and they sum to one. Each game provides different expected payoffs, and the rulers have differentiated priorities on the outcomes of the games. As such, in order to optimize the total PO, a regime might have sub-optimal outcomes for individual games. For the reform era in Vietnam and China, this is reflected in the external accountability game: while Vietnam tended to be more accommodating to popular demands, China insisted on retaining low external accountability.

Although authoritarian regimes prefer to keep their populations in check, their choices are affected both by internal politics and foreign pressure. In the case of Vietnam, the regime's choice here appears to be sub-optimal because it puts it at risk of regime change. This is because high accountability is associated with democratization:

the more political rights the citizenry has to hold the government accountable, the greater the chance they will press for change. As shown by Tuong Vu and Thuy Nguyen in Chapter 1 of this book, a rising civil society challenges the legitimacy of the VCP and makes the task of "renovation without changing political colours" much more challenging, even with huge investments in its repressive capacity. Although accountability might serve as a "safety valve" to reduce public pressure, it is hardly possible to find a threshold at which the level of accountability is "safe" for the regime. Most non-violent democratization, such as the Polish Solidarity movement, takes hold gradually. And when the rulers decide to act it is often too late. This explains why both the Vietnamese and Chinese regimes place a strong emphasis on preventing what they dub as "peaceful evolutions".

The choice made by the VCP can be justified, however, if the outcomes of the internal and foreign pressure games are considered. As a middle power that is highly trade-dependent, Vietnam's economic prosperity—and thus the regime's performance-based legitimacy—relies on its relationship with the West. And this has been particularly the case following the Cold War. Consequently, Hanoi needs to take foreign pressures seriously and must weigh the West's stance in implementing its domestic policies. In addition, as the result of a more balanced ruling coalition since the 1980s, the internal politics in Vietnam have become more democratic, with the principle of collective leadership being largely upheld. On the one hand, this has helped the "reformist" faction cement its position in the VCP's policymaking process. On the other, it indirectly pushes the regime towards addressing popular demands (Malesky, Abrami and Zheng 2011), which the regime does not always possess the capacity to deliver. This high internal accountability—with its tendency for the decentralization of power—also makes the VCP's anti-corruption efforts less effective than those of its Chinese counterpart, as shown in the excellent comparison by Duy Trinh (Chapter 12 of this book). These outcomes change the VCP's payoff order in Game 1 and moves it towards a high-accountability equilibrium.

China has adopted a different path. As a global power, Beijing tends to be less affected by foreign pressure. In some cases, pressure can even be counterproductive as the regime resorts to aggressive action as a defensive response. Such a scenario took place after the Tiananmen incident, as the event created fear among the Chinese leadership of the risk of foreign-backed uprisings (Shambaugh 1994). The 1989 incident represents a "critical juncture" that has shaped the CCP's emphasis on maintaining social and political stability. In addition, as a result of the tendency towards personalization that was analysed in Game 2, there is less room for any "reformist" group within the Chinese ruling coalition to challenge the conservative position. As such, keeping low external accountability is the main priority, which moves it towards a low-accountability equilibrium.

The above analysis is undoubtedly simplified and does not consider specific cases or incidents. For example, keeping low external accountability does not mean that China would not give any concessions at all to the population. For the past few decades, China has implemented a series of social and political reforms that give more rights to its citizens (Fewsmith 2013). In the same vein, although Vietnam tends to be more accommodating to the pressures of the West, it has categorically rejected demands that could directly threaten the VCP's monopoly on power. Instead, the nested game analysis aims to explain the general tendency that each regime has taken during the course of their development. This helps understand the logic of the decision-making process and the logic behind the configuration of state capacity in the regimes over the long term.

Note

1. Foreign influences certainly include pro-regime support such as the enormous amounts of aid from the Soviet Union and China that helped Hanoi survive the Vietnam War and the economic crisis that followed. To reduce the complexity of the analysis, however, this chapter assumes the effects of pro-regime support are internalized within the regime's capacity. By focusing on the pressure for democratization from the West, it is also easier to compare this chapter with other studies that examine the impact of Western links and leverage on regime change. For more on this issue, see Levitsky and Way (2010).

References

Abrami, R., E. Malesky, and Y. Zheng. 2013. "Vietnam through Chinese Eyes: Divergent Accountability in Single-Party Regimes". In *Why Communism Did Not Collapse: Understanding Authoritarian Regime Resilience in Asia and Europe*, edited by M. Dimitrov, pp. 237–76. New York: Cambridge University Press.

Abuza, Z. 2002. "The Lessons of Le Kha Phieu: Changing Rules in Vietnamese Politics". *Contemporary Southeast Asia* 24, no. 1: 121–45.

Ang, A., and D. Peksen. 2007. "When Do Economic Sanctions Work? Asymmetric Perceptions, Issue Salience, and Outcomes". *Political Research Quarterly* 60, no. 1: 135–45.

Ash, R. 1989. "Quarterly Chronicle and Documentation". *China Quarterly* 119: 666–734.

Baum, R. 1994. *Burying Mao: Chinese Politics in the Age of Deng Xiaoping*, rev. ed. Princeton University Press.

Chen, T.C. 2010. "China's Reaction to the Color Revolutions: Adaptive Authoritarianism in Full Swing". *Asian Perspective* 34, no. 2: 5–51.

Chinese Communist Party. 2011. 十三大以来重要文献选编(上) [Selections of important documents since the 13th National Congress (part 1)]. 中央文献出版社 [Central Literature Publishing House].

Cima, R.J. 1990. "Peasants and Regime in Vietnam: Perspectives on Transition". *Problems of Communism* 39, no. 6: 90–95.

Dang Phong. 2008. *Tư duy kinh tế Việt Nam, 1975–1989* [Vietnamese economic thinking, 1975–1989]. Hanoi: Knowledge Publishing House.

———. 2009. "'Phá Rào' Trong Kinh Tế Vào Đêm Trước Đổi Mới" ['Fence-breaking' in the pre-reform economy]. Hanoi: Knowledge Publishing House.

Dang Phong and M. Beresford. 1998. *Authority Relations and Economic Decision-Making in Vietnam: An Historical Perspective*. Copenhagen: NIAS.

De Mesquita, B.B., A. Smith, J.D. Morrow, and R.M. Siverson. 2003. *The Logic of Political Survival*. London: MIT press.

Deng, X. 1984. *Selected Works of Deng Xiaoping (1975–1982)*. Beijing: Foreign Languages Press.

———. 1994. *Selected Works of Deng Xiaoping – Volume III (1982–1992)*. Beijing: Foreign Languages Press.

Duc Trong. 2018. "Đoàn người quá khích tràn vào trụ sở UBND tỉnh Bình Thuận" [Agitated mob vandalizes Binh Thuan provincial headquarter]. *Tuoi Tre*.

Duiker, W. 1989. "Vietnam: A Revolution in Transition". *Southeast Asian Affairs 1989*, edited by Ng Chee Yuen, pp. 351–68. Singapore: Institute of Southeast Asian Studies.

Duong, N.B. 2020. "Nâng cao cảnh giác và kiên quyết đấu tranh làm thất bại âm mưu, hoạt động 'diễn biến hòa bình' và thúc đẩy 'tự diễn biến', 'tự chuyển hóa' của các thế lực thù địch" [Raising vigilance and determination to fight "peaceful evolution", "self-development", "self-transformation" of hostile forces]. *Vietnamese Communist Review*.

Economy, E. 2018. *The Third Revolution: Xi Jinping and the New Chinese State*. New York: Oxford University Press.

Esterline, J.H. 1987. "Vietnam in 1986: An Uncertain Tiger". *Asian Survey* 27, no. 1: 92–103.

Ewing, R.D. 2003. "Hu Jintao: The Making of a Chinese General Secretary". *China Quarterly* 173: 17–34.

Fewsmith, J. 2013. *The Logic and Limits of Political Reform in China*. New York: Cambridge University Press.

Fforde, A., and S.D. Vylder. 1996. *From Plan to Market: The Economic Transition in Vietnam*. Boulder, CO: Westview Press.

Geddes, B., E. Frantz, and J. Wright. 2018. "Autocratic Seizures of Power". In *How Dictatorships Work: Power, Personalization, and Collapse*, edited by B. Geddes, E. Frantz, and J. Wright, pp. 25–43. Cambridge: Cambridge University Press.

Gray, M. 2015. "Control and Dissent in Vietnam's Online World". *Tia Sang Vietnam Initiative.*

Harvie, C., and T.V. Hoa. 1997. *Vietnam's Reforms and Economic Growth.* London: Palgrave Macmillan.

Horn, R.C. 1987. *Alliance Politics between Comrades: The Dynamics of Soviet-Vietnamese Relations.* Santa Monica, CA: RAND Corporation.

Huan, G. 1986. "China's Open Door Policy, 1978–1984". *Journal of International Affairs* 39, no. 2: 1–18.

Huntington, S.P. 1993. *The Third Wave: Democratization in the late Twentieth Century.* Norman: University of Oklahoma Press.

Huy Duc. 2012. *Ben Thang Cuoc* [The winning side] (2 vols.). Boston: OsinBook.

Irvin, G. 1995. "Vietnam: Assessing the Achievements of Doi Moi". *Journal of Development Studies* 31, no. 5: 725–50.

Jesse, N.G., U. Heo, and K. DeRouen, Jr. 2002. "A Nested Game Approach to Political and Economic Liberalization in Democratizing States: The Case of South Korea". *International Studies Quarterly* 46, no. 3: 401–22.

Kennedy, R. 2010. "The Contradiction of Modernization: A Conditional Model of Endogenous Democratization". *Journal of Politics* 72, no. 3: 785–98.

Koh, D. 2001. "The Politics of a Divided Party and Parkinson's State in Vietnam". *Contemporary Southeast Asia* 23, no. 3: 533–51.

Levitsky, S., and L. Way. 2010. *Competitive Authoritarianism: Hybrid Regimes after the Cold War.* New York: Cambridge University Press.

Li, Y. 2019. "A Zero-Sum Game? Repression and Protest in China". *Government and Opposition* 54, no. 2: 309–35.

Li, Y., and A.C. Drury. 2004. "Threatening Sanctions When Engagement Would Be More Effective: Attaining Better Human Rights in China". *International Studies Perspectives* 5, no. 4: 378–94.

Liu, M. 2019. "30 Years after Tiananmen: How the West Still Gets China Wrong". *Foreign Policy*, 4 June 2019.

Malesky, E., R. Abrami, and Y. Zheng. 2011. "Institutions and Inequality in Single-Party Regimes: A Comparative Analysis of Vietnam and China". *Comparative Politics* 43, no. 4: 409–27.

Mann, J. 1991. "Many 1989 U.S. Sanctions on China Eased or Ended". *LA Times*, 30 June 1991.

Manyin, M.E. 2005. "The Vietnam-US Normalization Process". Washington, DC: Library of Congress.

McMillan, J., and B. Naughton. 1992. "How to Reform a Planned Economy: Lesson from China". *Oxford Review of Economic Policy* 8, no. 1: 130–43.

Meisner, M. 1996. *The Deng Xiaoping Era: An Inquiry into the Fate of Chinese Socialism 1978–1994.* New York: Hill and Wang.

Moore, B. 1993. *Social Origins of Dictatorship and Democracy.* Beacon Press.

Nathan, A. 2003. "Authoritarian Resilience". *Journal of Democracy* 14, no. 1: 6–17.

Nathan, A. J. 1986. *Chinese Democracy.* Berkeley: University of California Press.

O'Donnell, G., P.C. Schmitter, and L. Whitehead. 1986. *Transitions from Authoritarian Rule: Tentative Conclusions about Uncertain Democracies.* Baltimore: Johns Hopkins University Press.

Olson, M. 1971. *The Logic of Collective Action: Public Goods and the Theory of Groups*. Harvard University Press.

Quang, L.V., and N.X. Duong. 2015. "'Những việc cần làm ngay' – dấu ấn Nguyễn Văn Linh trong cuộc đấu tranh chống tiêu cực ['Things must be done immediately' – the influence of Nguyen Van Linh in fighting negativity]. *Lý luận Chính trị* [Political theory].

Reuters. 2019. "Vietnam's Social Media Crowd Swells with New Entrant to Take on Facebook, Google". Reuters, 17 September 2019.

Schellhorn, K.M. 1992. "Political and Economic Reforms in Vietnam". *Contemporary Southeast Asia* 14, no. 3: 231–43.

Shambaugh, D. 1994. "Peking's Foreign Policy Conundrum since Tiananmen: Peaceful Coexistence vs. Peaceful Evolution". In *Contemporary China and the Changing International Community*, edited by B.-J. Lin and J.T. Myers. South Carolina: University of South Carolina Press.

———. 1996. "Containment or Engagement of China? Calculating Beijing's Responses". *International Security* 21, no. 2: 180–209.

Shirk, S.L. 1993. *The Political Logic of Economic Reform in China*. Berkeley, University of California Press.

———. 2018. "China in Xi's 'New Era': The Return to Personalistic Rule". *Journal of Democracy* 29, no. 2: 22–36.

Svolik, M.W. 2012. *The Politics of Authoritarian Rule*. Cambridge: Cambridge University Press.

Thayer, C.A. 2010. "Political Legitimacy in Vietnam: Challenge and Response". *Politics & Policy* 38, no. 3: 423–44.

Tismaneanu, V. 1989. "Personal Power and Political Crisis in Romania". *Government and Opposition* 24, no. 2: 177–98.

Unger, J. 2016. *The Nature of Chinese Politics: From Mao to Jiang*. Armonk: Routledge.

Vietnam Communist Party. 1986. "Phương hướng, mục tiêu chủ yếu phát triển KT - XH trong 5 năm 1986–1990" [The main directions and targets of socio-economic development in the next five years 1986–1991].

———. 1986. "Báo cáo chính trị của BCHTW khóa V trình tại Đại hội đại biểu toàn quốc VI" [Political report of the 5th Central Committee presented in the 6th National Party Congress].

———. 2006. *Van kien Dang toan tap* [Compilations of the Vietnam Communist Party documents], vol. 47. Hanoi: National Political Publishing House.

Vo, N.T. 1990. *Vietnam's Economic Policy since 1975*. Singapore: Institute of Southeast Asian Studies.

Vu, Tuong. 2016. *Vietnam's Communist Revolution: The Power and Limits of Ideology*. New York: Cambridge University Press.

Vuving, A.L. 2017. "The 2016 Leadership Change in Vietnam and Its Long-Term Implications". *Southeast Asian Affairs 2017*, edited by Daljit Singh and Malcolm Cook, pp. 421–35. Singapore: ISEAS – Yusof Ishak Institute.

White, G. 1993. *Riding the Tiger: The Politics of Economic Reform in Post-Mao China*. Basingstoke: Macmillan.

Womack, B. 1987. "The Party and the People: Revolutionary and Postrevolutionary Politics in China and Vietnam". *World Politics* 39, no. 4: 479–507.

World Bank. 2019. World Bank data – Trade (per cent of GDP).

Zhang, X. 2010. "Deng Xiaoping and China's Decision to Go to War with Vietnam". *Journal of Cold War Studies* 12, no. 3: 3–29.

Zhu, J.-H., and S. Rosen. 1993. "From Discontent to Protest: Individual-Level Causes of the 1989 Pro-democracy Movement in China". *International Journal of Public Opinion Research* 5, no. 3: 234–49.

Zweig, D. 1997. Freeing China's Farmers: Rural Restructuring in the Reform Era. New York: Routledge.

Chapter 12

The Where and Why of Political Protection in Vietnam's Anti-Corruption Campaign

Duy Trinh

In November 2018, when general secretary of the Vietnamese Communist Party (CCP) Nguyen Phu Trong became the first leader of post-war Vietnam to hold simultaneous control of both party and state leadership positions, many could not resist the comparison between him and his counterpart Xi Jinping in China. Yet, years before opinion pieces started debating whether Trong is the new Xi,[1] parallels between them had already existed. They go back to the start of their anti-corruption campaigns—China's in 2012 and Vietnam's in 2016. In these campaigns, both leaders promised an unprecedented war against corruption that would leave no stone unturned. While Xi vowed to target "both the tigers and the flies" (*laohu cang ying yiqida*), Trong also declared that his campaign would leave "no restricted zone and no exception" (*khong co ngoai le, khong co vung cam*).

Fast forward to 2020. Four years after the start of Trong's campaign and eight years after the start of Xi's, to what extent have the two leaders delivered on their promises? Besides the unsurprising ovation in both countries' state media, the two campaigns have attracted as much praise as criticism from outside observers and experts. On one hand, the campaigns have been criticized as veiled excuses for political infighting—a popular sentiment among scholars and even within the party ranks (Thayer 2017; Zhu and Zhang 2017; Hutt 2020). More broadly, the criticisms echo a political science literature that casts doubt on the willingness and ability of authoritarian regimes to mount effective anti-corruption efforts. To this research body, the unwillingness of autocrats comes from the fact that not only can they use corruption rents to attract supporters (Geddes 1999; Bueno De Mesquita 2003), but they can also easily respond to corruption-related discontent with censorship or repression (Wintrobe 1998). The lack of capacity, on the other hand, is rooted in the absence of the democratic checks and balances that enable deterrence, detection and disciplining of corrupt acts such as free media, electoral accountability or civil society (Rose-Ackerman 1996, 1999; Johnston 2005).

From another perspective, a sizable strand of the literature has pointed to the role of authoritarian accountability institutions. In contrast with the aforementioned scepticism, this strand argues that, despite serving a different function from their democratic counterparts, these institutions are nevertheless able to help regimes oversee their bureaucratic agents and provide credible commitment to deter corrupt activities (Malesky and Schuler 2013; Brancati 2014). Specific arguments along this line have found their way into the discussion of Vietnam's and China's ongoing anti-corruption campaigns, with some scholars urging others to take them seriously as not only *sincere* (e.g., Manion 2016) but also *effective* attempts at curbing corruption (e.g., Carothers 2020).

With the campaigns still ongoing, any debate on their effectiveness is bound to be premature. Results of corruption-control efforts often take years to materialize: early gains may be lost, while long-term improvements cannot be immediately observed. This chapter is therefore dedicated instead to a discussion on the sincerity of Vietnam's and China's anti-corruption campaigns, with specific focus on the former campaign. To examine the extent to which they adhere to their original rhetoric of "leaving no restricted zone", I engage in a comparative analysis of the current results of the campaigns as well as of the core institutions that produce them; most notably, the Central Committees for Disciplinary Inspections (CCDI). Through this comparison, I argue that, while both campaigns have made similar and equally impressive progress in investigating the high-ranking "tigers", the breadth of the campaigns, especially when it comes to investigating the rank-and-files in the regimes, remains uneven. Vietnam in particular appears to have a more limited campaign with fewer investigations compared to China's. Through a quantitative model that considers cross-provincial variations in socio-economic performance, administrative capacity and latent corruption level, I then trace Vietnam's lower disciplinary records to political protection along factional lines by local elites. Between 2016 and 2018, provinces whose party secretaries have informal ties with the general secretary experienced much fewer inspections and investigations compared with similar provinces without such ties. To explain why this pattern of political protection exists in Vietnam, and why its effect manifests specifically in depression of the investigation rate, I then point to a key institutional explanation: reforms to the accountability structure of the CCDI, which took place in China but not in Vietnam. Specifically, whereas institutional reforms that are part of China's anti-corruption campaign place a strong emphasis on strengthening the CCDI's independence from executive, judiciary and local party organs, Vietnam's reformers prioritized other institutional problems and allowed their CCDI to remain vulnerable to political interference, especially from local party elites.

The arguments made in this chapter, while preliminary, renew the discussion on the motivations and potential impacts of Vietnam's anti-corruption campaign. Whereas existing works attempt to characterize the campaign's motives in a black-and-white fashion as either sincere or politicized, the evidence here suggests a more nuanced picture—one of a sincere anti-corruption effort from the top leadership undermined by political interference at local levels. From a policy perspective, the chapter points to the need for more radical reforms to the VCP's disciplinary system, especially with respect to the complex local network of accountability and dependence between the party, the state and the disciplinary organs. More generally, the chapter urges scholars to look deeper than news headlines and national statistics in their attempts to analyse political behaviours in Vietnam, and, more broadly speaking, in other authoritarian regimes as well. Finally, it demonstrates that even political puzzles that seemingly belong to the realm of elite politics can benefit from greater attention to the micro-foundations—in other words, the incentives and constraints of local actors, who turn lofty rhetoric and policies into concrete actions and outcomes.

Vietnam and China's Anti-Corruption Regimes: Structural and Institutional Similarities

When it comes to political regimes, few in the world are as comparable to one another as Vietnam and China. The two neighbours share more than just geographic location and a common border. Historically, pre-modern Vietnam and China intertwined, and the former moved back and forth in status, but rarely straying too far outside the Sinosphere.

In the modern era, both countries witnessed the rise of communism in the early 1920s with the founding of the Chinese Communist Party (CCP) in 1921 and the Thanh Nien, predecessor to the VCP, in 1925. Interestingly, both parties traced their formation to southern China (Shanghai and Guangzhou, respectively). The two communist parties then rose to power through a series of revolutionary wars: the CCP battled the Japanese and then the Nationalist Party during the Sino-Japanese War and the Chinese Civil War, while the VCP fought off the French, followed by the South Vietnamese government, backed by the United States, during the two Indochina Wars.

After the two communist parties took over China and Vietnam, both regimes attempted to reorganize and revitalize their economies through central planning, before economic stagnation forced them to embark on marketization reforms in the 1970s and 1980s. The two reforms followed a similar recipe that involved, sequentially, the dismantling of agricultural collectives and state-owned enterprises, the acceptance of private enterprises, and a move towards an export-oriented economy (Kerkvliet, Chan and Unger 1998). These reforms ultimately allowed the regimes to survive the collapse of communism in the 1990s. With the survival of their regimes, however, Vietnam and China also managed to avoid the political liberalization that took place elsewhere in the post-communist European states. The two regimes today are still under firm control of the communist parties, whose track records on political freedom and human rights issues have frequently been a topic of criticism. For example, the 2019 World Report by Human Rights Watch denounces China as "an exporter of human rights violations" and Vietnam's human rights record as "appalling".

The parallels between Vietnam and China do not stop at their political system. When it comes to specific organs for corruption control, Vietnam and China are also very similar. Altogether, three main disciplinary bodies supervise and investigate public sector corruption in each country. First, bureaucrats, like any citizen, are subject to legal sanction by the judicial system, which includes the People's Procuratorate and the People's Court. In both countries the Criminal Code also defines a wide range of violations applicable specifically to government officials, such as treason, espionage or dereliction of duty, as well as specific provisions for abuse-of-power and corruption violations. Second, each executive branch has a dedicated organ for the inspection of government officials: the Government Inspectorate in Vietnam, and the Ministry of Supervision in China. Both organs are tasked with policymaking and policy consultation with the head of government and other government offices in public administration and corruption control. In addition, they handle accusations and investigate violations related to public official malfeasance and corruption. But neither organ holds the power to issue sanction—they can only forward cases to other "relevant offices."[2]

In practice, the head of all ministry-level agencies and of the People's Procuratorate and People's Court at all levels are required to be Communist Party members. Furthermore, every governmental organ contains an embedded party committee that assumes de facto control of the organ. As a result, political sanctions are ultimately orchestrated through party apparatuses. Party disciplinary actions, while formally following a separate procedure, take precedence over legal and government sanctions.[3] They are coordinated at the very top by the *Uy ban Kiem tra Trung uong* in Vietnam and *Zhongyang Jilu Jiancha Weiyuanhui* in China—both translatable to Central Commission for Discipline Inspection (CCDI).

There are few major differences in the organizational structure of the Vietnamese and Chinese CCDI. As typical of democratic centralist principles, every five years, delegates at the National Party Congress elect a Central Committee from among its members. The Central Committee in turn has the power to decide the CCDI's membership. To exercise its power, it either elects members of the CCDI directly (Vietnam) or approves the members that the National Party Congress has elected (China). These members then elect their own leader, who has traditionally been a member of the party's highest body, the Politburo in Vietnam (since 1991) and the Politburo Standing Committee in China (since 1978).[4] The newly formed CCDI is then expected to serve a five-year term until the next National Party Congress.

In addition to the central office, the CCDIs also oversee a hierarchy of local inspection commissions (ICs). In both China and Vietnam, every non-primary-level party committee—including regional committees from province down to district (Vietnam) or county level (China), as well as committees at ministries, government-affiliated associations and state-owned enterprises—is required to elect its own IC. Each IC's membership is jointly decided by its party committee as well as by the IC directly above it in administrative level. The director of an IC, in turn, is required to be a standing member of the respective party committee.

Altogether, the national CCDI offices and their local ICs share responsibility for monitoring party discipline and investigating violations. These violations are broadly defined to include not only ideological infractions but also moral and lifestyle offences, "violations of democratic centralism and government socio-economic policies", as well as other offences already governed by the Criminal Code (Wedeman 2004; Vietnam Communist Party 2017). Both party codes also specifically place a range of corruption-related offences, such as nepotism, and appropriation and misuse of authority, within the CCDI's jurisdiction. The central office is directly responsible for the supervision and investigation of central-level officials. Local ICs, on the other hand, are responsible for members of party organizations that rank equal to or immediately below them (Vietnam Communist Party 2009, chapter VII, article 32; Communist Party of China 2012, chapter VIII).[5] Whether at the local or central level, however, neither the Vietnamese nor Chinese CCDI possesses the power to independently sanction any case it investigates. When an IC in China discovers a disciplinary violation, it must secure approval from the party committee at the corresponding level before beginning a formal investigation. Afterwards, they must also report to the same committee on "the results of their handling of cases of special importance or complexity" (Communist Party of China 2012, chapter VIII, article 44).[6]

Similarly, in Vietnam an IC can issue lesser sanctions (warnings and reprimands) against party cadres in organs immediately below it. For major sanctions against these cadres, or for any sanction against cadres in a party organ at a corresponding level, the IC must refer the case to the party committee at the corresponding level and to the upper-level IC for the final verdict. The national office of Vietnamese CCDI can decide on lesser sanctions against central party cadres but not against members of the Central Committee, Politburo or Secretariat. Rather, sanctions against those are within the purview of the Politburo and ultimately the Central Committee.

Anti-corruption Campaigns in China and Vietnam: Similarities and Divergences

In Vietnam, as much as in China, the anti-corruption campaign started with intense rhetoric. In China, the official start date of the campaign can be traced to Xi Jinping's inauguration speech of 15 November 2012 where he explicitly identified corruption as the first among the problems the party would need to "make every effort to solve". Subsequently, on his first day in office, Xi doubled down on the message by vowing to "kill all tigers and flies alike"—a slogan that has since become emblematic of the entire campaign (Branigan 2013). Around the same time, the Vietnamese leadership also made initial preparations for their own campaign. In February 2013, General Secretary Nguyen Phu Trong secured passage through the Politburo of Decision No. 162-QD/TW on the Creation of the Central Anti-Corruption Steering Committee. This decision, combined with an earlier Revised Anti-corruption Law that the National Assembly had passed three months prior,[7] transferred anti-corruption authority from the jurisdiction of the prime minister to that of the Politburo and gave Trong its directorship. The actual campaign did not officially start, however, until the VCP's 12th National Party Congress, which was held in January 2016. Similar to Xi's inauguration speech, the document from the 12th National Party Congress also lists corruption as one of the four threats facing the party.[8] And not being one to shy from metaphors, the incumbent Trong also immortalized his commitment to fighting corruption with an equally catchy slogan. On 31 July 2017, in a televised meeting with the CCDI, he warned that "once the [anti-corruption] furnace has heated up, even wet firewood would burn" (Vietnamnet 2018).

The campaigns soon began to make headlines for more reasons than rhetoric. In stark contrast to the many campaigns that preceeded them, they quickly resulted in several high-profile investigations of "tigers" in the regimes. The first salvo in China occurred in the latter half of 2013, and was directed at Zhou Yongkang, a former Politburo Standing Committee member, along with his network of associates in the China National Petroleum Corporation, Sichuan province (where he served as Party Secretary) and in the national security organ. Over the next five years a total of thirty-five full and alternate members of the Central Committee had been disciplined. Vietnam's track record was no less extensive: In a five-year period from 2016 to the end of 2020 alone, the campaign has disciplined twenty-seven current and former Central Committee members in addition to four current or former members of the Politburo (VnExpress 2020).

These campaigns by Vietnam and China have so far delivered on their promises to target the "tigers" and the "wet firewood". But once we begin to look beyond the news headlines to examine the breadth of the campaigns—specifically, the extent they target the rank and files across the country—a contrast begins to emerge. A Vietnamese CCDI report reveals that by the end of 2018 it had managed to investigate and punish a total of 35,000 party

FIGURE 12.1
CCP Membership and Disciplined Cadres, 2012–18

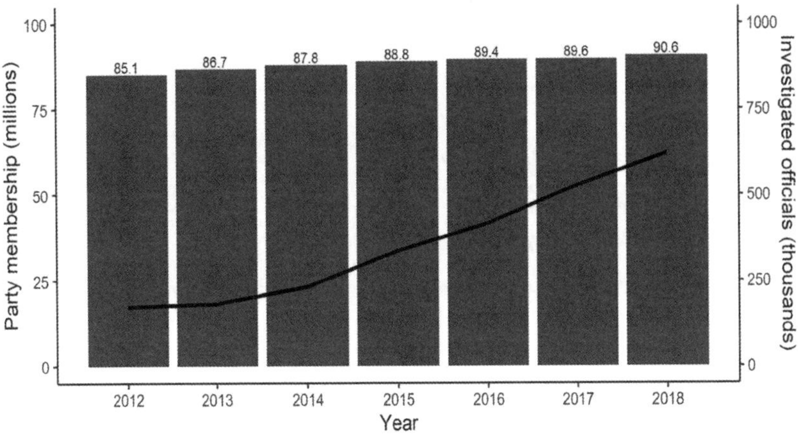

Source: CGTN, Xinhua, CCP Department of Organization.

cadres (Vietnamnet 2018). Based on the VCP's membership of a little more than 5.2 million members, this translates to a ratio of around 6.7 party members investigated per 1,000. The number is celebrated as "unprecedented" in the Vietnamese press, and is indeed much higher than any anti-corruption campaign achieved before it (Carothers 2020). Yet, within the same time period, the Chinese CCDI has investigated and disciplined many more officials, measured both in terms of raw figures and as a share of total party membership. From 2016 to 2018, a total of 1.56 million party cadres have been disciplined, or more than 17 party members for every 1,000 (Xinhua 2019; Yiwei 2020). This is more than three times the Vietnamese figures. Even if one uses the first three years of the CCP's anti-corruption campaign as the frame of reference, the ratio still comes down to 8.4 members investigated per 1,000. Between 2012 and 2014, the CCDI investigated 750,000 party cadres out of a membership of 88.8 million (see Figure 12.1).

This comparison in the number of investigations, if it had been made between any two other countries, would be likened to comparing apples to oranges. But when it comes to Vietnam and China, their striking similarities in geography, history, economics, politics and culture makes it reasonable to raise doubts about the sincerity of the Vietnamese anti-corruption campaign, at least relative to its Chinese counterpart. Further fuelling this suspicion is the fact that in terms

FIGURE 12.2
Vietnam and China's Corruption Perceptions Index score, 2012–18

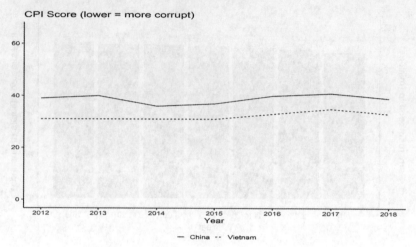

Source: Transparency International.

of international rankings, while Vietnam and China are much more similar to each other than to other countries, the former has typically been ranked as more corrupt than the latter. In 2016, for example, the Corruptions Perception Index gave Vietnam a score of 33 and ranked it as the 117th least corrupt country, while China was ranked 87th with a score of 39 (see Figure 12.2). As a result, one would expect two equally sincere anti-corruption campaigns to reveal more corrupt cases in Vietnam than in China, and not, as we have observed, the other way around.

In this chapter, I bring in quantitative evidence using novel data from the Vietnamese CCDI itself to argue that, among the many possible reasons for the relatively low breadth of Vietnam's anti-corruption campaign, political protection might play quite an influential role. In this case, protection manifests in the lower rate of investigations and disciplinary sanctions in provinces whose leaders have informal connections with the incumbent regime leader. Whether by active intervention from the top or by a failure to investigate and prosecute from the bottom, these provinces—after considering variations in socio-economic performance, government capacity and latent level of corruption—saw fewer investigations; and investigations also resulted in fewer punishments compared with provinces without such ties.

Identifying the Missing Cases

Data

Anti-corruption Investigations

To examine where and how political protection occurs during Vietnam's anti-corruption campaign, I collected an original dataset of the Vietnamese CCDI's disciplinary activities. I developed a web scraper to retrieve all the official releases ever published on the website of the CCDI (ubkttw.vn) since it first went online in June 2016. The scraper yielded 1,428 official releases between June 2016 and October 2018. These releases report on various activities conducted by both the central office and the local ICs. These activities, while wide ranging, can be broadly organized into four categories: (1) reports of internal meetings by CCDI officials and meetings with the press and delegates from other party and state organs ("Meetings"); (2) reports of routine supervisory and inspection activities ("Routine inspections"); (3) reports of training workshops and study tours conducted for and by CCDI officials ("Training workshops"); and (4), most importantly, reports of the results of investigation and of disciplinary action taken against party cadres or party cells ("Disciplinary action").

The articles of the last category, which account for 477 out of 1,428 articles in my dataset, are particularly useful for the empirical analysis in this chapter. They follow a set formula and contain the same basic information: the date of the meeting where the sanction decision was made; the specific IC that made the decision; the name(s) and current position(s) of the investigated individual(s); the location and other details of their disciplinary violations, including the party-designated level of seriousness, which ranges from "of little seriousness" (*it nghiem trong*) to "serious" (*nghiem trong*), "very serious" (*rat nghiem trong*) and "extremely serious" (*dac biet nghiem trong*); and finally, the level of punishments given, from reprimands (*khien trach*), to warnings (*canh cao*), dismissal (*cach chuc*) and expulsion (*khai tru*). Using this information, I then aggregated the count of investigations at the province level to identify the number of investigations each year between 2016 and 2018 in each of Vietnam's sixty-three provinces. This measure serves as the main outcome variable of my analysis.

Informal Ties

In addition to the disciplinary data, I also collected a range of biographical data of top officials in Vietnam. Specifically, I developed several web scrapers to extract information from the

Vietnamese-language Wikipedia and from the official websites of the VCP (www.dangcongsan.vn), the Vietnamese National Assembly (www.quochoi.vn) and various provincial-level party newspapers. This information allowed me to construct an original biographical dataset for all eighty-nine past and present Politburo members and for all the provincial party secretaries from the 10th to the 12th Party Congress (from 2006 to 2020).[9]

The record for each individual includes their name, gender, birthplace, religion and ethnicity. In addition, it includes their educational attainment and history as well as their year-by-year career trajectory in the party and government.

Similar to previous research on CCP factional networks (Meyer, Shih and Lee 2016; Keller 2016), I use the biographical data of VCP leaders and provincial party secretaries to derive a measure of informal connections. An investigated official is coded to have informal ties to the general secretary if the party secretary of the province in which the violation occurred is (1) born in the same province as General Secretary Nguyen Phu Trong, (2) had worked at the same ministerial-level unit with him for at least a year by 2016, or (3) went to the same university as the general secretary (Vietnam National University's University of Science). To avoid over-identifying ties, I do not include Central Committee career overlaps since the general secretary and all provincial party secretaries are by default included in the Central Committee.

Admittedly, overlaps in background—whether in the form of a common workplace, hometown or educational origin—do not necessarily lead to a factional connection, which is defined as a "network of reciprocity" in which a superior provides a subordinate with political favours in exchange for support and loyalty (Shih, Adolph and Liu 2012). Such factional connections require time, effort and resources to cultivate and often involve under-the-table dealings that cannot be easily observed.[10] Nevertheless, these informal ties are instrumental as a necessary condition for factional relationships, or at least a foot-in-the-door advantage that gives a subordinate a better chance of cultivating such relationships with a political elite. In his seminal work on factionalism, for example, Nicholas (1965) argues that a leader "makes use of all possible ties to draw supporters into his faction". As a result, informal ties serve as a good if imperfect proxy for actual factional connections. The literature on Chinese factionalism has indeed used this proxy to great effect to study the effect of elite factionalism on a wide range of political economy outcomes (Shih 2008; Hillman 2010; Meyer, Shih and Lee 2016; Chen and Hong 2020).

Controls

To infer the intention of a political purge, existing studies in the literature on intra-regime violence often analyse the demographic makeup of its targets and attempt to identify certain overrepresented subgroups, either relative to previous purges or to the general population. In his analysis of the current anti-corruption campaign in China, for example, Wedeman (2017) notes an unprecedented presence of foreign companies among investigation cases as well as a high number of investigations in the provinces of Sichuan, Shanxi and Jiangxi compared with the rest of the country. In this analysis, I adopt a similar approach in order to identify the scale and extent of political protection in Vietnam. Specifically, I compare investigation reports from across Vietnam's sixty-three provinces to identify locations that experienced an uncharacteristically low number of investigations and disciplinary actions.

Intuitive as it is, however, the approach is easier said than done. In practice, the act of purging an individual and of protecting an individual from a purge is not exactly two sides of the same coin. A corrupt official who is protected from disciplinary investigation by a powerful elite is observationally equivalent to an upright official who does not engage in corrupt activities. He or she is observationally equivalent, too, to another corrupt official whose corrupt acts have (so far) eluded investigation. As a result, before we can make inferences about the kind of officials or provinces that are shielded from the anti-corruption campaign, we need to take into consideration variations in the latent likelihood of these individuals engaging in corruption as well as them being investigated in the first place.

While it is impossible to directly measure these quantities, in this analysis I proxy for them by controlling for provincial variations in the proximity and presence of the CCDI. In bigger provinces—and particularly in Hanoi, where the CCDI headquarters is located, for example—the mere availability of CCDI resources might allow for more investigations to take place, with or without political interference. CCDI presence is measured by the total mentions of a province across all categories of the CCDI's news articles each year. Second, I control for variations in population and in socio-economic performance, as measured by provincial GDP. These variations influence both the opportunities for corruption and the local government's resources to detect corruption. Additionally, I proxy for the pervasiveness of

TABLE 12.1
Descriptive Statistics for Provincial
Socio-economic and Governance Variables

Statistic	N	Mean	St. Dev.	Min	Max
Province mentions in all CCDI-V reports	189	8.68	8.82	0	65
Investigations taken place in province	189	2.59	2.80	0	13
2011 population (thousands)	189	1,394.29	1,188.85	299	7,521
GDP (billion VND)	189	332,134.50	3,259,941.00	8,358.02	44,850,176.00
Concurrent leadership	189	0.47	0.50	0	1
PCI aggregate score	189	61.53	3.34	52.99	70.69
Unweighted PAPI aggregate score	189	36.24	1.83	25.33	39.57

corruption using the aggregate score of the Provincial Competitiveness Index (Malesky et al. 2020) and the Public Administration Performance Index (CECODES et al. 2019). The two indices, derived from surveys of firms (PCI) and citizens (PAPI), provide a measure of public-sector corruption as well as of government administrative capacity at the provincial level. Finally, I control for the personal power of provincial leaders by including a dummy indicator for whether an incumbent party secretary is simultaneously the head of the People's Committee of the province. This concurrent leadership suggests a high concentration of power, which has implications for a local leader's ability to manipulate disciplinary resources regardless of factional connections to the centre.

Findings

The regression models reveal a fascinating picture of politicized anti-corruption investigations in Vietnam. At first glance it does not seem that provinces whose party secretaries have informal ties with the VCP general secretary are particularly different from others in terms of investigation intensity. These party secretaries include Nguyen Nhan Chien of Bac Ninh province, who shares birth province (Bac Ninh) with Nguyen Phu Trong, and Pham Quang Nghi of Hanoi, who succeeded Trong when the latter became chairman of the National Assembly in 2006. Nghi stayed in Hanoi until 2016, when he was succeeded by Hoang Trung Hai, whom Trong had no tie with. However, after controlling for variations in socio-economic performance, latent corruption and local government capacity, it becomes apparent that these provinces saw much fewer disciplinary visits than similar provinces without such ties. Specifically, depending on the controls in the model, a province's informal connection to the general secretary is associated with between 1.56 and 1.74 fewer investigations per year,

TABLE 12.2
Informal Tie to VCP General Secretary
Associated with Fewer Investigations

	Dependent variable:					
	Number of mentions in CCDI investigation announcements					
	(1)	(2)	(3)	(4)	(5)	(6)
Informal tie to GS	−1.64***	−1.56***	−1.74***	−1.69***		
	(0.63)	(0.55)	(0.50)	(0.53)		
Informal tie to ex-PM					2.09	
					(1.30)	
Informal tie to incumbent PM						−0.26
Mentions in all CCDI reports	0.18***	0.20***	0.20***	0.20***	0.19***	0.20***
	(0.05)	(0.05)	(0.04)	(0.05)	(0.04)	(0.04)
GDP (logged)		0.13	0.09	0.15	−0.11	0.08
		(0.29)	(0.34)	(0.30)	(0.30)	(0.30)
2011 population (logged)		−0.69	−0.58	−0.46	−0.34	−0.45
		(0.47)	(0.52)	(0.46)	(0.46)	(0.46)
Concurrent leadership			0.67**	0.71**	0.83**	0.69**
			(0.32)	(0.31)	(0.33)	(0.33)
PCI score				−0.09	−0.07	−0.09
				(0.06)	(0.06)	(0.06)
PAPI score (unweighted)				−0.03	−0.02	−0.04
				(0.07)	(0.07)	(0.07)
Constant	0.83***	4.24*	3.59*	8.78*	8.89*	9.67**
	(0.26)	(2.24)	(2.17)	(4.82)	(4.67)	(4.67)
Observations	189	189	189	189	189	189
R2	0.38	0.40	0.41	0.42	0.43	0.41
Adjusted R2	0.37	0.38	0.39	0.39	0.40	0.38

Notes: *p<0.1 **p<0.05 ***p<0.01.

holding everything else constant. The effect is both statistically (at 0.05 significance level) and substantially significant: Given a total of fewer than 500 investigations in the dataset, each province on average saw only a little more than 2.5 investigations per year.

Figure 12.3 further illustrates the scale and direction of the political protection that appears to have taken place during Vietnam's anti-corruption campaign. A much higher number of the CCDI's activities took place in provinces that had informal ties to the VCP general secretary. This on its own is not surprising given that the CCDI headquarters—where the bulk of routine meetings, visits and training activity occurs—is located in Hanoi. When it comes to actual disciplinary investigations, however, the fortune is reversed: provinces with ties to Trong experienced as many routine inspections as provinces without such ties, and indeed fewer formal investigations that result in disciplinary punishments.

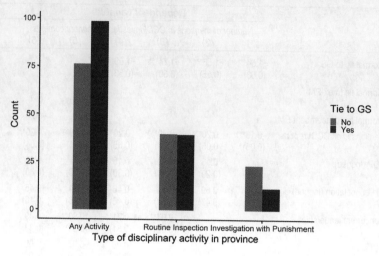

FIGURE 12.3
Provinces with Informal Ties to VCP General Secretary Experienced More CCDI Activities but Fewer Actual Investigations

Notably, the negative relationship between informal ties and number of investigations is specific to ties with the incumbent general secretary. When one examines ties with Nguyen Tan Dung, the former prime minister and Trong's alleged political rival, there is no statistically significant effect of informal ties on investigation rate whatsoever. This finding casts doubt on the narrative that the anti-corruption campaign is merely a pretext to dismantle Dung's factional network. Similarly, ties to the current prime minister, Nguyen Xuan Phuc, who contends with Trong for a seat in the Thirteenth VCP Politburo as an "exception candidate" (in this case, a candidate who exceeds the age of sixty-five at the time of his nomination), also does not explain variations in investigation rate. At the same time, it, together with the cross-national comparison between Vietnam and China, further points to the role of political protection in the limited scope of Vietnam's anti-corruption campaign.

Potential Explanation: CCDI's Vulnerability to Political Interference

Having identified evidence of political protection in Vietnam's ongoing anti-corruption campaign, I propose an explanation for the phenomenon. Specifically, I argue that there are weaknesses in the institutional design of the Vietnamese and Chinese CCDIs; these weaknesses have been partially addressed in China's most recent anti-corruption campaign but not in Vietnam's. As previously discussed, the CCDIs in Vietnam and China are governed under a dual leadership structure in which individual ICs are answerable both to upper-level ICs all the way up to the central headquarters and to the party committees at their administrative level. This leadership structure leaves them exposed to political interference. At the top of the leadership chain, the general secretary of the VCP and that of the CCP, as first among equals in their respective Central Committee and Politburo or Politburo Standing Committee, hold the power to protect party officials suspected of violations in two ways. First, in both parties there are stipulations requiring the CCDI to seek the approval of the Politburo or Politburo Standing Committee before initiating a formal investigation against members of the Central Committee. Even after the conclusion of a formal investigation, the CCDI still requires further approval to issue sanctions if the investigation leads to major sanctions against central-level cadres (Vietnam Communist Party 2009, chapter 7, article 36; Guo 2014).[11]

These stipulations enable the highest leaders of the regimes to delay or terminate investigations they deem undesirable. CCDI investigators, anticipating the possibility of intervention from the top, are also incentivized to propose minor sanctions even if a violation warrants a more serious punishment (Guo 2014).

Second, the regime leaders exert indirect control over the CCDI through their authority over its personnel matters. In Vietnam and China, the CCDI head is required to be a member of the Politburo or Politburo Standing Committee, respectively. Additionally, the Central Committee elects members of the CCDI in Vietnam, and it approves the CCDI's standing committee, secretary and deputy secretary in China. This allows the leadership of the regime, and in particular the party head, to appoint a closely aligned elite as the party's chief disciplinary inspector. Indeed, recent appointments as heads of the CCDIs, such as Wang Qishan in China or Tran Quoc Vuong in Vietnam, have been reported to be very close to their respective general secretaries.

Below the level of the Politburo and Central Committee, similar channels exist for local party elites to undermine the activities of the IC in their jurisdiction. During an investigation—which entails many steps, from a preliminary review to case opening, evidence collection, case hearing, implementation of sanctions, and appeal (Guo 2014)—heads of local party committees can create delays by withholding approvals or modifying, overriding and vetoing sanctions. Local leaders also hold informal influence through control by the Party Committee over IC personnel. CCDI staff at all levels are rotated on a five-year basis, and it is often the case that they will end up working in the same locality and/or with the same party cadres they used to investigate. This creates pressure for disciplinary inspectors to avoid "stirring the pot" and to prioritize the goodwill of local party cadres over their responsibilities (Guo 2014, p. 611). In fact, party cadres in the same province generally look out for one another: party committees and IC staff alike are reluctant to open new cases unless they receive clear instructions to do so from the top.

Institutional Reforms

The vulnerability of the CCDIs to political interference speaks to a broader obstacle to the efforts by Vietnam and China to control corruption: a lack of independence in function and responsibility across institutions. To the VCP's and CCP's credit, besides rhetoric and high-profile arrests, their anti-corruption campaigns have also tackled this core problem by paving the way for significant institutional reforms. In doing so they have distinguished themselves from the campaigns launched by previous generations of leaders.

But despite both regimes having made big strides in the institutional realm, only in China has the CCDI itself become a target for reform. The first series of reforms, which took place around 2013–14, were aimed at decoupling the CCDI from party-based constraints, at least at local levels. Specifically, since 2013 the regime has transferred two significant aspects of authority from the hands of local party committees: the power to approve an investigation conducted by the ICs at their administrative levels, and the power to nominate their chiefs and deputy chiefs. These powers were subsequently given to the superior-level ICs in a move that strengthens the vertical accountability of the CCDI. At the same time, ICs also consolidated their departments and reduced the number of disciplinary issues they were responsible for—from 125 to only 14—in order to focus on corruption-related investigations. IC members were also required to shed concurrent duties in other organs and become fulltime disciplinary cadres so as to limit any conflict of interest (Beijing News 2014; Xinhua 2014; Manion 2016).

No less significant and controversial, the second round of reforms strengthened the authority of the CCDI vis-à-vis the regime's executive and judicial organs. In 2018 the regime passed a new National Supervision Law. Among other provisions, the law dissolved the Ministry of Supervision in China and created a new anti-corruption body called the National Supervision Commission (NPC). This NPC has been designed as the fourth branch of the government and enjoys equal status with the State Council, the Supreme People's Court, and the Supreme People's Procuratorate. Its operations are in turn integrated into the CCDI. On paper the reform was intended to give the regime's anti-corruption authorities more legal power by simultaneously allowing the NPC to investigate party cadres in state organs (which the old Ministry of Supervision was not allowed to) and by enabling the CCDI to make use of legal procedures and resources on top of its own internal channels in its investigations. In practice the re-organization empowers the CCDI much more than it does the NPC. Even though the functions of the two organizations are "integrated", the CCDI ultimately retains superiority over the NPC; indeed, the head of the NPC is the deputy director of the CCDI—an arrangement that signals the subordinate status of the NPC to the CCDI.

These reforms have by no means turned China's CCDI into an independent anti-corruption agency, nor have they freed it from all sources of political interference. Nevertheless, they have had the effect of changing how political interference manifests in the localities. Previously, the power over personnel enabled local party elites, especially strong elites with factional connections to top central leaders, to fill their local ICs with loyalists. These loyalists would then be incentivized, either voluntarily or under the threat of retaliation from their benefactor, to refrain from creating trouble. Even on the rare occasions that a local IC attempted to launch an investigation on its own initiative, the power to authorize formal investigations ensured that there would be no investigation that the party committee—and, by extension, the local party head—disapproved of. After the reforms to China's CCDI, however, local CCP elites for the first time could not guarantee that the interests of their IC's staff would be aligned with theirs. Since local IC staff are now chosen by superior-level ICs, and since they no longer hold concurrent duties in organs in which local elites hold influence, there is greater freedom for local ICs to pursue cases against the wishes of their local committees. While local party bosses still retain the power to interfere in the investigation process through delays and obstructions, their protection can only manifest during an ongoing investigation, not before it. In other words, they can *obstruct* but no longer *prevent* a corruption investigation in their jurisdiction.

Vietnam, for its part, has also made several significant moves towards reforming its institutions. Among its many regulatory changes, the most major reform since 2016 came in the form of a brand-new Law on Anti-Corruption in 2018. The law greatly expands on and clarifies its 2005 predecessor; first, by expanding the scope of prosecution. Unlike the 2005 Law, which only covers "individuals who engage in corrupt acts", the 2018 law omits the reference to individuals and thus opens up a legal channel to prosecute both individuals and organizations. It also broadens the definition of "office-holders" responsible for prosecution, making heads of private and non-profit organizations liable for corruption charges as well. Other important provisions include a redefined set of regulations on giving and receiving gifts, as well as specific provisions for protecting whistle-blowers. Another significant reform came from the party side of the regime. In August 2017 and then in February 2020, the VCP passed, respectively, directives No. 90-QD/TW and No. 214-QD/ TW, which clarified qualifications for positions of leadership in the regime's highest organs, including the central and local party, the government, the National Assembly, the judiciary and the Vietnam Fatherland Front (Vasavakul 2020). Another regulation, No. 205-QD/ TW, passed in September 2019, spells out further prohibitions on various manifestations of office buying.

The reforms in Vietnam are substantial and are consistent with the narrative that the campaign is more than just a factional purge. Nevertheless, they touched on a different set of issues than the reforms in China did. Thus, the Vietnamese regime left its disciplinary investigation apparatuses, especially the CCDI, with the same constraints they had to cope with prior to the anti-corruption campaign. Even even during the campaign, local elites in Vietnam still enjoy power over their local CCDIs and can exercise it to prevent corruption investigations from taking place. The only check against local party elites comes from higher-level party committees. But this check is likely to be weaker against local elites who have a factional connection directly to the highest echelon of the leadership. This, indeed, is the likely mechanism by which provinces whose leaders are connected to General Secretary Nguyen Phu Trong saw far fewer inspections and sanctions than other provinces.

Conclusion

Those who look at news headlines will be inclined to believe that the anti-corruption campaigns of Vietnam and China have delivered on the promises of their leaders. Indeed, at least half of Trong's and Xi's original promises have been fulfilled: the campaigns have led to an unprecedented downfall of the "tigers" and the "wet firewood" in the regimes. There is evidence, too, of extensive institutional reforms that have the potential to bring about lasting change not only to the availability of corruption opportunities but also to the anti-corruption capacity in Vietnam and China.

Beyond the high-profile arrests and impressive statistics, however, the question of insincerity remains, especially with respect to Vietnam's anti-corruption campaign. This chapter demonstrates that despite promises to the contrary, there indeed remain "restricted zones" around the investigation of lower-ranked party cadres in Vietnam. Through a rudimentary quantitative analysis, I have demonstrated that missing cases—potential corrupt incidents that were never investigated—have tended to be concentrated in provinces whose party secretaries have informal ties to the general secretary. The lower number of cases in these provinces does not reflect provincial differences in socio-economic performance, in administrative capacity or in latent corruption levels to the extent that these factors can be measured and controlled for. Rather, it appears that the very ties of these leaders indeed has something to do with political protection.

Building on this evidence, I propose a possible explanation as to why this phenomenon should manifest in Vietnam. Unlike in China, whose institutional reforms during the anti-corruption campaign focused on empowering the CCDI and strengthening its autonomy from local party organs, the Vietnamese regime focused their efforts elsewhere and did little to address the indirect and direct institutional channels of political interference in the CCDI's operations. As a result, local party elites—especially powerful elites who enjoyed factional connections to the central leadership and hence a lower level of scrutiny from their patrons—can limit the extent that incidents of corruption in their locality could lead to formal investigations.

Scepticism about the sincerity of an anti-corruption campaign is not uncommon and is certainly not unique to the case of Vietnam. At the same time, empirical evidence to support or disprove such scepticism is often hard to come by. Even with evidence, the conclusion one arrives at still depends heavily on the specific choice of methodology. The empirical analysis in this chapter, with all its shortcomings, thus does not aim to pass a definitive judgment of the intention of the Vietnamese anti-corruption campaign. Nor does it claim that its proposed explanation is the one true one for the observations made.

At the same time, the pattern of political protection that has been highlighted invites more scholarly attention to the scale and scope of Vietnam's anti-corruption efforts beyond mere headlines and national statistics. Examining the subtle distributions of cases, whether along provincial or sectoral lines, may reveal even more interesting insights.

Future research should subject the proposed causal claim to a more rigorous test. To see whether, indeed, the lack of CCDI reforms is responsible for the missing cases in Vietnam, a comparative analysis of anti-corruption investigations taken in China both before and after these reforms could prove useful. More generally, one can look broader to cross-national studies of legal and institutional reforms to anti-corruption authorities in the world and their effects on corruption-control capacity. To what extent is political protection more prevalent in regimes whose anti-corruption agencies are dependent on local political elites? Do reforms that give greater autonomy to anti-corruption investigators actually lead to more investigations? And, if so, why? Answering these questions could shed more light not only on the political logic of corruption control in Vietnam but also for other political settings across the world.

For the case of Vietnam, the coming years could be crucial both for understanding the current campaign and for the future trajectory of its anti-corruption efforts. Since the analysis ended in 2018, several key personnel changes have taken place at the local level, with the notable removal of a provincial party secretary in Binh Duong province and a People's Committee chairman in Hanoi. The VCP's 13th National Party Congress in 2021 also brought forth a new batch of leadership. While Nguyen Phu Trong remains the VCP's general secretary (thus breaking the informal two-term limit set by his predecessors), his concurrent seat as the president has been transferred to Nguyen Xuan Phuc, who in turn gave up his post of prime minister. Alongside Trong and Phuc, Pham Minh Chinh and Vuong Dinh Hue, two familiar faces from the 12th Politburo, have risen to assume the remaining two pillars of the party's leadership quad (*tu tru*)—the head of government and head of the National Assembly, respectively. Altogether, the 13th Politburo features ten new members, outnumbering the eight re-elected members of the previous Politburo.

This leadership shuffle has so far to introduce any new faction to the political arena. Nonetheless, in due course it will shake up the delicate factional balance of power that was established at the 12th Congress. Even if Trong's current anti-corruption campaign is motivated by more than just factionalism, as this chapter has shown, factional concerns will continue to weigh heavily on the various outcomes. Whether the campaign intensifies or dies down thus rests on delicate personnel decisions following the Congress, and no less importantly, on the political bargains behind them.

Notes

1. See, for examples, the opinion pieces by Hutt (2018) or Murray (2018).
2. This stipulation is defined in China's 1997 Law on Administrative Supervision and Vietnam's Decree 55/2005/ND-CP on the Function, Responsibilities, Powers, and Organizational Structure of the Government Inspectorate.
3. According to Huy Duc (2012), for example, a Central Committee member can only be prosecuted by the court after the party has "met and decided on the level of Party sanction".
4. In China, this has become a formal requirement since the 15th National Congress in 1997.
5. The Vietnamese Party Code (e.g., Decision 102-QD/TW in 2017 on Disciplinary Actions against Cadre Violation, issued by the Central Committee) explicitly distinguishes between supervision (*giam sat*) and investigation (*kiem tra*). The former refers to routine monitoring of the performance of cadre/party organ; the latter refers to actions in response to disciplinary violations and accusations of disciplinary violations.
6. If the case involves a standing member of the local party committee, it should "report to both that party committee and then to the IC at the next higher level for approval".
7. Law no. 27/2012/QH13 Amending and Supplementing a Number of Articles of the Anti-corruption Law.
8. Alongside "peaceful evolution", ideological and moral decay, and "self-evolution and self-transformation".
9. The dataset also includes all historical and current ministerial-level officials in the Vietnamese government, all historical and current Central Committee and Alternate Central Committee members, and all members of the National Assembly since 1946. Data for these individuals were not used in this analysis.
10. For an anthropological discussion of gift-giving and bribery as a practice of building social capital, see Smart (1993).
11. When the officials in question are members of the Politburo, or when the proposed sanction involves dismissal or expulsion, the Central Committee holds the final say on the sanction decision, which it does through a closed vote.

References

Beijing News. 2014. "31 Ge sheng ji jiwei gaige fang'an huo pifu 12 sheng yi wancheng jiwei 'chongjian'" [31 provincial IC reforms approved; 12 provinces completed IC 'reconstruction']. http://news.ifeng.com/a/20140613/40714652%7B%5C_%7D0.shtml (accessed 21 February 2021).

Brancati, Dawn. 2014. "Democratic Authoritarianism: Origins and Effects". *Annual Review of Political Science* 17, no. 1: 313–26.

Branigan, Tania. 2013. "Xi Jinping Vows to Fight 'Tigers' and 'Flies' in Anti-corruption Drive". *The Guardian*, 22 January 2013. https://www.theguardian.com/world/2013/jan/22/xi-jinping-tigers-flies-corruption.

Bueno De Mesquita, Bruce. 2003. *The Logic of Political Survival*. Cambridge: MIT Press.

Carothers, Christopher. 2020. "Taking Authoritarian Anti-corruption Reform Seriously". *Perspectives on Politics*: 1–17.

CECODES et al. 2019. *The 2018 Viet Nam Governance and Public Administration Performance Index (PAPI): Measuring Citizens' Experiences*. Tech. rep. Hanoi.

Chen, Ting, and Ji Yeon Hong. 2020. "Rivals Within: Political Factions, Loyalty, and Elite Competition under Authoritarianism". *Political Science Research and Methods*: 1–16.

Communist Party of China. 2012. *Constitution of the Communist Party of China*.

Geddes, Barbara. 1999. "What Do We Know about Democratization after Twenty Years?" *Annual Review of Political Science* 2, no. 1: 115–44.

Guo, Xuezhi. 2014. "Controlling Corruption in the Party: China's Central Discipline Inspection Commission". *China Quarterly* 219, no. 6: 597–624.

Hillman, Ben. 2010. "Factions and Spoils: Examining Political Behavior within the Local State in China". *China Journal*, no. 64: 1–18.

Hutt, David. 2018. "Vietnam's Communist Chief Is No Xi Jinping". *The Diplomat*, 16 November 2018. https://thediplomat.com/2018/11/vietnams-communist-chief-is-no-xi-jinping/.

————. 2020. "Battle Lines Drawn for Vietnam's Future Leadership". *Asia Times*, 9 January 2020. https://asiatimes.com/2020/01/battle-lines-drawn-for-vietnams-future-leadership.

Huy Duc. 2012. *Ben thang cuoc: Quyen binh* [The winning side: Power game]. Nguoi Viet Books.

Johnston, Michael. 2005. *Syndromes of Corruption: Wealth, Power, and Democracy*. Cambridge: Cambridge University Press.

Keller, Franziska Barbara. 2016. "Moving beyond Factions: Using Social Network Analysis to Uncover Patronage Networks among Chinese Elites". *Journal of East Asian Studies* 16, no. 1: 17–41.

Kerkvliet, Ben, Anita Chan, and Jonathan Unger. 1998. "Comparing the Chinese and Vietnamese Reforms: An Introduction". *China Journal* 40, no. 40: 1–7.

Malesky, Edmund, and Paul J. Schuler. 2013. "Star Search: Do Elections Help Nondemocratic Regimes Identify New Leaders?" *Journal of East Asian Studies* 13, no. 1: 35–68.

Malesky et al. 2020. *The Vietnam Provincial Competitiveness Index: PCI 2019*. Tech. rep. http://eng.pcivietnam.org/publications/2018-pci-full-report/.

Manion, Melanie. 2016. "Taking China's Anticorruption Campaign Seriously". *Economic and Political Studies* 4, no. 1: 3–18.

Meyer, David, Victor C. Shih, and Jonghyuk Lee. 2016. "Factions of Different Stripes: Gauging the Recruitment Logics of Factions in the Reform Period". *Journal of East Asian Studies* 16, no. 1: 43–60.

Murray, Bennett. 2018. *Vietnam's Quiet New Autocrat Is Consolidating Power*. *Foreign Policy*, 7 November 2018. https://foreignpolicy.com/2018/11/07/ vietnams-quiet-new-autocrat-is-consolidating-power/.

Nicholas, Ralph. 1965. "Factions: A Comparative Analysis". In *Political Systems and the Distribution of Power*, edited by Michael Banton, pp. 21–62. London: Tavistock.

Rose-Ackerman, Susan. 1996. "Democracy and 'Grand' Corruption". *International Social Science Journal* 48, no. 149: 365–80.

———. 1999. "Political Corruption and Democracy". *Connecticut Journal of International Law* 14, no. 2: 363–78.

Shih, Victor C. 2008. *Factions and Finance in China: Elite Conflict and Inflation*. New York: Cambridge University Press.

Shih, Victor C., Christopher Adolph, and Mingxing Liu. 2012. "Getting Ahead in the Communist Party: Explaining the Advancement of Central Committee Members in China". *American Political Science Review* 106, no. 1: 166–87.

Smart, Alan. 1993. "Gifts, Bribes, and Guanxi: A Reconsideration of Bourdieu's Social Capital". *Cultural Anthropology* 8, no. 3: 388–408.

Thayer, Carlyle A. 2017. "Vietnam: Dinh La Thang Victim of Factional In-Fighting?" Thayer Consultancy Background Brief.

Vasavakul, Thaveeporn. 2020. "Vietnam Fights Corruption: Towards More Inclusive Initiatives?" *ISEAS Perspective*, no. 2020/92, 26 August 2020.

Vietnam Communist Party . 2009. *Dieu Le Dang Cong San Viet Nam* [Vietnamese Communist Party Statute]. Hanoi: National Political Publishing House.

———. 2017. *Regulation 102-QD/TW: Quy dinh xu ly ky luat dang vien vi pham*.

Vietnamnet. 2018. "Mot nam 'Lo nong, cui tuoi cung phai chay' cua Tong bi thu" [One year since general secretary's 'even wet firewood would burn' campaign]. https://vietnamnet.vn/vn/thoi-su/media/mot-nam-lo-nong-cui-tuoi-cung-phai-chay-cua-tong-bi-thu-416274.html (accessed 21 February 2021).

VnExpress. 2020. "Hon 110 can bo dien Trung uong quan ly bi ky luat trong 5 nam" [More than 110 central-level cadres disciplined in 5 years]. 12 December 2020. https://vnexpress.net/hon-110-can-bo-dien-trung-uong-quan-ly-bi-ky-luat-trong-5-nam-4188923.html.

Wedeman, Andrew. 2004. "The Intensification of Corruption in China". *China Quarterly* 180: 895–921.

———. 2017. "Xi Jinping's Tiger Hunt: Anti-corruption Campaign or Factional Purge?" *Modern China Studies* 24, no. 2: 35–94.

Wintrobe, Ronald. 1998. *The Political Economy of Dictatorship*. Cambridge: Cambridge University Press.

Xinhua. 2014. "CPC Graft Watchdog Stronger and Cleaner". http://www.chinadaily.com.cn/china/2014-03/19/content%7B%5C_%7D17361589.htm (accessed 21 February 2021).

———. 2019. "CPC Members Exceed 90 Million". http://www.chinadaily. com.cn/a/201906/30/WS5d1825c6a3103dbf1432b08f.html (accessed 21 February 2021).

Yiwei, Hu. 2020. "In Numbers: China's Anti-graft Campaign after Achieving 'Sweeping Victory'". CGTN, 16 January 2020. https://news.cgtn.com/

news/2020-01-16/In-numbers-China-s-anti-graft-campaign-NikJlOTb8s/
index.html.

Zhu, Jiangnan, and Dong Zhang. 2017. "Weapons of the Powerful: Authoritarian
Elite Competition and Politicized Anticorruption in China". *Comparative
Political Studies* 50, no. 9: 1186–220.

Index